For Claude Rawson: teacher, scholar, friend

Contents

Illustrations

Contributors

BARBARA M. BENEDICT is Charles A. Dana Professor of English at Trinity College, Hartford. She is author of *Framing Feeling: Sentiment and Style in English Prose Fiction, 1745–1800* (1994), *Making the Modern Reader: Cultural Mediation in Early Modern Literary Anthologies* (1996), and *Curiosity: A Cultural History of Early Modern Inquiry* (2001).

JENNY DAVIDSON is Assistant Professor of English at Columbia University. She is author of *Hypocrisy and the Politics of Politeness: Manners and Morals from Locke to Austen* (2004).

HOWARD ERSKINE-HILL is Emeritus Professor of Literary History, Peterhouse College, University of Cambridge. He is author of many books, including *The Augustan Idea in English Literature* (1983), *Poetry of Opposition and Revolution* (1996), and *Poetry and the Realm of Politics* (1996).

IAN HIGGINS is Reader in English at The Australian National University. He is author of *Swift's Politics: A Study in Disaffection* (1994) and *Jonathan Swift* (2004), and editor (with Claude Rawson) of *Gulliver's Travels* (2005).

NICHOLAS HUDSON is Professor of English at the University of British Columbia. He is author of *Samuel Johnson and Eighteenth-Century Thought* (1988), *Writing and European Thought, 1600–1830* (1994), and *Samuel Johnson and the Making of Modern England* (2003).

THOMAS KEYMER is Professor of English at the University of Toronto. He is author of *Richardson's "Clarissa" and the Eighteenth-Century Reader* (1992) and *Sterne, the Moderns and the Novel* (2002); he is editor of *The Cambridge Companion to English Literature, 1740–1830* (2004).

JONATHAN LAMB is Andrew W. Mellon Professor of Humanities at Vanderbilt University. He is author of *Sterne's Fiction and the Double Principle* (1989), *Rhetoric of Suffering: Reading the Book of Job in the Eighteenth Century* (1995), and *Preserving the Self in the South Seas, 1680–1840* (2001).

HAROLD LOVE was Emeritus Professor in the Department of English at Monash University's School of Literary, Visual, and Performance Studies. He was author, most recently, of *Attributing Authorship: An Introduction* (2002) and also of *Scribal Publication in Seventeenth-Century England* (1993).

JAMES MCLAVERTY is Professor of Textual Criticism at Keele University. He is one of the general editors of the Cambridge University Press edition of the works of Jonathan Swift and author of *Pope, Print, and Meaning* (2001).

RONALD PAULSON is William D. and Robin Mayer Professor Emeritus of the Humanities, Johns Hopkins University. He is author of many books, including *Popular and Polite Art in the Age of Hogarth and Fielding* (1979), *Hogarth* (1991), and *Hogarth's Harlot: Sacred Parody in Enlightenment England* (2003).

MARJORIE PERLOFF is Professor Emerita at Stanford University. She is author of many books, including *The Poetics of Indeterminacy: Rimbaud to Cage* (1981), *The Futurist Moment: Avant-Garde, Avant-Guerre, and the Language of Rupture* (1986), and *Wittgenstein's Ladder* (1996).

PAT ROGERS is DeBartolo Professor of Humanities, University of South Florida. He is author and editor of many books, including *Grub Street: Studies in a Subculture* (1972), *The Augustan Vision* (1974), *Essays on Pope* (1993), *Johnson and Boswell: The Transit of Caledonia* (1995), and *Pope and the Destiny of the Stuarts* (2005).

DAVID ROSEN is Associate Professor at Trinity College, Hartford. He is author of *Power, Plain English, and the Rise of Modern Poetry* (2006).

PETER SABOR is Canada Research Chair at McGill University and Director of the Burney Centre. He is co-author, with Thomas Keymer, of *Pamela in the Marketplace: Literary Controversy and Print Culture in Eighteenth-Century Britain and Ireland* (2005) and editor of many books, including *The Complete Plays of Frances Burney* (1995) and Jane Austen's *Juvenilia* (2006).

AARON SANTESSO is Assistant Professor in the School of Literature, Communication, and Culture at the Georgia Institute of Technology. He is author of *A Careful Longing: The Poetics and Problems of Nostalgia* (2006) and co-editor (with Claude Rawson) of *John Dryden (1631–1700): His Politics, His Plays and His Poems* (2004).

DAVID WOMERSLEY is Thomas Warton Professor of English Literature at the University of Oxford, and a Professorial Fellow of St. Catherine's College. He is the author of *The Transformation of 'The Decline and Fall of the Roman Empire'* (1988) and *Gibbon and the Watchmen of the Holy City* (2002), and editor of Gibbon's *The History of the Decline and Fall of the Roman Empire* (1994). He is one of the general editors of the Cambridge University Press edition of the works of Jonathan Swift, for which he is editing *Gulliver's Travels*.

STEVEN N. ZWICKER is Stanley Elkin Professor of Humanities at Washington University. He is author of *Dryden's Political Poetry: The Typology of King and Nation* (1972), *Politics and Language in Dryden's Poetry: The Arts of Disguise* (1984), and *Lines of Authority: Politics and English Literary Culture, 1649–1689* (1993).

Acknowledgments

We wish to acknowledge the encouragement and support of Linda Bree, without whom this volume would not have been produced. Thanks are due also to the University of Nevada Department of English, Esra Mirze, and Deb Taniwa. Partial funding for the volume was received from the Social Sciences and Humanities Research Council of Canada. Finally, we thank the contributors to the volume for their patience, co-operation, and support.

Introduction

The essays in this collection concern "Swift's travels" both forward and back across the literary tradition. Together they build a picture of a kind of satire that we might recognize as traditionally British, and as having achieved a dark apogee in the satires of Swift. Behind Swift's achievements, however, lie a range of precedents and influences that not only make his own literary journeys and achievements clearer, but also, viewed through the lens of Swift's reinterpretations and reformulations, cast the British satirical tradition itself in a different light. Swift entered into a literary arena marked in many ways by a self-conscious sanity – utopian speculation, the rational calculus of Thomas Hobbes, political and religious dissent, satiric reflections on fops and ladies, the classicism of John Dryden. In transforming so much of this rationality into a supremely controlled madness, Swift redirected his age, and inspired the uncertainty, instability, and anger of those works that followed in his shadow. Pope, Fielding, Austen, Beckett – none could forget Swift, and all wrote in a satiric Brobdingnag ruled by one giant. Even today, the name of Swift conjures a particular mode of satire – acerbic, unrelenting, unbounded. "A modern-day Jonathan Swift"[1] remains an honorific title for any writer of bitter truths and dark comedy.

This collection thus differs from other books on eighteenth-century satire, not in making Swift its central focus, but by moving outward from that mysterious and hostile center to offer a new understanding of British satire in general as a mode more radical, more troubled, and more ambitious than previously imagined. In developing this method, the editors and contributors have been inspired by perhaps the best living scholar on eighteenth-century satire, and perhaps on British satire itself. Claude Rawson's writing has consistently circled back to Swift, whom he portrays as a figure of virtually archetypal importance in understanding the subtleties of satiric language and the darker paradoxes of human nature itself. But in his own scholarly travels, Rawson has taken in a wide orbit of authors from classical times to the present – Lucian, Rabelais, Montaigne, Pope, Fielding, Johnson, Wilde, Shaw, Céline, Mailer, and Laing, to name only a few. The methodologies of Rawson's writing will be recognized in many of the following essays. These include a sharp awareness of the unresolved polarities at the heart of Swiftian satire, a keen ear for the modulations of narrative voice, a sensitivity to what is not only said but implied in satire, and above all a belief that there is something abiding in the revelations of satire, something which seems rooted in human experience. The essays in this book treat diverse aspects of satire in various different ways. But the reader will recognize the common admiration of the contributors for Claude Rawson and what he has taught us about satire.

The book is divided into three parts – "Swift and his antecedents," "Swift in his time," and "Beyond Swift." The first part concerns models in Renaissance and seventeenth-century literature which Swift drew upon for his satiric purposes, beginning with the speculative utopian tradition examined by David Rosen and Aaron Santesso. As these authors observe, Swift's satire recalls the social allegory of More's *Utopia*, although "the organizing system is brutally absent" (12). Swift's utopias, nowhere more clearly than the Flying Island, are disconnected from the transcendental authority that underwrote the vision of humanists like More. In Swift's age, idealized visions (even highly skeptical ones like More's) inevitably disintegrate into a harsh and uncanny "afterlife of allegory" (23). Jonathan Lamb also begins with Swift's reworking of a speculative political tract. In this case he recasts Hobbes's political trope of the "Leviathan," the state ordered under the authority of a Sovereign, who bestows order, ownership and meaning on the Commonwealth. But as Rosen and Santesso had observed, the higher authority that would legitimize even an absolutist state has vanished in Swift's world. Swift's Grub Street authors claim, like Hobbes's Sovereign, to possess authority over a community of readers, but Swift's society is more like the State of Nature, a chaos of individuals without language, without meaning, without property. Authors, words, and things never transcend their status as insignificant objects.

Ian Higgins's "Killing no murder" traces Swift's satire back to another genre: the political pamphlets of the seventeenth and eighteenth centuries. The justification for killing and even genocide that characterized a vicious edge of political writing during the English Revolution and its aftermath became the subject of parodies like Defoe's *The Shortest Way with Dissenters* and numerous parts of Swift's writing, most famously *A Modest Proposal* and the fourth part of *Gulliver's Travels*. Swift, however, raises the following question: how close can parody come to espousing actual murder and genocide? Higgins follows Claude Rawson in detecting in Swift, and in others like Céline, an implied sympathy for genocide, "a diffused aggression,"[2] born from Swift's genuine rage against humanity and what Orwell called his "Tory anarchism" (39). "Swift's generalizing imaginative satires," writes Higgins, "sometimes appear to be rehearsals for the invective found in the more dangerously focused polemic" (50). Swift's "literalism," his impatience with "the sanitizing or protective operations of fiction,"[3] is also a theme in Harold Love's "Satirical wells from Bath to Ballyspellan." Those who satirized Bath, Tunbridge Wells, and England's spa towns before Swift, such as Lord Rochester and Francis Fanes, often used these places as springboards for mythological fantasies and erotic comedy. Swift brings these settings down to earth, excoriating "the trivial, wholly self-centered life of the London beau monde," and "almost gleefully" joining in with the "engrained heartlessness" (68) that often characterizes this world. While performative and tinged with grief, this heartlessness reveals what Rawson has judged "a certain violence and immoderation of character"[4] that separates Swift from his more moderate predecessors. Whereas previous ironists like Dryden, as Steven N. Zwicker argues, sought positions of moderation and reconciliation, Swift rejects any middle ground, preferring instead to sharpen those contradictions and conflicts that others sought to resolve. Dryden's effort to balance the merits of the ancients and moderns, for example, is reduced in *The Battle of the Books* into "the clatter of ill-fitting armour and the rustle of self-promotion" (87). To cite Rawson again, Swift confronts the reader with "a sense of irreconcilable opposition between two absolutes."[5]

These themes – reductive realism, aggression, immoderation, the juxtaposition of opposites – reappear in part II, which is devoted to Swift himself. Like Jonathan Lamb, Barbara M. Benedict surveys the clutter of bare, insignificant *things* in Swift's satire, a materiality that aggressively dissolves people into objects, souls into clothes, essences into surfaces. "Through his satirical deflation of the Scriblerian mode of literalistic description," writes Benedict, "[Swift] demonstrates that language can construct and de-construct not only things, but human bodies, and thus identity itself" (105). Sheer "thingness" relates paradoxically to "Swift's shapeshifting," as David Womersley calls a related technique, the blurring and reversal of oppositions, the desiccation of language and identity. Swift's friends had to beware of his own personal habit of showing affection through scorn, friendship through irritable indifference. Surely, there is no more scabrous portrait of the "Fair Sex" than

Corinna in "A Beautiful Young Nymph Going to Bed." Yet even if we "spew" at the end of this poem, as Swift expects we will, the poem is not without its edge of sympathetic anger on Corinna's behalf against male brutality and self-righteous moralism. Perhaps Swift even personally identified with Corinna's wounds, as Womersley suggests.

For Swift, like Corinna, thought of himself as a wounded outcast, an exile in Ireland. It was a position that called up some of his most complex and subtle modulations of irony. A central irony of Swift's long sojourn in Dublin, Pat Rogers argues, is that so much of his writing from this period was set in London. What does the predominance of London in much of Swift's major poetry tell us about the Dean of St. Patrick's and the psychology of an exile? Certainly there is a sense of loss and alienation underlying much of Swift's work, as well as a yearning to address a larger audience and larger human themes than the parochial world of Anglo-Ireland seemed to accommodate. The acidity of Swift's satire derives from the reader's keen awareness that it is *personal* – never more so than in "Verses on the Death of Dr. Swift," examined in subsequent essays by Howard Erskine-Hill and James McLaverty. In the difference between the early "Bathurst" edition of this poem and the later "Faulkner" edition, Erskine-Hill finds, above all, a profound and self-effacing candor on Swift's part, the product of his vulnerability and alienation as a self-styled exile. It was a frankness too strong for even his friends Pope and William King, who directed Bathurst to censor large portions of the manuscript. What Swift restored in the Faulkner edition were political allegiances dangerously close to Jacobitism, deep and even humiliating reservations about the durability of his literary reputation, and a Christianity that falls curiously short of full piety. Furthermore, Swift's willingness to name names, or at least to leave broad indications about whom he meant, would appear to contradict his own, perhaps ironic, boast in the "Verses" that "he lash'd the Vice but spar'd the Name,"[6] as McLaverty points out. Both he and Pope (who made a similar claim about himself) pillory their satiric targets with a bluntness curtailed by few considerations besides the possibility of lawsuits. Of the two writers, surprisingly, Swift may have been more constrained by tact and political caution, yet he joined with Pope in creating a satire characterized by unprecedented personal invective.

Pope was the greatest satirist in the immediate orbit of Swift, and his work also opens part III, "Beyond Swift." These essays explore the continuing legacy of the themes examined in parts I and II, the shadow cast by Swift from his own time to the twentieth century. Nicholas Hudson focuses on the formation of the "middle class," an ideological construct of enduring significance that framed and shaped the work of the Scriblerians. These men generally derived from modest social backgrounds, and Pope's satire is marked by a desire for acceptance by the elite combined with an awareness of his own marginal status as the Catholic son of a linen draper. This awareness gives rise to various rhetoric postures, some aggressive, but generally Pope's satire is characterized not by irreconcilable polarities, as in Swift, but rather by "oscillations of mood."[7] This is also the phrase that Rawson used to describe Fielding's literary musings on social rank – yet Tom Keymer finds a dark, unsettling irony in Fielding's writing that is in some ways comparable to Swift's. Fielding indulged an "uneasy relish" (207) in gallows humor, the kind of gruesome witticisms sometimes made by judges in condemning criminals to hang, and collected in popular jestbooks. In Fielding, therefore, we find a version of the polarized irony typical of Swift: "On one hand [Fielding] enjoys, and invites readers to enjoy, a comedy of victimization . . . On the other he distances himself, with defensive irony, from the supercilious malice of the bullies and tormentors involved" (207).

Swift's influence can indeed be found in unexpected places, as in the writing of Jane Austen, the subject of essays by Peter Sabor and Jenny Davidson. Austen could share Swift's aggression and irreverence, as Sabor indicates in his examination of her annotations of Goldsmith's *History of England*. In these private notes, Austen unleashes her own satiric impulses, pouring forth pro-Jacobite sympathies mixed with a relish for the disgrace of the Stuarts' enemies, even to the point of ribald innuendo. Rawson's own excellent studies of Austen's novelistic narrative have identified precisely this asperity beneath the decorous formality of Austen's prose. As argued by Jenny Davidson, we can indeed compare the strategies of *Gulliver's Travels* and Austen's novels, for Austen's narrative modulations recall "Swift's remarkably unstable first-person voices" (235). She detects in "Austen's voices" versions of an "oblique mode of operating" (243) and an "indeterminate quality" (244) that keeps the readers of both Swift and Austen unsettled and off balance.

And yet the durable legacy of Swift is less his subtle control of narrative technique than his somber illumination of the human condition. A master of language, he is nonetheless among the most visual of British writers, for his satires typically direct us to see the world in unconventional and often unwelcome ways. There is, not surprisingly, a pictorial analogue for Swift's vision, as explored by Ronald Paulson. Paulson pursues a long-standing theme in Rawson's studies of Swift's satire, the theme of cannibalism, through the visual art of Hogarth, Goya, and Domenico Tiepolo. In

Hogarth's unpublished *Enthusiasm Delineated*, a Methodist congregation literally eats images of Christ in a grotesque parody of the Eucharist; in *The Four Stages of Cruelty*, a criminal's body is dissected before a congregation of doctors, another mock-Eucharist that reminds us that the real sacrificial victims "eaten" by eighteenth-century society were its poor and outcast (as does *A Harlot's Progress*). Hogarth reduces "the spiritual image to the physical" (259), a Swiftian literalness that can also be found in the paintings of Goya and Tiepolo. Again, therefore, satire in the Swiftian vein submerges the audience in the gross materiality and barbarity of human life. Yet Swift understood well the irony that we feel a visceral attraction to the most noxious and shameful dimensions of our corporeality, a recognition echoed in Samuel Beckett's confession that he did not find the smell of corpses unpleasant. As Marjorie Perloff argues in the collection's concluding essay, Beckett's mixture of disgust and stimulation in the face of "The Yahoo nature of man, the defecating animal" (286) also stimulated his profound admiration for Swift. Beckett shared Swift's immoderation, his materiality, and to some degree also his pessimism. Yet this volume ends with the bleak solace Beckett identifies as available to people of the twentieth century. Surrounded by the wars and brutality of his era, Beckett envisaged humanity struggling on through its own muck and suffering. Final redemption was not possible, but possibly we could "Fail better" (282).

At the conclusion of his *Travels*, Gulliver, less stoic than Beckett, rants madly at the stench of Yahoo bodies, forgetting the stench of his own. For all the vaunted "Teachableness" of Yahoo nature,[8] Gulliver has learned nothing. Or rather learned too much. The lessons of the Swiftian satiric tradition cannot be imagined as taking the world to a particularly better place. "The chief end that I have proposed to my self," wrote Swift famously, ". . . is to vex the world rather then [*sic*] divert it."[9] Yet, unlike Yahoos, we at least *travel*. In their own journey through the following volume, we hope readers will encounter intellectual engagement, critical frankness, and a willingness to question received truths. These human potentials, at least, seem the reassuring lessons of Swift and the satiric tradition he did so much to shape.

NOTES

1 We find the habit practiced on book-cover blurbs (*Entertainment Weekly* praises Dean Koontz as "A modern Swift . . . a master satirist"), newspaper reviews (*The New York Times* suggests that Kramer wishes to be "a contemporary Jonathan Swift" but that "the playwright is no Jonathan Swift": Mel Gussow, "Skewers for the Political in Kramer's 'Just Say No'" [October 21, 1988]; the

Boston Globe opines that "Christopher Buckley has been touted as a modern-day Jonathan Swift so often he's begun to believe it"), and academic studies (a paper at the 2007 ASECS conference suggested that "Dave Chappelle and Spike Lee [are] the New Jonathan Swift(s)").

2 Claude Rawson, *God, Gulliver, and Genocide: Barbarism and the European Imagination, 1492–1945* (Oxford: Oxford University Press, 2001), p. 310.

3 Rawson, *God, Gulliver, and Genocide*, p. 12.

4 Claude Rawson, *Order from Confusion Sprung* (London: George Allen & Unwin, 1985), p. 27.

5 Rawson, *Order from Confusion Sprung*, p. 83.

6 *The Poems of Jonathan Swift*, 2nd edn., ed. Harold Williams, 3 vols. (Oxford: Oxford University Press, 1958), vol. II, p. 571, l. 460.

7 Claude Rawson, "Gentlemen and Dancing-Masters," in *Henry Fielding and the Augustan Ideal under Stress* (London and Boston: Routledge and Kegan Paul, 1972), pp. 3–34.

8 *Gulliver's Travels*, ed. Claude Rawson and Ian Higgins (Oxford: Oxford University Press, 2005), pt. 4, ch. 3, p. 219.

9 *Correspondence of Jonathan Swift*, ed. Harold Williams, 5 vols. (Oxford: Clarendon Press, 1965), vol. III, p. 606.

PART I

Swift and his antecedents

CHAPTER I

Swiftian satire and the afterlife of allegory

David Rosen and Aaron Santesso

Gulliver himself refers to only one work of English literature. In the prefatory letter to his "Cousin Sympson," he notes that readers have "gone so far as to drop Hints, that the *Houyhnhnms* and *Yahoos* have no more Existence than the Inhabitants of *Utopia*."[1] Moreover, the famous "*Sextumvirate* to which all the Ages of the World cannot add a Seventh," described by Brutus in Glubbdubdrib, is rounded out by More, the group's only Englishman, and only non-classical figure.[2] Needless to say, there are many reasons why Swift would have evoked More in his masterpiece. As numerous critics have pointed out, the idealized aspects of Houyhnhnmland recall the society on More's fictional island, and indeed Book IV can be read as a long meditation on utopian thought.[3] In Claude Rawson's elegant argument, the "Utopians [are] in some ways the ancestors of the Houyhnhnms." Be that as it may, in this essay, we will suggest that Swift's deepest engagement with More is to be found earlier on, in Book III; to be precise, *Utopia* is among the earliest works to acknowledge a crisis in the allegorical articulation of culture – a crisis that receives its most dramatic depiction, two centuries later, on the flying island of Laputa. Though both men understood this crisis to be a disaster, it nevertheless had a seminal and lasting effect on the development of modern satire.

ALLEGORICAL CULTURE: THE CASE OF *UTOPIA*

On the face of it, it makes little sense to call either *Utopia* or *Gulliver's Travels* "allegorical": while both have allegorical elements (often of a parodistic kind), neither belongs to the genre of *Piers Plowman* and *The Faerie Queene*. More to the point, how or why one would conceive of a culture in allegorical terms is far from self-evident. Some explanation of premises, then. When we call the culture of Renaissance England "allegorical" – our chief underlying assertion – we are not making the

obvious point that allegory was the dominant literary form from Lang-
land to Spenser, nor are we claiming that the Renaissance was particularly
conducive (though it most certainly was) to the production of literary
allegory; our interest in the *genre* per se is limited. Rather, we are arguing
that allegory, *as a mode*, involves certain habits of thought and ways of
organizing reality that are as operative in everyday life – socially, politically, ideologically – as in the aesthetic structure of a romance or poem.
As Gordon Teskey observes,

> A poetics of allegory can achieve stability only by grounding itself on an
> unambiguous determination of the "other" in the word *allegory* as that to which
> the discourse refers, the ideal "meaning." This determination is formalized in
> poetics as what I call the *singularity*, the ineffable presence into which, it is
> supposed, everything in the allegorical work ultimately is drawn. The singularity
> operates in an allegory as does the vanishing point in a linear perspective: it is
> never visible itself, but everything that *is* visible directs the eye toward it.[4]

That is to say: in any allegory, the tension between vehicle and tenor,
between images as they are deployed on the page and the larger belief
system they are meant to represent, is inevitably a destabilizing force. The
two are made to cohere only by a transcendental verifier, Teskey's
"singularity," which necessarily exists beyond representation itself. We
may observe a social equivalent to this literary process in the way strongly
authoritarian societies seek to overcome the centrifugal force between
national ideology and lived reality – a process underwritten by the
godhead or (more tendentiously) by a secular surrogate. In such a society,
immense pressure is exerted from above to ensure that the inner life of the
ordinary civilian conforms to his or her social role or persona. The most
vivid recent depiction of these pressures is to be found in novels provoked
by Stalinism (think of Zamyatin, his "Benefactor," and "numbers"), but
surely every government of a totalizing disposition aspires finally to be the
allegorical author of its citizenry.

Social allegory of this sort, however problematic in the twentieth
century, was at least conceivable during the Middle Ages, a period of
relatively sedentary populations and fixed feudal hierarchies, a social order
still underwritten by the *logos* of God.[5] For reasons that are well known
(the dwindling prestige of the Holy Roman Empire and papacy, the
loosening of feudal loyalties, the first stirrings of Protestantism, a particular volatility amongst the lower gentry), the Renaissance made such
thinking at once more attractive and less likely to succeed.[6] The rise of
strong nations under despotic kings coincided with a gradual withdrawal

of the divine *logos* and its replacement by an altogether less stable ideology of monarchy by divine right. The immense and tortured complexity of literary allegories like *The Faerie Queene* is ample witness to the tendentiousness of the times, as authors like Spenser struggled to give state power adequate and convincing textual representation, as a means of (to paraphrase Angus Fletcher) indoctrinating and putting people in their place.[7] More relevant to our topic, the problems of social allegory during the Renaissance produced works like *Utopia*.

To put it into a phrase: *Utopia* is an imagining of the conditions under which a functioning social allegory would be possible. Practically, More was well aware that his republic was an impossibility: as countless commentators have pointed out, his narrator's name ("Hythlodaeus") means "dispenser of nonsense" in Greek, and "utopia" itself means "no place." More, in his very public role as an MP (he would soon be appointed Henry VIII's Privy Counsellor and subsequently Lord Chancellor) knew all too well that the early modern nation-state was unmanageable. While the second, and longer, of *Utopia*'s two books is mainly a description of the island, the first begins with a litany of everything amiss in England and on the continent. The "More" who appears as a character in the dialogue (as Hythlodaeus's polite but skeptical intellectual adversary), while finding society's ills deplorable, nevertheless seems to believe them pragmatically beyond any full solution. Progress, when it comes, comes through compromise and accepting human imperfection.

If you can't completely eradicate wrong ideas, or deal with inveterate vices as effectively as you could wish, that's no reason for turning your back on public life altogether. You wouldn't abandon ship in a storm just because you couldn't control the winds.

On the other hand, it's no use attempting to put across entirely new ideas, which will obviously carry no weight with people who are prejudiced against them. You must go to work indirectly. You must handle everything as tactfully as you can, and what you can't put right you must try to make as little wrong as possible. For things will never be perfect, until human beings are perfect – which I don't expect them to be for quite a number of years![8]

Even if we grant the distance between "More" the character and More the author, this pragmatism suggests a way to read Utopian society: rather than being, primarily, a set of proposals for the reform of the English state – which it may well be, in a "tactful" and "indirect" way – *Utopia* shows us an allegorical mind solving the problems of society unimpeded by the hindrances of everyday, sixteenth-century life.

Thus, simplification. If the allegorical project of early Tudor statecraft was defeated at every turn by an increasingly diverse and complex social structure, the obvious answer for More was not – as it would be two centuries later – to refine the means of inspection and observation, but rather to simplify, and thus render legible, the citizenry itself. Indeed, the social conditions most thoroughly imagined by More are those that permit the state immediately to comprehend its subjects. Thus, while More's countrymen had considered imposing different uniforms on different social ranks, the Utopians take the next logical step, assigning convicts and slaves instantly recognizable badges and distinctly colored uniforms. Mere felons are spared the gallows, but wearing the wrong color means death.[9] Utopia is a monoculture: individuality is all but erased, and the worst possible sin is one against regimentation and order. Everyone wears the same clothing and although, necessarily, different people pursue different trades, everyone is compelled to farm. The cities are identical: "They're all built on the same plan, and, so far as the sites will allow, they all look exactly alike ... when you've seen one of them, you've seen them all ..." (*Utopia*, 50, 52). Diversity is the enemy of transparency, More has intuited, so everyone must be more or less the same.

In short, *Utopia* is the vision of a society that functions as an efficient allegory, with the meaning of each citizen superficially apparent, and the state, through persistent surveillance, the ultimate reader. When More describes the social body as "one big household," he means, essentially, that no one has any privacy, ever.

> You see how it is – wherever you are, you always have to work. There's never any excuse for idleness. There are also no wine-taverns, no ale-houses, no brothels, no opportunities for seduction, no secret meeting-places. Everyone has his eye on you, so you're practically forced to get on with your job and make some proper use of your spare time. (*Utopia*, 65)

Anything that leads to differentiation is conspicuously absent on the island; even the houses are "changed round every ten years" (*Utopia*, 53), for fear that habits, attachments, personal feelings may develop. And yet More's aim is not, as has been claimed, "a cancellation of identity itself."[10] Rather, he is attempting to bring inner and outer identity, tenor and vehicle, into concord – or, more precisely, to preserve the sense that inner and outer identity are one and the same thing, even if it means paring down individuality to a degree that most people would now find inhuman. Even in More's own time, of course, the likelihood of this ever coming to pass was slim; within a hundred years of his death, with the rise of a new dispensation based on premises entirely different from those of the Tudor age, the only genre in which More's program could be taken seriously was the last place people would look.

A GENEALOGY OF SATIRE

A standard explanation of the rise of satire is literary-historical: sometime shortly after the publication of *Paradise Lost*, epic died and satire took its place.[11] Confronted by an astounding masterpiece, by a display of overwhelming imaginative force, a subsequent generation could only approach the genre with self-conscious gestures of futility: works of palpably diminished ambition or – more relevant to the history of satire – parody (e.g. *MacFlecknoe, The Rape of the Lock, The Splendid Shilling*). There is likely some truth to this: all genres undergo a natural rise and fall, and the appearance of *Paradise Lost* was a cataclysm in the history of modern epic, as well as the literary culture more broadly. Tellingly, the eighteenth century was a great age for the *appreciation* of epic. Addison's papers on Milton, for instance, marked a revival rather than a decline of interest in the form – and in the modern English epic particularly – even as they foreclosed practically on the possibility of another *Paradise Lost* getting written any time soon. And yet, we would suggest that to ascribe the rise of satire to a single event in publishing is to miss the forest for the trees; nor, we would add, is the decline of epic, as a genre, of central relevance to the ascent of satire. Rather, this decline, and the malaise felt by many writers in Milton's wake, was part of the broader cultural crisis that we have begun to trace; it is in this crisis that the genealogist of satire must look for origins. Comparing Utopia with Houyhnhnmland, John Traugott concludes that the writers were linked by "the whole mad vision of utopia which lies behind [Swift's] passion and More's."[12] A profoundly Augustan remark. Certainly there is a notable correspondence of thought between the two authors; we find it inspired, however, less by the mad vision of Utopia, than by Swift's vision of an allegorical world, More's world, gone mad.

The reasons for the decline of the *genre* allegory at the turn of the eighteenth century have been explored elsewhere at great length; the decline of allegorical *culture*, and the relevance of this collapse for literature, far less so. Despite the problems inherent in conceiving of a state allegorically – problems that More had diagnosed with great acuteness – there had still been considerable motive among the Tudors and early

Stuarts to do precisely that. As Lacey Baldwin Smith has commented, the fading of the medieval *logos* necessitated a recouping of divine prestige in the persons of "kings and emperors...God's attested leaders among men."[13] The idea of divine-right monarchy was allegory at its most tendentious: an ideology of society as a divinely ordained array, with everyone in their proper place, and the king (or queen) as God's vassal; a cult of personality surrounding the despot so intense as to make him (or her) indeed seem both divine and all-seeing, a master interpreter. The (literally) crowning image of this dispensation in its last phase was Gloriana, the virgin queen, whose body was at once her own and the entirety of her nation. So long as this vision of the state persisted, the writing – and adequate reception – of powerful *literary* allegory remained possible. *The Faerie Queene* is underwritten in the most explicit way imaginable by the "singularity" of the sovereign, and the conception of society (and indeed reality itself) that the sovereign sustained. Within living memory of Elizabeth's death, however, forces philosophical (the empiricist and materialist critique of received wisdom), political (the parliamentary system), and social (the rise of religious and economic strata with no investment in the king), to restrict ourselves to the obvious, had shaped a new society no longer able (or willing) to conceive of itself in allegorical terms.

For authors of a traditionalist bent two unpleasant options remained open. The first was to continue writing allegory despite the loss of a transcendental verifier (God's eye, manifested physically in the eye of the king) and the waning of the social faith that had made the genre a plausible and powerful representation of reality. The result, as has been widely acknowledged, was a hollowed-out form of allegory, a self-consciously artificial didactic tool. In place of the powerful ambiguities of Renaissance allegory, authors now offered the crystalline clarity of mathematical equations, the meaning of the texts no longer lying beyond representation, but now explicitly political or intellectual. As Teskey has commented, Enlightenment allegory was "an artifact to be considered by the mind from a distance and appreciated for its simplicity and propriety."[14] For *Absalom and Achitophel* to succeed, that is, there must be no confusion about its one-to-one matches – matches whose unfailing "propriety" one cannot but admire. The only cost of Dryden's success, perhaps, is a rigidity that prevents the poem from ever springing fully to life, and a restriction to topicality that turns it into an instant period piece.

The history of post-Restoration allegory is largely a record of authors' increasing dissatisfaction with their own medium. Thus Pope's "Preface" to his *Temple of Fame*, which begins with a blunt admission: "Some modern Criticks, from a pretended Refinement of Taste, have declar'd themselves unable to relish allegorical Poems."[15] He defends himself against this criticism ("The ancients constantly made use of Allegories") but admits that some writers "have rather errr'd by insisting on it too closely, and carrying it too far... [Allegories] should never be spun too long, or much clog'd with trivial Circumstances, or little Particularities." His defense of allegory has the feeling of protesting too much, an admission that he is defending a paradigm that is no longer socially relevant.[16] Even *The Rape of the Lock* is carefully glossed when Pope publishes the "Key" – his gesture towards a public that expects only a game of find-the-correspondence. Johnson's proclamation, at mid-century, that "allegories drawn to great length will always break," reflects a radical undervaluing of the genre: it would never have occurred to Spenser that *The Faerie Queene*, however long it got, might "break."[17]

The second option for writers nostalgic for an allegorical social order was satire – a more complex tactic, since the relation between the two *genres*, allegory and satire, is by no means self-evident. In Fletcher's well-known argument, satire can be understood as a *continuation* of allegory, not so much a successor genre as a perverse extension, "[directing] allegory against allegory, irony against irony."[18] This strategy may be seen, perhaps, in authors who anticipated Johnson's warning, and wrote satires that, to use Rawson's term, "exploded" allegory from the inside. In *The Dunciad*, the greatest instance of such a work, "a new world to Nature's laws unknown, / Breaks out refulgent, with a heaven its own." The clarity and propriety of post-Restoration allegory is replaced by a surreal world in which "Nature's laws" break down: "The forests dance, the rivers upward rise, / Whales sport in woods, and dolphins in the skies." Rawson imagines *Gulliver's Travels* as making a similar gesture: "Whole allegorical sequences, whose straightforward message has Swift's full endorsement, dissolve in a self-undercutting inconsistency, or explode in violence." In these sequences, what begins as "initially straightforward allegory" gradually moves "outside the clean outlines of the allegory," and ultimately "explode[s] the emphasis away from the domain of allegorical correspondence as such."[19]

Yet *Gulliver's Travels*, and indeed Swiftian satire in general, complicates any straightforward notion of exploded allegory. For one thing, even the most "exploded" works still reveal something of the primal eighteenth-century drive for coherence; thus, with no irony intended by Pope, the bizarre and fragmented shards of allegory that litter *The Dunciad* are all carefully glossed. Swift, who must have laughed bitterly at the appearance of "keys" to *Gulliver's Travels* (such as *"Gulliver Decypher'd"* [1728]), had no faith in coherence – quite the opposite – and scorned all palliatives. Much more to the point, we would argue that, on the most basic level, the relation between Swiftian satire and Renaissance allegory *cannot be understood in generic terms at all.* Though the fragments of literary allegory are to be found from Lilliput to Laputa, and all points in between, Swiftian satire is neither the ruin of allegory nor its blasted remainder: it is not, in any simple or direct way, a successor genre. In contrast to Pope and Johnson, who both attributed the failure of allegory to a fundamental flaw in the form, Swift recognized a fundamental flaw in society: the *modal* forces that had underpinned Tudor–Stuart culture, and which had made a stable social allegory possible (or at least, as More proved, imaginable), had now given way to a crass materialism embodied, in different ways, by Walpole, Defoe, and Locke. Swift frequently imagines himself as fighting this new society; as he comments in a letter to Pope: "Drown the world! I am not content with despising it, but I would anger it, if I could with safety" (November 26, 1725). The lines express something more than simple disgust or dismissal, as Swift moves from violence (drowning) to contempt (despising) to spite ("anger" is used here to mean "hurt" – but only if it can be done "with safety"). This final turn is telling: Swift is not "content" merely to reject the world, but rather feels an irresistible desire to engage with it. If social allegory – and, almost in passing, truly potent literary allegory – was no longer feasible, the task of the satirist was to analyze and diagnose the modal sickness ravaging the body politic. In this sense, the nearest analogue for Swift's project is not to be found in Spenser, still less in Dryden and Pope, but rather Sir Thomas More.

SWIFT'S NEGATIVE THEOLOGY

Swift may well have been the last person to remember what an allegorical society was like. Having written, early in his career, what might be considered a late Renaissance allegory (*The Battle of the Books*), a friend to both Sir William Temple and Alexander Pope, he bridged two cultural dispensations. For this reason, he was uniquely attuned to the social and literary consequences of a post-allegorical world. To begin measuring the distance fallen, consider the Swiftian grotesque: why, specifically, does much of Swift's imagery strike us as distorted? The most common explanation, of course, is that Swift is satirizing empiricism and the canons of realism that follow from it. Thus, as the Lilliputians puzzle over the contents of Gulliver's pockets, with everyday items examined in microscopic detail, Swift's point is obvious: myopic realism leads to estrangement, and a defamiliarizing of the world, not the reverse. When Swift calls Defoe a "stupid illiterate scribbler," he is expressing also a broader disgust at the kind of writing an empirical society has inspired.[20] But what, then, to make of the Renaissance grotesque, in which imagery very similar to Swift's strikes the reader as entirely appropriate? Here, contrapasso, or its absence, offers a partial explanation: it is immediately clear why Spenser's Argante (whose monstrous lust "devours" men) is gigantic, but by no means obvious why the Brobdingnagians must be – particularly after the charming miniature fairies of Lilliput (which most readers familiar with fairy tales would have expected to be virtuous) turned out to be astonishingly vicious, and what is more, vicious in a depressingly human way.

For Swift, the logic of contrapasso is inadequate. Why should horses represent the perfection of human reason? Swift's fantastic landscape and characters offer no clear and consistent pattern. And yet, we would argue, to approach the problem this way (*why is Swift's imagery so incoherent?*), is to miss the bigger picture. The more pregnant question, in addressing the gap between Renaissance and Swiftian grotesquerie, is instead: "what is the fate of representation in a world where the eye of God no longer has any correlate in the social body?" Allegory, as both a mode and genre, had relied for its energy on a sense of the vital link between the social formation and the godhead. The presence of God insured a stable system of representation, even as God's transcendence necessitated that the representation would be, on at least some level, non-mimetic: though Spenser is no less grotesque or fantastic than Swift, his imagery strikes us as decorous, appropriate and powerful. With the severing, however, of the royal connection between divine and human worlds, non-mimetic representations could no longer seem *natural*; artists were left with the choice of either self-conscious artifice (the impotent political allegories of the Restoration), or the mimesis of an empirical, secularized world (Defoe and the novel). Swiftian satire disturbs us, and retains an uncanny power, precisely because it disdains both of these alternatives: neither allegorical nor novelistic, it offers a kind of negative theology, in which the numinous power of the divine, though still strongly felt, can find no manifestation in the state, or indeed in any worldly object. The world itself, in consequence, appears distorted, a place where nothing can be recognized clearly; images that *remind* us of allegory abound, but the organizing system is brutally absent.

And thus we return to More. *Utopia* was a visionary imagining of the conditions under which a social allegory might function. Instead of surrendering to the impossibility of a Morean project, Swift shows the significance of this impossibility by illustrating what such a project might look like in his own, materialist age. His analysis, like More's, is from the perspective of a social allegorist – but where More, at the flood stage of Tudor prestige, could at least imagine the harnessing of existing modal energies to produce a perfect state, Swift, living a century too late, can only observe those energies misdirected or in chaos. Laputa in particular provides a vivid counterpoint to – or inverse image of – Utopia: it is the great emblem of Swift's recognition, expressed here and elsewhere, that the very pursuit of perfection, under false modal pretenses, will inevitably pull individuals and nations further into imperfection and chaos.

This insight can be quantified. Though the age of allegory has passed, Swift reasons, there nevertheless persist basic human desires and motives that allegory had once satisfied, and which still cry out for satisfaction. A post-allegorical culture will therefore strive to meet those needs but, in the absence of any ontic authority, will fail in certain predictable ways. And so Book III of *Gulliver's Travels* revolves around two famous images: the Academy of Lagado and the Flying Island of Laputa. The Academy, of course, is a frontal assault on the Royal Society, an attack on the institutional incarnation of the empirical worldview. Here, the basic human drive to coherence inexorably fails when it relies upon human ingenuity. Thus various projects reflect a reversal of cause and effect (e.g. the "Project for extracting Sun-Beams out of Cucumbers"; the "Operation to reduce human Excrement to its original Food"), and a misunderstanding of the relation between things (witness the attempt "to calcine Ice into Gunpowder"). Perhaps most telling, on the flying island, the aristocracy have convinced themselves that, through their observations, they have learned to hear the "Musick of the Spheres"; in fact, the music they have designed, far from corresponding with a divine harmony underlying the universe, is a meaningless cacophony – data with no organizing narrative.

To pursue the analysis further: because of the desires and motives from which they spring, the actions and products of a post-allegorical culture will inevitably resemble, morphologically, the products of allegory itself – indeed, this will be the very sign of their inversion. The Laputans, for example, have come to place "great Faith in judicial Astrology" (150); lacking the master narratives conferred by allegory (and underwritten by the divine word), they create and impose random narratives based on their minute yet uncomprehending stellar observations (this a revisiting of a theme explored earlier in the Bickerstaff papers). The sheer effort required to create artificial coherence is so great that the Laputans have lost any ability to comprehend events on earth (leading, most notably, to rampant adultery by the wives of the astronomers). The natural outcome, finally, of this obliviousness (to the very events they hope will be explained by the stars), is paranoia – that is, the creation of master-plots to avoid facing an unpleasant or baffling reality.[21] Laputan society is plagued by "Apprehensions . . . of impending Dangers" (151). That their "apprehensions" are commonly wrong does not assuage their terror; the astronomers simply continue to collect massive amounts of data and speculate wildly as to what new disasters they might predict. In much the same way, at the Academy of Lagado, harmless messages are transformed, via the state-sponsored delusion of the "Anagrammatick Method" (179), into the information the decoders want to hear. Signs and tokens abound, but with no referent in sight – and thus, more stress and paranoia. Laputan astronomy, like Lagadan decoding, is the gathering of information that can make sense only when understood as part of a greater coherence to which the Laputans do not have access, and which they cannot artificially reconstruct.

Their entire society, in short, can be seen as the negative image of Utopia. If More, imagining the conditions under which an allegorical society might thrive, had preached a simplification of the social body, a monoculture, Laputan society is complex beyond legibility. If the functioning of the Utopian state was made possible by unremitting and omnipresent surveillance, both Laputa and Lagado suffer from surveillance gone mad – at once despotic and utterly ineffectual. It was palpably obvious to Swift that no one apart from God can see into the soul. Thus we are presented with Laputa as a perversion of the state's attempt to create an empirical replacement for the divine eye. The absurdity of the device is apparent to all except those who have created it: faced with the loss of a watching God, a new one is constructed out of magnets and telescopes. The flying island is at once one of the great panoptic images in literature and (quite literally) π in the sky. It is not just a spying device used to discipline the population below, but also a weapon to punish and crush them – yet problems with employing this power are immediately apparent: the Island might shatter upon hitting the ground, or it might be heated from below by rebels until it cracks, or its magnetic core might be drawn in with lodestones and trapped – all weaknesses that the populace understands and exploits. Be that as it may, the Laputans in practice take "no Notice" of things around them: Gulliver's hosts are not only "altogether unmoved by the Sight of [his] Foreign Habit and Countenance" (contrast this with the impact of a similarly countenanced foreigner appearing in Utopia), but also "by the Shouts of the Vulgar" (147). The King has "not the least Curiosity" about "Laws, Government, Religion," or indeed anything besides Mathematics (153). Finally, while there is never a question in Utopia of the administrators' ability to comprehend and employ the fruits of their observations, the Laputans, unable even to understand themselves, are clearly ignorant as to what they would do with their power, were the system working correctly, and their attention properly occupied. The ultimate irony of the Flying Island is its own status as a literary allegorical figment elucidating the unfeasibility of social allegory. It embodies, in its impracticality, the allegorical ambition of Utopia literally separated from the material reality of the world, and ideologically alienated from the habits of mind and spirit that make allegory possible. Unable to comprehend what it sees, unsure even of what to look for, it is Utopia blinded.

SPLENDIDE MENDAX

It should come as no surprise that, after the publication of *Utopia*, More was accused of being a liar.[22] Writing at a time when *historia* had not yet divided unambiguously into *fact* (true history) and *fiction* (story), More indeed purposely commingled the two. Real people (Peter Gilles, "More" himself) converse with figments (Hythlodaeus); Hythlodaeus, in turn, sounds almost like an empiricist when certifying that Utopia, a fantasy, is "real": "if you'd been with me in Utopia, and seen it all for yourself as I did...you'd be the first to admit that you'd never seen a country so well organized" (46). One can sympathize, therefore, with More's enemy, Tyndale, when he commented, "if I were come whom [home] out of a land where never man were before, and where sure never man should come, I might tel as many wonders as *Master More* doth of *Utopia*, and no man could rebuke me."[23] Swift, of course, deploys many of the same reality-blurring techniques as More – but it's far harder to understand a contemporary reader's declaration that the "Book was full of improbable lies, and for his part he hardly believed a word of it."[24] One's first instinct is to write off the reader (an Irish bishop, according to the well-known anecdote) as a hopelessly naïve rube who, in the age of the novel, should have known better. And yet there is something in this reaction to which we still respond. Swift's medium, in *Gulliver's Travels* and elsewhere, is not the mimetic "formal realism" (to use Watt's term) of the novel, but neither is it the licensed fantasy of a Spenser. He writes not of a *deus absconditus* so much as a *civitas abscondita*, and if one accepts the premise underlying his work – that without adequate divine representation in the social body, the only honest depiction of reality must be fantastic – his work can seem more realistic, oddly, than the superficial and misleading mimesis of the novel. While no one is likely to book passage to Crusoe's island, still less the Bower of Bliss, Swift's work continues to owe much of its power to this uncanny reality effect. On the deepest level, satire is a form of realism; this is the afterlife of allegory.

NOTES

1 *Gulliver's Travels*, ed. Claude Rawson and Ian Higgins (Oxford: Oxford University Press, 2005), p. 9. All future references are to this edition.

2 Elsewhere, Swift simply calls St. Thomas "the only Man of true Virtue that ever England produced." (Marginalia in Swift's copy of Lord Herbert of Cherbury's *Life and Raigne of Henry VIII*, in *The Prose Works of Jonathan Swift*, ed. Herbert Davis, 13 vols. [Oxford: Basil Blackwell, 1939–68], vol. V, p. 247.)

3 Claude Rawson, *Gulliver and the Gentle Reader* (London: Routledge & Kegan Paul, 1973), p. 19. The classic study remains John Traugott's "A Voyage to Nowhere with Thomas More and Jonathan Swift," in *Swift: A Collection of Critical Essays*, ed. Ernest Tuveson (Englewood Cliffs, NJ: Prentice-Hall, 1962), pp. 143–69. See also Eugene R. Hammond, "Nature–Reason–Justice in *Utopia* and *Gulliver's Travels*," *SEL* 22:3 (1982), 445–68; and Jenny Mezciems, "Utopia and 'the Thing which is not': More, Swift, and Other Lying Idealists," *UTQ* 52 (1982), 40–62, which both concentrate on comparing Utopia with Houyhnhnmland. In "The Unity of Swift's 'Voyage to Laputa': Structure as Meaning in Utopian Fiction," *Modern Language Review* 72:1 (1977), 1–21, Mezciems suggests that the "divided figure" of Gulliver likely derives from Hythlodaeus. Brian Vickers argues that *Utopia* was more of a model for Book IV, and for Swift's satire in general, than has commonly been supposed ("The Satiric Structure of Gulliver's Travels and More's *Utopia*," in *The World of Jonathan Swift*, ed. Brian Vickers [Oxford: Blackwell, 1968], pp. 233–57); Hermann Real, on the other hand, argues that the influence of *Utopia* is exaggerated ("Voyages to Nowhere: More's *Utopia* and Swift's *Gulliver's Travels*," in *Eighteenth-Century Contexts*, ed. Howard D. Weinbrot *et al.* [Madison: University of Wisconsin Press, 2001], pp. 96–113).

4 Gordon Teskey, *Allegory and Violence* (Ithaca: Cornell University Press, 1996), p. 5.

5 See S. K. Heninger, Jr., *The Subtext of Form in the English Renaissance* (University Park, PA: Pennsylvania State University Press, 1994), p. 22.

6 Lacey Baldwin Smith, *Treason in Tudor England: Politics and Paranoia* (Princeton: Princeton University Press, 1986), p. 5.

7 Angus Fletcher, *Allegory: The Theory of a Symbolic Mode* (Ithaca: Cornell University Press, 1964), pp. 22–3, 120.

8 Thomas More, *Utopia*, trans. Paul Turner (New York: Penguin Books, 1965), p. 42. All future references are to this edition.

9 *Utopia*, pp. 30–1.

10 Stephen Greenblatt, *Renaissance Self-Fashioning* (Chicago: University of Chicago Press, 1980), p. 32.

11 Thus even Fredric V. Bogel, who attempts to complicate the move from Miltonic epic to Augustan mock-epic, concludes that "The distinctive character of Augustan satire and related forms may be understood as a literary consquence of – at least, a direct parallel to – the rewriting of Miltonic difference" (*The Difference Satire Makes* [Ithaca: Cornell University Press, 2001], pp. 19, 21). See also Weinbrot, *Eighteenth-Century Contexts*, pp. 189ff.

12 Traugott, A Voyage to Nowhere," p. 160.

13 Smith, *Treason in Tudor England*, p. 132.

14 Teskey, *Allegory and Violence*, p. 99.

15 *Twickenham Edition of the Works of Alexander Pope*, general ed. John Butt, 11 vols. (London: Methuen, 1938–68), vol. II, p. 243.

16 In his most confident work, *The Dunciad*, Pope is nonetheless nervous about his use of allegory, as in the remarkably defensive note to 3:28: "The allegory of the souls of the dull coming forth in the form of books, dressed in calf's leather, and being let abroad in vast numbers by Booksellers, is sufficiently intelligible."

17 Johnson, *Lives of the English Poets*, ed. George Birkbeck Hill, 3 vols. (Oxford: Clarendon University Press, 1905), vol. I, pp. 436–7.

18 Fletcher, *Allegory: The Theory of a Symbolic Mode*, p. 151.

19 Rawson, *Gulliver and the Gentle Reader*, pp. 55–6.

20 Swift, *Examiner* 15, in *The Prose Works of Jonathan Swift*, vol. III, p. 13.

21 The definition is adapted from Freud. See *The Schreber Case (Psychoanalytic Remarks on an Autobiographically Described Case of Paranoia (Dementia Paranoides))*, trans. Andrew Webber (New York: Penguin Books, 2002).

22 William Nelson, *Fact or Fiction: The Dilemma of the Renaissance Storyteller* (Cambridge, MA: Harvard University Press, 1973), p. 7.

23 William Tyndale, *The Whole Workes of W. Tyndall, Iohn Frith, and Doct. Barnes...* (London, 1573), p. 223. See also Rainer Pineas, "Thomas More's 'Utopia' and Protestant Polemics," *Renaissance News*, XVII (1964), 197–202.

24 Swift passed this anecdote along to Pope in November 1726 (*The Correspondence of Jonathan Swift*, ed. Harold Williams, 5 vols. [Oxford: Oxford University Press, 1963], vol. V, p. 189).

CHAPTER 2

Swift, Leviathan, *and the persons of authors*

Jonathan Lamb

Swift's references to Locke are few and insignificant, but Hobbes's *Leviathian* made a bigger impression on him. Claude Rawson has drawn attention to this as "a notion of radical restlessness," a shared intuition of "teeming perversity" that joined Swift closely to an author whom he did not like, and yet who encouraged in him techniques of reflexive excess that anticipate the modernist effects of Sterne and Beckett. This association runs deep, Rawson points out, infecting Swift's own irony and taking his writing as a whole to a level "where no act of containment, however complete and resourceful, can in the end be validated."[1] It is this problem of validation in Swift's early satires, signaled by authors who are merely "authors," that I want to probe in this essay, hoping to specify a link between restlessness and modernity in the shape of the printed book.

Abraham Bosse's design for the frontispiece of *Leviathan,* showing a single figure composed of a multitude of tiny ones, is the icon that draws Swift immediately to Hobbes.[2] Swift returns to it whenever he is thinking of associations of individuals, especially authors, or whenever he needs a metaphor for the functions of the brain. It seems also that the artificial person of the commonwealth, which bears the persons of all those little individuals and which is borne in turn by the sovereign, and thereafter by all the magistrates and office-holders that bear his person, represents for Swift a peculiarly fallible political organization. It exhibits the opposite of what Hobbes presents as a coherent distribution of intensive and extensive authority; instead it fosters the perpetual threat of aggression that is called in *Leviathan* a state of war. The two key terms in Hobbes's analysis of the accumulation and delegation of power are *author* and *own.* He says, "For that which in speaking of goods and possessions is called an Owner . . . speaking of Actions is called an Author . . . he that owneth his words and actions, is the AUTHOR."[3] The various persons within the commonwealth are *actors,* functioning on behalf of the original authors who long ago forwent their rights of action in order to escape the state of war. Consequently their authority is now purely virtual. It is the virtuality of

authors that Swift finds so bountifully represented in Hobbes, and which
for him seems most expressive of the emptiness of modernity and its
inevitable descent into nonsense. As far as he is concerned Leviathan is just
another name for mob, and everyone inside that kind of whale professes an
authority that never can be vindicated. This is how Swift discovers a
relationship between authors and their books of an exclusively material and
impermanent kind: an indistinct blend of mind and body that successive
commentators on the law of copyright struggled to define. Without
Hobbes he would not have made this discovery, based as it is upon his
analogy between political and literary representation and his idea of the
artificiality of the persons who perform it.

In the Preface to *A Tale of a Tub* the author explains the allegory behind
the title of his work. Like the tubs thrown overboard by mariners to divert
the violence of whales, his performance is intended to attract the attention
of pamphleteers who otherwise might attack the institutions of church and
state. The whale in this case is Hobbes's *Leviathan*, "which tosses and plays
with all schemes of Religion and Government," and the ship is the state or
commonwealth. His diversionary tactic will "prevent these Leviathans from
tossing and sporting with the Commonwealth (which of itself is too apt to
fluctuate)."[4] *Leviathan* is deployed for another analogy in *A Discourse on the
Mechanical Operation of the Spirit*, where the image of a multitude of small
creatures formed into a figure is applied to the brain, "a Crowd of little
Animals ... [which] cling together in the Contexture we behold, like the
Picture of Hobbes's Leviathan, or like Bees in perpendicular swarm upon a
Tree" (p. 279). In both examples Swift's modern author mistakes Levia-
than-as-Commonwealth for a crowd, ignoring the unity which Hobbes's
"artificiall Man" is supposed to embody, whether in the form of a person
or a mind. The factional pamphleteers represented by the whale put the
state in danger not because they are a rival unity but because they are
inchoate and represent nothing but themselves. As for the little creatures,
the bites of whose teeth cause us to think and feel, they are like Mandeville's unregenerate bees, each engaged on its own particular business
with no thought for the ultimate end or meaning of its activity.

Hobbes explained the difference between a crowd and Leviathan in his
De Cive as follows:

What actually is a Crowd of men? ... they are not a single entity but a number of
men, each of whom has his own will and his own judgement about every proposal ... There will be nothing about which the whole crowd, as a person distinct
from every individual, can rightly say, this is mine more than another's. Nor is
there any action which should be attributed to the crowd as their action ... For

this reason a crowd is not a natural person. But if the same crowd individually agree that the will of some one man or the consenting wills of a majority of themselves is to be taken as the will of all, that number then becomes one person.[5]

Once the crowd is represented by a person it is transformed into a Leviathan that cannot possibly menace the state because it is fundamental to the representational structure that renders the commonwealth a governable unity: one person, an artificial man, a mortal god, the body of the king, sovereign power, and so on through a series of personifications. But while it is still a crowd it dwells in a miniature state of nature where property cannot be held, nothing can be owned, and authorship means nothing.

Swift's modern author acts as an individual in a crowd and cannot conceive of a figure fit to represent his relation to it, although he tries very hard. He talks boastfully of the vast number of his fellow writers, the immense bales of paper they use, the ten thousand ways their works go out of the world never to be seen again, the multifarious symptoms of madness, the innumerable followers of zealous Jack, and so on, as if he were about to synthesize them all. But he is dogged by particularity, confessing that it is as hard to get quit of number as of hell (p. 55). His Leviathan is an undigested mass, the shape of shapelessness, like Milton's Death. It exhibits none of the symmetry of a corporate entity. Having mistaken a crowd for a person, the author is without any body of individuals to represent, and without any action to own. Defining "the Republick of Dogs" as "an Institution of the Many" where rights of possession lie in common and where everyone is in a "State of War, of every Citizen against every Citizen," the author of *The Battle of the Books* reduces politics from a commonwealth to a state of war, and the study of literature to combat (pp. 218–19). The nature of this combat is specified in *A Tale of Tub* as the use of gun-quills for firing missile ink at sheets of paper, which then confront other sheets in a per-petual strife of print. This warfare originates in a quarrel over property that cannot be arbitrated, arising as it does from the false claim for the pos-session of the territory of Parnassus made by the colonial Moderns in defiance of the customary rights of the aboriginal Ancients.

It follows that all titles to authorship among the Moderns (whether they are assumed or alleged) remain suspect and contestable, and any system of representation on which their authority depends is correspondingly impotent. *The Battle of the Books*, and the dispute about ancient and modern learning on which it is based, began with Richard Bentley's and William Wotton's challenge to Sir William Temple's attribution of authorship of Aesop's fables to Aesop and of Phalaris's letters to Phalaris. These are really the names of a succession of editors and interpolators, argued Bentley, who was satisfied with the authenticity of no writer who was not fully annotated by himself, as Bentley's Horace, Bentley's Milton, and so on. From the pro-Ancient point of view this sort of editorship was not a judicious assignment of property, just a more elaborate form of theft. The ladder or gallows, the favorite oratorical machine among the British, stands so eminent because it institutionalizes the relationship between theft and authorship, being ascended only by those remarkable for confounding the distinction between *meum* and *tuum* (p. 63). Bentley's Milton is no longer Milton, therefore, but Bentley. The ladder is not so much the penalty for literary felony as it is the necessary circumstance of modern authorship, for without pillage there would be nothing to write, nothing falsely to claim, and no position from which to make announcements. For his part the modern author of *A Tale of a Tub* owns that none of the 738 flowers and shining hints in his commonplace book, all of which he has incorporated into his treatise, in fact belongs to him (p. 209). Yet it is solely on the basis of these borrowings that he has set up as author. He pretends to authorship on the basis of what he does not own, in a world where everyone is doing the same. The corollary is that no one owns any thing, no one shares a common cause with another, nor does any person represent individuals. In the war with the Ancients he notices widespread defections to the enemy, "and our nearest Friends begin to stand aloof, as if they were half-ashamed to own Us" (p. 416). Authors have challenged "Authors, as unworthy their established Post in the Commonwealth." And as if authors and owners and their representative bodies were not already acting in a sufficiently perplexed, fantastic, and futile relation to one another, he adds, "This is the utmost I am authorized to say upon so ungrateful and melancholy a Subject" (pp. 64–5), speaking in the person of this non-community. Similarly in his apostrophe to Prince Posterity, where the author once more wishes to cite copiousness of wit as proof of commonwealth, he can produce no evidence, because the wit is not owned, therefore it is not kept or preserved. It instantly turns to waste, and is consigned to the "Abyss of Things" (p. 32). On a broad front the modern author stands vindicated by nothing but his bare assertions, which are necessarily dubious even if they purport to be true ("I have stolen this"). Like Gulliver he is forced to say only the thing which is not, and to affirm that which is neither ownable nor evident, because he keeps no company but with a mob or crowd.

Notwithstanding the problems he faces in establishing himself the person or vicar of "the Institution of the Many," the author persistently refers to himself as a representative of communities. At different times he speaks on behalf of a "vast flourishing Body" of authors and "our Corporation of Poets" (p. 33); he mentions that he is the official agent of a Grand Committee and the sponsor of "a large Academy" (pp. 40–1). His most valiant attempt in this regard is to speak for the inhabitants of Bedlam, "that honourable society, whereof I had some time the happiness to be an unworthy member" (p. 176). Here the analogy between crowds and brains is perfected as reciprocal disorder, and the only authority the author can cite for representing the insane – those who, like children and fools according to Hobbes, are incapable of conferring authority – is the history of his own insanity.[6] The structure of his brain is as weak as their social bond. He aims at what Hobbes would call actorhood rather than an authorship, but the person he claims to be is unstable as the cloud he points to when explaining to Prince Posterity the metamorphoses of a modern community – now a bear, now an ass, now a dragon. His Leviathan is just such an ephemeral image, and there is no authority by which he can represent it, and no symmetry that might allow it to be embodied in his person. He is only virtually an author, and not even virtually an actor. He is what Hobbes would call an idol, the material form of something that doesn't exist and which therefore represents nothing at all. All that is left of such an empty sign is "the matter of the Image, which is Wood, Stone, Metall, or some other visible creature" (*Leviathan,* p. 449).

This is no impediment to the grandeur of the illusion. The author's aim is the universal benefit of mankind, to be achieved by means of the advancement of universal knowledge, first enlarged to all spheres of learning and then distilled into a universal system (pp. 180, 106, 126). His cabbalistic and alchemical agendas are aspects of a mystical cult of unity and abridgment – the *Iliad* in a nutshell – that Michel de Certeau finds typical of all mystical and proto-modernist enterprises in the seventeenth century, when coalitions of menacing and violent circumstances throughout Europe weakened or removed traditional sources of authority, tempting isolated egos to invent utopian dialectics of "the nothing and the all."[7] Although this dialectic was pitched at the conjunction of knowledge and practice, or what Bacon called the union of contemplation and action, its novelty necessarily divided it from institutional norms and received forms of expression, leading to exaggerations, improprieties, and barbarisms, particularly in usage.[8] He says that mystics were notorious not only for their pseudo-synthetic programmes of knowledge, but also for the jargon and obscurity of their universal languages, and for the extravagance of their metaphors and tropes (pp. 113–19). The modern author refers to this modern state of nonsense and glossolalia when he complains that

Time ("Author of this universal Ruin") has destroyed the works of authors who could not write English: "Unhappy infants! Many of them barbarously destroyed before they have so much as learnt their mother-tongue to beg for pity" (pp. 32–3). Similarly, the author of *The Mechanical Operation of the Spirit* notices that the rhetoric of the modern saints issues as "insignificant Words, Incoherences, and Repetition" and sometimes just as noise – sighs and humming (p. 290).

When Swift's "real" author writes his Apology in order to distinguish his own irony from the imbecile panegyric of his false counterpart, the difference between true and false authorship is presented as almost exclusively social. The real author belongs to a club resembling the community of wit praised by Shaftesbury in his *Letter on the Freedom of Wit and Humour*. His community is as solid and real as his authorship, committed to the pursuit of good taste and a relish for what is just and seemly. His meaning is evident to his company even when the expression is oblique; and he is aware that his social circle extends from the past to the future. He mentions with disgust the unhappy turns of phrase, *impedimenta literarum*, such as William Wotton's fondness for colloquial expressions ("it is all a Farce and a Ladle") and modern slang ("Banter") (p. 19), or Bentley's ill-manners (he called Aesop's editor "that idiot of a monk").[9] Wotton's and Bentley's impoliteness indicates with what little authority they censure a work of wit. Although Pope compared Bentley to a whale in *The Dunciad*, he is no Leviathan of letters, and every attempt he makes to speak as one collapses into the vituperation, theft, and violence of the crowd. He and Wotton are the blind proofs that ownership, authorship, representation, and governance are the fictions of a modernity scarcely capable of disguising its savagery. Bentley is chief exemplar, having steeped himself in literature not in order to civilize and polish himself, but to become more brutal in his combat with other authors. Scaliger tells him, "Thy Learning makes thee more barbarous, thy Study of Humanity more inhuman; thy converse among Poets, more groveling, miry, and dull" (p. 253).

With the introduction of a real author as a counterpart to these individual ones, a difficulty emerges. As it was not sufficient merely to describe the savage traits and ill language of crowd-authors, wit – specified as irony – was introduced to distinguish Ancient taste from Modern prejudice, raillery from railing, and so on. Nevertheless the real author is obliged to defend and explain his use of irony, even though he asserts that within his community its value is self-evident. Clearly that club is not as large or powerful as the public which has found his piece outrageous. Being forced therefore to instance and explain examples of his wit, so destroying it, the true author finds that his impersonation of a false one has implicated him in the *mise en abyme* of false authorities so typical of modern self-representation. How can a natural person (the true author) represent a *soi-disant* artificial person (the modern author) who is so insubstantial it is equivalent to representing nothing, and not be caught up in the crowd's state of war? How for that matter can the true author represent the closed community of wit without becoming an artificial person, the Leviathan of irony, more artificial than the author he impersonates? In his efforts to justify what ought to have been instantly demonstrable, he contradicts the authority he set out to maintain. The further he gets from self-evidence, the further he is driven from figurative language to literalisms; and the further he gets from the common sense of propriety, the more he sounds like a dunce. In a strangely self-annihilating gesture, the true author's last shift as ironist is aggressively to declare his own anonymity, daring anyone to own what he himself cannot put his name to.

This problem is to some extent understood by the modern author, too, as one that allies representative personhood with wit. He begins his treatise by stating that all meaning lies hidden beneath occult figures and fables, and that all wisdom is shut up in allegories whose personified actors drive the action and make the point. His "Scheme of Oratorial Receptacles" is a vast plan of wit ("a Type, a Sign, an Emblem, a Shadow, a Symbol, bearing Analogy to the spacious Commonwealth of Writers" [p. 61]). Because this commonwealth is no more substantial than Leviathan in the allegory of the tub, its signs and emblems are as incapable of representing meaning as the author is of representing the crowd of writers. He has no other relation to the many but that of an individual; so these figures have no other relation to a body of ideas than single literal terms. Exactly the same insufficiency that afflicts the author when he tries to act as the person of a commonwealth overwhelms his words when he tries to make them represent more than they simply say. We observe metaphors contradicting one another (wisdom is first a fox and then a hen) or collapsing into literalism (words are made of air, therefore learning is nothing but wind). Personification is especially vulnerable. The genealogy of the true critic dissolves into a haphazard collection of hieroglyphic possibilities – critic as ass, serpent, beggar, brass, rat, and dog – just like the clouds on a windy day that represented the modern commonwealth of authors successively as a bear, an ass, and a dragon. Eventually he determines to meddle with this kind of wit no longer, parting company with those whose converting imaginations "dispose them to reduce all Things into Types...whose peculiar Talent lies in fixing Tropes and Allegories to the Letter, and refining what is Literal into Figure and Mystery" (p. 190).

The tale itself is an allegory, a fable of parental authority, which contrives its own ruin, for "coats" end up as heterogeneous pieces of fabric, and the "will" is reduced to a body of words that can be made to mean literally whatever its readers desire. The allegory of the *Tale* runs out of steam when finally there is no text left worth interpreting and no authority left to dispute. Then everything is literalized. Nothing remains of the tension between the story and its application that might preserve interest or suspense. At this point the author finds his commonplace book empty and his material for digressions all used up, an embarrassment running parallel with the emptying of the will and the coats of deeper meaning. So he is driven to his last shift and commences to write upon nothing – owning in effect that his authority extends neither to allegory nor even to literal meaning, just to nonsense. His treatise disintegrates into noise, the sound of scratching made when "the Pen still move[s] on; by some called the Ghost of Wit" (p. 208).

Each attempt made to invest a symbol or figure with significance descends first into literalism or tautology, and at last into nonsense. The material form of this nonsense is always the same, a dark liquid draining from the individuals that compose crowds. Whether a crowd is understood as a brain or a Leviathan, its particles yield phlegm, snot, sperm, poison – fluids that ultimately take the form of ink. The little commonwealth of the brain, for instance, is subject to a looseness of the bowels that flows from the head as snot-verse and rheum-rhetoric, and can be improved by orators: "A Master Work-man shall *blow his Nose so powerfully* as to pierce the Hearts of his People" (p. 281). The war of all against all is fought with ink derived from the brains and gall of modern authors, seasoned with extra supplies from the teats of the goddess Criticism. In the introductory fable of the spider and the bee in *The Battle of the Books*, the odious self-sufficiency of the spider is explained by Aesop as an allegory of modern authors, whose originality is nothing but poison distilled from their own insides and spat at the public, "excrement and venom." No sooner is it received than it is returned in a perpetual cycle of projectile waste. Thus the Bedlam professor survives on his own excrement, expelling it, then re-ingesting it (p. 178); and the Aeolist congregation join a circle, blowing each other up with wind that is then belched and farted backwards and forwards (p. 154). The serpent-critic "emit[s] a poisonous juice: whereof whoever drinks, that person's brains fly out of his nostrils" (p. 100). The modern books in St. James's Library are in the same plight, either emitting this malignant spirit or doused with it, the occasion and the means of their endless warfare. The true author declares in his Apology, perhaps too confidently, that his work is so much his own as never to suffer from this poisonous effluvium, proof against being "battered Dirt-Pellets however envenom'd the Mouths may be that discharge them" (p. 10).

If the spider is the type of modern authors, then the person of this crowd is not our author, who owns nothing and has no authority to represent anyone, but the goddess Criticism. She evinces spider-like habits, being a divinity who feeds her subaltern agents ("Noise and Impudence, Dulness and Vanity") from her spleen, which they suck like a breast, imbibing the black liquor that will foment the war of all against all. When Criticism enters the field of battle she flings some of this liquid into Bentley's mouth, provoking such a disturbance in his brain that when he starts fighting, "an atramentous Quality, of most malignant Nature, was seen to distil from his Lips" (p. 251). Like the circulation of unspent sperm in the Digression on Madness, which evaporates into clouds and then distils into madness, ink courses through the system, alternating between the status of physical excrement and a big idea, a private embarrassment and a public outrage, but never finally transcending its material form of sewage or its tendency to sustain a state of war. In personifying this process Criticism does not assemble it into a real Leviathan, nor does she act as a true Hobbesian person. She preserves the accidents of crowds – their atomization, pugnacity, and disorder – literally by circulating ink. She is like the god worshiped by Jack's disciples, "a new Deity, who hath since met with a vast Number of Worshippers, by some called Babel, by others, Chaos" (p. 194). Such deities embody unrepresentable incoherence by manipulating its most obvious physical attributes – noise, waste, and dirt. They are not representations, visible or audible, of a summary idea of disorder; nor are they projections of human qualities. Like Death, War, Fate, Madness, History, or even Samuel Johnson's Observation, theirs is a force to which human beings are blindly subject because no one is able to penetrate its closed circuit of causes and effects.

And here it is worth distinguishing between personifications that serve human purposes and those that don't. When the modern author meditates on the religion of the Aeolists, he adapts an observation of Lucretius on the invention of gods and devils: "As the most unciviliz'd Parts of Mankind have some way or other, climbed up into the Conception of a God, or Supream Power, so they have seldom forgot to provide their Fears with certain ghastly Notions, which instead of better, have served them pretty tolerably for a Devil" (p. 158). Thus the Aeolists worship wind, and fear all enemies of their god, such as windmills and chameleons, that assault or eat it. The undulation between a higher metaphorical point of good (inspiration) and a lower point of evil (belching) corresponds to others, such as ironic wit and duncely literalism, representative persons and inchoate crowds, emblematic meaning and leaking ink, afflatus and flatulence. Personifications at the lower level operate outside the zone of figurative representation by making singular, univocal, and material affirmations of what they are. Whatever they discharge they reincorporate; whatever they distribute they gather back. They embody nothing but their own repetitive individuality. Personifications are wrapped up in their tautological perfection, being cause and effect of the same thing: "If the personification knows anything at all, it knows itself, with a symmetrical purity unmatched by anything in empirical consciousness."[10] They are not the result of the human "propension to spread a resemblance of ourselves over all other things."[11] They have no significance beyond what they do and are; and what they do is indifferent to human concerns, "removed from our Affairs...from Sorrow free, secure from Danger...neither pleased with Good, nor vexed with Ill," as Lucretius says of the gods.[12]

Lucretius wished to write a poem on the mobility of matter and the impermanence of forms that would rely on no deities or personifications. Except the very general figure of Venus, who represents the appetence of a poet undistracted by false resemblances, there are no gods in *De rerum natura*. Lucretius' neglect of all the arts of music and painting is consistent with this design, since their representations provide only fainter impressions of impressions, weaker images of images that fly directly from the superficies of things. In his theatre there are no actors, no figures bearing the persons of others, just the vivid colors of the awnings dyeing the audience different hues.[13] Eventually Swift's modern author arrives at the same position as Lucretius, content with his total failure to abstract the qualities of things or to represent meaning in a public and ownable form. Things get left as things, despite the grand gestures towards system and synthesis, and persons are traceable only in the material residues they leave as stains on the pages of books. Our author has no name, no genealogy, no home, no society, and no future. His book does not record his actions or indeed anything that is properly his own. What remains of *it* is all there is of *him*. Failing as history his book becomes something like a diary of the moments of writing: "I profess...that what I am going to say is literally true this Minute I am writing" (p. 36).

John Dunton, who is acknowledged in the Introduction as eminent among those booksellers publishing the eloquence of the British gallows, was eminent also in this modern way of writing. In his *Voyage round the World,* a peculiar autobiography often thought to anticipate *Tristram Shandy,* he reduces all experience to the model of voyaging ("We take shipping at our birth"), and all writing to a journal or log.[14] He confesses that his pocket-book is "a man's own private history from breakfast to dinner time, from dinner to supper etc. . . . By this method, which is wholly of modern invention . . . a gentleman can see at a minute's warning as well what he is, as where he is to be, or what he is to do, or whither he is to go" (vol. I, p. 103). Recording the same pointless succession of moments, Swift's modern author advises his readers to put themselves in the same "Circumstances and Postures of Life, that the Writer was in, upon every important Passage, as it flow'd from his Pen" (p. 44). De Certeau distinguishes this sort of writing as an adventure with language itself. It replaces the owning of an author's actions with what he calls "a manner of speaking" (p. 183). This personal signature or style is implicated in the accumulations of pointless minutiae designed to let the author as well as the world know (as Dunton puts it) who he is. "So great a Glory do I esteem it to be the Author of these Works, that I cannot . . . endure that any should own 'em who have nothing to do with 'em . . . there is such a sort of whim in the style, something so like my self" (1691: 1.19). The self disclosed by this whimsical style is authenticated however not in the world but in the text, for Dunton is as attached to anonymity as the ironical author of the *Tale*: "[No] other Person[s] yet named or suspected, are the real Authors of this Book, or the real Evonder, but that I, and I only am be; and who I am, is yet, and ever shall be a Secret" (1691: 1.23). What is written by these haphazard interventions of the pen has nothing to do with the tendency or providence of a series of known events or with the intention of a consistent agent; its interest lies solely in the resources of the writer as they are exhibited from moment to moment. Like Dunton, de Certeau compares this to a traveler's log or an epistolary novel, where the pen responds to the passing event, and the authenticity of the record relies purely on the turn of a timely word (p. 117). Out of these the author constructs what de Certeau calls "the mansion of the soul," namely a fiction that authorizes writing (p. 180).

By a specifically literary route we arrive at Hobbes's notion of idols as fictions which represent nothing but the materials of which they are composed. Instead of "Wood, Stone, Metall, or some other visible creature," here they are made of paper and ink. The metamorphosis of Criticism during the war of all against all is the pattern for all her worshipers: "She therefore gathered up her Person into an Octavo Compass: Her Body grew white and arid, and split in pieces with Driness; the thick turned into Pastboard, and the thin into Paper, upon which, her Parents and Children artfully strowed a Black Juice, or Decoction of Gall and Soot, in Form of Letters" (p. 243). These elements of the visible creature are still faithful to the "Phantasmes of the brain" in which all idols originate (*Leviathan*, p. 449), thanks to the black juice flowing from one to the other. In *The Battle* it is reported of the volumes-at-arms, "In these Books, is wonderfully instilled and preserved, the Spirit of each Warrier, while he is alive; and after his Death, his Soul transmigrates there, to inform them . . . So, we may say, a restless Spirit haunts over every Book, till Dust or Worms have seized upon it" (pp. 222–3). It is already clear that the book does not represent its author any more than Criticism represents writers, or than the book she turns herself into represents her. There is nothing of the author as author except the material constituents of the book. The other idols in the *Tale* are the same. The apt conjunction of lawn and black satin which makes a bishop is the bishop, not a sign of episcopality, nor the token of an office of state which a human creature assumes and represents. In the sensible impression of the fabric alone does its importance inhere, which explains why all systems of dress are reducible in the *Tale* to fashion: the function of clothes from moment to moment. The wind of Aeolists in its downward motion is the same: it signifies only what it is – farts, belches, vagitus, not some other idea or meaning. Wit and the sublime are not found in figurative language, not in snot and phlegm and their cognate substance, ink, as they are traced on cloth or paper. The triumph of the "Digression Concerning the Use and Improvement of Madness" is the unequivocal and commanding paraphrase of Lucretius in praise of the surface appearances of things, most beautiful when they are appreciated solely for what they are, the material residues of themselves, "the Films and Images that fly off . . . from the Superficies of Things" (p. 174). The splendor as well as the squalor of things is perceived in the image of the visible creature. "How fading and insipid do all Objects accost us, that are not conveyed in the Vehicle of Delusion!" (p. 172). The vehicle of delusion is not something that stands for something else: it is a self-conveying fiction.

The spirit of modern books is related to what Mark Rose calls the "ownness" of copy, a quality in marketed writing that passes with the book from hand to hand, never to be monopolized or even fully understood by its possessor.[15] The ownness of a book coincides with its alienation from its original owner and its subsequent metamorphosis into an independent printed thing. In the case of modern authors, however, there are extra factors contributing to this autonomy of their works. Not only did they never really own the copy, their war of all against all insures that books, like other things in a war, act without reference to the humans who pretend to the ownership of them. When the narrator of *The Battle* says, "Things were in this Ferment," or "Things were at this Crisis," (pp. 227, 229) he means things "Ancient and modern Creatures called Books" (239), whose conflict will be decided not by a human or even a god, but by another book, "the Book of Fate . . . three large Volumes in Folio, containing Memoirs of all Things" (p. 239). These books offer mansions for the soul in the same way that the stool or throne of a prince offers a dwelling for the royal spirit, that is to say solely by means of a materialized fiction (*Leviathan,* p. 449). What is real is the thing, and what is fantastic is the notion that its spirit or soul could refer to anything but itself. Its soul is not the abstract form or essence of either the author or the prince, a Pythagorean immaterial substance capable of metempsychosis. Instead it is a Lucretian aggregate of matter and mind, temporarily cohering as the paper, ink, pasteboard, and calf of the book, or the wood and metal of a throne. Criticism, it turns out, is Clinamen's sister. The more a book performs as an unowned thing, the more spirit it exhibits; whereas the more it functions as a vehicle for the identity and meaning of its author, the less there is of its own. Modern books in the universe of the *Tale* never have to convey identity or meaning. Thanks to the inconstancy and inanity of their modern authors, they are entirely in charge of their own affairs.

Things that represent nothing but images of themselves stay as they are for as long as their atoms hold together. The words that attach to them may try to act as metaphors but they will be reduced to univocality in the end. Humpty Dumpty always organizes his words like this, ensuring that they mean only what he says; for he is careful never to say what he means. It is a distinction on which the extravagance of the modern manner of speaking is established. The humans who claim to be authors of books according to Humpty Dumpty's doctrine prove, like the egg himself, to be extremely fragile. Swift's modern author has been intermittently mad; his health is ruined by venereal disease; he is alternately the secretary of the universe and a singleton in a garret. Dunton talks of his "soul's luggage" as a compendium of metamorphoses: "I may have a piece of roaring lion rambled into me . . . one leg of me may have been rambled out of a whole, and a piece of my left hip from the shoulder blade of an elephant."[16] In a more extreme form these modern authors experience the predicament of even the truest of true authors in having such temporary mansions for their souls that authorial identity can never be preserved for very long. Apuleius' Lucius is transformed into an ass, a metamorphosis consequent upon another, foretold him by Diophanes: "I will become a long story, an unbelievable tale, a book in several volumes."[17]

NOTES

1 'The Character of Swift's Satire,' in Claude Rawson ed., *The Character of Swift's Satire* (Cranbury NJ: Associated University Presses, 1983), 22, 35; *Gulliver and the Gentle Reader* (London: Routledge and Kegan Paul, 1973), 59.

2 Horst Bredekamp, *Thomas Hobbes Der Leviathan*, 3rd edn. (Berlin: Akademie Verlag, 2006), pp. 31–51.

3 Thomas Hobbes, *Leviathan*, ed. Richard Tuck (Cambridge: Cambridge University Press, 1996), p. 218. All future references are to this edition and will be cited parenthetically in the text.

4 Jonathan Swift, *A Tale of a Tub*, ed. A. C. Guthkelch and D. Nichol Smith (Oxford: Clarendon Press, 1920) p. 40. All future references are to this edition and will be cited parenthetically in the text.

5 Thomas Hobbes, *On the Citizen*, ed. Richard Tuck (Cambridge: Cambridge University Press, 1998) pp. 75–6.

6 See Hobbes, *Leviathan*, p. 113.

7 Michel de Certeau, *The Mystic Fable*, vol. I, *The Sixteenth and Seventeenth Centuries*, trans. Michael B. Smith (Chicago: Chicago University Press, 1986), p. 156.

8 de Certeau, *Mystic Fable*, pp. 119, 133.

9 Richard Bentley, *Dissertations upon the Epistles of Phalaris*, 2 vols., ed. Alexander Dyce (London: Francis Macpherson, 1836), vol. II, p. 233.

10 Steven Knapp, *Personification and the Sublime* (Cambridge, MA: Harvard University Press, 1985), p. 4.

11 Hugh Blair in Ian Balfour, *The Rhetoric of Romantic Prophecy* (Stanford: Stanford University Press, 2002), p. 67.

12 Lucretius, *Of the Nature of Things*, 2 vols. (London: Daniel Browne, 1743), vol. I, p. 153.

13 Lucretius, *Of the Nature of Things*, vol. II, p. 13.

14 John Dunton, *The Life, Travels, and Adventures of Christopher Wagstaff*, 2 vols. (London: J. Hinxman, 1762), vol. I, p. 50. First published as *A Voyage Round the World: or, a Pocket Library*, 3 vols. (London: Richard Newcombe, 1691). References in the text are to both editions, distinguished by date.

15 Mark Rose, *Authors and Owners: The Invention of Copyright* (Cambridge, MA: Harvard University Press, 1993), p. 118.

16 Dunton, *Voyage round the World*, vol. I, p. 43.

17 Apuleius, *Metamorphoses*, 2 vols., trans. J. Arthur Hanson (Cambridge, MA: Harvard University Press, 2001), vol. I, p. 85.

CHAPTER 3

Killing no murder: Jonathan Swift and polemical tradition

Ian Higgins

This chapter considers Swift's response to pamphlets and pamphleteers and sees his invective against Whigs and Dissenters as belonging to a polemical tradition in which, to adapt the title of a famous tyrannicide tract, "killing is no murder." This polemical extremism was strongly identified with crypto-Jacobite High Churchmen in Swift's day, whose printed sermons and pamphlets Daniel Defoe notoriously mimicked in *The Shortest-Way with the Dissenters*, producing a sensational epitome of the polemical kind. It has avatars in twentieth-century literature in the invective of the French novelist and pamphleteer Louis-Ferdinand Céline, a reactionary or right-wing anarchist with whom Swift, famously described as a "Tory anarchist" by George Orwell, has been compared.

What I am calling the killing-no-murder tradition of invective is characterized by black humor, blatant exaggeration, and elision of its homicidal rhetoric with actual menaces. It evinces what Walter Benjamin in a study of Baudelaire called "the metaphysics of the *provocateur*" and a technique he called the *"culte de la blague."* Benjamin saw the technique as integral to Fascist propaganda and exhibited in Céline's pamphlet (or extended polemic) *Bagatelles pour un massacre*.[1] As Nicholas Hewitt remarks, Céline's use of the technique "which consists in stating the outrageous in such a way that it appears as a joke, but has in fact a deadly serious meaning," of "saying apparently in jest things which are in reality intended to be taken as true" has important precedents in eighteenth-century polemical literature, and especially in Swift and Defoe.[2] After his pillorying for *The Shortest-Way with the Dissenters* (1702), Defoe claimed that he had been punished "for telling that Story in Earnest which the Church men Preach'd, Printed, and Talkt about only in Jest."[3] What Benjamin would call the *"culte de la blague"* was perhaps being witnessed by Swift's contemporaries in their response to the extremism of the satire on Popery and Dissent in *A Tale of a Tub* and *The Mechanical Operation of the Spirit.* It was described as a "JOKE" in which Swift "*certainly discover'd the* Shortest way with CONTROVERSY"[4] or as a "Banter," as in William Wotton's appalled response to Swift's book: "one of the Prophanest Banters upon the Religion of *Jesus Christ*, as such, that ever yet appeared. In the *Tale*, in the *Digressions*, in the *Fragment*, the same Spirit runs through, but rather most in the *Fragment*, in which all extraordinary Inspirations are the Subjects of his Scorn and Mockery, whilst the Protestant Dissenters are, to outward appearance, the most directly levelled at."[5] Swift's invective provides exemplars of the kind of polemical extremism imitated by Defoe. His writings against Whigs and Dissenters were an imaginative "literary" transposition of contemporary demotic polemical language, as indeed were Céline's anti-Semitic pamphlets.[6] Swift, Defoe's *Shortest-Way with the Dissenters*, and Céline are major presences in Claude Rawson's searching examinations of extermination rhetoric across literary genres and European history, and Rawson provides the now standard account to which this essay is indebted.[7]

SWIFT, POLEMICAL TRADITION, AND
KILLING NOE MURDER

Swift expressed an aversion to pamphlets, describing them as "usually the vilest things, in nature."[8] Pamphlets are found at the rear of the Moderns in *The Battle of the Books*: "In the last Place, came infinite Swarms of *Calones*, a disorderly Rout led by *Lestrange*; Rogues and Raggamuffins, that follow the Camp for nothing but the Plunder; All without *Coats* to cover them."[9] This disdain reflects an old pejorative association of pamphlets with prostituted writing and scurrility, even though pamphlets had become in the early modern period a major print medium for writing on affairs of church and state, and in many cases were not mere ephemera but enduring literary works.[10] Swift made a performance of not mentioning the names of high-profile contemporary Whig pamphleteers, implying that they were unspeakable, forgettable, and beneath notice. In the *Examiner* of May 17, 1711 we learn everything but the name of the "little whiffling *Frenchman*" who writes *The Political State of Great Britain*, in which Swift is attacked. "*One* A. BOYER" was added as a footnote to the 1735 collected edition of Swift's writings.[11] Daniel Defoe was treated in a similar manner, as Claude Rawson and Maximillian Novak have discussed.[12] When Swift expressed doubt as to whether his own pamphlets that "were temporary occasional things" would be thought worth including in Faulkner's edition of his *Works*, his friend

Charles Ford replied that they were an important part of the canon of his writings. Ford paralleled Swift's Tory pamphlets with a famous tyrannicide tract of 1657, *Killing Noe Murder*, and with the *Letters* of Cicero (an important classical authority for tyrannicide invoked in *Killing Noe Murder*). Ford wrote: "I see no reason why all the pamphlets published at the end of the Queen's reign might not be inserted. Your objection of their being momentary things will not hold. *Killing no Murder*, and many other old tracts, are still read with pleasure, not to mention *Tully's Letters*, which have not died with the times."[13]

Although Swift's library contained pamphlets by some prominent Whigs and Tory High Churchmen, pamphlets are remarkably under-represented in the extant catalogues of his library.[14] However, Swift is often operating in allusive fields outside the purlieu of his known library. Swift certainly knew the work of high-profile and fugitive contemporary pamphleteers, alluded to them, and appropriated from them. His correspondence reveals his professional interest in what pamphlets were coming out and his polemic explains the art of pamphleteering practice: the use of "Caution and double Meaning, in order to prevent Prosecution" and the "several Ways here of abusing one another, without incurring the Danger of the Law."[15] His pamphlets and satires attest to his reading in the pamphleteering of the early Stuart period, the Civil War and Interregnum, and the Restoration.[16] Violent passages in Swift's great satires, *A Tale of a Tub* and *Gulliver's Travels*, seem to be palimpsests of pamphlets from the world of seventeenth-century pamphleteering.

The satiric extremism of *A Tale of a Tub* is a literary transposition of earlier but now forgotten polemical texts. For example, a Restoration Tory propaganda sheet of 1682 entitled *The Whig Rampant: or, Exaltation* imputing that the Whigs are avatars of the rebellious Puritan Enthusiasts illustrates its text with a picture of a Tub preacher and, as in Section I of Swift's *Tale*, the "exalted" Tub preachers are elevated to the gallows. In the fifth edition of Swift's *Tale* there is an illustrative plate juxtaposing a Dissenting preacher in a wooden tub with a hanging on the "wooden tree" or gallows.[17] In Section IX of the *Tale*, "*A Digression concerning the Original, the Use and Improvement of* Madness *in a Commonwealth*," the author applies to leading Tory Opposition MPs to bring in a bill to release the inmates of Bedlam to take up their natural appointments as military officers, lawyers, financiers, courtiers, and physicians in the post-Revolution Williamite state. A blaspheming Bedlamite foaming at the mouth should be given command of a regiment of dragoons and sent to join the rest in Flanders, for example.[18] There had been such ironic recommendations before for the improvement of madness in a Commonwealth. A royalist satiric pamphlet entitled *Englands Mad Petition to the Right Honourable the, &c. . . . Presented to the Houses on Thursday, August 26. 1647* has the insane people of England, who have abandoned their king and episcopacy, petition parliament to "take into mature consideration" releasing all the "Mad people" confined in Bedlam and to open the prisons and make "the maddest of us all," John Lilburne, "Commander in Chiefe of all our Mad multitude."[19] Swift's violent derision of the Williamite Whig establishment in this passage of the *Tale* appears to be a palimpsest of Anglican royalist satire against the Puritan government.

One pamphlet from the world of Leveller and royalist conspiracy against Cromwell certainly enjoyed a Jacobite Tory afterlife in the first half of the eighteenth century. The pamphlet is not present in Swift's library but it seems to have a presence in *Gulliver's Travels*. *Killing Noe Murder* was written by the Leveller, New Model Army Agitator, and fugitive conspirator against Cromwell Edward Sexby, perhaps in collaboration with others (possibly with the Presbyterian royalist conspirator Silius Titus), and was published in 1657 under the name of Sexby's fellow Army Agitator William Allen. The pamphlet invites Oliver Cromwell to accept the tribute of assassination and the proffered opportunity of dying for his people. The aim of the pamphlet is to incite members of the army to assassinate Cromwell, adducing biblical and humanist republican antityrannical authorities to prove it a glorious and lawful action which will deliver an enslaved people from bondage. *Killing Noe Murder* was well received by exiled royalists.[20] And despite its radical republican principles and provenance it was seasonally reprinted at times of Jacobite subversion and conspiracy in the first half of the eighteenth century. The *English Short Title Catalogue* records editions in 1708, 1715, 1734, 1741, 1743, and 1745.[21] This pamphlet advocating the assassination of Cromwell and justifying the good work with Cicero's authority and the classical exemplum of Caesar's assassination by Marcus Brutus may well have been a distant model for the anti-Julian passages in Swift's Tory ministerial writings directed against the Duke of Marlborough, but it is part of the polemical foreground of Swift's writings under the Hanoverian monarchy. It is interesting that Ford should have thought to compare Swift's pamphlets with *Killing Noe Murder*. Just as royalists and disaffected parliamentarians in the Interregnum made menacing comparisons of Cromwell with Julius Caesar,[22] so, after the Hanoverian accession, King George was compared in print to Caesar, and to Cromwell, as Swift witnessed in his correspondence.[23] In 1724, as M. B. (perhaps Marcus Brutus) Drapier, Swift incites direct action against William Wood, the manufacturer of a copper coinage being imposed arbitrarily on Ireland. But there are also subtle menaces against King George when the ostensibly loyal M. B. Drapier notes that Wood's coin is stamped "with His Majesty's *Image and Superscription*." The Drapier asks: "If any Foreigner should ask us, *Whose Image and Superscription* there is on *Wood*'s Coin? We should be ashamed to tell him it was *Cæsar*'s."[24] The allusion is to Christ's words in St. Matthew 23:20–1 ("Whose is this image and superscription? They say unto him, Cæsar's. Then saith he unto them, Render therefore unto Cæsar the things which are Cæsar's; and unto God the things that are God's"), which, along with Romans 13, was a key text for proponents of passive obedience to the ruling monarch. The texts, however, were given a homicidal inflection by proponents of tyrannicide, where the words were understood to mean render stabs with a dagger, as Brutus did to Caesar.

The homicidal black humor of *Killing Noe Murder*, particularly in the parodic introductory epistle "To His Highness Oliver Cromwell," might be thought to anticipate the passage in Part III of *Gulliver's Travels* where Gulliver in Glubbdubdrib has Brutus and Caesar conjured into his presence by the island's governor. "*Cæsar* freely confessed" to Gulliver "that the greatest Actions of his own Life were not equal by many Degrees to the Glory of taking it away" and Gulliver "had the Honour to have much Conversation with *Brutus*."[25] Caesar is not exactly murdered in Swift: he welcomes the taking away of his life as a glorious act for Rome. Similarly, *Killing Noe Murder* delights in euphemism for the unspeakable. In *Killing Noe Murder*, killing becomes an obscene joke, lurking off the page, meant but not said. Cromwell is told:

> To your Highness justly belongs the honour of dying for the people; and it cannot choose but be unspeakable consolation to you in the last moments of your life to consider with how much benefit to the world you are like to leave it. 'Tis then only, my Lord, the titles you now usurp will be truly yours. You will then be indeed the deliverer of your country, and free it from a bondage.

The people hope not for Cromwell's murder, but for "your Highness's happy expiration": "few . . . have expired more to the universal benefit of mankind than your Highness is like to do." And readers are reminded that "Julius Caesar . . . himself thought Brutus worthy to succeed him."[26] Swift took the Suetonian account of Caesar welcoming his death and transposed it into the killing-no-murder idiom.[27] Among the ghosts

of Glubbdubdrib Gulliver happily watches a live theatrical version of
Killing Noe Murder: "I chiefly fed mine Eyes with beholding the Des-
troyers of Tyrants and Usurpers, and the Restorers of Liberty to oppressed
and injured Nations" (p. 183).

The kind of real-world menace, unspoken but present, in the ghosts
of Glubbdubdrib passage is disclosed in a sardonic letter to William
Pulteney of May 12, 1735 where Swift fears he "might outlive liberty in
England" and reflects on the king (George II) desiring "unlimited power"
and the "chief minister" (Robert Walpole) endeavoring to make "his
master absolute":

As to the lust of absolute power, I despair it can ever be cooled, unless princes
had capacity to read the history of the Roman emperors, how many of them were
murdered by their own army; and the same may be said of the Ottomans by their
janissaries; and many other examples are easy to be found. If I were such a
minister, I would go farther, and endeavour to be king myself. Such feats have
happened among the petty tyrants of old Greece, and the worst that happened
was only their being murdered for their pains.[28]

Thomas Hobbes wrote that reading the "Histories of the antient Greeks,
and Romans" had dangerous consequences:

From the reading, I say, of such books, men have undertaken to kill their Kings,
because the Greek and Latine writers, in their books, and discourses of Policy,
make it lawfull, and laudable, for any man so to do; provided before he do it, he call
him Tyrant. For they say not *Regicide*, that is, killing of a King, but *Tyrannicide*,
that is, killing of a Tyrant is lawfull.[29]

Swift mentions this "Remark of *Hobbes*" in several places, but the references have a sharp edge in the pamphlets written under the regime of King
George and Walpole. In *A Vindication of his Excellency John, Lord Carteret,
from The Charge of favouring none but Tories, High-Churchmen and Jacobites* (1730), Swift wrote: "*Hobbes* most judiciously observes, that the
Writings of the *Greeks* and *Romans*, made young Men imbibe Opinions
against absolute Power in a Prince, or even in a first *Minister*" and in *The
Presbyterians Plea of Merit* (1733) he confesses "that I am now justly liable to
the Censure of *Hobbs*, who complains, that the Youth of *England* imbibe ill
Opinions, from reading the Histories of ancient *Greece* and *Rome*, those
renowned Scenes of Liberty and every Virtue."[30] In his references to the
passage in Hobbes, Swift is silent about the fact that the specific opinions
Hobbes was complaining about and Swift is imbibing endorse king-killing.
After the Revolution of 1688–9, approval of assassination had Jacobite
polemical provenance and valency. When this language was explicitly

focused, it was vigorously prosecuted, as in the case of George Harbin's *The Hereditary Right of the Crown of England Asserted* (1713), for which the nonjuror Hilkiah Bedford was fined and imprisoned. This work, defending hereditary right, was denounced as the Pretender's "declaration in folio." It insinuates that to kill a usurper is not murder.[31]

Swift's cold-blooded animus against Whigs (including Whig kings and first ministers) and Dissenters might be thought to make him also liable to another censure of Hobbes. John Aubrey reports Hobbes remarking that some "take a delight in killing men more than I should to kill a bird."[32] Writing to Alexander Pope on November 26, 1725, Swift commented "I am no more angry with — than I was with the Kite that last week flew away with one of my Chickins and yet I was pleas'd when one of my Servants shot him two days after."[33] Editors traditionally fill the blank with "Robert Walpole" but "King George" is just as likely to be meant. Aubrey had also heard the anticlerical Hobbes "inveigh much against the Crueltie of Moyses for putting so many thousands to the Sword for Bowing to the Golden Calf."[34] Moses was a model for the High Church speaker of Defoe's *Shortest-Way with the Dissenters*, who not only approves of Moses when he "cut the Throats of Three and thirty thousand of his dear *Israelites*, that were fallen into Idolatry," but inflates the biblical figures of the numbers slain.[35] Swift also looked to the Old Testament and the history of the early Church for exempla on the treatment of liberty of conscience. Swift wrote in his "Remarks" upon Tindal's *The Rights of the Christian Church* that "we see in the Old Testament, that Kings were reckoned good or ill, as they suffered or hindered Image-Worship and Idolatry" and he observed that "if Heresies had not been used with some Violence in the primitive Age, we should have had, instead of true Religion, the most corrupt one in the World."[36] As for the Dissenters, Swift expressed approval for the idea of extirpating all Scots Presbyterians in Ireland. When Edward Hyde, Earl of Clarendon, in his *History of the Rebellion* reports that parliament alleged against the Earl of Strafford: "That at his coming from Ireland the Earl had said in council there; That if ever he returned to that sword again, he would not leave a Scottishman in that kingdom," Swift commented: "And it was a good resolution."[37] Swift's animus against Presbyterian Scots in the annotation to his copy of Clarendon's *History* is matched in published works, such as "On the Words 'Brother Protestants and Fellow Christians'" (1733), in which a delirium of hatred directed against Protestant Dissenting "vermin" in Ireland inspires an exuberant stylistic performance in rhyming and imagery.[38]

SWIFT AND *THE SHORTEST-WAY WITH THE DISSENTERS*

The Shortest-Way with the Dissenters at face value appears to be the work of an indiscreet Jacobite High Churchman, his punitive exasperation not under stylistic control, who is calling for the destruction of Dissent through the extirpation of Dissenters by hangings and deportations. There are features of the style and content of the text that might have indicated that this was some kind of sinister jokerie and not simply to be taken straight. These features include the shameless exaggeration, mistakes with facts and figures, and the appalling elision of euphemism and ambiguous diction into explicit violent proposal. The evident Jacobitism of the pamphlet might have also seemed just too suspiciously open and given pause to readers. Defoe did claim that "it seems Impossible to imagine it should pass for any thing but an Irony."[39] But it was taken straight by High Churchmen, Dissenters, and by the government. If those aspects of the text that might have suggested authorial deniability were registered by readers, they nevertheless seem to have understood these features as being in the *culte de la blague* style of the killing-no-murder tradition. It was apparently outrageous but meant in earnest. One pamphleteer wrote, for example, that whether the author is "*serious or otherwise,*" *The Shortest-Way* plainly "*speaks the Language*" of the Jacobite High Churchmen against the Dissenters, even in "all the extravagant Passages" such as the call to "a general Massacre" of Dissenters, and the violent reflections on the French Protestants, the Act of Succession and House of Hanover, William III and his government, and the Presbyterian Scots.[40] Defoe was indicted for the seditious design of alarming Protestant Dissenters that their Toleration was to be taken away and for attempting to persuade conforming Anglicans to procure the destruction of these same Protestant Dissenters.[41] Defoe later claimed that his aim had been "to speak in the first Person of the *Party* ... not only speak their Language, but make them acknowledge it to be theirs."[42]

Swift alludes obliquely to the controversy surrounding *The Shortest-Way with the Dissenters* and to one of its sequels, *The Experiment: or, The Shortest-Way with the Dissenters Exemplified* (1705) in a passage in his position statement of 1708, *The Sentiments of a Church-of-England Man* (published 1711), a work in which Swift is ostensibly avoiding "the Extreams of *Whig*" and "the Extreams of *Tory*." Swift comments that if "Mr. *Lesly*" "could make the Nation see his Adversaries, under the Colours he paints them in; we had nothing else to do, but rise as one Man, and destroy such Wretches from the Face of the Earth." And if, on the other side, what the "Advocates for *Moderation*" say of the Tories "were true, and believed" we should have to hang them: "But, I suppose it is presumed, the common People understand *Raillery*, or at least *Rhetorick*; and will not take *Hyperboles* in too literal a Sense; which, however, in some Junctures might prove a desperate Experiment."[43]

The Jacobite High Churchman Charles Leslie denied (and confirmed) Defoe's imputation of extremism when he wrote:

This *Shortest Way* is a New *Engine* of the *Faction*, being wrote in the *Stile* of a *Church-man*, with an Air of *Wit* and a great deal of *Truth*; which they thought would make the *Severity* to Pass as coming from the *Church-Party*, to have the *Dissenters* Treated according to what he had prov'd to be their *Deserts*, that is, the *Preachers* to be sent to the *Gallows*, and the *Hearers* to the *Galleys*.

In fact, said Leslie, there has not been "the least Infringement so much as Attempted" upon the Toleration that the Dissenters enjoy, "on the Contrary, all the Assurance has been given them that any *Government* can give."[44] Swift, like Leslie, was charged with a predilection for massacre. Citing the "*Examiner*" and "*Publick Spirit of the Whiggs*, &c.," Matthew Tindal later wrote that the invectives of the High Church party were inciting a "*General Massacre*" of "*Whiggs*."[45] Swift's attitude to the toleration of Dissent and to accusations of rhetorical violence with actual menaces can be juxtaposed with Leslie's. Swift's highly qualified view of Toleration in the *Sentiments* was that: "Sects, in a State, seem only tolerated, with any Reason, because they are already spread; and because it would not be agreeable with so mild a Government, or so pure a Religion as ours, to use violent Methods against great Numbers of *mistaken* People, while they do not manifestly endanger the Constitution of either."[46] As Tory "*Examiner*" Swift denied that he had ever literally menaced the Whigs, writing in the *Examiner* of April 19, 1711: "I never once invoked the Assistance of the *Gaol* or the *Pillory*, which upon the least Provocation, was the usual Style during their Tyranny."[47] Swift, of course, soon did seek short ways with Whigs and Dissenters with the assistance of Henry St. John. On September 21, 1711 Swift reports to Stella that the "pamphleteers begin to be very busy against the ministry: I have begged Mr. secretary to make examples of one or two of them, and he assures me he will." The space between High Church "tantivy" rhetoric and actual physical threat is closed when on October 10, 1711 a Whig writer (Abel Boyer) who reflected on Swift as "an ambitious Tantivy" is, at Swift's instigation, taken up by the secretary of state: "he shall have a

squeeze extraordinary … I'll *Tantivy* him with a vengeance." On
October 16 Swift confides to Stella that "One Boyer, a French dog, has
abused me in a pamphlet, and I have got him up in a messenger's hands:
the secretary promises me to swinge him … I must make that rogue an
example for warning to others."[48]

It is indicative of Swift's extremism that Defoe's *Shortest-Way with the
Dissenters* turns out to be a proleptic imitation of Swift's writings against
Whigs and Dissenters. Those passages that modern critics have supposed
are ironic triggers and indices of Defoe's satiric exaggeration might be
compared with what Swift was writing. For example, it has been said that
when Defoe's speaker compares suppressing the Dissenters and the spirit
of Whiggism to melting old coin, the brutality of the inhuman equation
of killing people with reworking metal is a clear hint that we are being
invited to recoil from the speaker, that *The Shortest-Way* is clearly a work
of satiric irony rather than an imitation.[49] However, Swift used the trope
in answering Matthew Tindal's *The Rights of the Christian Church*, a work
he thought deserved to be burnt and its author punished.[50] And Swift
matched Defoe's speaker's violence, when inciting a short way with
William Wood, in his poem, "Wood, an Insect." Wood should either be
scalded in "his own melted copper" or boiled in oil: "Then choose which
you please, and let each bring a faggot, / For our fear's at an end with the
death of the maggot."[51]

It has been said that in pushing its High Church persona "over the line
from orthodox Tory allegiances into Jacobitism" (in those "extravagant
Passages" identified by contemporaries) Defoe's work violates imitation
and becomes parody.[52] But this crossing was precisely what Defoe witnessed in *The Conduct of the Allies*, Swift's pacifist pamphlet arguing the
Tory case for peace with France, a work which was construed as enter-
taining the possibility of altering the succession.[53] The High Church
speaker of *The Shortest-Way* refers to William III's rule as "the Oppression of the Stranger" under which the Dissenters "crope into all Places of
Trust and Profit" and "suppress the Episcopal Government" of the
Church in Scotland.[54] This language is also Swift's Tory idiom, both
in print and in private. Swift wrote that with the "new King from a
Calvinistical Commonwealth" came in "new Maxims in Religion and
Government." Alluding in *An Argument Against Abolishing Christianity* to
the Whig Comprehension Bill at the beginning of William's reign,
Swift's sardonic extremism is unleashed. The "Abolishing of Christianity"
will answer "the great Ends of a Scheme for Comprehension, by opening
a large noble Gate, at which all Bodies may enter; whereas the chaffering

with *Dissenters*, and dodging about this or the other Ceremony, is but like opening a few Wickets, and leaving them at jar, by which no more than one can get in at a Time, and that not without stooping and sideling, and squeezing his Body." For Swift, William III was "a Native of *Holland*," "a perfect Stranger to our Laws and our People" who "abolished Episcopacy" in Scotland. In *A Tale of a Tub*, it is in William III's reign that "Jack" is no longer creeping but is on his high horse, having risen to be Lord Mayor of London.[55]

Defoe's High Church speaker's use of diminution in diction and biblical extermination rhetoric against the Dissenters has its parallels in Swift's punitive satiric rhetoric. The notorious Swiftian instance of it, of course, is in Part IV of *Gulliver's Travels* where the Houyhnhnms debate whether to exterminate the Yahoos or to effect a genocide in a generation. The degenerate Yahoos are the pariah species in Houyhnhnmland. They have been thought to resemble the "native Irish" as described in accounts by Swift and English writers.[56] The Yahoos are a subversive threat to the island plantation economy of Houyhnhnmland: "restive and indocible, mischievous and malicious: They would privately suck the Teats of the *Houyhnhnms* Cows; kill and devour their Cats, trample down their Oats and Grass" (p. 253). It is feared that they could be brought "in Troops by Night to destroy the *Houyhnhnms* Cattle" (p. 261). However, the Yahoos are explicitly said not to be native to the country.[57] If they are "Irish" then they are perhaps to be paralleled with the Scots Presbyterians in Ireland against whom Swift deployed epithets and imagery he also uses for the Yahoos. In an early barnyard allegory, for example, Swift depicts odious Scotland, "a Presbyterian of the most rank and virulent Kind," as encouraging rogues, thieves and pickpockets to rob England's "Hen-roosts, steal his Corn and Cattle, and do him all manner of Mischief."[58] For Swift the "Scotch" were "worse than Irish" but "worst" when Scots Irish.[59] The High Church speaker begins *The Shortest-Way with the Dissenters* with a fable of High Church horses being preached to by an unperched rooster (the Dissenters). Defoe imputes a penchant for the fable among High Church writers as a carapace for their violent politics. When Swift sought to explain the affronts the Church has endured from heretical and anticlerical authors, the latest being Matthew Tindal, he would also resort to fable: "the Church appeareth to me like the sick old Lion in the Fable, who, after having his Person outraged by the Bull, the Elephant, the Horse, and the Bear, took nothing so much to Heart, as to find himself at last insulted by the Spurn of an Ass."[60] And, of course, his horses in *Gulliver's Travels* threaten to stamp out the Yahoos.

Swift has had a varied afterlife in literary and polemical tradition. He has certainly been compared with some of the twentieth century's most extreme and scandalous writers. Many of Orwell's observations about Swift in an essay published in *Polemic* in 1946 labeling him as a "Tory anarchist" have been applied to Céline, who, like Swift, is one of Rabelais's literary heirs.[61] It has been said that the "crux of the Célinian 'scandale'" is the case of a great writer who sustains and furthers his literary experimentation through and not in spite of his violent and unacceptable anti-Semitic polemic.[62] Swift's literary satire was coterminous with his pamphleteering, and in his own lifetime and afterwards his extremism scandalized readers. The principal targets of Swift's polemic seem to be identified primarily by religious confession and political allegiance, rather than by what we would now call race, as in Céline's case. The range of Swift's imaginative satire is more radical than his polemic. If the Yahoos resemble one of Swift's pet hates, they are also identified with all humankind. Yet, interestingly, in "Verses on the Death of Dr. Swift," it is Swift the pamphleteer who is given pride of place. Swift's generalizing imaginative satires sometimes appear to be rehearsals for the invective found in the more dangerously focused polemic. The famous "Woman *flay'd*" and dissected "Carcass of a *Beau*" of *A Tale of a Tub* might be seen as the prototypes for the Whig victim of a later pamphlet, Viscount Joshua Allen, who is under the knife of Swift the political surgeon:

Who, without waiting for his Death, will *flay*, and *dissect* him alive; and to the View of Mankind, lay open all the disordered Cells of his Brain, the Venom of his Tongue, the Corruption of his Heart, and Spots and Flatuses of his Spleen – And all this for *Three-Pence*.[63]

This experiment in satiric anatomy is presented in the pamphlet as Swift's coda to a joke, his application of the "Humour" of a Dublin surgeon who took posthumous revenge on the carcass of an unjust Earl. It is a "Metaphor" and no doubt the reader is to "understand *Raillery*, or at least *Rhetorick*."[64] This shortest way with a Whig is *de la blague*.

NOTES

1 Walter Benjamin, *Charles Baudelaire: A Lyric Poet in the Era of High Capitalism*, trans. Harry Zohn (London: New Left Books, 1973), p. 14; Louis-Ferdinand Céline, *Bagatelles pour un massacre* (Paris: Denoël, 1937).
2 Nicholas Hewitt, *The Golden Age of Louis-Ferdinand Céline* (Leamington Spa, Hamburg, New York: Berg, 1987), p. 198 (see also pp. 32–3, 197); Nicholas

Hewitt, "Louis-Ferdinand Céline: Anti-Semitism and Modernism," in *The Pen and the Sword: Right-wing Politics and Literary Innovation in the Twentieth Century*, ed. Richard Griffiths (London: Centre for Twentieth-century Cultural Studies, School of Humanities, King's College London, 2000), pp. 81–94 (p. 93). Céline is persuasively viewed as a right-wing anarchist in Nicholas Hewitt, *The Life of Céline* (Oxford: Blackwell, 1999).

3 Daniel Defoe, *More Short-Ways with the Dissenters* (1704), in *The Genuine Works of Mr. Daniel D'Foe* ..., 2 vols. (London, [1721]), vol. II, p. 274.

4 [Charles Gildon], "The Epistle Nuncupatory, To the Author of *A Tale of a Tub*," in *The Golden Spy* ... (London, 1709).

5 *A Defense of the Reflections upon Ancient and Modern Learning ... With Observations upon The Tale of a Tub. By William Wotton B.D.* (London, 1705), pp. 62–3.

6 On Céline's sources, see Alice Yaegar Kaplan, *Relevé des sources et citations dans "Bagatelles pour un massacre,"* Céline Études (Tusson, Charente: Du Lérot, 1987).

7 Claude Rawson, *God, Gulliver, and Genocide: Barbarism and the European Imagination, 1492–1945* (Oxford: Oxford University Press, 2001); Claude Rawson, *Satire and Sentiment 1660–1830* (Cambridge: Cambridge University Press, 1994; new edn., New Haven and London: Yale University Press, 2000), p. 5: invective's "great masters (Rabelais, Swift, Céline) are fantasists of an enormity which signals that the calls to hatred or to massacre don't really mean what they say, but don't not mean it either."

8 *The Correspondence of Jonathan Swift, D.D.*, ed. David Woolley, 5 vols. (Frankfurt: Peter Lang, 1999–2007; hereafter *CW*), vol. I, p. 150 (Swift to the Rev. William Tisdall, February 3, 1703/4).

9 *The Prose Writings of Jonathan Swift*, ed. Herbert Davis and others, 16 vols. (Oxford: Basil Blackwell, 1939–74; hereafter *PW*), vol. I, p. 152.

10 See Joad Raymond, *Pamphlets and Pamphleteering in Early Modern Britain* (Cambridge: Cambridge University Press, 2003), esp. ch. 1, pp. 4–26.

11 *PW*, III, pp. 156–7. On the French Huguenot writer Abel Boyer, see *Oxford DNB*.

12 See *PW*, II, p. 113; Claude Rawson, in *TLS* (August 17, 2001), 3–4 and *TLS* (September 10, 2004), 3–4; Maximillian E. Novak, "Swift and Defoe: Or, How Contempt Breeds Familiarity and a Degree of Influence," in *Proceedings of the First Münster Symposium on Jonathan Swift*, ed. Hermann J. Real and Heinz J. Vienken (Munich: Wilhelm Fink Verlag, 1985), pp. 157–73 (pp. 166–7).

13 *CW*, III, p. 709 (Swift to Charles Ford, November 20, 1733); *CW*, IV, pp. 475–6 (Charles Ford to Swift, November 22, 1737).

14 For Swift's library and reading: Dirk F. Passmann and Heinz J. Vienken, *The Library and Reading of Jonathan Swift: A Bio-Bibliographical Handbook, Part I: Swift's Library in Four Volumes* (Frankfurt am Main: Peter Lang, 2003; hereafter *Library*) and A. C. Elias, Jr., "Swift's Corrected Copy of *Contests and Dissensions*, with Other Pamphlets from His Library," *Philological Quarterly* 75 (Spring 1996), 167–95.

15 *PW*, vol. III, pp. 155–6; vol. VIII, pp. 14–15.

16 *PW*, vol. XII, p. 264; *PW*, vol. IV, p. 62.

17 *The Whig Rampant: or, Exaltation* ... [London, 1682]; *PW*, vol. I, pp. 33–6.

18 *PW*, vol. I, pp. 111–13.

19 *Englands Mad Petition to the Right Honourable the, &c.* ... *Presented to the Houses on Thursday, August 26. 1647* (London, 1647), pp. 4, 5.

20 William Allen (i.e. Edward Sexby), *Killing Noe Murder. Briefly Discourst in Three Quaestions* (1657), in *Divine Right and Democracy: An Anthology of Political Writing in Stuart England*, ed. David Wootton (Harmondsworth: Penguin, 1986), pp. 360–89. On Sexby and *Killing Noe Murder*, see James Holstun, *Ehud's Dagger: Class Struggle in the English Revolution* (London and New York: Verso, 2000), pp. 305–66; Nigel Smith, *Literature and Revolution in England 1640–1660* (New Haven and London: Yale University Press, 1994), pp. 151–3; David Norbrook, *Writing the English Republic: Poetry, Rhetoric and Politics 1627–1660* (Cambridge: Cambridge University Press, 1999; paperback edn. 2000), pp. 324–5. On its reception by Charles II's party, see Smith, *Literature and Revolution*, p. 153, and Holstun, *Ehud's Dagger*, p. 332.

21 On the pamphlet and its publication and application history, see Olivier Lutaud, *Des Révolutions d'Angleterre à la révolution française: le tyrannicide & Killing No Murder (Cromwell, Athalie, Bonaparte)* (The Hague: Martinus Nijhoff, 1973).

22 See Holstun, *Ehud's Dagger*, p. 312.

23 R. Browne, "A George for an Oliver," *FACTOTUM: Newsletter of the XVIIIth century STC*, British Library, 8 (April 1980), 14–17; *Mist's Weekly Journal*, 130 (May 27, 1721); *CW*, vol. II, p. 383 (Swift to Knightley Chetwode, June 10, 1721). *The Weekly Journal: or, British Gazetteer* (January 6, 1722) pointed out the Jacobite application of "*Julius Caesar*" to "King GEORGE."

24 *PW*, vol. X, p. 21.

25 *Gulliver's Travels*, ed. Claude Rawson and Ian Higgins (Oxford: Oxford University Press, 2005), p. 183. All future references are to this edition and will be cited parenthetically in the text.

26 *Killing Noe Murder*, pp. 360, 361, 376.

27 In Suetonius, Caesar is said to have desired the sudden and unexpected manner of his death, see Suetonius, *The Lives of the Caesars*, vol. I, p. 87.

28 *CW*, vol. IV, pp. 106, 107.

29 Thomas Hobbes, *Leviathan*, ed. Richard Tuck (Cambridge: Cambridge University Press, 1991), ch. 29, pp. 225, 226.

30 *PW*, vol. II, p. 17; vol. XII, pp. 161, 278. See also: *PW*, vol. VIII, p. 37.

31 *The Hereditary Right of the Crown of England Asserted* ... (London, 1713). The Whig cleric White Kennett in his answer focused on its apologia for attempts to murder kings; see *A Letter to the Lord Bishop of Carlisle* ... *On Occasion of a New Volume for the Pretender, Intituled, The Hereditary Right of the Crown of England Asserted* (London, 1713).

32 Oliver Lawson Dick, ed., *Aubrey's Brief Lives* (London: Secker and Warburg, 1949), p. 157.

33 *CW*, vol. II, p. 623.

34 *Aubrey's Brief Lives*, p. 157.
35 [Daniel Defoe], *The Shortest-Way with the Dissenters: Or Proposals for the Establishment of the Church* (London, 1702), p. 20. The number given in Exodus 32:28 is "about three thousand men." In Numbers Moses is commanded by God to "Take all the heads of the people, and hang them up before the LORD" (25:4). The highest number of dead Israelites in the plague is given as "twenty and four thousand" (25:9).
36 *PW*, vol. II, pp. 89, 103–4.
37 *Library*, Part I, vol. II, p. 942; *PW*, vol. V, p. 298.
38 Jonathan Swift, *The Complete Poems*, ed. Pat Rogers (Harmondsworth: Penguin, 1983; hereafter *Poems*), pp. 537–9, 879.
39 *A brief Explanation of a Late Pamphlet, Entituled, The Shortest Way with the Dissenters*, in *A Collection of the Writings of the Author of the True-Born English-Man* (London, 1703), p. 215.
40 *Reflections upon a Late Scandalous and Malicious Pamphlet* (London, 1703), esp. pp. iii, 22.
41 Paula R. Backscheider, *Daniel Defoe: His Life* (Baltimore and London: The Johns Hopkins University Press, 1989), p. 104 (for the Old Bailey indictment).
42 [Daniel Defoe], *The Present State of the Parties in Great Britain* (London, 1712), p. 24.
43 *PW*, vol. II, p. 13, see p. 25. This passage is noticed and more generally discussed in Rawson, *God, Gulliver, and Genocide*, pp. 252–3, and see pp. 13, 184–5.
44 *The New Association, Part II* (London, 1703), pp. 6, 10. Swift owned this pamphlet (his *Contests and Dissentions* of 1701 is interrogated in "A Supplement" at the end of the pamphlet), see *Library*, Part I, vol. II, p. 1072. It would have been one of Leslie's pamphlets which Swift referred to in February 1704 as being "violent against Presbyterians and Low Churchmen" (*CW*, vol. I, p. 150).
45 [Matthew Tindal], *The Defection Consider'd* ... (London, 1717), pp. 13–14.
46 *PW*, vol. II, p. 5.
47 *PW*, vol. III, p. 136.
48 *PW*, vol. XV, p. 365; vol. XVI, pp. 381, 384–5. Boyer's reflections on Swift in his journalism and pamphlets are reprinted in David Woolley, " 'The Author of the *Examiner*' and the Whiggish Answer-Jobbers of 1711–1712," *Swift Studies* 5 (1990), 91–111.
49 *The Shortest-Way*, pp. 14–15; Robert Phiddian, *Swift's Parody* (Cambridge: Cambridge University Press, 1995), p. 62.
50 *PW*, vol. II, p. 80 ("melt this refined Jargon into the *Old Style*"), and see vol. II, p. 69 (book deserves burning) and vol. II, p. 98 (author should be punished).
51 *Poems*, p. 288.
52 Phiddian, *Swift's Parody*, p. 61.
53 [Daniel Defoe], *An Account of the Swedish and Jacobite Plot* ... (London, 1717), p. 21.
54 *The Shortest-Way*, pp. 2, 9, 10.
55 *PW*, vol. VII, p. 5; vol. II, p. 34; vol. VI, p. 11; vol. VII, p. 102; vol. V, p. 290; vol. I, p. 131.

56 See the evidence assembled in Donald T. Torchiana, "Jonathan Swift, the Irish, and the Yahoos: The Case Reconsidered," *Philological Quarterly* 54 (1975), 195–212, and Claude Rawson, *Order from Confusion Sprung: Studies in Eighteenth-Century Literature from Swift to Cowper* (London: George Allen & Unwin, 1985), pp. 121–44.

57 *Gulliver's Travels*, pp. 253–4.

58 See *PW*, vol. IX, pp. 3–4.

59 *PW*, vol. XII, p. 306. And see Christopher Fox, "Swift's Scotophobia," *Bullán* 6 (2002), 43–65.

60 *The Shortest-Way*, pp. 1–2; *PW*, vol. II, p. 72.

61 George Orwell, "Politics vs. Literature: An Examination of *Gulliver's Travels*," in *The Collected Essays, Journalism and Letters of George Orwell*, ed. Sonia Orwell and Ian Angus (London: Secker & Warburg, 1968), vol. IV, pp. 205–23 (p. 216); Louis-Ferdinand Céline, *Fable for Another Time* [*Féerie pour une autre fois I*], trans. with intro. by Mary Hudson, preface and notes Henri Godard (Lincoln: University of Nebraska Press, 2003), pp. xxviii–xxx.

62 Hewitt, *The Life of Céline*, pp. 282–3.

63 *PW*, vol. I, p. 109; *PW*, vol. XII, pp. 157–8.

64 *PW*, vol. XII, pp. 157–8; *PW*, vol. II, p. 13.

CHAPTER 4

Satirical wells from Bath to Ballyspellan

Harold Love

A linkage between satire and wells can claim both modern and ancient precedents. The emergence of the spa as a gathering place for invalids and holidaymakers, which in England dates from the mid-seventeenth century, led to the composing of group lampoons directed at visitors for a particular season. These were both a means of maintaining social propriety among such promiscuous assemblages and one of the expected entertainments when taking the waters. In the case of Tunbridge Wells, one or more lampoons from every year would usually achieve scribal circulation in the metropolis and beyond.[1] A similar tradition of social satire at Bath, later in developing, and best represented by Christopher Anstey's *The New Bath Guide* (1766), overflowed into prose fiction, notably *Humphry Clinker*. But there was also a much older connection between place and genre arising from the belief that sacred springs were an avenue for communication with the powers of the underworld. Curse tablets inscribed on lead were often deposited in them: several Roman examples have been retrieved from the hot spring at Bath.[2] The older wells, most famously St. Winifred's in Wales, were represented as magical places giving rise to miraculous cures.[3] Such influences could be invoked for destructive as well as benevolent ends, as at Bath, where in ancient times the presiding deity was invoked both to restore health to the suffering and to destroy that of the targets of the curse tablets.

In Britain, Tunbridge Wells and Bath each nourished traditions of satire that mirror their differing characteristics as places of assemblage. The Restoration vogue for Tunbridge began from its being patronized in the 1660s by Catherine of Braganza. Anthony Hamilton has left a lively account of court visits to the Kentish wells during this decade.[4] Later in the century the place was described by Narcissus Luttrell, Celia Fiennes, and other travelers, and made the subject of socio-topographic depictions in verse by Peter Causton and John Lewkenor.[5] Tunbridge was as distinctly modern as Bath was ancient. It had been discovered as recently as

1606, when the valetudinarian Dudley, Lord North, having refreshed himself with some reddish water seeping from the ground, became convinced that it possessed medicinal properties. The well's repute, therefore, owed nothing to legend or sanctity: from the beginning it was regarded as a scientific spa whose curative powers derived from the iron content of the water. Lewkenor is particularly insistent that Tunbridge cures were the work of nature, not of angels (pp. 60–1). The area had long been a site of iron and steel production. The wife in Rochester's "Tunbridge Wells" considers the benefits of steel to a young girl suffering from the green sickness before dismissing them for a more practical alternative (ll. 147–8). In *Tunbridgialia* Causton describes drinkers listening to an exposition of this very matter:

> Here one, forsooth, plays the Philosopher
> Upon the Wells, describes the secret power
> Of *Spaws* and Mineral Waters, how they come,
> With Steel impregnate, thro the Earth's cold Womb;
> Whence springs their force that they so nearly can
> Make clean this foul *Augean* Stable Man;
> How first found out, and when the Mode began. (p. 205)

Patrick Madan, writing in 1687, gives an elaborate account of the powers of the water as they were understood by the science of the time:

they are impregnated with a *Chalcanteous* or *Vitreolate Juice*, which, with its *Sulphureous Particles* irritates and moves the Belly to *Blackish Excretion*, and by Frequent Drinking thereof, it *Blackneth* the Tongue, because this member being of a *Spongy Substance* imbibes some *Sooty Sulphureous Minims* into its *Porosity*, occasioning this *Tincture*.

   Through its more subtiler piercing Chalchantous Spirits, it provokes Urine in a plentiful manner.

   To these is admixt some *Ferrugineous Juice*; which contains a great deal of the *Volatile Salt*, which is it that is dissolv'd in the *Chalybeat-Wine*, now so much in Vogue amongst *Physicians*.[6]

One effect of this cocktail was "the *Nidorolent Belches*, and *Eructations* after taking 'em, as if one had eaten hard Fryed Eggs" (p. 5). Owing to a belief that the palliative substances were dispersed by the rays of the sun, it was recommended that the waters should be taken as early as possible. Thus in "Tunbridge Wells"

> Att five this Morn: when Phœbus rais'd his head
> From Thetis Lapp, I rais'd my selfe from bed (ll. 1–2)

and from Causton

> Refresht with sleep, which Natures loss repairs[,]
> Soon as the day on the streak'd hills appears,
> Up with the Sun we mount and travel, We
> To the fam'd Spring, He to the Western Sea. (p. 203)

The waters were to be swallowed rather than absorbed through the skin by immersion, as was the case by preference at Bath. Science recommended that this be done in very large quantities. Luttrell explains that one would begin with three to five half-pint glasses, which would be increased at the rate of two or three a day until as many as thirteen were consumed (pp. 232–3). Madan advised preparing the body for Tunbridge with three or four days of Epsom or North Hall waters, either raw, boiled, or "altered with Milk," then to undertake an hour to an hour and a half of steady, moderate drinking with intermissions of walking, to be conducted every day for a month or six weeks (p. 10). Women "dippers" were in attendance at the wells to fill glasses. The resultant purging, spewing and copious urination were part of the cure, which was particularly recommended for bladder stones in males, which the waters were reputed to "break." A lavatory for women was available close to the pumps but not for men, who presumably made use of the nearby trees. The place's reputation for curing barrenness in women is dismissed by Rochester with typical sarcasm:

> For here walk Cuffe, and Kick
> With brawny back, and leggs, and Potent Prick
> Who more substantially will cure thy wife
> And on her halfe dead womb bestow new life:
> From these the waters gott the reputation
> Of good assistants unto generation. (ll. 155–60)

Madan preferred to believe that the dissolved salts gave rise to a "sweet *Balsamick*, *Spirituous*, and *Sanguineous Temperament*, which naturally incites and inspires men and Women to *Amorous Emotions* and *Titillations* ... enabling them to *Procreation*" (p. 7), making them an aphrodisiac.

Other aspects of Tunbridge kept it firmly aligned with the up-to-date. Its closeness to London and a reaction, encouraged by Queen Catherine herself, against strict protocol ensured a greater social mix among its attenders than at the more remote and hierarchic Bath. To take the waters at Tunbridge involved entering the human turbulence of the two parallel "walks," which were lined with stalls selling a variety of foodstuffs and trinkets. The atmosphere of the place is strikingly captured in Rochester's poem:

> Amidst the Crow'd, next I my selfe convey'd
> For now were come, white wash and paint be'ng laid,
> Mother, and daughter, Mistress, and the Maid
> And squire with wigg, and Pantaloon displaid;
> But ne're could conventicle, play, or faire
> For a true Medley with this herd Compare:
> Here Lords, Knights, Squires, ladyes, and Countesses,
> Channdlers, mum-bacon women, semptressess
> Were mixt together, nor did they agree,
> More in their humours, then their Quality. (ll. 88–9)

The long period of open-air drinking, alternating with walking, was another prompt to sociability, whether desired or otherwise. Religion at Tunbridge was democratic, too, owing to the presence near the wells of the chapel of King Charles the Martyr (1678) and on a hill nearby "a large Chapple where the Presbiterians have preaching."[7] Both were new constructions built by subscription. Lewkenor remarks on the presence of Dissenters, who seem not to have been frequent at Bath:

> Dire Sects may here of grim Devotion talk,
> Whilst Moderater-Men just by 'em walk.
> Th' Enthusiastick with his Brain as full
> Of Fury as *Geneva* Pulpit-Bull,
> Yet here walks quiet, peaceable and dull. (p. 49)

"Tunbridg satyr" laments that whereas in a former time "Free Conversation was Esteem'd no Crime" the place had now become divided between "The starch'd Fanatick and the Libertine."[8]

Because the area round the wells was not yet built up, visitors would distribute themselves widely across the surrounding countryside, creating little communities of the like-minded. A journey to the wells did not involve detaching oneself from the everyday concerns of the capital; indeed, in some ways the place represented a kind of distillation of enlightened, secular urbanism. Madan lists intelligent conversation among its diversions (p. 21), while Lewkenor portrays it as conducive to writing:

> Some excellent Poet yonder makes his Verse,
> Another here takes pleasure to reherse;
> The Wits that hear, admire; all Wits delight,
> These hear with Pleasure, those with Pleasure write. (p. 71)

What was written was read eagerly, even when unflattering:

> Since I came last, I've seen a Lampoon here,
> The Ladies talk and read it every where;
> And thô 'tis leud almost in every Place,
> Not the least Blush adorns the Palest Face:
> To such great Impudence they're now arriv'd,
> They care not if 'tis known by whom they're s–d;
> Heaven have Mercy on the Men are Wiv'd!⁹

Rawlins's *Tunbridge Wells* introduces Poet Witless with his pocket stuffed with verses. When he inadvertently drops a lampoon, it is immediately picked up by a bystander and sung aloud.¹⁰ This was the Town and the City at play, always happy to inspect themselves narcissistically in the mirror of writing.

Tunbridge satire shares this orientation.¹¹ Its method is descriptive and empirical, in the manner of Rochester's poem and its many successors. A typical Tunbridge lampoon takes the form of a series of vivid satirical snapshots of individuals present for the season, joined with reflections on their behavior, liaisons, and motives for coming. Much information is presented only glancingly on the assumption that the reader is already in possession of it through gossip, the other principal occupation of the day. The natural stance for the satirist was as a Baconian observer of the passing concourse on the walks:

> Arise, Arise my Muse
> Hast to the Morning Rendezvous
> Then take thy stand and Observation make
> Due Measures take
> Let Quality advance
> And in thy Character lead up the Dance.¹²

When Tunbridge satire becomes more thoughtful, it is in order to reflect on its victims as moral and psychological types. The extended series of political fables, "Aesop at Tunbridge," which was reprinted in the second volume of *Poems on Affairs of State* (London, 1703), is not specifically *about* Tunbridge, but was presented to the public as a distillation of the critical spirit of the place:

Riding of late, to take a little Air, and crossing by some chance the *Tunbridge* Road, it was my Fortune to find a parcel of Papers, which were doubtless dropt by some unwary Passenger, who had made more Haste than good Speed; and taking them up, I found they were the following *Fables*: which, I imagine, some young Gentleman of Wit and Leisure had diverted himself in composing, whilst he was obliged to drink the Waters. (p. 47)

Satire in this context was itself a kind of purgative, provoking the spewing out of folly from the communal body, and the satirist a kind of adjunct diagnostician – no alienated Persius or Juvenal. Tunbridge lampooning is written from within the social world it describes as a means of regulating that world for the better pursuit of health and diversion. The writers adopt the role of moderator so as to champion a civilized in preference to a destructive hedonism. The one partial exception is Rochester's "Tunbridge Wells," which betrays an unusual degree of repugnance and concludes with the proto-Swiftian gesture of declaring the poet's horse a "wiser Creature" than the variety of humankind on display (ll. 184–7); but the satirist is still speaking *to* Tunbridge and will presumably be back to take the waters just as early the following morning.

Bath had a very different atmosphere and satirical style. It had been a spa since pre-Roman times, dedicated to Sulis, the Celtic Minerva, and appears to be the city described in the Anglo-Saxon elegy "The Ruin" from the Exeter Book. More remote from the capital than Tunbridge, it was also closer to the magical springs of Celtic Britain, of which it could claim to be an example. Many visitors would be aware of Geoffrey of Monmouth's account of King Bladud being cured of leprosy by contact with its black mud and his creating its springs by magic. A sense of unearthly transformative powers at work is present in the opening stanza of Strode's Caroline "A Song on the Baths":

> What Angel stirs this happy Well,
> Some Muse from thence come shew't me,
> One of those naked Graces tell
> That Angels are for beauty:
> The Lame themselves that enter here
> Come Angels out againe,
> And Bodies turne to Soules all cleere,
> All made for joy, noe payne.[13]

The site was certainly difficult of access: "the wayes to the Bath are all difficult," noted Fiennes around 1686, "the town lyes low in a bottom and its steep ascents all ways out of the town" (*Journeys*, p. 17). At the time with which we are now concerned it was not yet the orderly, purpose-built pleasure city created by Ralph Allen and Beau Nash. Fiennes found the houses "indifferent." Like Tunbridge, it was resorted to by women who found difficulty in conceiving, but whereas success in that endeavor at Tunbridge, as we have seen, was likely to be attributed either to the action of salts or to sexual misbehavior, at Bath claims were still made for a supernatural influence, as in the case of Mary of Modena who, after many years of barrenness, finally became pregnant after taking the waters in 1687. Her attribution of this to the intervention of the Virgin attracted satire in a splenetic piece *The Miracle; How the Duchess of* Modena *(being in Heaven) prayed the B. Virgin that the Queen might have a Son, and how our Lady sent the Angel* Gabriel *with her Smock; upon which the Queen was with Child.*[14] Fiennes on revisiting the Cross Bath in 1698 noted the addition of "fine carving of stone with the English arms and saints and cupids according to the phancye and religion of King James the Seconds Queen Mary of Modina, as part of her thanks and acknowledgments to the Saints or Virgin Mary for the Welsh Prince she imposed on us" (p. 236) – "imposed" because the Old Pretender was believed by Protestants to be a suppositious child smuggled into the birth chamber in a warming pan. Whereas Nonconformists, given the choice, would have preferred Tunbridge, Catholics were clearly happier at Bath, which was also much closer to their traditional heartland. Anglicans of the reign of Charles II, worshipping at the Abbey Church, would have been subject to the ministrations of Joseph Glanvill, that doughty foe of Sadducism and champion of the intervention of spirits in the activities of everyday life.

Their temporal maladies might have been treated by Henry Stubbe, a thinker of a very different cast who was an admirer of the political and religious system of Islam. But Stubbe's was a dissonant presence in still holy Bath and when he drowned after falling from his horse into a few inches of water, his fate was represented as divine retribution upon a scoffer.[15] Bath was linked with cthonic energies in a more tangible way than Tunbridge because of the heat of its springs, the noxious smell of the water, and the volume with which it rose up from the earth; also because the site of treatment was subterranean. The method of consumption was certainly more resonant of the sacral. While some only drank, the most commonly used cure was by immersion through a kind of mimic baptism, preceded by purging. Women clad in shape-disguising robes of yellow canvas resembling "a parsons gown" and men in drawers and waistcoats of the same canvas had a choice of sitting covered up to the neck on a stone bench, walking under the guidance of assistants to protect them from the force of the stream, or being pumped with hot water while wearing broad-brimmed hats with the crown cut out. Drying off afterwards was an even more complicated and secretive ritual that concluded with sufferers being carried to their lodgings in sedan chairs and left at their bedsides, where a fire would be lit to encourage sweating.[16] Whatever might happen at other times of day, the prolonged ritual of immersion involved none of the easy sociability of taking the waters at Tunbridge.

The special qualities of Bath are reflected in two linked satires of close to the same date as "Tunbridge Wells" – Rochester's "Say Heav'n-born Muse" and Francis Fane's "Iter occidentale." "Say Heav'n-born Muse" is attributed to Rochester in my OUP edition but was rejected by Vieth and Walker on the grounds that Rochester is himself the central figure of the satire and that he is far from kindly treated.[17] The same is, however, true of "Verses on the Death of Dr. Swift," which has never been placed under question on that count. My reasons for favoring the attribution are first that Rochester was certainly present in Bath at the time of composition and that this dazzlingly written, intricately allusive, and (even today) outrageously obscene satire would be hard to sheet home to any other poet of his generation. To these qualifications I would add how perfectly it conforms to Claude Rawson's masterful account in *Satire and Sentiment* of the aristocratic social "ease" or "headlong grace" that Pope so resented in Rochester.[18] The poem dates from his attendance during the summer of 1674 at the miniature court of the king's *maîtresse-en-titre*, the Duchess of Portsmouth. A letter from Henry Stubbe reveals that Portsmouth, despite dining in state every day with people admitted to watch "as were she Queen," had been snubbed by the adherents of Catherine.[19] The satire has every appearance of an act of revenge against these disrespectful loyalists. It takes the form of a mock-heroic narrative built around a version of the judgment of Paris. Three well-born ladies, two of them widows and the third the daughter of one of them, are living riotously at "bawdy Bath." Rochester, represented as a Satan-like spirit of malice, resolves to disrupt their Edenic amity. In order to do this he leaves the place to consult "a *Hagg*, deep red in Charms, and Spells," who turns out to be Lady Sanderson, the *gouvernante* to the Queen's maids of honor at court. He informs her of the reason for his hostility, beginning with an account of Bath itself:

> There is a place, a down a gloomy Vale,
> Where burthen'd Nature, lays her nasty Tail;
> Ten Thousand Pilgrims, thither do resort
> For ease, disease, for letchery, and sport:
> Thither Two Beldames, and a jilting Wife
> Came to Swive off, the tedious hours of life: (ll. 39–44)

Depending on whether "burthen'd" is read as referring to excretion or pregnancy, Bath is metaphorically either an anus or a vagina. Making it a site of pilgrimage obliquely acknowledges its sacred character and might even suggest an allusion in the following couplet to an earlier wife of

Bath. In the story, Rochester, having offered his erotic services to the daughter, is told by her mother that he must earn this privilege by having sex twelve times successively with herself; however, the competition is rigged and, despite clear evidence to the contrary, the twelfth ejaculation is declared a "dry bob." The hag agrees to assist his revenge, which she does by presenting him with a gigantic dildo inscribed with the motto of the Garter:

> This pious *Son* (said she) nail up in *Box*,
> By *Carryer*, send it these salt burning *Nocks*.
> Directed thus. To the Lady most deserving
> Who's made most Slaves, and kept most Pricks from Starving. (ll. 85–8)

The ruse is successful: no sooner is the prize delivered than the three women join in "Mortal Fray" to possess it. Their strife is ended only by the arrival of a clergyman, partly modeled on Father Patrick, the queen's almoner, and partly on Joseph Glanvill (whose *Plus ultra* earns a mention). The newcomer solves the problem by a combination of sage advice and sexual ministrations, after which,

> . . . all well pleas'd to *Church* away they go,
> To sing *Te Deum*, for their dear *Dildoe*. (ll. 153–4)

This conclusion identifies the poem generically with the ancient Priapeia, which include Horace's *Satire* 1.8. An insult to Priapus and his secular priest, Rochester, has been revenged and then atoned for by the veneration of his image.[20] This bare description gives no sense of the poem's hyperingenious intertextualities, which include allusions to or direct quotations from *Paradise Lost*, *Macbeth*, *The Faerie Queene*, the New Testament, the *Aeneid*, and the *Iliad*.[21] A poem so packed with resonances and surreal imaginings is a direct reflection of the place, with its ancient associations and insistence on engaging visitors in disorienting, putatively timeless subterranean rituals.

The other major Bath satire of this early period is little known and so far has no modern edition. Variously titled "Le temple del' L'Amour" and "Iter occidentale, or the Wonders of Warm Water," it survives in six currently known manuscript sources, divided between three lampoon anthologies compiled around 1680 and three very large retrospective collections compiled around 1700.[22] This degree of circulation suggests that it was quite widely copied and read when it first appeared in the 1670s and again after a new scribal edition of the late 1690s. The three later sources attribute the poem to Sir Francis Fane, while one of the earlier ones gives it to Rochester and the other two name no author. Certainly, the influence of Rochester is strongly evident. Fane, who admired Rochester both personally and as a writer, was to dedicate his fine Venetian comedy of 1675, *Love in the Dark, or, the Man of Business*, to him in fulsome terms. Rochester, in return, both contributed an epilogue to the play and gave it "impartial corrections."[23] He may easily have done the same for "The Wonders," which in the three later sources is dated 1674. Rochester, as we have just seen, was present at Bath during that summer, which could also have been the occasion of his assistance with *Love in the Dark*, first performed in the following spring. Fane also addressed two poems to Rochester (one a funeral elegy) and wrote a masque for inclusion in Rochester's revision of Fletcher's *Valentinian*.[24] He was a gifted poet and dramatist whose works deserve to be brought together in a scholarly edition. The title burlesques that of at least seven earlier poems called *Iter boreale*, *Iter australe* or *Iter orientale*, the best known of which were a genial Caroline account by Richard Corbett of four Oxford scholars on a vacation ramble and Robert Wild's popular paean on Monck's march from the North to bring about the Restoration.[25]

Fiennes recorded that "the baths in my opinion makes the town unpleasant, the aire thick and hot by their steem, and by its own situation so low, encompassed with high hills and woods" (p. 17). Fane takes these facts a metaphorical step further:

> Deep in an unctious Vale 'twixt swelling Hills,
> Curl'd o're with Shady Tuffs, spending hot Rills,
> Lyes *Englands C_t*, call'd Bath in modest British.
> That Animal that is elswhere so skittish
> Here's frig'd with Pumps, and warbling out soft Ayres,
> Like Virgins spending, whilst they say their Prayers,
> With scalding Sperm, five marble pisspots fills,
> Form'd for the cure of Ach, and amorous Ills . . .[26]

These lines introduce the main tendency of the poem's wit, which is its ingenious troping of the vagina as an animal, as land to be ploughed, as a goal of pilgrimage, as varying according to nation and region, as dancing to music, as the bear at a baiting, as a beast fought by a gladiator, as a cooking pot producing broth, as a magnet, as hell, as the quarry in a hunt, as a duck in a lake, as a seacoast with bay and pier, as the moon, as a becalmed ship, as a boxer, as a mouth, as a book, as the gate, entry, and rooms of state of a mansion, as a creek, as a whale, as a "well train'd Soldier," as the touchhole of a cannon, as a pool, as Wookey Hole, as the ocean, as St. Paul's Cathedral, as the church militant, as a rock in the sea (see below), and as a member of parliament. In the most elaborate of these metaphors it becomes the world soul as conceived by Plato and Aristotle:

> Here is a thing, that can contract, dilate,
> Move from it self with reason, Love and Hate,
> Stretcht to the *Indies*, and still nere the thinner,
> Less solid, or more wide, seeking at dinner[;]
> At *London*, fuckt, at Bath a minute after,
> T'is all in all, and all in every Quarter:
> Ask Moor, and Scaliger, and Peter Martyr.[27]

"Moor" being Henry of that name. Here again one can hardly not quote Rawson: "No isms are more doctrinaire or persistent than isms of excess, which readily pursue metaphysical exhaustiveness as much as physical exhaustion."[28] The poem is also a formal epyllion dealing mock-heroically with a combat of a single hero against a host of assailants, resembling that of Perseus in Book V of the *Metamorphoses*. Having set the scene in one of the warm baths, the poet introduces as his protagonist

> . . . a nymph of the inspired Train.
> Some said a Quaker; but most did agree,
> She came to set up *C_ts* fifth Monarchy. (fol. 12v)

The identification of the woman as a Dissenter was presumably in order to distance her from Portsmouth, whose free behavior with Rochester in the pool had been noted by Stubbe. By exposing her "Pitt Infernall" she encourages "All Zealous Youths" present to divest themselves of their drawers and swim after her; however, their various attempts to copulate in the water are either unsuccessful or leave them exhausted while the "nymph" remains active and unsatiated. At the climax

> Then twice twelve *P_ks* attaqu'd her severall Ways;
> And twice twelve times *C_t Militant* bore the Bayes:
> Even as a Rock, that braves the Wind and Tides[,]
> The Waves that dash against her painfull sides
> Loosing themselves in Fome so *C_t* abides. (fol. 14v)

(The "twice twelves" anticipate the "twice six Vultures" of *MacFlecknoe*, l. 131.) At the conclusion of the encounter the males retire baffled, leaving the woman in possession of the field, whereupon

> All Judges, that had Conscience, did ascribe
> The fighting Garland to the Female Tribe: (fol. 15r)

The theme of female triumph and male sexual humiliation situates the poem as an allegorical "Triumph of Venus," to set against the elevation of Priapus in "Say Heav'n-born Muse." A veiled political message is reserved for a short elegy in tetrameters spoken by "an attentive Matron that stood by," which after running through a shorter series of metaphors for the penis concludes

> How great a Soveraign would'st thou be,
> If poor C_t did not master thee! (fol. 15v)

It is hard not to see this as a reflection on Charles II's subordination to the mock-Queen, Portsmouth, perhaps regretful or perhaps thankful, in that it is what keeps him from becoming an absolute tyrant. Unlike the Tunbridge satires, "Iter occidentale" makes no attempt whatsoever to represent the everyday realities of wells life: instead it moves the reader directly to an allegorical realm, in which a superhumanly gifted Amazon revenges her sex's oppression by exposing the hollowness of male sexual boasting. "Say Heav'n-born Muse" performs a similar transmutation. The satirist, far from being an adjunct doctor, is a kind of poetic hydromancer through whose powers then recognizable Bath identities or types are subjected to surreal transformations. Something similar occurs in the Fleet Ditch episode of Book II of *The Dunciad*, itself distantly modeled on the practice of diving for pennies at Bath.

Yet there is no suggestion of such a transformation in Swift's Bath satire, found in the closing lines of "The Progress of Marriage," written in January 1722.[29] The poem's grimly realistic picture of a doomed union between an elderly clergyman and a much younger aristocratic woman was supposedly based on the real-life marriage of Benjamin Pratt, Dean of Down, and Lady Philippa Hamilton. The pair have no interests in common. The flighty bride continues her fashionable lifestyle independently of her colorless husband, who has soon "dwindled to a Lath" in his attempts to become a father. After a series of miscarriages, she insists on going to Bath, bribing her physician with a double fee to secure his recommendation. The springs are allowed a supernatural power of sorts but it is not through either Celtic or Christian tradition but a burlesque of classical fable in a hybrid of the legend of Acheloüs from Ovid's *Metamorphoses* Book IX with that of Alpheus diving under the ocean in his pursuit of Arethusa from Book V.

> For Venus rising from the Ocean
> Infus'd a strong prolifick Potion,
> That mixed with Achelous Spring,
> The *horned* Floud, as Poets sing:

> Who with an English Beauty smitten
> Ran under Ground from Greece to Brittain,
> The genial Virtue with him brought,
> And gave the Nymph a plenteous Draught;
> Then fled, and left his Horn behind
> For Husbands past their Youth to find;
> The Nymph who still with Passion burnd,
> Was to a boiling Fountain turn'd,
> Where Childless wives crowd ev'ry morn
> To drink in Achilous' Horn.
> And here the Father often gains
> That Title by anothers Pains. (ll. 107–22)

Denied any intrinsic life-enhancing powers, Bath still nourishes the malevolent energies invoked by satire – those of the dark Sulis. The wife enjoys "all Diversions of the Place" and

> . . . in the *cross-bath* seeks an Heir
> Since others oft have found one there (ll. 137–8)

Here Swift repeats the Protestant taunt at Mary of Modena's architectural adornments earlier uttered by Fiennes. The Dean is shamed from bathing by "his Cassock and his Years." The place had a gallery from which it was possible to converse with the bathers but he is banished even from this by "Coxcombs Raillery." By now his fruitless philogenitive strivings have so exhausted him that he dies of a fever, leaving his wife his estate and "swarms" of new lovers. The place of curing has become the place of death. Swift farewells her savagely enough:

> Oh, may I see her soon dispensing
> Her Favors to some broken Ensign
> Him let her Marry for his Face,
> And only Coat of tarnish't Lace;
> To turn her Naked out of Doors,
> And spend her Joynture on his Whores:
> But for a parting Present leave her
> A rooted Pox to last for ever. (ll. 159–66)

Bath so pictured is more recognizable as a social reality than in Rochester's and Fane's satires of half a century earlier but the poem concurs that it is a place of men's servitude to women and that a principal means by which women humiliate men is by encouraging them, in Rawson's rich phrase, to a "machismo of sexual debility" (7). The common fate of "Rochester," the swimmers in "Iter occidentale," and Swift's uxorious Dean is to be worn

out in a vain attempt to live up to an unrealizable ideal of Priapic masculinity. But where Rochester and Fane had at least been prepared to
celebrate Bath as the alchemist's limbeck that transported its devotees into
new realms of the erotic imagination, Swift can see no more than an
extension of the mindlessly trivial, wholly self-centered life of the London
beau monde. He becomes a predator on predators, leaving little to choose
between the cold-hearted ruthlessness of the wife and his own savaging of
her in verse. Rochester sideslips the charge of savagery by explicitly
including himself and his malice among the objects of the satire. Fane does
likewise by reducing his victims to a robotic infantilism rather than a
Yahoo-like brutishness. Swift stays formally outside the scene of his satire
while almost gleefully embracing that scene's engrained heartlessness. Both
satirist and subject belong to a Hobbesean world in which it is difficult to
claim any moral superiority for the satirist. Neither does one detect any
sympathy for a brother cleric led astray by a designing minx. The Dean of
Down was a fool and deserved everything he got for becoming involved
with a younger woman (a transgression of which the Dean of St. Patrick's
was doubly guilty). The satire comes from a place that has its own moral
strangeness, about whose origins the poem is typically evasive.

Two other poems from the Swift canon touch on the difference discussed earlier between sacral and non-sacral wells, one of them conducting
a formal act of desacralization. Dublin's healing well was named after
St. Patrick, who was said to have created it as a miracle. In 1729 it inex-
plicably ceased to flow. "Verses Occasioned by the Sudden Drying up of
St. Patrick's Well near Trinity College, Dublin," whose attribution to Swift
has been questioned but which is strongly Swiftian in manner, is spoken by
the saint himself.[30] Most of the poem is concerned with demonstrating the
degeneracy of modern Ireland in its subjection to England. Patrick has sent
three warning omens – magpies (English bishops appointed to Irish sees),
frogs (English soldiers, lawyers and judges), and "Vermin . . . from the
Land of *Huns*" (court-favoured entrepreneurs and absentee landlords).[31]
The drying up of the well represents the saint's abandonment of his patronage of Ireland out of disgust at the nation's failure to defend its liberty.
Among the victims of this act will be Swift's *alma mater*:

> Here, from the neighbouring Nursery of Arts,
> The Students drinking, rais'd their Wit and Parts;
> Here, for an Age and more, improv'd their Vein,
> Their *Phœbus* I, my Spring their *Hippocrene*.
> Discourag'd Youths, now all their Hopes must fail,
> Condemn'd to Country Cottages and Ale;

> To foreign Prelates make a slavish Court,
> And by their Sweat procure a mean Support;
> Or, for the Classicks read th'Attorney's Guide;
> Collect Excise, or wait upon the Tide. (ll. 69–78)

The passage identifies the satirist as a Protestant, negating any sense that the saint's founding miracle could have been other than Popish legend. For this wholly secularized St. Patrick, the spiritual influence of the well is reduced to its influence on the studies and career prospects of Trinity men; but an unseen wider influence will undermine the entire nation:

> Not half thy Course of Misery is run,
> Thy greatest Evils yet are scarce begun.
> Soon shall thy Sons, the Time is just at Hand,
> Be all made Captives in their native Land . . . (ll. 87–90)

The theme is the extinction of a once potent patriotic force founded in the love of liberty.

In "An Answer to the Ballyspellin Ballad" Swift again touches on the theme of desacralization through a picture of a spa which is not only useless for health but physically disgusting.[32] Ballyspellan near Kilkenny, a chalybeate spring like Tunbridge, had been praised in a poem by Swift's friend Thomas Sheridan. The stanza form of the two works was one used for a genre of sung improvised verse based on discovering strange and unusual rhymes for an invarying refrain: a widely known earlier example is the outrageous "A Song on Danby" (1678), partly written by the second Duke of Buckingham.[33] In a letter of September 28, 1728 Swift explained his aim of a double response that would both invert Sheridan's praise and discover additional strained rhymes for Ballyspellin. His invective is directed at the patrons as well as the place:

> Howe'er you flounce,
> I here pronounce
> Your Med'cine is repelling,
> Your Water's mud,
> And sowrs the blood
> When drank at Ballyspellin
> Those pocky Drabs
> To cure their Scabs
> You thither are compelling
> Will back be sent
> Worse than they went
> From nasty Ballyspellin (ll. 7–18)

The point of contrast is "our Well" at Markethill, Armargh, where the
bathers wear linen as opposed to "smocks hempen" and where "Sheelah"
and "bony Jane" outshine the dowdies of the better-known venue. But
the bathers of Markethill are not ladies of fashion but village girls who
otherwise spend their time shelling sowins (a form of oatmeal). Their
disrobing is public and designed for the voyeuristic pleasure of men,
including the lascivious poet. When Sheelah obligingly stripped to bathe
"A Bum so white / Ne'r came in sight" (ll. 40–1). Ballyspellan, a place for
drinking not bathing, allowed no such exposure. The poem does not need
to deny Ballyspellan spiritual powers, since none have been claimed for it,
but sets out to destroy its aspirations to social elegance and medical efficacy.
As in the Tunbridge satires, the fashionable spa is treated as a theatre for
the display of pretence and folly. Swift seems to have been particularly
offended by Sheridan's emphasis on the power held by women

> Our Ladies are as fresh and fair
> As Ross, or bright Dunkelling:
> And *Mars* might make a fair Mistake,
> Where he at *Ballyspellin*.
> We Men submit as they think fit,
> And here is no rebelling;
> The Reason's plain, the Ladies reign,
> They're Queens at *Ballyspellin*.[34]

In Swift's reverse account the women at Ballyspellin are characterized as
drabs, jades, "Maukins," "Grisetts," and blowses. They arrive as disease-
ridden whores and depart no better.

   This essay began by proposing two basic orientations for wells satire.
The first grew from the maturation of the spa or wells as a place of
assembly for summer visitors. Satires in this tradition were for the most
part written from within the wells community as a mode of social discipline and entertainment; however, some use the wells as a stage for the
exhibition of folly for a wider audience who were not themselves sharers
in the social experience. Rochester's "Tunbridge Wells" can be read in
this way. Alternatively, the speaker of the satire might dissociate himself
entirely from the community, except in so far as he displayed knowledge
of goings-on at the place. "The Progress of Marriage" and "An Answer to
the Ballyspellin Ballad" fall into this category. The second orientation
drew on the mythic associations of wells as places of communication with
supernatural powers, which in England is primarily associated with Bath.
These communications could either be benevolent, leading to the restoration of health or the bestowal of fecundity, or malevolent, leading to

the worsening of illness and even death. "Iter occidentale," if read as an allegorical triumph of Venus, might be squeezed into the benevolent category. "Verses Occasioned by the Sudden Drying up of St. Patrick's Well" also invokes hydro-supernaturalism, but ironically, since it records the cessation of an act of benevolent guidance in which the Protestant author makes no pretence of believing. Satire most patently invoked the malevolent powers through its incorporation of the curse. "The Progress of Marriage" ends with an actual curse, not all that different in its substance from those inscribed in ancient times on lead tablets sent down to Sulis. "Say Heav'n-born Muse" narrates the origins, casting, results, and eventual exorcism of a curse. It is to be feared that Mary of Modena did serious damage to wells satire by her attempt to reassert the sacral status of Bath. Fane and Rochester, writing before her intervention, while unsympathetic to Catholicism, are able to play in an imaginatively liberating way with the notion of the waters being a source of supernatural energy. Burlesque in their hands becomes an oblique form of celebratory ritual, one poem ending with an apotheosis of female sexual performance and the other with a parodic religious offering to a sanctified dildo. But once anti-Jacobites like Fiennes and Swift had forbidden themselves to acknowledge the legitimacy of the "Welsh prince," satire was forced to reject the rich mythopoetic possibilities of the well as a place of miracles. Swift's Saint Patrick appears only in order to quash a miracle, which had in any case already been reallocated to the realm of the secular. "The Progress" and "Ballyspellin" eschew the supernatural entirely. Yet while wells have ceased to be places for invoking the healing gods, they retain a connection with their darker peers who impel their votaries to lust, humiliation, murder, and satire.

NOTES

1 So "Tunbridg Satyr" (Northamptonshire Record Office MS, E(S)1209, item 2) begins "Though Satyr does admonish Every year / Yet no Amendment does appear . . ." For further examples of Tunbridge lampooning see Harold Love, *English Clandestine Satire 1660–1702* (Oxford: Oxford University Press, 2004), pp. 93, 155–7, 160, 165–6, 207–12.

2 An example is reproduced in Simon Hornblower and Anthony Spaworth (eds.), *The Oxford Companion to Classical Civilization* (Oxford: Oxford University Press, 1998), p. 201. See also R. S. O. Tomlin, "The Curse Tablets," in *The Temple of Sulis Minerva at Bath*. Vol. II, *The Finds from the Sacred Spring*, ed. Barry Cunliffe (Oxford: Oxford University Committee for Archaeology, 1988), pp. 59–280, and the website of the Centre for the Study of Ancient Documents, Oxford.

3 St. Winifred's and its miracles are the subject of a study in progress by Alison Shell.

4 *Memoirs of the Count de Gramont: Containing the Amorous History of the English Court under the Reign of Charles II. By Count Anthony Hamilton*, ed. Henry Vizetelly, 2 vols. (London, 1889), vol. II, pp. 152–73.

5 Narcissus Luttrell, *Notes of Travels*, Yale MS Osborn b 314, pp. 231–7, recording a visit of August 1680; *The Journeys of Celia Fiennes*, ed. Christopher Morris (London: The Cresset Press, 1947), pp. 132–7; Peter Causton, *Tunbridgialia* (London: typis J. Richardson, 1686), English version in *State-Poems; Continued from the Time of O. Cromwel to this Present Year 1697* (London, 1697), pp. 202–12; John Lewkenor, "A Journey to Tunbridge Wells," in *Metellus His Dialogues* (London, 1693), pp. 1–79. The place was also the basis of scenes in two London comedies, Thomas Rawlins's *Tunbridge Wells: or a Day's Courtship* (London, 1678), and Thomas Baker's *Tunbridge Walks* (London, 1703). Bath had its turn in D'Urfey's *The Bath, or, the Western Lass* (London, 1701), whose first act is actually set in the baths themselves, and Epsom in Shadwell's *Epsom-Wells* (London, 1673).

6 *A Phylosophical, and Medicinal Essay on the Waters of Tunbridge* (London, 1687), A2.

7 *Journeys of Celia Fiennes*, p. 135.

8 "Tunbridg Satyr," p. 1.

9 "The Second Tunbridge Lampoon 1690," Yale University Library. MS Osborn fb 70, p. 81.

10 III.i (pp. 23–4). Discussed in Harold Love, "That Satyrical Tune of Amarillis," *Early Music* 35 (2007), 39–47.

11 For examples see note 1.

12 "Tunbridg satyr," p. 1.

13 *The Poetical Works of William Strode (1600–1645)*, ed. William Dobell (London, 1907), p. 9.

14 *State-Poems; Continued*, pp. 184–5.

15 For Stubbe see James Jacob, *Henry Stubbe, Radical Protestantism and the Early Enlightenment* (Cambridge: Cambridge University Press, 1983).

16 *Journeys of Celia Fiennes*, pp. 19–20. By Anstey's day they might actually be collected from their beds.

17 *The Works of John Wilmot, Earl of Rochester*, ed. Harold Love (Oxford: Oxford University Press, 1999), pp. 81–5, 414–20, 594–5.

18 Claude Rawson, *Satire and Sentiment 1660–1830* (Cambridge: Cambridge University Press, 1994), pp. 3–4, 26.

19 BL MS 35838, f. 276r–v; reprinted in Jacob, *Henry Stubbe*, pp. 135–6.

20 Claude Rawson reminds us that in 1671 Rochester had been chosen general by his friends to conduct war against the customs farmers, after the latter had destroyed an illegally imported consignment of dildos (*Satire and Sentiment*, pp. 10–11).

21 Identified in Rochester, *Works*, pp. 414–20.

22 BL MS Harl. 7312, pp. 100–5; BL MS Harl. 7319, fols. 11v–15v; Edinburgh University Library MS DC 1 3/1, pp. 42–3; Harvard University Library, MS Eng. 636f, pp. 32–9; Österreichische Nationalbibliothek, Cod. 14090, ff. 131v–134v; Victoria and Albert Museum, MS Dyce 43, pp. 248–54.

23 (London, 1675), A2r.

24 Reprinted in Rochester, *Works*, pp. 232–40.

25 Texts in *The Poems of Richard Corbett*, ed. J. A. W. Bennett and H. R. Trevor-Roper (Oxford: Clarendon Press, 1955), 31–49, and *Poems on Affairs of State. Augustan Satirical Verse, 1660–1714*, gen. ed. George deForest Lord, 7 vols. (New Haven: Yale University Press, 1963–75), vol. I, pp. 3–19. For similarly titled poems by Richard Edes, Thomas Master, Thomas Bispham, George Wither, and Jeremiah Wells, see Corbett, *Poems*, pp. 118–9.

26 British Library, MS Harl. 7319, 11v (repunctuated for clarity).

27 Folio 14v. The fifth line has been editorially reconstructed on the basis of other MS versions. The lame ending of the fourth could well be a scribal corruption.

28 Rawson, *Satire and Sentiment*, p. 8.

29 *The Poems of Jonathan Swift*, ed. Harold Williams, 2nd edn. (Oxford: Clarendon Press, 1958), vol. I, pp. 289–95. Curiously, there seems to be no record of Swift visiting Bath. The references in the correspondence are largely excuses for not going.

30 Swift, *Poems*, vol. III, pp. 789–94.

31 The "magpie" jibe was associated with Dissenters (see Love, *English Clandestine Satire*, p. 252) but that need not apply here since the point stressed is nationality not objection to the prelacy as an institution.

32 Swift, *Poems*, vol. II, pp. 437–43.

33 Text and variants in *Plays, Poems, and Miscellaneous Writings Associated with George Villiers, Second Duke of Buckingham*, ed. Robert D. Hume and Harold Love (Oxford: Oxford University Press, 2007), vol. II, pp. 20–30, 426–34, 517–29.

34 "Ballyspellin. By Dr Sheridan," in Swift, *Poems*, pp. 438–40.

CHAPTER 5

Dryden and the invention of irony

Steven N. Zwicker

I would like to begin with a little piece of irony. If you look up the word "irony" in the *Oxford English Dictionary* there are no definitions or instances of usage drawn from texts written or published between 1660 and 1700. If you seek further, asking after "ironic," "ironical," "ironize," "ironist," or "ironism," you hit a similar wall: none of the variants are cited from the Restoration.[1] There are definitions and applications before and after the Restoration, but from those years of mischief and malfeasance there is not one instance cited, no definition offered, no refinement enumerated. It is as if a philological act of oblivion had been passed over the age whose modes of political, social, and literary consciousness were most deeply and most pervasively characterized by irony. Perhaps this is a shadow of the Victorian high-mindedness that has fallen across the Restoration, even from the origins of the *New English Dictionary* in the 1850s to the online *OED*, but it is also true that Jonathan Swift – Dryden's near-contemporary and irony's most brilliant student – seems to have had some difficulty in allowing irony's signal position in Restoration culture, and a particular disability in reckoning with the example of John Dryden.[2] Dryden had offered Swift and his generation the model of a career devoted to the practices of irony, but from his handling of Dryden it would be difficult to discern Swift's awareness of that model, or indeed any sense of indebtedness to Dryden at all.[3]

"Cousin Swift, you will never be a poet" – Dryden may have made that remark in the 1690s, and Swift's occlusion of Dryden may have begun here, but a personal slight is insufficient to explain either the seeming oblivion that Swift passed over Dryden's lessons in irony or the deep hostility in Swift's representations of Dryden.[4] I want eventually to turn to Swift's hostility and especially to his send-up of Dryden in *The Battle of the Books* (1704), but I would like to begin with origins – with Dryden's invention of irony – and to ask what effect his ironies may have had on the possibility of literary relations with cousin Swift, who tells us that Dryden "though my near relation, is one I have often blamed as well as pitied."[5] Pity and blame are part of the mix, and the advantages of condescension are obvious, but there are other elements in this story, certainly Swift's indebtedness to Dryden but as well his contempt for Dryden's uses of irony to protect himself, to maintain precarious balance, to forestall commitment, to embrace contingency, and at times to perform a kind of disappearing act in the midst of argument and assertion. Such uses of irony must have seemed to Swift a spectacle of equivocation.

Of course, Dryden did not invent irony. He understood how the ancients had fashioned this voice; he admired Lucian as an ironist of genius; and he knew very well and as a translator the ironies of Horace, Juvenal, Persius, and Tacitus.[6] But if Swift had looked for English exemplars, he would have found none before Dryden who had so widely explored the uses of irony, who had turned a mere figure of speech into an arresting mode of literary self-consciousness, and who used irony not only to humiliate antagonists but as well to refuse simplifications and singularity. From early in his career, Dryden was engaged with a progressive unfolding of the ways irony might furnish a shield against commitments and enable a writer to walk away from the most overt demonstration of damaging truths while at the same time insinuate them into his writing. It was this opening of irony – self-irony but as well irony at the expense of others, and of a number of others – that stood before Swift. He may well have ignored or diminished Dryden as an exemplar in order to imagine his own literary existence, but this was not a simple killing of the literary father; Swift's violence, his aggression and indignation, his uses of irony to expose barbarism and excoriate bad faith surely blocked the figure of Dryden in other ways. Some of Dryden's work with irony could be accommodated to Swift's themes and obsessions, but there was much else about his uses of irony that fits awkwardly with Swift's moral intensities. As Claude Rawson has so powerfully demonstrated, everywhere Swift aims to disallow readerly complacency: he imposes moral dilemmas; he denies the solace of competing points of view; he anatomizes the depths of human depravity even while "entertain[ing] these in himself at a level of 'cruel' play."[7] Whatever Dryden's considerable self-awareness, such readerly discomforts and disruptions were not his way; moral outrage was a country that Dryden hardly ever visited.

BEGINNING WITH IRONY

At the opening of Dryden's career there is nothing to suggest an ironist. His set pieces on Lord Hastings or on the Restoration, like his

commendatory poems to Clarendon, Sir Robert Howard, and Walter
Charleton, are straightforward, univocal. His verse on Cromwell's demise
hints at the capacity to walk away from events at hand, though the whole
performance is sufficiently strange as to deny the kind of settled intention
that would soon allow Dryden to think simultaneously on the surface of
and somewhere deeper within an argument. Things began to change by
the mid-1660s when Dryden emerged with a new armamentarium. In the
summer of 1665, with the plague raging in London and with a few plays
behind him, he retreated to his father-in-law's estate in Wiltshire and
produced a different kind of theatricality and a new self-presentation in
An Essay of Dramatic Poesy (1668). This set of arguments about the theater
is fashioned as a conversation on the rival literary merits of the ancients
and moderns and of English and French playwriting. The topics need not
concern us here, but what we should notice is Dryden's creation of
different voices that at once expose persons and ideas. This simultaneity
and its contrapuntal and skeptical methods, as well as the turns of
exaggeration, needling, and understatement, begin to define Dryden's art
as an ironist.[8]

Part of Dryden's development in that art is a growing mastery of
ventriloquism, a nearly dispassionate articulation or occupation of positions and characters with which he may well agree but also with which he
cannot quite agree, or with which he somewhat disagrees, or with which
he strongly disagrees. Writing for the theater was one source of this
capacity, but Dryden's mastery of ventriloquism in the *Essay* is not simply
a piece of theatricality. It involved a more elaborate set of moves – yes, a
cultivation of appearances, but also an ability to stand to the side of his
characters, and to be seen standing to their side, while they argue con-
tradictory and uncompromising positions. The ventriloquism at its most
damaging is seen in the figure of Crites who displays himself, or rather
whom Dryden displays, as arrogant and self-regarding, stiff in opinions,
but not always in the wrong. The personal and derisory force of Dryden's
portrait of his brother-in-law, Sir Robert Howard, is clear, but what is
also clear is Dryden's own regard for the ancients, for the literary models
that Crites defends and for the aesthetic which could not simply be put
aside as a consequence of Crites' self-importance. A different kind of
ventriloquism can be heard in Dryden's production of his own voice in
the person of Neander, whom he allows an unconscionable amount of
argumentative and digressive space to theorize and defend those new
idioms of dramatic art that Dryden and his collaborator, Sir Robert
Howard, had already put on the London stage. At the same time Dryden

allows a touch of self-mockery to deflate Neander; he has a bit of fun with his own digressive self and perhaps too with the ways in which Neander represents the casual disorder and hybridity of English literary culture. Dryden's capacity to see himself and to create himself as a character is played out repeatedly in prefaces and dedications, though nowhere more daringly and disinterestedly than in the figure of Melantha from *Marriage-à-la-Mode* (1673), who represents, to hilarious and humiliating effect, Dryden's habitual borrowings and adaptations and interpolations of French idioms and fashionable language in his writings, and his own courtly ambitions. Dryden is able to see himself in the comic and distorting mirror of *Marriage-à-la-Mode*, to see his social over-reaching, his need to caress the great and to ape and abet courtly manners; at the same time he allows the harmless vanity, even the inventiveness and cultural productivity driven by those ambitions. Starting with the *Essay*, what Dryden displays is an uncanny capacity to interrogate his own habits and habituations, his space within the cultural economy, his pretensions and achievements, and to see them simultaneously in the light of self-irony and self-regard.

By such means he maintained proximity and distance: he stands next to a character or an idea even while he is in the midst of moving away, perhaps not principally as a mode of equivocation – though sometimes it is that – but as a way of holding off, not wholly committing himself to one position.[9] We know what Dryden's enemies would make of such mobility; what they did not appreciate was the argumentative force, the intellectual bearing, or the psychological vulnerabilities that impelled mobility, or the art that emerged from skittish uncertainties and ironic reversals and removals. Of course there are striking shifts in Dryden's politics and religions, and they did happen at opportune moments, and there was a fair amount of equivocation and perhaps some social climbing in Dryden's character. But he was also busy over almost his entire career moving away from fixed positions. Mobility is important to Dryden's style; it is part of his fluency, his abundance, his literariness. But mobility is also a balancing act and a way of resisting dogmatism. Mobility eased his relations to policy and pragmatism; at one point during the Exclusion Crisis Dryden has Charles II, in the guise of King David, assert with a mock and hollow defensiveness that "a king's at least a part of government," claiming one of the fundamentals of the mixed and ancient constitution and at the same time and by ironic diminution suggesting how radical and how absurd was the position to which the Exclusionists would drive the commonweal. Mobility was also important to the poet's advocacy of religious toleration and to the expression of his lifelong contempt for priestly impositions and religious authoritarianism, a set of convictions that put him in the surprising spiritual company of John Milton and Andrew Marvell. Within his complex maneuvering over charity in the preface to *Religio Laici* (1682), for example, Dryden managed at once to regret – and with a touch of anti-popery – the "infallibility in the private Spirit" that marked the pretensions of dissent, to deride the failure of charity among the Anglican high-flyers, and to denounce the king-killing doctrines of Rome, and all the while, and quoting with marvelous fluency and offhandedness a variety of theological texts and opinions, to claim his own naïvety, his innocence of technical sophistication in matters of belief, his spiritual simplicity. By means of a sinuous chain of analogy and argumentation Dryden manages in *Religio Laici* to skate between various theological strictures and to assert spiritual diffidence, charity, and ease. When the poet then turned about and made his awkward embrace of Roman Catholicism what is most striking about the presentation of this new spiritual home is not the infallibility of Rome but its mysteries, even equivocations, and the intricacy and ambiguity of holy writ. A similar blurring of outlines had taken place when Dryden handled the sanctity of lineal descent, that leitmotif of Stuart politics, tying patriarchy to the profligate body of the monarch and hedging the divinity of kingship with an acknowledgment of its frailties, at one point displaying that theme as if it were an idea lifted from a Restoration comedy. Dryden did not mean to dispense with ideals, but his embrace is partial, protected from absolutes. This is the posture and the intellectual formation that we begin to discover in the *Essay of Dramatic Poesy*. He would spend an entire career refining on and transmuting the techniques that allowed him such space.

DEDICATING *ANNUS MIRABILIS*

The *Essay* provided Dryden with the first occasion to explore ways of holding arguments and commitments in tension with one another, and of using irony to veil convictions and counterpoint ideals. Soon he visited the broader canvas of civics and political history in the brief exercise that forms the Dedication of *Annus Mirabilis* (1667). We might first ask if there is to be found here any discomfiture at all, the least sign of irony clouding the high and perfumed rhetoric of the Dedication. It has been read as perfectly straight, a set of tropes and exaggerations with which any student of Dryden's exercises in dedication and digression would be familiar, and Dryden already knew how to play the various hand of suave and efficient sincerity. But something else marks the language of this performance. The poem itself indulges a series of baroque exaggerations that highlight English heroics and royal sacrifice, and surely these set pieces of celebration are meant to prop their subjects without the deflection of second guessing or misgiving, though it is, admittedly, difficult for us, as perhaps it was for the poem's first readers, not to pause over the figure of Charles II out-weeping the hermit and out-praying the saint (ll. 1041–2). But in the Dedication, Dryden displays a sharper hold on discomfiture, aiming at once to caress the city and to remind its aldermen and sheriffs and common council of difficult and compromised times. What seems to be in play in the Dedication is a way of writing that holds together aspirations and misgivings. Irony allows two stories to be told at once, though in this instance it might be more accurate to say something like one and a half stories to be told simultaneously. First, the seamless and ostensible narrative of the Dedication, its recital of the city's loyalty, honor, and love for her monarch and her own afflictions, perseverance, and wonders. Such a recital in the aftermath of civic disaster is entirely plausible, eminently suitable given the occasion, the rhetorical context in which Dryden is writing, and the narratives of the poem itself, though we know that very different stories had been spun out of the materials that Dryden handles in this poem. But there is also a counter-narrative in the Dedication, not a full inversion, but a set of turns that allow local reversals and more oblique angles of reflection to complicate without canceling the overt narrative.

In the Civil Wars London had been the center of religious nonconformity and political dissent, the foundation of the parliamentary effort to wage war against the king. Now in the mid-1660s, the City had again become home to "nests" of fanatics, a site of plots and intrigues, of jealousies and fears.[10] Could Dryden possibly have written of London and Charles II as "a pair of matchless Lovers" unaware of the strains that political, social, and spiritual history exerted on this language?[11] The figure of that loving body politic belongs to a traditional vocabulary of state, but the way in which Dryden unfolds the metaphor puts considerable pressure on the convention: "Other Cities have been prais'd for the same Virtues, but I am much deceiv'd if any have so dearly purchas'd their reputation."[12] The many rivals for London's affections, the violent ravishing, the withholding from desire, the dearly purchased reputation: this language pointedly twins political and sexual misdemeanor. In *Astraea Redux* (1660), Dryden had visited this figure, the king there yearning to embrace "Our first Flames and Virgin Love" (l. 20). In that poem the sense of political eros was naïve; here it is coy and urbane.

What Dryden is able to do in a few lines of this Dedication frames and counterpoints his 1,200 lines of verse in *Annus Mirabilis*. He is aware of the limits of loyalty and constancy to be discovered in London, and hints at the pleasures taken and appetites indulged both in the City and at court. While it is possible to read the Dedication straight – nor would such a reading have disappointed a poet who was, among other things, busy soothing relations between the king and the City in the midst of fiscal crisis – the deftness of the prose allows the Dedication to be read in more than one way. The straight and ironic narratives may seem to cut against one another, but we might think of them working surreptitiously together, one script offering a conventional and idealized vision of the City and its relations with Stuart monarchy, the other instructing the poem's most immediate audience – the Lord Mayor, those aldermen rumored to be in collusion with radicals, the sheriffs, and the common council that had to be warned against taking up arms against the king – that the memory of the past was not lost on those who wrote of London's history, reputation, and civic life in the summer and fall of 1666. The pamphlet literature of dissent and nonconformity had urged the interpretation of London's disaster as evidence of divine wrath, God's anger at a whoring king and debauched court. Rather than deny or contradict that story, Dryden seems to ignore it; in turn he implicates the City in its own misfortunes, perhaps even in the king's misadventures. Who, after all, had been yielding to the king's many rivals, whoring herself in the process, and withholding from the king his "matchless lover?" For those who would read the relationship of London and her monarch as a seamless whole, the story of innocent desire and celebration would be enough; but if that were too naïve, then Dryden hints at another story that he allows to occupy the fringes of this text.

MATURE ENCOUNTERS

The intention of irony in the Dedication to *Annus Mirabilis* is to complicate life slightly, to unsettle things, to allow a touch of frayed edges to show. When Dryden returns to the themes of civic life in *Absalom and Achitophel* (1681), he is in an altogether different place – laureate, a kind of star literary spokesman for the crown, and now an old hand at the give and take of paper scuffles and at violence that went beyond the printed page. Not only have the poet's literary and civic identities matured, his uses of irony have gathered assurance, grown in complexity. With

Absalom and Achitophel there is no possibility of univocal reading; everywhere Dryden's lines are brightened by irony – sometimes turned against partisans and politicians, at other moments undermining the themes of Whiggery; at some points proffering false modesty, at others leveling enemies with devices of scorn and derision. Is there anything in ironic abuse quite so perfectly managed as the portrait of Buckingham? "A man so various, that he seem'd to be / Not one, but all Mankinds Epitome . . . Rayling and praising were his usual Theams; / And both (to shew his Judgment) in Extreams: / So over Violent, or over Civil, / That every man, with him, was God or Devil. / In squandering Wealth was his peculiar Art: / Nothing went unrewarded but Desert" (ll. 545–60). The poem has been much admired for such satiric uses of irony, and rightly so, though in the shadow of this brilliant portraiture we may overlook Dryden's deployment of irony in a more experimental or investigative mode, irony as a set of conjectures and possibilities. And *Absalom and Achitophel* gives us some wonderful instances of irony where Dryden is clearly trying things out. He leavens the fierce mood of anti-popery, for example, by seeming to join in such abuse. The wonderful send-up of Egyptian rites "Where Gods were recommended by their Tast" (l. 119), is simultaneously a piece of laughter at popish ritual and at those who fear a religion that proffers the same deities "for Worship and for Food" (l. 121). Daring in a slightly different way is Dryden's glance at the conversion of the Duke of York which allows the poet to conflate courts and stews – both exactly the right place, indeed perhaps the same place, to "rake" for converts to Roman Catholicism (l. 127). Such conflation makes a joke out of popery, and at the seeming expense of its most prominent convert; at the same time and by ironic diminution Dryden ridicules those who would stir the fear of popery on behalf of political experimentation and Exclusion. I suspect that Dryden did not know exactly how such passages would turn out – he is juggling argumentative and tonal possibilities, hoping to keep everything in the air at the same time, and in these passages he does so brilliantly. We may find the uses of *Paradise Lost* (1667) a bit heavy-going in the way Dryden deploys the Miltonic sublime to undercut the figure of Absalom (l. 372), a character whom Dryden seems unable to treat without condescension. But in both instances above, irony works in an experimental fashion – the poet not fully in control of the ripple effect of his ironies. Such uncertainty makes these moves exhilarating, a satiric high-wire act.

Perhaps even more interesting in this regard are the poem's opening lines. The passage has been often and observantly read, but it is still worth noting the kinds of direction and indirection at play in these lines. What makes this set of gestures so intriguing is the touch of moral uncertainty that Dryden allows to move against the strictures of priestcraft. Of course Dryden argues against priestly regulation of the state, but does he recommend installing a regime of waste and indiscriminate sexuality in its place? This is where irony takes on its complex argumentative life. On the one hand, irony's job here is to deflate false pretensions to authority, to take a bit of wind out of the sail of moral criticisms leveled at the promiscuity of court. Scattering "his maker's image" is not what Charles II had most in mind as he practiced the art of sexual generosity, and Dryden's knowingness blurs the lines of morality – his courtly sophistication in such matters is clear. But what would replace the inflexible codes of monogamy and moral regulation or the laws strictly governing the uses of the royal body and the descent of such properties as the crown? Here the deflecting agency of irony comes alive – not exactly the work of truth-seeking, but a generous indecision, a refusal to settle for the simplest solutions, a willingness to keep uncertainty in play. How fitting such play seems in a poem that is hesitant about theories of state, a poem that imagines restorative politics as patch-work and fine tuning. We might even think of *Absalom and Achitophel* as a kind of "un-Patriarcha," a work where nothing is argued from first principles. And how closely allied in this project are the poetics of irony with their uncertain and equivocal movement between possibilities of meaning and statecraft by half measures.

MODERNS AND ANCIENTS

Relations among poets are almost always fraught with ambiguities, with admiration as well as competition, deep indebtedness as well as denial, and Dryden's relations with his contemporaries and predecessors constitute a virtual transcript of mixed messages. We know, for example, of Dryden's ambivalent relations with the vernacular tradition in the theater, both his admiration of Shakespeare and Jonson and his competitiveness and ambivalence, and we have learned something too of his difficulties with his contemporaries – the living great and even not so great, as in the beautiful verses that allow hedging admiration to the memory of John Oldham, or his nervous attention to the Earl of Rochester.[13] But his relations with Milton provide the most curious and challenging site of literary competition among the moderns; indeed, these relations seem emblematic of Dryden's uses of irony simultaneously to achieve proximity and distance. I want to pause over a particular moment in that relationship, Dryden's adaptation of *Paradise Lost*, since *The State of Innocence* (1677) together with its Dedication and the essay on heroic poetry printed with the play form a case-study in mixed messages and uncertain affinities.

The poets met when neither was practicing poetry: in the office of the secretariat for Foreign Tongues in the 1650s, where Dryden joined Marvell as an assistant to Milton; they met again when Dryden asked permission to create an opera from Milton's epic.[14] The result was a hybrid production, a piece of theater based on *Paradise Lost* that radically reduced and redesigned the epic, filled with echoes of Milton's poem but cast in a spare and pointed idiom. *The State of Innocence* is neither a send-up of *Paradise Lost* nor an act of homage to the Miltonic sublime. Its work of uncertain affiliation begins in the opera's Dedication to Mary of Modena, where we hear Dryden in full panegyric flight, indulging in fantastic exaggeration, slavish adoration of the young princess, and out-rageously toying with the idioms of Roman Catholic adoration and mysticism even while deriding the stubborn English devotion to liberty and the ancient constitution.[15] What could provide a sharper, a more ironic subversion than Dryden's dedication of Milton's masterpiece of dissenting spirituality and republican idealism to the person of the Princess of Modena on the occasion of her marriage to the most visible, the most notorious convert to the religion which above all others Milton identified with political absolutism and spiritual idolatry? But is there not also something strange in Dryden's choice of texts for such a dedication, something that upsets our notions of easy partisanship in Dryden's thrusting of Milton into the midst of royal ceremonial, aiming with his masque to ornament a royal and Roman Catholic marriage with an adaptation of the poetry of that notorious regicide and divorcer John Milton? These acts of exaggeration and aggression destabilize our sense of Dryden's relations with Milton so that the texts of *The State of Innocence* seem to stage something of a disappearing act, forcing us to ask after Dryden's location in the midst of contrary moves.

But if the Dedication compromises Milton, "The Authors Apology for Heroique Poetry" asserts alliance and protects the epic and the epic poet's ambitions against a carping, illiterate, and censorious age. The essay defends heroic verse by celebrating its sinews, its bold figuration and strong metaphors, the lively images and heightened elocution that epic demands. Dryden's defense of heroic poetry fits exactly and at every turn with Milton's achievement in *Paradise Lost*, and Dryden makes sure in the essay carefully to align Milton with Homer, Virgil, and Tasso, though we should remember that in the Dedication Tasso is explicitly linked with aristocratic patronage.[16] If the Dedication to Mary of Modena opens a gap between courtly culture and republican poetics, the essay on heroic poetry mostly closes it, and if there were any discomfort for Dryden in shuttling between positions, it almost never shows; it is of course the set of moves that irony most dexterously allows.

Of the text itself, Dryden aims neither to depend on *Paradise Lost* nor to deny Milton the dignity of his achievement. The most striking aspect of Dryden's style is the heroic couplet, a daring choice given the hostile note on verse that Milton added to the 1668 issue of *Paradise Lost*, which not only denies the affinity of rhyme and heroic poetry but as well derides heroic drama and Restoration court culture and perhaps Dryden himself. And Dryden's couplets certainly shift the tone and range of Milton's style, they proffer epigrammatic closure and refuse the syntactical freedom and digressive elaboration that are at the heart of Milton's style and not only style, they are at the heart of Milton's vision, his way of extending the range of his myths and themes deeply into fallen time.[17] Although Milton uses the imperative "haste" throughout *Paradise Lost*, the slowness and the variety of tempos in which the epic unfolds over and through time are never more obvious than when we turn to *The State of Innocence*, which moves with such rapidity and at the nearly uniform theatrical tempo of repartee. This is not to say that Milton's masterful elaboration of different schemes of time is mindlessly flattened by the rhythms of theatrical writing, but that the genres of *Paradise Lost* and its textures, its allusiveness, its imagining of times past and present and future demand rhythms that cannot be supported on stage. Dryden reshapes *Paradise Lost* to claim ownership over the epic, to assert the stage over text, but the competition is fraught, complex, and uncertain, and perhaps even more so when we recall that *The State of Innocence* was never performed, known in Dryden's own time as a closet drama, perhaps something closer to *Samson Agonistes* (1674) than to his own *Indian Emperor* (1667) or *Conquest of Granada* (1672). On first reading *Paradise Lost*, Dryden was reported to have said "that poet has cut us all out" – surely an acknowledgment of genius, but a suggestion too of the wounding force of literary competition.[18]

Dryden's poems and plays display his literary relations with a host of moderns, and in his prose he was often a superb advocate of modernity, a vocation that Swift mercilessly ridiculed. But Swift also ridiculed Dryden's relations with the ancients. No figure from antiquity was more important to Dryden than Virgil, whom he acknowledged early and late and whose style he everywhere imitates, echoes, and adapts. Yet Dryden is not all admiration; his relations with Virgil are also animated by an odd and defensive hesitancy that discovers other ancients favored in little ways over Virgil, and Virgil removed from the center of his literary life near its very close when he had spent a lifetime chasing after Virgil and four years translating the whole of Virgil's works. The story is complex, as is often the case with looming literary models, but I want to take a moment from Dryden's *Dedication of the Aeneis* (1697) to ask after its argument and its affect.

First, we need to acknowledge that the *Dedication* includes a very large amount of very conventional praise of Virgil and of epic poetry, so conventional that Dryden does not even try to hide his footsteps among those who had been here before him. Perhaps he is perfectly happy to praise Virgil in borrowed terms so that he might allow Virgil his due but at the same time allow his utter conventionality – not an uninteresting critical tack. But Dryden has other things to say in defense and admiration and these seem more personal and more complex, indeed more compromised and more affecting. For the *Dedication* displays a deep and touching effort to see Virgil as a poet whose circumstances reflect Dryden's own, and to see in the figure of Virgil all the compromises that Dryden himself had made: his own need to curry favor with the great, to instill a kind of simple-minded nationalism in the English people, to justify political stability and power by endorsing what may have been even in his own mind a corrupt political regime – to explain himself away through Virgil. And of course what Dryden contrives to see in the mirror that he creates is not always a shining image, not always a heroic figure of the poet, but one shaded by compromise and complicity. It is so especially when Dryden defends Virgil's responsiveness to "Obligations," his treating with patrons and with power: Virgil's willingness for example to personate Augustus in the figure of Aeneas, to accommodate to circumstance, to allow anachronisms and to slight chronology.[19] And further, and at some length, Dryden both acknowledges and defends the need to flatter and caress; Virgil was, indeed,

a finer Flatterer than Ovid; and I more than conjecture that he had in his eye the Divorce which not long before had pass'd betwixt the Emperour and Scribonia. He drew this dimple in the cheek of Aeneas, to prove Augustus of the same Family, by so remarkable a Feature in the same place. Thus, as we say in our home-spun English Proverb, "He killed two Birds with one stone", pleased the Emperour by giving him the resemblance of his Ancestor; and gave him such a resemblance as was not scandalous in that Age. For to leave one Wife and take another, was but a matter of Gallantry at that time of day among the Romans . . . If the Poet argued not aright, we must pardon him for a poor blind Heathen, who knew no better Morals.[20]

This may simply be part of the contextualizing work that Dryden performs throughout the *Dedication*, explaining in historical terms what seem the compromised morals of Virgil's poem, compromised because the poet stooped to caress, to "sooth the vanity of the Romans," and compromised too because, Dryden seems to say, Virgil was after all only a heathen.[21] But the critique turns back on itself, and the lovely exaggerations and ironies of Dryden's description rescue Virgil's manners as poet and moralist, as indeed "our contemporary." Perhaps the heathen knew no better than to wink at divorce, but if that were the case then he would have been utterly at home with the morals and manners of Restoration England, as Dryden intimately knew them. And there are many other moments in the *Dedication* that work just to this effect, that seem to allow critique even while rescuing Virgil from misunderstanding. The *Dedication* protects Virgil from his critics and excuses him for his imperfections; but in this defensive economy the critics are perhaps too often conjured, the imperfections too frequently on display. Even as Dryden reconciles the reader to Virgil and even as he identifies with and appropriates Virgil, he moves away from him, drifting in and out of focus as apologist, admirer, protector, and explainer. The specter of hostile criticism haunts this text, which is a masterpiece of adjustments and refinements, of accommodation and admiration, and of distance and denial as well. These complex and contradictory moves aim to open a space somewhere beside Virgil, not wholly covered by Virgil's shadow but not wholly outside the aura of his master, somewhere between ancients and moderns.[22]

When Swift takes up Dryden's appropriations he is utterly unresponsive to the mixed motives that define Dryden's relations with literary precedents, to Dryden's uses of irony to allow proximity and distance, and while Swift's portrait of Dryden is deeply ironic it is also wholly unambiguous.[23] Swift flattens to hilarious and wounding effect Dryden's advocacy of the ancients, first to identify him exclusively with what he considers an appalling canon of moderns, then to reduce Dryden's lifelong apprenticeship to Virgil and the masterful translation to a humiliating comedy of misalliance. The encounter is staged as an episode in *The Battle of the Books* where the two are arrayed as combatants, and where

Virgil's grandeur and diffidence everywhere trump the servility and impotence of his translator:

On the left Wing of the Horse, Virgil appeared in shining Armor, completely fitted to his Body; He was mounted on a dapple grey Steed, the slowness of whose Pace, was an effect of the highest Mettle and Vigour. He cast his Eye on the adverse Wing, with a desire to find an Object worthy of his valour, when behold, upon a sorrel Gelding of a monstrous Size, appear'd a Foe, issuing from among the thickest of the Enemy's Squadrons; But his Speed was less than his Noise; for his Horse, old and lean, spent the Dregs of his Strength in a high Trot, which tho' it made slow advances, yet caused a loud Clashing of his Armor, terrible to hear. The two Cavaliers had now approached within the Throw of a Lance, when the Stranger desired a Parley, and lifting up the Vizard of his Helmet, a Face hardly appeared from within, which after a pause, was known for that of the renowned Dryden. The brave Antient suddenly started, as one possess'd with Surprize and Disappointment together: For, the Helmet was nine times too large for the Head, which appeared Situate far in the hinder Part, even like the Lady in a Lobster, or like a Mouse under a Canopy of State, or like a shriveled Beau from within the Penthouse of a modern Perewig: And the voice was suited to the Visage, sounding weak and remote. Dryden in a long Harangue soothed up the good Antient, called him Father, and by a large deduction of Genealogies, made it plainly appear, that they were nearly related. Then he humbly Proposed an Exchange of Armor, as a lasting Mark of Hospitality between them. Virgil consented (for the Goddess Diffidence came unseen, and cast a Mist before his Eyes) tho' his was of Gold, and cost a hundred Beeves, the others but of rusty Iron. However, this glittering Armor became the Modern yet worse than his own. Then, they agreed to exchange Horses; but when it came to the trial, Dryden was afraid, and utterly unable to mount.[24]

Swift travesties Dryden's claims of intimacy and ridicules his outsized ambitions; he mocks Dryden with a torrent of diminutions that would deny literary authority. This is surely one effect of that counterpointing of steeds and geldings at the opening of the passage and of the closing image of Dryden's failure "to mount" and as well of the derisive figure of Dryden as the "lady in the lobster," all images that assault masculinity and miniaturize literary achievement: a wounding personal slight, of course, but also an attack on generative power. Dryden's relation to Virgil is staked on imitation and translation, and Swift caught the scent of the ambivalence and discomfort that Dryden wove through the *Dedication*, but in Swift's hands all of Dryden's maneuvering, his aim to open a space between originary force and imitation and between ancients and moderns is reduced to the mere clatter of ill-fitting armor and the rustle of self-promotion; those complex genealogies that claim affinity are ridiculed as transparent and self-serving devices. Perhaps it was Dryden's efforts to align his own political and patronage circumstances with those that he imagined Virgil had endured that goaded Swift to his indignation, to dismiss Dryden's self-appointed affinity as comic posturing. But there are other issues at stake in dismissing Dryden's claims as translator, arbiter, and defender of the ancients and of disallowing that space that Dryden opened for himself between ancients and moderns. Swift's version of Dryden's encounter with Virgil intends mockery, it aims to catch Dryden out, to remove the little equivocations, to reduce Dryden's affection to mere self-promotion; it intends to reposition Dryden and to deny him the comfort of the middle ground.

Dryden may not, could not, have known that he would aim throughout at a position in between: in between, of course, ancients and moderns, but in between so many other aesthetic models, political affinities, spiritual identities, social discourses, and literary patrons. These shifting, temporizing, uncertain, and experimental modes of affiliation are beautifully caught in the sentence that opens the Preface to *Fables* (1700) – Dryden's last prose – where he aims to occupy the shifting ground of fable, miscellany, and translation:

'Tis with a Poet as with a Man who designs to build, and is very exact, as he supposes, in casting up the Cost beforehand: But, generally speaking, he is mistaken in his Account and reckons short of the Expence he first intended: He alters his Mind as the Work proceeds, and will have this or that Convenience more, of which he had not thought when be began. So has it hapned to me; I have built a house where I intended but a Lodge: Yet with better Success than a certain Nobleman, who beginning with a Dog-kennil, never liv'd to finish the Palace he had contriv'd.[25]

Though Swift would have admired the ironies at the close of this self-portrait, Dryden pausing once again to glance at the Duke of Buckingham, he could not have lived in the house that Dryden built with its alterations and contingencies, its casual assurance, and its simultaneous touches of self-irony and self-regard, and perhaps too Dryden's disregard for the moral complicities and complacencies of his readers. This is of course not to deny Swift the complexities of his own ironic modes, but, whatever the arc of Swift's journeys between Dublin and London, Dryden's endemic "in between" was not a place that Swift could have discovered as home. It is surprising how much Dryden made out of contingency, out of irony's superb unfixedness, its maneuvering and dislocations. What does not surprise, in the end, is how little of this ironist Swift could allow himself to acknowledge.

NOTES

1 The only Restoration variant cited is an obscure and rare application of "ironically," which is said to mean "with dissimulation or personation," this from Sir Thomas Browne's *Christian Morals*, a work held in manuscript until its eighteenth-century publication; see *OED* online, www.dictionary.oed. com/ (accessed April 21, 2007), s.v. "ironically," adverb.

2 In Swift's library there is nothing to be found of Rochester and no mention of him in Swift's work; see *Rochester: The Critical Heritage*, ed. David Farley-Hills (New York: Barnes and Noble, 1972), p. 13; further, there is nothing of Etherege, Savile, Buckingham, or Dorset among Swift's books, and while Swift mentions Wycherly, he hardly notices Sedley, and, most strikingly, nothing of Dryden is to be found in Swift's library; see Dirk F. Passmann and Heinz J. Vienken, *The Library and Reading of Jonathan Swift: A Bio-Bibliographical Handbook*, 4 vols. (Frankfurt: Peter Lang, 2003). On Swift's antagonisms towards Restoration compromises and settlements, see Robert Phiddian, *Swift's Parody* (Cambridge: Cambridge University Press, 1995), pp. 24–51; and on Swift's ideological incompatibility with the apostate and anticlerical Dryden, see Ian Higgins's illuminating discussion, "Dryden and Swift," in *John Dryden: His Politics, His Plays, and His Poets*, ed. Claude Rawson and Aaron Santesso (Newark: University of Delaware Press, 2004), pp. 217–34.

3 Irvin Ehrenpreis, *Swift: The Man, His Works and the Age*, 3 vols. (Cambridge, MA: Harvard University Press, 1962–83), catalogues a number of Swift's echoes, allusions, and adaptations of Dryden's works; see also, Higgins, "Dryden and Swift," pp. 217–18, 220.

4 On this anecdote, see Maurice Johnson, "A Literary Chestnut: Dryden's 'Cousin Swift'," *PMLA* 68 (1953), 1232–40.

5 *The Correspondence of Jonathan Swift*, ed. Harold Williams, 5 vols. (Oxford: Oxford University Press, 1963–5), vol. IV, p. 321.

6 See Dryden's "Life of Lucian," *The Works of John Dryden*, ed. H. T. Swedenberg, Jr., *et al.*, 20 vols. (Berkeley and Los Angeles: University of California Press, 1953–2002), vol. XX, p. 221; all further citations of Dryden's works are to this edition.

7 Claude Rawson, *God, Gulliver, and Genocide: Barbarism and the European Imagination, 1492–1954* (Oxford: Oxford University Press, 2005), p. 258; see especially Rawson's readings of *A Modest Proposal*, pp. 227–54, and *Gulliver's Travels*, pp. 92–108, 256–98.

8 On the *Essay* and Dryden's modes of doubling and dialectic, see Stuart Sherman, "Dryden and the Theatrical Imagination," in *The Cambridge Companion to John Dryden*, ed. Steven N. Zwicker (Cambridge: Cambridge University Press, 2004), pp. 15–18; see as well Joseph Levine, *Between the Ancients and the Moderns* (New Haven: Yale University Press, 1999), pp. 39–48, and Cedric Reverand, "Dryden and the Canon: Absorbing and Rejecting the Burden of the Past," in *Enchanted Ground: Re-imagining John Dryden*, ed.

Jayne Lewis and Maximillian E. Novak (Toronto: University of Toronto Press, 2004), pp. 203–25.

9 He would call the method "Sceptical, according to that way of reasoning which was used by Socrates, Plato, and all the Academiques of Old . . . and which is imitated by the modest Inquisitions of the Royal Society" (*A Defence of an Essay of Dramatique Poesy*, in *Works*, vol. IX, p. 15, ll. 8–11).

10 See *Calendar of State Papers, Domestic Series*, 28 vols. (London: Longmans, Green, 1860–1939), vol. V (1864), *1665–1666*, p. 270.

11 *Works*, vol. I, p. 48, l. 17.

12 *Works*, vol. I, p. 48, ll. 6–7.

13 Dryden addresses Rochester in the dedication of *Marriage-à-la-Mode*, where he offers a fawning appreciation of the wit and elevation of Rochester's conversation but also allows his anxiety over Rochester's invasion of his own terrain as professional writer. See *Works*, vol. II, pp. 221–4.

14 See James Winn, *John Dryden and His World* (New Haven: Yale University Press, 1987), pp. 80, 264.

15 *Works*, vol. XII, p. 83, ll. 30–3.

16 *Works*, vol. XII, p. 81, ll. 18–20.

17 On Dryden's aphoristic style in, and the libertine cast of, *The State of Innocence*, see Nicholas von Maltzahn, "Dryden's Milton and the Theatre of Imagination," in *John Dryden: Tercentenary Essays*, ed. Paul Hammond and David Hopkins (Oxford: Oxford University Press, 2000), pp. 32–56, esp. p. 43.

18 See Winn, *John Dryden and His World*, p. 80.

19 *Works*, vol. V, p. 280, l. 12; and p. 283, ll. 18–20.

20 *Works*, vol. V, p. 303, ll. 1–24.

21 *Works*, vol. V, p. 314, l. 10.

22 On Dryden and this theme see Levine, *Between the Ancients and the Moderns*, pp. 77–95, and, as well, Michael Gelber, *The Just and the Lively: The Literary Criticism of John Dryden* (Manchester: Manchester University Press, 1999), pp. 186–200.

23 See Phiddian, *Swift's Parody*, pp. 127–32, on Swift's animosity towards Dryden in *A Tale of a Tub*.

24 *A Tale of a Tub to which is added the Battle of the Books and the Mechanical Operation of the Spirit*, ed. A. C. Guthkelch and D. Nichol Smith, 2nd edn. (Oxford: Oxford University Press, 1958), pp. 246–7.

25 *Works*, vol. VII, p. 24, ll. 1–10.

PART II

Swift and his time

CHAPTER 6

Self, stuff, and surface: the rhetoric of things in Swift's satire

Barbara M. Benedict

Things – clothes, cosmetics, tools, refuse, Flappers' bladders, and Celia's chamber pots – appear everywhere in Jonathan Swift's satire. While they collect, clog, and compose both the city and the human body, they dramatize the relationship of materiality to subjectivity, of surface to depth. Several critics have recently explored the literary representations of things as a commentary on selfhood, stressing the cultural agency in objects and their re-enactment of enslaved, impoverished, or inadequate humans.[1] Many argue that, as things lose their physical fixity, humans acquire it: as the thing becomes human, the human becomes thing-like, a process that uncovers the "essential and unproblematic core" of human identity beneath delusive appearance.[2] This essay argues, however, that Swift's poetic satires, by exploring the ambiguity of materiality in language, demonstrate a parallel absence of human fixity. Through his depiction of things and the corresponding human thing, the body, Swift shows that stuff supposedly subordinate to human use escapes both definition and possession, and so, correspondingly, does the self. Swift's satire reveals that behind the appearances cherished by a commodifying, consuming society lies an instability of form itself that erases the border between surface and soul.[3]

Swift characterizes objects as physically ambiguous. Represented in poetry, they change, even as they enact a permanence that radically contrasts with human decay. "A Meditation upon a Broom-Stick," for example, mocks the transformative power of rhetoric, yet it also shows that things hold a Promethean promise through their ability to meta-morphose into other things, agents, and/or subjects. Objects can thus serve human purposes by simultaneously embodying and escaping firm meanings. In "The Virtues of Sid Hamet the Magician's Rod" (1710), a satire on Lord Godolphin, the rod alternates between being a piece of upright and inflexible "honest English wood" and "a devouring serpent."

It represents not only a political staff of office, but objects in "scripture, myth, and fiction."[4] These include a broomstick, a witch's besom, a divining rod, Hermes' magical branch, a fishing-rod, a magician's wand, a scepter, a whipping-stick, and, of course, a penis, the fleshly embodiment of disobedience. By his roller-coaster through rods of history and legend, Swift transforms the object into a mythic motif symbolizing human mutability. Finally a Rochesterian "rod in piss," the object becomes a human tool, as the human Godolphin has become a political one. In the course of the poem, the absolute form of the rod, the Platonic ideal, dissolves into a series of imitations, animate and inanimate.[5] The rod, rather than symbolizing the fixity of the material world, dramatizes its entire dependence on poetic rhetoric and imaginative context.[6]

Swift's exploration of the permeability of form and rhetoric reflects the cultural and philosophical atmosphere of the early eighteenth century. Especially since the Restoration, things were symbols of progress, opulence, and novelty; ubiquitous in collections and museums; commodified in advertisements and shops; desirable, fungible, and lauded in newspapers, auctions, and literature. For cultural commentators, they incarnated the empirical philosophy of the New Science, for whose advocates nature's appearances provided the key to unlocking her mysteries. Members of the Royal Society had energetically promoted the empirical and experimental approach, arguing that, by examining phenomena through minute observation of material substances, natural philosophers would avoid individual error and bias, and provide a common ground for understanding reality. Thomas Sprat, himself a bishop, poet, and member of the Society, argued in *The History of the Royal-Society of London, for the Improving of Natural Knowledge* (1667) that the scientific method would not only banish insurrection, civil strife, and entanglement in "the passions and madness," but even simplify language by replacing the fuzzy metaphors of poetry with precise definitions.[7] John Locke, albeit contentiously, explained the formation of individual identity itself as the human encounter with empirical reality in *An Essay Concerning Human Understanding* (1690). Joseph Glanvill, a cleric yet also a member of the Royal Society, enthusiastically demonstrated that empiricism could reveal mysteries even beyond the grave through his investigation of supernatural manifestations, *A Philosophical Endeavour towards the Defence of the Being of Witches and Apparitions* (1666), republished as *Saducimus Triumphatus* (1681) and popular throughout the following century. Things both natural and manufactured were seen as testaments to a new, factual understanding and mastery of nature.

At the same time, physical nature also appears in human bodies and cultural products: material selves that decay and commodities fashioned to disguise or confute nature, both of which compromise the ideal of nature's stability.[8] Empiricism thus supplied contemporary writers with a rich source of ridicule. Seizing on the single-minded earnestness of the Royal Society's members, satirists such as Samuel Butler, Thomas Shadwell, Aphra Behn, and Alexander Pope depict empirical thinkers as besotted by surfaces.[9] Much of this satire targets the idealism lurking beneath supposedly pragmatic empiricism: philosophers' earnest faith that the empirical enterprise would lead society out of conflict and religious confusion into a new world of progress and hope. Sprat even declares that science will "increase the Powers of all mankind, and . . . free them from the Bondage of Errors," yet his rhetoric echoes the Puritan fanaticism of the Civil War (dedication). Moreover, the scientific style he endorses eschews figurative language and innuendo for a dogged literalism. For Swift and the Scriblerians, Sprat's ideal language violates traditional registers of fine writing by trusting apparent meanings, words' surfaces, to convey thought. The threat empiricism offers traditional thinkers and writers thus centers on where to locate meaning: in changeless substance or slippery style?

In *Gulliver's Travels* (1726), Swift dramatizes the flaws of Scriblerian empiricism. These include accounting so manic that quantities, calculations, and numbers replace moral evaluations; a dedication to accurate description so engrossing that the nature of what is described ceases to matter; and a resulting moral relativity that leads to the evaporation of a stable self. When Gulliver describes Lilliputian political rituals of leaping and creeping, for example, he omits any judgment, and his conviction that his writerly task necessitates including *every detail* of his experience leads him to inform his readers of his arrangements for defecation.[10] Such self-absorption confuses the describer with the described: although he believes himself to be objectively recording what he sees, Gulliver dwells on his own experience – an experience eerily free of emotion. His unawareness of the way he appears in his own language invalidates his authority as eye-witness since he cannot convey reality. As Brean Hammond observes, "The Scriblerian target is *homo mechanicus*, a species both produced by and producing the new scientific learning, but at a cost to fundamental humanity, to naturalness, and to good writing."[11] By the end of the four parts, as Swift finally arranged them, Gulliver's moral compass has spun so thoroughly out of orbit that he tries to remake his human nature as an animal.

Gulliver's stylistic tin ear demonstrates another of Swift's objections to empirical culture. The enterprise of analyzing material reality by acquiring, collecting, dissecting, and examining it, either through physical possession or simply by observation, reflects for Swift the problematic notion that one could own the world by categorizing it. This gesture of possession imitates Adam's privilege of naming the creatures in Eden, but Swift's work suggests that contemporary empiricists lack both God's guidance and Adam's innocence. In addition, the assumption that seeing phenomena constitutes in some fashion possessing them credits both the act of seeing and object seen with a permanence dubious at best. Swift thus often represents the decay of contemporary culture as a misguided preoccupation with the physical nature of apparent phenomena, nature, things, and people. He locates the flaws of this preoccupation in both epistemology and morality: empirical, materialist thinking mis-perceives both the nature of physicality and the relationship between humans and the world. It assumes the possibility of knowing and naming – in language – the world and the self, and thus of owning them.

Swift's "Desire and Possession" (1727?) illustrates the delusiveness of ownership by partnering possession with transience. The poem ostensibly opposes the fleet but spendthrift Desire, who tumbles "in the gulph profound" while reaching for "the crown," to his brother, the steady Possession, who gathers all his brother strews (ll. 49, 47, 36). "[D]oomed to whirl an endless round," Desire's essential insubstantiality becomes his fate. However, Swift's final stanza shows that Possession too becomes insubstantial as, crushed by the weight of his things, his dying body is cannibalized by birds of prey:

> The raven, vulture, owl, and kite,
> At once upon his carcass light;
> And strip his hide, and pick his bones,
> Regardless of his dying groans. (ll. 55–8)

Possession's torture is apparently the opposite of his nature: to lose, rather than to keep. Swift's verse reveals that, ironically, Possession's things, his very substantiality, evaporate in time and space, and just as his goods scatter, his very body is recycled into the innards of scavengers. He becomes the stuff possessed by others; possession is thus an impossibility.

Although "Desire and Possession" exhibits poetic control over the human relationship to materiality, Swift often shows how language also refuses to be owned. The Projectors in Part III of *Gulliver's Travels* dramatize this problem by carrying Things on their backs to avoid using imprecise language: rather than serving their owners, however, these Things literally ride people as language refuses to express meaning. Similarly, once uttered or written, a poet's or politician's words become part of commodity culture. The loss of control over his language entails the loss of the poet's ownership of his identity. In "The Life and Character of Dr. Swift" (1733), for example, Swift's "two special friends" agree that Swift meant well yet argue about *what* he meant: "Sir, our accounts are different quite, / And your conjectures are not right'" (ll. 194–5). While enacting social repartee, this exchange dramatizes the impossibility of controlling words and meaning beyond the self.

The poem describes social interaction itself as a parade of verbal items, sent into the void. By juxtaposing things, words, and feelings, it illustrates the overlap between these categories:

> When you are sick, your friends, you say,
> Will send their *how d'ye's* every day:
> Alas! That gives you small relief!
> They send for manners – not for grief:
> Nor, if you died, would fail to go
> That evening to a puppet-show:
> Yet, come in time to show their loves,
> And get a hatband, scarf, and gloves. (ll. 58–65)

The formulaic inquiry, "*how d'ye*," italicized to insulate it from the poet's own language, parallels the garb of mourning, "hatband, scarf and gloves." Even the friends' objectified "loves" are poetically reified, extant only in "show." Indeed, the spectacular "puppet-show" trumps Swift's dead self: the puppets' artificial bodies replace the poet's. Material forms thus constitute social essence. As the poet remarks, "I could give instances enough, / That human friendship is but stuff" (ll. 22–3). "Verses on the Death of Dr. Swift" similarly chronicles the clash between physicality and immaterial significance. When the bookseller Bernard Lintot confesses that he sent Swift's writings "with a load of books, / Last Monday to the pastry-cook's. / To fancy they could live a year!", Swift satirizes the ephemerality of fame, language, and good intentions by portraying them all doubly corporealized – in a book and as pie-paper (ll. 259–61). The poem dramatizes the impossibility of owning one's own meanings in a culture where even language is reified.

The reification of language, however, betrays the insubstantiality of meaning by showing that words, rather than ideas, are material. "Verses Wrote in a Lady's Ivory Table Book," for example, focuses the encounter of lover and mistress on a material object used to record fashionable purchases and amorous clichés: "(Madam, I die without your Grace.) / *Item*, for half a yard of lace" (ll. 15–16). Defined by Samuel Johnson as "A book on which any thing is graved or written without ink," the table-book mixes and mirrors the stylized languages of the lover and the shopper: poetry and purchases, love and luxury, fashion and feeling meld.[12] Certainly this object parodies its similarly superficial owner, like things in later eighteenth-century sentimental it-narratives which, as Lynn Festa observes, "*see through* the duplicitous surfaces of humans they encounter."[13] Here, however, the underlying self remains insubstantial since there is nothing to see *beyond* the surface. In "The Furniture of a Woman's Mind" (1727?), Swift catalogues the fashionable acquirements that construct a modern lady to exhibit this inner emptiness:

> A set of phrases learned by rote;
> A passion for a scarlet coat;
> When at a play to laugh, or cry,
> But cannot tell the reason why . . .
> Her learning mounts to read a song,
> But, half the words pronouncing wrong;
> Has every repartee in store,
> She spoke ten thousand times before.
> Can ready compliments supply
> On all occasions, cut and dry . . .
> In choosing lace a critic nice,
> Knows to a groat the lowest price;
> Can in her female clubs dispute
> What lining best the silk will suit . . . (ll. 1–4, 10–14, 27–30)

> O yes! If any man can find
> More virtues in a woman's mind,
> Let them be sent to Mrs. Harding;
> She'll pay the charges to a farthing:
> Take notice, she has my commission
> To add them in the next edition;
> They may outsell a better thing;
> So halloo boys! God save the King. (ll. 57–64)

Words and feelings dwindle to items equivalent to a suit's silk lining: costumes clothing vacuum. Both "virtues" and patriotic jingles become commodities produced by Swift's printer Sarah Harding.

Even as Swift satirizes empirical philosophy and a commodifying culture, however, he also sympathizes with the empirical insistence on the importance of physicality in reaction to superstition and Puritan mysticism.[14] John Sitter has suggested that "Augustan wit *embodies* concerns that comprise a materialist understanding of experience," and observes that Augustan satirists "portray the desire to transcend or penetrate the surfaces of bodies available to humans as in fact the most hazardous superficiality."[15] The "hazard" that Swift finds in looking beneath the surface, however, is not merely the replacement of real surface for imagined depth. Rather, it is the conviction of the difference between surface and depth. As James Noggle explains, "Writers repeatedly describe skepticism in its extreme form as the over-riding of the boundaries between the subject and the world he tries to know."[16] Albeit not a radical skeptic, Swift explores this inter-penetration to cast doubt on readerly assumptions about identity, and knowability.[17] As Claude Rawson points out, his "strategy of undermining doubt" in *Gulliver's Travels* invalidates the authority of both surface and depth.[18] Swift's poems thus suggest that disregarding exteriority not only smacks of divisive Puritan mysticism but also threatens a loss of self. By rejecting the "order from confusion sprung," seekers and peekers return to the con-fusion; by dismissing the forms that structure culture and nature, they veer toward substance-less mass or empty space. The danger of looking beneath the surface, Swift shows, is that nothing lies within: the very no-thing that is also the surface and the self.

Swift's attack on empiricism thus employs things to symbolize the folly both of trusting and of distrusting appearances. Things incarnate this paradox because, in much eighteenth-century literature, they both derive significance from their social context, and also manifest a meaning beyond it: they thus touch the contested margin between magical and rational thinking. Advertisements, museum and auction catalogues, and a swath of Tory verse from Alexander Pope's *Rape of the Lock* (1714) to John Gay's *Trivia; or, The Art of Walking the Streets of London* (1716) dem-onstrate the contemporary exploration of things as simultaneously spir-itual and material. Swift's satire, however, juxtaposes materiality and insubstantiality to undermine both. In "A Beautiful Young Nymph Going to Bed" (1734), for example, Corinna's body is both reified and absent, and it both epitomizes and evades her identity. While the first stanza describes the collection of things – a crystal eye, mouse-skin brows, artificial teeth, hip bolsters – that fill out her hollowed body, the second recounts the parallel dreams that fill her polluted imagination. These possess both psychological and physical urgency: when she dreams "Of Bridewell and the compter," she "feels the lash, and faintly screams" (ll. 41–2). When "struck with fear, her fancy runs / On watchmen, constables, and duns" (ll. 51–2). Thus, her mind produces physical sensations based on her experience while her body has vanished into objects. Both mind and body are constructions.

The confusion of her self and her stuff dramatizes Corinna's emptiness. As the artificial remedies of venereal disease and brutality have supplanted her body, so the social injuries of abuse, punishment, and transportation replace the dreams of love or hope that she might once have had. The result is a scattering of the self as much moral as physical. The penultimate stanza describes this in the ruination of Corinna's beauty aids and the disappearance of her man-made "crystal eye," itself a symbol of the fusion of surface and depth since, designed to deceive others' eyes, it is both transparent and opaque: it cannot see yet, as "crystal," can be seen through to reveal Corinna's empty socket. Finally the poet abandons description:

> The nymph, though in this mangled plight,
> Must every morn her limbs unite.
> But how shall I describe her arts
> To recollect the scattered parts?
> Or show the anguish, toil, and pain,
> Of gathering up herself again? (ll. 65–8)

"Recollecting" involves the twin acts of physically reconstituting and psychologically remembering. Such a task cannot be described in poetic language, not only because the erotic and obscene topic falls beneath the conventional bar for public verse, but also because the process itself escapes the denotative power of words.[19] By using the categorical and denotative rhetoric of contemporary description, Swift demonstrates that literalistic language cannot describe the process of making an inner self when there is no material to make it.

While collected and recollected phenomena replace the self in "A Beautiful Young Nymph," "The Lady's Dressing Room" dramatizes the self-loss entailed by immersing oneself in perceived reality. The poem records the duality of an empiricism that expresses and conceals the nature of things and the things of nature. Peter Stallybrass and Ann Jones have argued that, in eighteenth-century culture, the exterior costume actually defines the interior: the essential self lies in appearances.[20] Swift's poem suggests rather that neither appearances nor essences contain the self. Celia's "counterfeit" chest, adorned with deceiving artistry but concealing excrement, seems to present the traditional opposition of surface to essence. Yet by comparing it to Pandora's box, the symbol of impious prying, the poet depicts it as a form that merely encases emptiness; refusing to grope, Strephon cannot find even hope within. Thus, although "No object Strephon's eye escapes," Scriblerian Strephon sees not artful transformation, but the horror of natural decay beneath (l. 47). He suffers from a double blindness: his idealism and his parallel reliance on what he sees.[21] When he peers through "Celia's magnifying glass," he perceives only his own "giant" visage, a still grosser surface that reveals yet disguises Strephon's human nature (l. 60). So thorough is the entanglement of shaped surface and messy depth that neither exists distinct from the other. Thus, Swift ends the poem by recommending a willful blindness that will enable Strephon and, by extension, the reader to admire the fusion of the two represented by art: if instead of peering "behind the scene," the "ravished eyes" focus on the surface, they will blissfully "see / Such order from confusion sprung, / Such gaudy *tulips* raised from *dung*" (ll. 133, 142–4). This conclusion ironically suggests that, since surface is depth, and depth surface, neither contains identity. Strephon's "strict survey" registers the ineluctable but ominous significance of things that both blend into and replace the human body.

This epistemological fusion of depth and surface unsettles not only the process of seeing and what is seen, but also who is seeing. The marvelous plenitude and specificity of Celia's things – "various combs for various uses" – seem to offer to Strephon and for the reader alike a fascinating power of identifying, registering, collecting, and possessing (l. 20). As they replace her absent body, the process of naming and knowing them seems to promise similar power over her. Like Corinna's body bits, however, these inventoried parts lack integrity, ultimate form. In "A Beautiful Young Nymph," Corinna experiences what critics have described as "the vanishing point of the subject into the commodified object [and] of the object into pure exchangeability" as her body evaporates into manufactured beauty aids.[22] She no longer has a center of self, and thus the poet cannot describe her. Similarly, in "The Lady's Dressing Room," the mesmerized observer, uncontrollably inventorying Celia's things and body bits, loses his control over his own perceptual processes: as things snatch his attention, he abandons his self-mastery, wandering in a world of objects smeared with human "stuff."

For his prying, however, he is eternally damned to a world of ugliness and contradiction. Tormented by the mechanical association of women and love with excrement and waste, his imagination fixes on the impossible similarity and contradiction between beauty and ugliness, art and nature, life and death: "By vicious fancy couple fast, / And still appearing in contrast" (ll. 127–8). As Pat Rogers notes, "contrast" was a

painterly term; here, it underscores the oxymoron of Strephon's perception, which vacillates hopelessly between surface and depth.[23] The
depth he fears is death, which appears everywhere in the poem, docu-
mented by the excrescences that record the body's decline: sweat, excrement, dandruff, hair, earwax, snot, eyebrow hairs, Tripsy's skin and her
puppy's bottle essence, the "worm in Celia's nose" that must come out
"alive or dead" (ll. 64, 68). Celia, like Corinna, is decaying or transforming:
unwonted and unwanted hairs and bristles grow on her face as she mutates
from a beauty to a monster (ll. 57–8). As the space between the natural
world of decay and the ideal world of immortal beauty, the Dressing Room
resembles purgatory holding the excremental coffin in which no "hope"
resides (l. 94). For Strephon, indeed, the Dressing Room operates analo-
gously to the room in Jean-Paul Sartre's play, *No Exit*: although he believes
hell is other people, Strephon like Milton's Satan becomes himself his
own hell when encountering "Those secrets of the hoary deep."[24]

The paradox of Strephon's (in)sight lies in his Platonic desire to find
absolute beauty, a form beyond form.[25] Such a desire rejects nature's
transformative processes; ironically, Strephon is indeed seeking a kind of
death. "The Lady's Dressing Room" dramatizes this conflict of ideal and
real by images of abundance and waste, absence and presence – a trope
that Sophie Gee has defined as the satirical portrayal of abundance as
loss: "material remnants are markers both of surplus and emptiness. In
representations of unwanted matter, surplus paradoxically marks the
place where value has been lost."[26] Swift's poem, indeed, opens by
counting the "Five hours" filled or emptied by "dressing," the process of
transforming Celia into a beauty, and Strephon's survey itself results from
his discovery that "the room was void," emptied of Celia and yet, as he
reveals, stuffed with "litter" (ll. 5, 8).[27] Swift, however, shows that this
cluttered void gives birth to a series of substitutions and transformations
as things and humans intermingle. Leading them is the replacement of
Celia by her besmirched smock, itself parodying her brocade, both gar-
ments substituting for her body, and, like that body, simultaneously so
insubstantial and so substantial that they defeat description: "In such a
case few words are best, / And Strephon bids us guess the rest" (ll. 15–16).
Strephon's inventory tracks the same paradoxes of excess and emptiness,
materiality and evaporation: the combs are "Filled up with dirt so closely
fixed" that they have no spaces between the tines, and the "night-gloves
made of Tripsy's hide" are empty (ll. 21, 29). The room's items have
shifted from their original shape or being in the service of Celia and the
beauty-making enterprise. Many of the items are full – too full – with

"washes ... paste ... pomatum, paints and slops," and finally the "basin" that "takes whatever comes, / The scrapings of her teeth and gums, / A nasty compound of all hues, / For here she spits, and here she spews" (ll. 34–5, 39–42). Concluding the poem is Swift's mock-heroic simile between meat and shit, lyrically chronicling the transformation of substance to smoke and beginnings to ends.

While these transformations parody natural processes, they also satirize the commodifying mentality consequent on empiricist epistemology. Once nature, bodies, and people become objects, they become exchangeable. Arjun Appadurai offers a theoretical account of this dynamic when he describes things as becoming social phenomena once they inhabit a "commodity situation ... *in which* [a thing's] *exchangeability (past, present, or future) for some other thing is its socially relevant feature.*"[28] The human Celia is exchanged for Celia as a sanitized, scented art object: as her smock, stockings, and handkerchiefs are exchanged for the "lace, brocade and tissues," Celia's body peels away: sweat, dirt, fingernail parings, hair. Appadurai further explains this dynamic by defining "the commodity context in which any thing may be placed" – the social or cultural circumstances which make a thing into a commodity (ll. 13–15). Swift's trope of "rotting Celia," the maiden remade by a market economy into a whore comprised of things illustrates Appadurai's notion of the "commodity context," indeed squares it: not only is her body exchangeable for money itself, but that body has already been exchanged for artificial parts. Yet Swift shows that this process of physical replacement entails also subjective decay. Humans' interiority or subjectivity melts into a commodity, as commodities melt into subjects.

The de-formation of objects and humans spreads also to the environment created by contemporary culture, an environment that penetrates the human body. Internal and external environment fuse, while both city and the urban body fragment into separate, sentient parts.[29] Swift's "A Description of a City Shower" (1710) illustrates this inter-penetration by descriptions of people whose interiority blends with exteriority, and of urban things personified as enemies. Although the speaker promises that the physical signs noted by "Careful observers" will reliably signal the coming shower, they do so by attacking human actors. Pedestrian things become violent and obtrusive: the odorous sewer "strike[s]" the home-bound urbanite. Even his own body fragments into prescient and painful parts: his "corns" "presage" the weather by "shooting" pains through him, while his "Old aches throb" and his hollow tooth "rage[s]." The animation of parts of the body that have escaped their subordination to the intellectual will parallels the intertwining of elements that makes the city itself a hybrid of filth: in the storm " 'Twas doubtful which was rain and which was dust." This mêlée causes the speaker's very clothes nearly to smother him: his "Sole coat, where dust cemented by the rain / Erects the nap, and leaves a cloudy stain" (ll. 29–30). Whereas the speaker's body produces only pains, his coat enacts the behavior of the body it veils, rising and staining in a parody of masculine sexuality. Once the rain begins, "daggled females" rush into "shops" to bargain over "goods," themselves sordid shop items as much as the objects they examine, and the "tucked-up seamstress" clutches her "oiled umbrella," herself becomes an enfolded garment (l. 37). Under the gaze of the "Careful observers" whom the poet invokes, things and people meld.

Swift's final stanza presents a dystopic vision of this fusion of human, thing, and waste. In the rush of urban refuse, each thing is differentiated: "Filths of all hues, and odours, seem to tell / What streets they sailed from, by the sight and smell" (ll. 55–6). At the same time, however, all merge: corpses and food, body parts and animals, offal and ordure all become part of the same river, swilling down Fleet Ditch.

> Sweepings from butcher's stalls, dung, guts, and blood,
> Drowned puppies, stinking sprats, all drenched in mud,
> Dead cats and turnip-tops come tumbling down the flood. (ll. 61–3)

While depicting the conflict between a world stuffed with things and the sweeping forces of nature, "A Description of a City Shower" ends by conflating nature and culture, just as the city full of things remakes and replaces nature as a poetic topic. Neither poetic form nor social form survive the torrent of waste and death.[30]

As the margin between the fluidity of nature and the forms of culture collapses, so too does the difference between object and subject, whether presented to the eye or represented by poetry. Both teeter on the verge of vanishing into formlessness, or death. In "The Progress of Beauty" (1719/ 20), Celia resembles a "Lusitanian dish" of white china, her rival as one of "Two brightest, brittlest, earthly things" enrobed in paint, but unlike the object, Celia's face refuses to retain the decorative coating, melting into a muddle – or puddle – of colors. Like the moon, Celia's face changes "in a different light," revealing beauty as "frightful" and "hideous" when the formless colors leak from one feature to another (l. 23). Echoing "A Description of a City Shower," the description of Celia's makeup and sweat streaming to a confluence at her chin shows how flesh threatens to dissolve until it is redefined through Celia's art, "By help of pencil, paint and brush" (l. 470). Indeed, "The best mechanic's hand must fail, / When nothing's left to work upon" (ll. 79–80).

> Matter, as wise logicians say,
> Cannot without a form subsist;
> And form, say I, as well as they,
> Must fail, if matter brings no grist. (ll. 81–4)

"Rotting" Celia, like the moon, which drops a bit of its face every night, loses her luxuriant hair, nose, teeth, chin, and eyes over time (ll. 102, 87–8). Although she tries to maintain "the materials of her face," she cannot fit into the formal perfection of the china dish (108). Celia's tricolored face – "black, and red, and white" (l. 21) – spreads into a mass of color, without either form or beauty.

Swift's satiric use of things radically questions the distinction between form and essence. By exploring the way language makes physicality ambiguous, Swift destabilizes the possibility of knowing by naming. Through his satirical deflation of the Scriblerian mode of literalistic description, he demonstrates that language can construct and de-construct not only things, but human bodies, and thus identity itself. As language becomes reified, things become linguistic. Despite their embodiment of a brutally consumerist, materialist reality, things in Swift's poems thus embody the interdependence of surface and essence. Things also mirror and parody the human self since, meaningful only in context and thus holding no firm meaning, their formal perfection is delusive. While as quintessentially formal phenomena things appear to embody materialism and validate empirical epistemology, they transform, decay, dissolve into subjects. Moreover, by their paradoxical fixity and fluidity, they – like the human body in the ceaseless process of transforming – both resist and incarnate death. At the same time, by revealing the fallibility of perception, Swift also challenges the possibility of knowing by seeing: his phenomenology undermines even Berkeley's skepticism. Both the seer and the seen become unstable, and the distinction between the two collapses. Swift's satires thus illuminate the way the contemporary passion for material meanings, acquisition, definition, and possession is a doomed quest for fixity in a world of flux.

NOTES

1 For example, Jonathan Lamb, "The Crying of Lost Things," *ELH* 71:4 (2004), 949–67; Mark Blackwell, "The People Things Make: Locke's *An Essay Concerning Human Understanding* and the Properties of the Self," *Studies in Eighteenth-Century Culture* 35 (2006), 77–94.

2 See Lynn Festa, *Sentimental Figures of Empire in Eighteenth-Century Britain and France* (Baltimore: The Johns Hopkins University Press, 2006), esp. p. 124; Deidre Shauna Lynch, *The Economy of Character: Novels, Market Culture, and the Business of Inner Meaning* (Chicago: University of Chicago Press, 1998), pp. 94–102.

3 See Dustin Griffin, *Satire: A Critical Reintroduction* (Lexington: University of Kentucky Press, 1993); Fredric V. Bogel, *Literature and Insubstantiality in Later Eighteenth-Century Literature* (Princeton, NJ: Princeton University Press, 1984).

4 Jonathan Swift, "The Virtues of Sid Hamet the Magician's Rod," ll. 7, 4. Irvin Ehrenpreis, *Swift: The Man, His Works, and the Age* (Cambridge, MA: Harvard University Press, 1967), vol. II, p. 388, n. 5.

5 Pat Rogers identifies an implied *"essential"* rod in "Swift the Poet," in *The Cambridge Companion to Jonathan Swift*, ed. Christopher Fox (Cambridge: Cambridge University Press, 2003), pp. 194–5.

6 Stephen Karian explores the concomitant instability of Swift's texts in "Reading the Material Text of Swift's *Verses on the Death*," *Studies in English Literature* 41:3 (2001), 515–44.

7 Thomas Sprat, *The History of the Royal-Society of London, for the Improving of Natural Knowledge* (London: J. Martyn, 1667), p. 53.

8 Carol Houlihan Flynn observes Swift's confrontation with the body in her seminal *The Body in Defoe and Swift* (Cambridge: Cambridge University Press, 1990).

9 Cynthia Wall, *The Prose of Things* (Chicago: University of Chicago Press, 2006), pp. 70–95.

10 See Jonathan Swift, *Gulliver's Travels*, ed. Claude Rawson and Ian Higgins (Oxford: Oxford University Press, 2005), p. 24.

11 Brean S. Hammond, "Scriblerian Self-Fashioning," *YES* 18 (1988), 108–124 (p. 118).

12 Samuel Johnson, *A Dictionary of the English Language* (London: W. Strahan, 1755). Samuel Johnson illustrates the meaning with quotations from Swift and, among others, John Dryden: "Put into your *table-book* whatsoever you judge worthy."

13 Festa, *Sentimental Figures*, p. 124.

14 Thomas Woodman, "Pope and the Paradoxical Centrality of the Satirist," *Studies in Literary Imagination* 38, 1 (2005), 9.

15 John Sitter, *Arguments of Augustan Wit* (Cambridge: Cambridge University Press, 1991), p. 124.

16 James Noggle, *The Skeptical Sublime: Aesthetic Ideology in Pope and the Tory Satirists* (Oxford: Oxford University Press, 2001), pp. 3–4. Christopher Fanning also identifies Swift's satire with the sublime in its "collapse of boundaries between subject and object," a process which "depends, of course, on a sense of the distinction to be erased," in "The Scriblerian Sublime," *Studies in English Literature* 45:3 (2005), 647–67 (p. 655).

17 Patricia Carr Brückman, *A Manner of Correspondence: A Study of the Scriblerus Club* (Montreal and Kingston: McGill–Queen's University Press, 1997), p. 100. For recent discussions of Swift's religious faith, see J. T. Parnell, "Swift, Sterne, and the Skeptical Tradition," *Studies in Eighteenth-Century Culture* 23 (1994),

221–42; Martin C. Battestin, "The Critique of Freethinking from Swift to Sterne," *ECF* 15:3/4 (2003), 341–420; John Bruce, "Plagued by Enthusiasm: Swift's Fear of Infectious Dissent and His Argument against Abolishing Christian Quarantine in *A Tale of a Tub*," in *Orthodoxy and Heresy in Eighteenth-Century Society*, ed. Regina Hewitt and Pat Rogers (Lewisburg: Bucknell University Press, 2002), pp. 89–111.

18 Claude Rawson, *Gulliver and the Gentle Reader*, 2nd edn. (Atlantic Highlands, NJ: Humanities Press International, 1991), p. 32.

19 See Pat Rogers, " 'How I want Thee, Humorous Hogart': The Motif of the Absent Artist in Swift, Fielding and Others," *Papers on Language and Literature* 42:1 (2006), 25–45.

20 Peter Stallybrass and Ann Rosalind Jones, *Renaissance Clothing and the Materials of Memory* (Cambridge: Cambridge University Press, 2000).

21 Christine Rees, "Gay, Swift, and the Nymphs of Drury-Lane," in *Jonathan Swift: A Collection of Critical Essays*, ed. Claude Rawson (Englewood Cliffs, NJ: Prentice Hall, 1995), p. 127.

22 Margreta DeGrazia, Maureen Quilligan, and Peter Stallybrass (eds.) "Introduction," in *Subject and Object in Renaissance Culture* (Cambridge: Cambridge University Press, 1996), p. 4.

23 *Jonathan Swift: The Complete Poems*, ed. Pat Rogers (London and New Haven: Yale University Press, 1983), p. 829, n. 128.

24 This line quoted from *Paradise Lost* (II, ll. 890–1). Swift's rendition of the dressing-room as hell glosses Pope's depiction of it as the space of art in *Rape of the Lock*.

25 See Claude Rawson, *Order from Confusion Sprung: Studies in Eighteenth-Century Literature from Swift to Cowper* (London: George Allen & Unwin, 1985), esp. pp. 165–77; also Tita Chico, *Designing Women: The Dressing Room in Eighteenth-Century English Literature and Culture* (Lewisburg: Bucknell University Press, 2005), pp. 135–7.

26 Sophie Gee, "The Sewers: Ordure, Effluence, and Excess in the Eighteenth Century," in *A Concise Companion to the Restoration and Eighteenth Century*, ed. Cynthia Wall (Malden, MA and Oxford: Blackwell Publishing, 1988), pp. 103, 101–20 (p. 119).

27 In "Seeing and the Difference It Makes: Ocularity, Gender, and Space in Swift's and Montagu's 'Dressing Room' Satires," Wendy S. Weise argues that the poem depicts a kind of rape as Strephon violates Celia's space, and even explores "fragile" gender boundaries, as "Structurally Swift's piece moves from inside out." *Women's Studies* 35:8 (2006), 707–38 (pp. 713, 709).

28 Arjun Appadurai, "Introduction: Commodities and the Politics of Value," in *The Social Life of Things: Commodities in Cultural Perspective* (Cambridge: Cambridge University Press, 1986), p. 13 (original italics).

29 Ehrenpreis comments that the poet "can see through the surface to the essence" of the city (*Swift: The Man, His Works, and the Age*, vol. II, p. 384).

30 Helen Deutsch, *Alexander Pope and the Deformation of Culture* (Cambridge, MA: Harvard University Press, 1996).

CHAPTER 7

Swift's shapeshifting

David Womersley

I defy you in all Shapes
   Lady Elizabeth Germain to Swift, November 4, 1731 (*Corr.*, III, p. 505)

they pretended to bring in Certain proofs of his [i.e. Swift's]
appearing in severall shapes
   The Earl of Peterborough to Swift, November 29, 1726 (*Corr.*, III, p. 192)

SWIFT IN SOCIETY

According to Laetitia Pilkington (not a witness upon whom one would wish always to rely) "the Dean always prefaced a Compliment with an Affront."[1] On this occasion, however, Mrs. Pilkington's observation about Swift is corroborated by others who knew him well, and upon whom his inverted social manner also registered. Orrery, for instance, concluded that Swift "must be viewed by a *camera obscura* that turns all objects the contrary way. When he appears most angry, he is most pleased; when most humble, he is most assuming."[2] Swift's letters frequently translate this feature of his social demeanor onto the page. For instance, writing to his friend the Earl of Peterborough in 1733, Swift disguised as a reproach his gratitude for practical help: "you were so cruel as never to give me Time to ask a Favour, but prevented me in doing whatever you thought I desired, or could be for my Credit or Advantage."[3] Orrery was paid with the same coin, as Swift turned inside out the pleasure he took in Orrery's company, and dwelt instead upon the distress he felt when that pleasure was withdrawn: "you have treated this Kingdom [Ireland] with great inhumanity, You will not stay long enough among us to spread your example, and you stay too long for all good men to have to be able to endure your absence."[4] Lord Bathurst, too, found that Swift's fondness for him wore the dress of indifference: "You threatened to pester me with letters if I will not write. If I were sure that my silence would force you to one letter in a quarter of a year, I would be wise enough never to write to you as long as I live."[5] And, as is so often the case with Swift, he subscribed also and equally to the corollary of these flayed compliments. Just as his ostensible contempt or resentment might be the shell of actual endearment and regard, so a necessary precondition for Swift's genuine contempt was, it seems, a measure of esteem. As he wrote to Robert Percival on January 3, 1730, "a Squire must have some merit before I shall honor him with my contempt. For, I do not despise a Fly, a Maggot, or a Mite."[6] It is an important feature of Swift's emotional economy that indifference came below (rather than above) contempt, because it sheds light on why it is that so often when we read Swift, we find ourselves negotiating, not smooth gradations of grayscale extending between opposites, but rather paradoxical intimacies of those very opposites themselves. Hence in Swift's letters we often find aggression to be the dress of affection. Of no correspondent is this more true than of Pope, to whom Swift wrote on October 12, 1727 that "if ever you made me angry, it was for your too much care about me."[7] Bolingbroke, too, inspired in Swift powerfully opposed sentiments, so that letters to him were always, it seems, written out of a divided mood of elation and dejection: "My Lord I hate and love to write to you, it gives me pleasure, and kills me with Melancholy."[8] These emotional doublets, yoking together sentiments both positive and negative, were not simply a characteristic of Swift's social relations. They migrated also into his writings, and we know that he admired such effects in the writings of others. Consider, for instance, his praise of Voiture: "And Fools would fancy he intends / A Satyr where he most commends."[9]

A NYMPH UNDRESSES

Swiftian fluidities of convergence and divergence (Claude Rawson, *Gulliver and the Gentle Reader*, p. 133)

A hard test for this view of Swift's emotional complexity would be the notorious poem, "A Beautiful Young Nymph Going to Bed." This poem was first published in 1734, but it had in fact been "*Written for the Honour of the Fair Sex, in 1731*" (as we learn from the version published in the 1735 edition of Swift's *Works* printed by George Faulkner).[10] This poem constitutes a hard test, because it is "often instanced as an example of unhealthy intensity and morbid body-hatred on Swift's part" – that is to say, as a purely and unpleasantly negative poem.[11] Nevertheless, and following the cue of another great critic of Swift's poetry, I see here evidence of Swift's general "capacity to be at once resistant and reciprocal," as well as corroboration of the particular judgment that "if Swift's view of Corinna is scarcely charitable neither is it unfeeling."[12] In other words, the poem's eventual rubric, "*Written for the Honour of the Fair Sex*," is a genuine irony, rather than a mere sarcasm, because "it is true, in some degree, in both senses."[13] The poem, I will argue, both defames and, in a subtle way, can be read as defending "*the Fair Sex.*"

The poem's earliest readers recognized the mode of the poem as prophylaxis, and identified a precise literary source for that mode, although the poem's most recent editors have not included this information in their notes.[14] In his *I ragguagli di Parnasso*, Traiano Boccalini tells of the world-famous physician from Bologna, Iovanni Zecca, who had "found out the true and secure receit to keep men from taking the French Pox." The *literati*, naturally eager to possess "a receit so necessary for these times," immediately flocked to Zecca, expecting to be given some ointment or electuary, but:

> they wondred exceedingly when they saw *Zecca* shew them a Picture drawn by the life, of a gallant Gentleman whose nose was eaten off with the French Pox; telling them the way how to use this receit, was, that just as they were about to lie with a woman whose health they suspected, they take this Picture out of their bosom, which he gave them, and which as many as should fixedly look upon, and seriously contemplate, they might be confident that this medicine taken in by the eye, would have such operation, as they should never be infected with that loathsom disease.[15]

The prophylactic effect of "A Beautiful Young Nymph Going to Bed" has received lengthy comment, particularly the "dry abruptness" of its ending, which according to some "surely subdues any previous overtones of playful fantastication":

> *Corinna* in the Morning dizen'd,
> Who sees, will spew; who smells, be poison'd.[16]

The violence of this ending is unmistakable, especially given that it comes without preparation following a lengthy section of the poem in which Corinna's nightmares of persecution, and the various disasters of the night which greet her on waking, seem to have moved Swift to a degree of imaginative sympathy with a whore:

> The Nymph, tho' in this mangled Plight,
> Must ev'ry Morn her Limbs unite.
> But how shall I describe her Arts
> To recollect the scatter'd Parts?

> Or shew the Anguish, Toil, and Pain,
> Of gath'ring up herself again?
> The bashful Muse will never bear
> In such a Scene to interfere.[17]

At this point, however, we face an interpretative dilemma. Do these apparently compassionate verses serve only to allow the final couplet to ambush the reader to more devastating and negative effect? That is the line taken by Geoffrey Hill: "The perfect dryness of 'recollect', the charged portentousness of 'dizen'd', inviting and awaiting the sharp crack of the final rhyme-word, have complete control over the plangencies of 'Anguish, Toil, and Pain'."[18] But do they in fact impose that control? Might it not equally be the case that Swift would like them to? In this second way of reading the end of the poem, the violence of its closure is required in order to cut off a drift towards sympathy with the nymph, discernible certainly in the "plangencies" to which Hill refers, but also prepared for earlier by Swift's quietly insistent and cumulative use of adverbs and adverbial phrases (here emboldened for the sake of clarity):

> Her Eye-Brows from a Mouse's Hyde,
> Stuck on **with Art** on either Side,
> Pulls off **with Care**, and first displays 'em,
> Then in a Play-Book **smoothly** lays 'em.
> Now **dextrously** her Plumpers draws,
> That serve to fill her hollow Jaws...
> **With gentlest Touch**, she next explores
> Her Shankers, Issues, running Sores,
> Effects of many a sad Disaster;
> And then to each applies a Plaister.[19]

Again, these adverbial touches place the reader in a characteristically Swiftian dilemma of reading, one which we will encounter again when we move on to Part III of *Gulliver's Travels*. Do they show Corinna bestowing a ridiculous, because inappropriate, degree of care upon something merely disgusting? Or do they rather show Corinna, with admirable tenacity, clinging to remembered norms of humane behavior despite the appalling adversity of her circumstances? For those tempted to reject this second possibility out of hand, the question to be faced is: "would you feel better about it if Corinna were doing these disgusting things in a *slovenly* manner?" Few, I suspect, would assent to that. It is of course the case that there is a strong, if submerged, mock-epic component in this poem. Corinna's exhausted self-dismantling shadows, as its at once pathetic and burlesque inverse, the epic *topos* of the arming of the hero before the day's combat.[20] I will return to the mock-epic aspect of the poem in the final section of this essay, and would merely note for the time being that the mode of mock-epic does not, particularly for the Scriblerians, preclude sympathetic engagement with its targets.

NOTES ON THE CHARACTER OF A PROJECTOR

Swift's mode [entails] placing the savage old Irish on a par with Indians, and asserting, in compassion or contempt or both, a species of fellowship with them.
(Claude Rawson, *God, Gulliver, and Genocide*, p. 5)

The coexistence of compassion and contempt lies, for a sensitive reader, on the linguistic surface of "A Beautiful Young Nymph Going to Bed." Elsewhere in Swift's writings, it may lie partially or completely obscured, to be retrieved as a result of editorial excavation. One such example occurs in chapter five of Part III of *Gulliver's Travels*. Gulliver visits the Academy of Lagado, and is disconcerted by the second projector on whom he calls:

I went into another Chamber, but was ready to hasten back, being almost overcome with a horrible Stink. My Conductor pressed me forward, conjuring me in a Whisper to give no Offence, which would be highly resented; and therefore I durst not so much as stop my Nose. The Projector of this Cell was the most Ancient Student of the Academy. His Face and Beard were of a pale Yellow; his Hands and Clothes dawbed over with Filth. When I was presented to him, he gave me a very close Embrace, (a Compliment I could well have excused.) His Employment from his first coming into the Academy, was an Operation to reduce human Excrement to its original Food, by separating the several Parts, removing the Tincture which it receives from the Gall, making the Odour exhale, and scumming off the Saliva. He had a weekly Allowance from the Society, of a Vessel filled with human Ordure, about the Bigness of a *Bristol* Barrel.[21]

Hitherto, no editor of *Gulliver's Travels* has felt it worth their while to discover the exact capacity of a "*Bristol*" Barrel," yet without that information we cannot know which of two characteristically Swiftian jokes we are being offered here. Is a Bristol barrel vast (and thus Swift is here in full Rabelaisian mode)?[22] Or is it small (and so Swift is here castigating a typical modern "refinement," namely bestowing an undeserved meticulousness on something disgusting)? Swift was, after all, equally the foe of gross physicality and mincing modernity.

Determining the capacity of a Bristol barrel is surprisingly difficult. No guidance is to be had from the *OED*, Johnson's *Dictionary*, or any of the various eighteenth-century dictionaries of trade. "Barrel," then as now, denoted both a particular kind of vessel, and a measure of a certain commodity. But that measure varied alarmingly depending on the commodity in question, as we can see in Charles Marriott's *New Royal English Dictionary* (1780):

The barrel contains in wine measure 31 gallons and a half, beer measure 36 gallons, and ale measure 32. When used for a certain quantity of weight, it differs according to the commodities it contains; a barrel of Essex butter weighing 106 lb. and of Suffolk 256. The barrel of herrings should contain 32 gallons wine measure, and 1000 herrings. The barrel of salmon is 42 gallons, the barrel of eels the same, and that of soap must weigh 256 lb.[23]

Outside Swift's writings, I have found three occurrences of the phrase. The first occurs in Arthur Young's account of his agricultural tour through Ireland in 1776, 1777, and 1778. In the section on "Prices," he records some of the yields achieved at Castle Oliver, in Limerick:

Mr. Oliver has known 150 Bristol barrels, each four bushels heaped of potatoes, which make six bushels, or 900 from an acre . . . The Bristol barrel, which is here charged at 4s. is heaped, and weighs 22 stone. The quality of the corn raised on these rich lands is much better than any other in the country; the quantity of barley, per acre, 12 Bristol barrels.[24]

This seems helpful, in that it links the capacity of the Bristol barrel to the bushel, which we know is equal to four pecks, or eight gallons. However, this does not in fact get us much further forward, as before the Imperial Measures Act of 1826 the bushel was no more determinate a measure than was the barrel:

The *imperial bushel*, legally established in Great Britain in 1826, contains 2218.192 cubic inches, or 80 pounds of distilled water weighed in air at 62° Fah. The *Winchester bushel*, much used from the time of Henry VIII, was somewhat smaller, containing 2150.42 cubic inches or 77.627413 pounds of distilled water; it is still generally used in United States and Canada. The bushel had a great variety of other values, now abolished by law, though often, in local use, varying not only from place to place, but in the same place according to the kind or quality of the commodity in question. Frequently it was no longer a measure, but a *weight* of so many (30, 40, 45, 50, 56, 60, 70, 75, 80, 90, 93, 220) pounds of flour, wheat, oats, potatoes, etc.[25]

Another lead is to be found in the letters of Roger Boyle. In a letter to the Duke of Ormonde, dated July 2, 1667, in the course of complaining about the difficulties of provisioning for his soldiers, he writes "I hope we may get for every Bristol barrel of wheat a hundred and fifteen pound of bisket delivered into the store."[26] The possibility suggested by this example, that "Bristol barrel" may be a phrase with a particular currency in late seventeenth-century Ireland, is corroborated by my third example. In a pamphlet on the deficiency of grain, the Irish peer Lord Sheffield reprinted a detail from a proclamation of James II dated February 28, 1689 which attempted to fix a maximum price for grain of "20s. the barrel, Bristol measure, for the best wheat in the neighbourhood of Dublin."[27] February 1689 was probably just before the twenty-two-year-old Swift fled Dublin on account of the disturbances arising from 1688.[28] So when we read in *Gulliver's Travels* of Bristol barrels, we are overhearing a fragment of the Dublin idiom of Swift's youth, a precious vestige of the language by which he had been surrounded before his transplantation to England.

It is when we pursue the particular Irish resonances of the phrase "Bristol barrel" that the full depth of this passage of *Gulliver's Travels* begins to emerge. Part III of *Gulliver* is, we know, preoccupied by the subject of colonial relations between England and Ireland. The flying island, which can descend and crush those beneath it, is commonly interpreted as an allegory of England's economic oppression of the Irish.[29] More specifically, the long manuscript passage describing the successful resistance of the city of Lindalino, which was appended to the end of chapter three of Part III in Charles Ford's interleaved copy of *Gulliver*, is unmistakably an account *à clef* of the successful Irish campaign against English attempts to impose on them the copper coinage manufactured by William Wood – a campaign in which Swift himself took a leading role, and for which he wrote the *Drapier's Letters*.[30] Swift began to publish the *Drapier's Letters* in 1724, and in order to compose them he broke off from composing *Gulliver* when he was in the middle of Part III, as we learn from his letter to Charles Ford dated January 19, 1724: "I have left the Country of the Horses, and am in the flying Island, where I shall not stay long, and my two last Journyes will be soon over."[31] In the *Drapier's Letters* Swift attacked the foisting of Wood's debased copper coinage on Ireland: "This WOOD, as soon as his *Patent* was passed, or soon after, sends over a great many *Barrels of those* HALF-PENCE, to *Cork* and other *Sea-Port Towns*."[32] Wood's coins were manufactured in Bristol before being transported to Ireland in barrels.[33] So in the mid-1720s, for Swift the barrel is an instrument whereby the English tried to oppress the Irish; and this was likely to be particularly true of barrels coming from Bristol.

Let us return to the description of the Projector. Of course, part of Swift's intention in this chapter is to satirize scientific presumption, embodied in the form of the Royal Society. But this filthy, misguided, wrecked figure, gratefully receiving his weekly Bristol barrel's worth of excrement, is, once we have explored some of the particular resonance of the phrase "*Bristol* Barrel," also an image of Irish abjection at the hands of England. As such, he is the object of not just Swift's satire, but also (like the hapless Irish) of his furious sympathy. The connection is strengthened when we note that Wood's halfpence were connected in Swift's mind with pollution. They were like (as Swift himself put it) "the accursed thing which . . . the children of Israel were forbidden to touch."[34] And we find that a further filiation between this passage and the drama of Wood's halfpence is to be found in the single earlier occurrence of the phrase "*Bristol* Barrel" in *Gulliver's Travels*. In chapter five of Part II, Gulliver is recounting the quotidian inconveniences of living amongst giants:

I should have lived happy enough in that Country, if my Littleness had not exposed me to several ridiculous and troublesome Accidents; some of which I shall venture to relate. *Glumdalclitch* often carried me into the Gardens of the Court in my smaller Box, and would sometimes take me out of it and hold me in her Hand, or set me down to walk. I remember, before the Dwarf left the Queen, he followed us one Day into those Gardens; and my Nurse having set me down, he and I being close together, near some Dwarf Apple-trees, I must need shew my Wit by a silly Allusion between him and the Trees, which happens to hold in their Language as it doth in ours. Whereupon, the malicious Rogue watching his Opportunity, when I was walking under one of them, shook it directly over my Head, by which a dozen Apples, each of them near as large as a *Bristol* Barrel, came tumbling about my Ears; one of them hit me on the Back as I chanced to stoop, and knocked me down flat on my Face, but I received no other Hurt; and the Dwarf was pardoned at my Desire, because I had given the Provocation.[35]

It is tempting to see this Gulliverian mishap as a satirical *rifacimento* of the famous episode from the biography of Isaac Newton, reporting that he had been prompted to think about the nature of gravity by watching the fall of an apple: intellectual heroism is rewritten as the chastisement of impertinent folly. If this passage in *Gulliver* does refer to Newton, then it becomes very significant, as it would be the first reference to that famous detail of Newton's biography (hitherto it has not been traced earlier than to a work of Voltaire's published in 1727).[36] And here the affinity between the phrase "*Bristol* Barrel" and the campaign against Wood's halfpence strengthens the possibility of this being an allusion to Newton, because Newton was the

Master of the Mint who had certified that Wood's halfpence were good coin, rather than excremental rubbish as Swift maintained:

Sir *Isaac Newton* reported an *Assay* taken at the *Tower*, of *Wood's* Metal; by which it appears, that *Wood had in all respects performed his Contract*. His Contract! With whom? Was it with the Parliament or People of *Ireland*? Are not they to be the Purchasers? But they detest, abhor, and reject it, as Corrupt, Fraudulent, mingled with Dirt and Trash.[37]

At this point, it is helpful to juxtapose the passage from *A Tale of a Tub* which Swift was re-writing and re-imagining when he described Gulliver's encounter with the Projector. It occurs in the "Digression Concerning Madness," and is part of the description of the visit to Bedlam:

Accost the Hole of another Kennel, first stopping your Nose, you will behold a surley, gloomy, nasty, slovenly Mortal, raking in his own Dung, and dabling in his Urine. The best Part of his Diet, is the Reversion of his own Ordure, which exspiring into Steams, whirls perpetually about, and at last reinfunds. His Complexion is of a dirty Yellow, with a thin scatter'd Beard, exactly agreeable to that of his Dyet upon its first Declination; like other Insects, who having their Birth and Education in an Excrement, from thence borrow their Colour and their Smell. The Student of this Apartment is very sparing of his Words, but somewhat over-liberal of his Breath; He holds his Hand out ready to receive your Penny, and immediately upon Receipt, withdraws to his former Occupations. Now, is it not amazing to think, the Society of *Warwick-Lane*, should have no more Concern, for the recovery of so useful a Member, who, if one may judge from these Appearances, would become the greatest Ornament to that Illustrious Body?[38]

The "Student" of Bedlam is clearly a forebear of the Projector in Lagado, but a very simplified one, who engages only Swift's disdain. By contrast, the Projector is not simply an image of scientific pride. When he gratefully accepts his weekly Bristol barrel of ordure, he is also an image of the suffering and tyrannized (as well as culpably servile and deluded) Irishry.

THE SLIGHTED SEA-CAPTAIN

Swift's imagination is powerfully exercised by notions . . . of merging identities, of categories under pressure from human impulse and activity. (Claude Rawson, *Gulliver and the Gentle Reader*, p. 109)

The double identity of the Projector of the Academy of Lagado is a vivid example of "the complex and nervous agilities of Swift's own voice."[39] My final example reveals a slightly different kind of shapeshifting, one between author and character: it is therefore one of "those highly-charged

Swiftian moments when formulaic distinctions" between author and authorial creation "dissolve."⁴⁰

Later in Part III of *Gulliver*, when the spirits of the dead are being summoned to the island of Glubbdubdrib, Gulliver's attention is particularly caught by one "whose Case appeared a little singular":

> He had a Youth about Eighteen Years old standing by his Side. He told me, he had for many Years been Commander of a Ship; and in the Sea Fight at *Actium*, had the good Fortune to break through the Enemy's great Line of Battle, sink three of their Capital Ships, and take a fourth, which was the sole Cause of *Antony*'s Flight, and of the Victory that ensued: That the Youth standing by him, his only Son, was killed in the Action. He added, that upon the Confidence of some Merit, the War being at an End, he went to *Rome*, and solicited at the Court of *Augustus* to be preferred to a greater Ship, whose Commander had been killed; but without any regard to his Pretensions, it was given to a Boy who had never seen the Sea, the Son of a *Libertina*, who waited on one of the Emperor's Mistresses. Returning back to his own Vessel, he was charged with Neglect of Duty, and the Ship given to a favourite Page of *Publicola* the Vice-Admiral; whereupon he retired to a poor Farm, at a great Distance from *Rome*, and there ended his Life. I was so curious to know the Truth of this Story, that I desired *Agrippa* might be called, who was Admiral in that Fight. He appeared, and confirmed the whole Account, but with much more Advantage to the Captain, whose Modesty had extenuated or concealed a great Part of his Merit.⁴¹

A curious feature of this passage concerns "*Publicola* the Vice-Admiral," whose favorite page was awarded the ship which should have gone to the anonymous but deserving sea-captain.⁴² Again, no previous editor of *Gulliver's Travels* has offered the reader any annotation on this point. Antiquity provides us with two main sources for the battle of Actium: Plutarch, in his *Life of Antony*, and Velleius Paterculus.⁴³ Both authors mention Publicola, but both specify that he served as vice-admiral to Antony. This is at variance with the clear implication in *Gulliver's Travels* that Publicola served under Augustus and Agrippa.

Why in *Gulliver's Travels* does Publicola migrate from Antony's fleet to that of Augustus? Is this just an example of an error of memory on Swift's part? Possibly. But another, more plausible⁴⁴ and more interesting possibility is revealed when we consider a publication by the author who in 1711 took over from Swift responsibility for the composition of *The Examiner*, namely Delarivier Manley. The book in question is the two-volume *Memoirs of Europe, towards the close of the eighth century, written by Eginardus, secretary and favourite to Charlemagne* (1710), a work of propaganda for the Tory party, which was later published as the third and fourth volumes of the *New Atalantis*. The first volume had been dedicated to the Earl of Peterborough, and on the strength of this Manley sought, with Swift's support, a pension from Peterborough on July 3, 1711.[45] In the *Memoirs of Europe* there is a character called "Publicola," who in the *Key* to the work is identified as "Lord Nottingham."[46] Who is this?

Daniel Finch, Earl of Nottingham (1647–1730), was detested by Swift as an apostate from the Tories, and repeatedly mocked and derided by him, not least in Part I of *Gulliver's Travels*, where he is the model for "Skyresh Bolgolam," the courtier in Lilliput who "was pleased, without any Provocation, to be my [i.e. Gulliver's] mortal Enemy."[47] Nottingham happened also to be Swift's mortal enemy. Nottingham bitterly resented Swift's lampoons of him (for instance, the half-sheet broadside, *A Hue and Cry after Dismal* [1712]).[48] And this resentment took its most dramatic form when Nottingham alluded to Swift in a speech in the House of Lords in June 1714 during the debates on the Schism Bill, saying that:

I tremble when I think that a certain divine, who is hardly suspected of being a Christian is in a fair way of being a bishop, and may one day give licences to those, who shall be entrusted with the instruction of youth.[49]

The attempts to obtain for Swift a bishopric, which had preceded his eventual appointment as Dean of St. Patrick's in April 1713, had, Swift felt, been chiefly frustrated by the Duchess of Somerset and the Archbishop of York,[50] who had exerted influence on Anne behind the scenes. But Nottingham's reference to him and to his reputation for irreligion (the consequences of his unacknowledged but widely known authorship of *A Tale of a Tub*), in such a public place, must have cemented Swift's despair of ever receiving the bishopric which he felt was his due for services rendered to the government in the years 1710–14, when he had been Harley's chief of propaganda. So this small detail of Part III of *Gulliver's Travels*, in which one of the hangers-on of "Publicola" receives the reward which was properly the due of the man who had really secured the momentous, world-changing victory of Actium, can, when we scratch below the surface, be read as an instance of encrypted or clandestine autobiography, provided we have understood the particular, early eighteenth-century significance of the name "Publicola" in Swift's circle. Swift believed that his efforts on behalf of Harley and St. John had been crucial to the conclusion of the War of the Spanish Succession and the signing of the Treaty of Utrecht. Certainly, the extraordinary impact of *The Conduct of the Allies* (1711) – in two months, six editions were called for, comprising a total of eleven thousand copies – makes the belief not ridiculous. But like the deserving sea-captain, Swift too was slighted in the division of the spoils of victory; and the captain's retirement "to a poor Farm, at a great Distance from *Rome*, [where he] ended his Life" is a translation into ancient Roman history of Swift's bitterly resented exile to Dublin. The migration in *Gulliver's Travels* of "Publicola" from the defeated to the victorious side at Actium is the vehicle for that almost indiscernible re-opening of old but unforgotten wound.

"EFFECTS OF MANY A SAD DISASTER"

Gulliver's account of the Academy of Lagado is, as we have seen, in part a re-writing of *A Tale of a Tub*, and the raising from the dead of the deserving sea-captain expresses a rising to the surface of a crucial period of Swift's past, which preoccupied his thought and imagination thereafter – namely, the "Four Last Years of Queen Anne," when he had acted as propagandist-in-chief to the Harley–St. John ministry, composing works such as *The Conduct of the Allies* (1711) and *The Examiner* (1711). These examples therefore illustrate the truth of the comment that "the vexation of former thoughts," as Swift put it in a letter, was one of the prime drivers of his literary creativity after he became Dean of St. Patrick's and was exiled (as he thought) to Dublin.[51] After the death of Queen Anne, much of Swift's writing can, without undue strain, be considered as a compulsive picking of figurative scabs.

Swift had a complicated attitude toward the years he spent working for the ministry.[52] On the one hand, they were the summit of his public career. On the other, he increasingly came to see them as a period of metaphorical prostitution, of contamination and infection by the activities he was obliged to undertake as a hired pen. Comments in the *Journal to Stella* show that such uncomfortable thoughts were in Swift's mind even at the time:

And the ministry all use me perfectly well, and all that know them, say they love me. Yet I can count upon nothing, nor will ... They think me useful; they pretended they were afraid of none but me. – Pox of these speculations! They give me the spleen; and that is a disease I was not born to.

See how my Stile is altered by living & thinking & talking among these People [i.e. the Ministry][53]

The language of love, disease, and pox is noteworthy here, as is the sense of an intimate contamination of thought and language. Similar implications are also latently present in Swift's expostulation to Arbuthnot in a letter of June 16, 1714, as his political frustrations with the ministry gathered to a head: "I have a Mind to be very angry, and to let my anger break out in some manner that will not please them, at the End of a Pen."[54] That outbreak was, literally, *Some Free Thoughts upon the Present State of Affairs* (composed 1714).[55] Metaphorically, however, the phrase "break out" likens the expression of Swift's anger to an imposthume, issue, sore or chancre, and the reference to its breaking out "at the End of a Pen" in an effluence of the contaminated language Swift had contracted amongst the ministry does nothing to diminish the expression's venereal qualities. Looking back on his life in a letter to Eaton Stannard of April 1735, Swift saw the years 1710–14 in terms of a waste of strength, and as the subject of belated penitence, when he spoke of "the Life I have led, which in the Strength of my days chiefly past at Courts and among Ministers of State, to my great Vexation and Disappointment, for which I now repent too late."[56] And in a letter of June 8, 1732 to Henry Jenney, Swift betrayed his feelings of being trapped in the political posture he had assumed in 1710–14: "You are an expectant from the world and from power. I have long done with both, having been an original offender against all principles set up since the death of the Queen, I could not think it worth my while to quit my old ones, and must have done it with an ill grace, though honour and conscience had been out of the question."[57] So, like Corinna, Swift suffered in later life from the painful consequences of love. Hence, perhaps, his sudden tone of tenderness in "A Beautiful Young Nymph Going to Bed" for Corinna's dreams of wandering forsaken through a treacherous landscape full of false friends.

That section of the poem contains an allusion to Virgil (pointed out by Swift himself in a footnote to the poem as first printed in 1734). It is to the *Aeneid*, IV, 467–8: "et longam incomitata videtur / Ire viam."[58] These verses are taken from the description of Dido's dream, when deserted by the faithless Aeneas, and their incorporation into "A Beautiful Young Nymph Going to Bed" is not simply a mock-heroic moment. For the beautiful nymph, repeatedly exploited by powerful men, and carefully inspecting her "Shankers, Issues, running Sores" is an image of Swift himself: Swift, who in later life was unable to prevent his imagination from re-exploring, re-writing, and re-expressing the "Effects of many a sad Disaster," and in particular the devastating disaster of 1714; Swift who was himself obliged every day to experience "the Anguish, Toil, and Pain, / Of gath'ring up [him]self again" by means of "Arts," and who experienced at first-hand how unavailing his art was to salve those "Shankers, Issues, running Sores" – as unavailing as Corinna's plasters and issue-peas, no matter how carefully and gently applied. And lest this final instance of shapeshifting between sexes should seem too unlikely, let us note that it had already been prepared for by an early eighteenth-century misremembering of the passage from Boccalini which, as we have already seen, lies behind Swift's poem. Recall that, in *I ragguagli di Parnasso*, Iovanni Zecca's receit against the pox is a portrait of a diseased *man*. When John Marten referred to that passage of Boccalini in his much reprinted *A Treatise of the Venereal Disease*, however, he remembered it as a portrait of a *woman*:

Take, says he, a well drawn Picture of the most perfect and faultless Beauty that ever appear'd in Flesh and Blood, and then with a Pencil touch it over again, with rotten Teeth, bleer Eyes, no Nose at all, in fine, let it be as Loathsome as Venom and Corruption can make it: Carry this Picture about with you, and when ever you have a Fancy for a Woman you suspect, do but take a sober View of this Piece, and seriously consider what you are going about, and the Consequences thereof, and my Life for yours, it shall keep you Safe and Honest.[59]

Safety and honesty were both comforts which Swift had, by his own account, to some extent sacrificed through his entanglements with Harley and St. John. From the vexation of that memory, however, sprang the extreme and stinging pleasures of Swift's later writings.[60]

NOTES

1 Laetitia Pilkington, *Memoirs* (Dublin, 1748), p. 59.
2 Orrery, *Remarks on Swift*, 2nd edn. (1752), p. 162.
3 *The Correspondence of Jonathan Swift*, ed. Harold Williams, corrected edn., 5 vols. (Oxford: Clarendon Press, 1965), IV, p. 168; hereafter cited as *Corr.*
4 *Corr.*, IV, pp. 144–5.
5 *Corr.*, III, p. 410.
6 *Corr.*, III, p. 368.
7 *Corr.*, III, p. 242.
8 October 31, 1729: *Corr.*, III, 355.
9 "To Mr. Delany," ll. 39–40, in *Swift's Poems*, ed. Harold Williams, 2nd edn., 3 vols. (Oxford: Clarendon Press, 1958), p. 216; hereafter cited as *Poems*.
10 *The Works of J.S.*, D.D. D.S.P.D. *in four volumes* (Dublin, 1735), II, 312.
11 Claude Rawson, *Order from Confusion Sprung* (London: George Allen & Unwin, 1985), p. 162.
12 Geoffrey Hill, "Jonathan Swift: The Poetry of 'Reaction'," in Geoffrey Hill, *The Lords of Limit: Essays on Literature and Ideas* (London: Andre Deutsch, 1984), pp. 67 and 80.
13 William Empson, *Some Versions of Pastoral: A Study of the Pastoral Form in Literature* (London: Chatto and Windus, 1935), p. 56.
14 *Poems*, pp. 580–3; *Jonathan Swift: The Complete Poems*, ed. Pat Rogers (Harmondsworth: Penguin Books, 1983), pp. 830–1.

15 *I ragguagli di Parnasso, or, Advertisements from Parnassus in two centuries: with the politick touch-stone written originally in Italian by that famous Roman Trajano Bocalini; and now put into English by the Right Honourable Henry, Earl of Monmouth* (1656), p. 168; "The First Century," advertisement 81. Swift's library seems to have contained the 1671 edition of Boccalini's *Pietra del paragone politico*, but no copy of *I ragguagli* (*A Catalogue of Books, The Library of the late Rev. Dr. Swift* [Dublin, 1745], p. 26; hereafter cited as *Catalogue*). However, he unmistakably refers to *I ragguagli* in *A Tale of A Tub* (*The Prose Writings of Jonathan Swift*, ed. Herbert Davis *et al.*, 16 vols. [Oxford: Basil Blackwell, 1939–74], I, p. 17; hereafter cited as *PW*); and *Gulliver's Travels* shows clear evidence of the influence of this work of Boccalini's on Swift.

16 *Order from Confusion Sprung*, p. 163. *Poems*, p. 583, ll. 73–4.

17 *Poems*, p. 583, ll. 65–72.

18 *The Lords of Limit*, p. 80.

19 *Poems*, pp. 581–2, ll. 13–18, 29–32.

20 *Iliad*, XIX, 365–403 (Achilles); *Aeneid*, XI, 487–91 (Turnus) and XII, 430–40 (Aeneas).

21 *PW*, XI, pp. 179–80.

22 Chapter 22 of Book Five of *Pantagruel* is a dominant presence in this particular chapter of *Gulliver*.

23 Charles Marriott, *The New Royal English Dictionary; or, Complete Library of Grammatical Knowledge* (1780), *sub*. 'Barrel'.

24 Arthur Young, *A Tour in Ireland; with General Observations on the Present State of that Kingdom* (1780), p. 316.

25 *OED*, I.

26 *A Collection of the State Letters of the Right Honourable Roger Boyle* (1742), p. 246.

27 John, Lord Sheffield, *Remarks on the Deficiency of Grain* (1800), p. 62, n. *.

28 In a letter to William Swift of November 29, 1692 Swift says that he resided at Trinity College, Dublin for seven years (*Corr.*, I, p. 12), which would place his departure in the spring of 1689, since he had been admitted on April 24, 1682; cf. Irvin Ehrenpreis, *Swift: The Man, His Works, and the Age*, 3 vols. (Methuen, 1962–83), I, pp. 43 and 88, n. 3; hereafter cited as Ehrenpreis. Cf. also *PW*, V, pp. 192–3.

29 See, for instance, Jonathan Swift, *Gulliver's Travels*, ed. Claude Rawson and Ian Higgins (Oxford: Oxford University Press, 2005), p. 325.

30 For the passage concerning Lindalino, see *PW*, XI, pp. 309–10.

31 *Corr.*, III, p. 5. The first of the *Drapier's Letters* was published in Dublin by John Harding in March 1724 (*PW*, X, p. 207).

32 *PW*, X, p. 5.

33 Marmaduke Coghill wrote to Edward Southwell, the Irish Secretary of State, on September 10, 1724, complaining about the arrival of "seven casks of these halfpence from Bristol" (Ehrenpreis, III, p. 245).

34 *PW*, X, p. 12; cf. Joshua 6:18.

35 *PW*, XI, p. 116. Given that the ratio of size between Brobdingnag and Europe is 1:12, the fact that in Brobdingnag a crab-apple was the size of a Bristol

barrel implies that the capacity of a Bristol barrel was such that it could hold approximately 1,728 (i.e. 12³) crab-apples. This is the most definite assessment of the size of a Bristol barrel in 1726 that I have been able to discover.

36 D. McKie and G. R. de Beer, "Newton's Apple" and "Newton's Apple – An Addendum," *Notes and Records of the Royal Society* 9 (1951–2), pp. 46–54 and 333–35; cf. also Anon., *Phino-Godol. A Poem. In hudibrastic verse* (1732), p. 4. Swift had met Voltaire in the summer of 1727 (*Corr.*, III, p. 214 and n. 1).

37 *PW*, X, p. 16; cf. pp. 187–8. Gravitation or *"Attraction"* is also belittled in Part III, chapter 8 of *Gulliver's Travels* (*PW*, XI, pp. 197–8).

38 *PW*, I, pp. 112–13. The "Society of *Warwick-Lane*" is the Royal College of Physicians.

39 Claude Rawson, *Gulliver and the Gentle Reader* (London: Routledge and Kegan Paul, 1973), p. 129.

40 *Ibid.*, p. 139.

41 *PW*, XI, pp. 200–1.

42 Lucius Gellius Publicola; deserted Brutus and Cassius for Octavian and Antony; consul, 36 BC; probably perished at Actium.

43 Plutarch, *Life of Antony*, lxv–lxvi; Velleius Paterculus, lxxxv.

44 Swift's library contained copies of both Plutarch's *Lives* and Velleius Paterculus: *Catalogue*, pp. 6 and 12.

45 Jonathan Swift, *Journal to Stella*, ed. Harold Williams, 2 vols. (Oxford: Clarendon Press, 1948), p. 306; hereafter cited as *Journal*.

46 *A Key to the Third Volume of the Atalantis, Call'd, Memoirs of Europe* (?1712), p. 3.

47 *PW*, XI, p. 42.

48 *PW*, VI, p. 210.

49 Ehrenpreis, II, p. 735; an allusion to the provision in the Schism Bill stipulating that schoolmasters had to be licensed by the appropriate bishop.

50 Who was also, as it happens, Swift's "mortall enemy" (*Journal*, p. 665; April 23, 1713).

51 *Corr.*, II, p. 334.

52 The full range of those emotional complexities would be best explored by means of a close reading of Swift's extraordinary imitation of Horace, "Horace, *Lib.* 2. *Sat.* 6. PART of it imitated," for which, however, there is no space in this essay (*Poems*, pp. 197–202).

53 *Journal*, pp. 303 (June 30, 1711) and 556 (September 15, 1712).

54 *Corr.*, II, p. 36.

55 *PW*, VIII, pp. 75–98.

56 *Corr.*, IV, p. 319.

57 *Corr.*, IV, p. 29. Cf. also the concluding lines of "Horace, *Lib.* 2. *Sat.* 6. PART of it imitated," ll. 105–7: "Thus in a Sea of Folly tost, / My choicest Hours of Life are lost: / Yet always wishing to retreat . . . ' (*Poems*, p. 202).

58 "She seems to be ever wending, companionless, on an endless journey."

59 John Marten, *A Treatise of the Venereal Disease*, 7th edn. (1711), pp. 386–7.

60 "I find a rebuke in a late Letter of yours that both stings & pleases me extreamly." Pope to Swift, August 1723 (*Corr.*, II, p. 457).

CHAPTER 8

Swift and the poetry of exile

Pat Rogers

Claude Rawson has been the most original and influential student in recent years of the British "age of satire." His achievement rests first on his remarkable skills as a critic and his ability to tease out the deeper meaning of texts with more finesse than anyone else. But he is also more of a historical critic than we often suppose. His understanding of Swift particularly derives from his familiarity with the cross-currents of eighteenth-century life, expressed in the nuances of tone and verbal texture. His grasp of the latent "Irishness" that pervades almost all Swift's work emerges most clearly in *God, Gulliver, and Genocide* (2001), which contains a startling revelation of links between *A Modest Proposal* and the writings of Shaw and Wilde. But almost everything Rawson has done in this area serves to locate Swift in an Anglo-Irish tradition, and to trace this line at the core of a wider British literary tradition.

Other scholars, from Louis Landa and Oliver Ferguson to Carole Fabricant and Andrew Carpenter, have helped to embed Swift within an Irish context. But nobody seems to have said much about one odd feature of his authorial career. This concerns his obsessive return to English materials in his poetry, for almost a decade following his visits to the metropolis of Britain in 1726 and 1727. During this period he kept going back to themes, events and personalities that lacked any authentic connection with Ireland. In one way this paradox is more apparent than real: Swift's exile, feigned or unfeigned, had been imposed on him. This marks him off from the individuals Terry Eagleton has taught us to view collectively as "exiles and émigrés" – writers such as Conrad, Joyce, Eliot, Koestler, Beckett, Auden – all of whom left their home-country with a degree of volition before embarking on a more nomadic life. To that degree Swift had more obvious reason to cast longing glances back to the place where he had enjoyed his former success. But this does not wholly explain his revulsion against his native land, or his willingness to take over the literally alien *topoi* of other writers. At least Joyce, poring in Trieste over Thom's *Directory of Dublin* and checking the omnibus schedules, had undertaken to write his novel about the city and its residents. On the other hand Swift does not profess overtly to be writing from Dublin about the political and literary scene in London. But that is just what he does, again and again.

I

Swift left England in September 1727 with a heavy heart. He had deep forebodings about the state in which he would find his "most valuable friend," Stella Johnson: indeed, he wondered if she might actually have died in his absence. When he got back to Dublin, her health had declined further, although she would survive until the following January. His mood was darkened, too, by his recognition that the visits he had paid to England in the past two years left him exactly where he was before. Everyone knew that *Gulliver's Travels* came from his pen, though he had not officially owned the book, and its scathing view of recent history (up to and including the Wood's Halfpence episode and the Atterbury affair) made it even less likely that those who held power would take him back into the fold.

At this moment Swift's long agony over his exclusion from English favor finally came to the surface of his writing. It seems as though he had embarked on a process of negotiating the stages of grieving: denial, anger, bargaining, depression, and acceptance. From this time on, he transferred his resentments into something more impersonal, cast in the form of his poems about English politics and letters. But initially his reaction was bleak, as he sat moldering at Holyhead in 1727, and waiting for the Irish ferry, which bad weather had delayed. Swift hardly ever wrote anything more bitter than the short poems which resulted. The verses headed "Holyhead, Sept. 25. 1727" begin in a savage tone, and do not get any softer as they proceed:

> Lo here I sit at holy head
> With muddy ale and mouldy bread
> All Christian vittals stink of fish
> I'm where my enemyes would wish. (ll. 1–4)

The danger in which Stella lies "With rage impatient makes me wait / A passage to the land I hate" (ll. 27–8).[1]

Another poem written during this stay, headed "Irel^d.," shows the same fury and sense of impotence, with a touch more of the chilly humor that often accompanies Swift's most blistering onslaughts: "Remove me from this land of slaves / Where all are fools, and all are knaves" (ll. 1–2). Although England bears a considerable share of blame for the troubles in her dependency, the emphasis here lies on the faults of the Irish themselves.

Naturally Swift's two visits to England in 1726 and 1727 had reawakened memories. They brought him back into personal contact with Pope, Gay, Arbuthnot, Bolingbroke, Peterborough, and others with whom he had been able to maintain only the virtual link of correspondence for more than a decade. Though the first Earl of Oxford was now dead, Swift could at least fraternize with his son, the second Earl. His friendship with Henrietta Howard meant that he still had some access to court circles, and he renewed acquaintance with Walpole. He also met members of the newly germinating opposition, most significantly William Pulteney. Naturally, during his sojourn in London, metropolitan affairs came to dominate his verse. One poem, "A Pastoral Dialogue between Richmond-Lodge and Marble-Hill," subtitled "Written June 1727, just after the News of the King's Death," provides the most obvious case in point. The two houses named in this title belonged respectively to the Prince and Princess of Wales, now on the verge of ascending the throne, and to Mrs. Howard. Swift chooses highly localized material, concerning the immediate environs of Richmond and Twickenham: the tone is strikingly intimate, with a good deal of in-group chatter embedded. As Marble Hill relates,

> Poor *Patty Blount* no more be seen
> Bedraggled in my Walks so green:
> Plump *Johnny Gay* will no elope;
> And here no more will dangle *Pope*. (ll. 47–50)

The easy matiness of these lines might mask our awareness that Martha Blount belonged in Pope's circle as a member of the Catholic gentry in the Thames Valley. She had developed strong ties with Gay, but had not enjoyed very close relations with Swift in the years up to 1714, and would never be a deep personal friend. (Just three letters survive between the two of them.) Not for the only time, Swift appropriated Pope's address book. The entire poem shows a marked desire on the writer's part to belong to the in-group, to share its secrets and retail its gossip. Thus, Marble Hill looks forward to more visits from Pope:

> Him twice a Week I here expect,
> To rattle *Moody* for Neglect;
> An idle Rogue, who spends his Quartridge
> In tipling at the *Dog* and *Partridge*. (ll. 95–8)

Faulkner's 1735 edition identifies Moody as the gardener. Swift slips the name in with colloquial fluency, to make us think that he regularly inhabited this world. Actually Marble Hill was the grand new house of a court lady, who permitted visits as an act of kind condescension. By the time Faulkner printed the poem, Swift had long been consigned to his distant outpost, and after 1727 he would never again meet a single one of the persons on whom the poem bestows such detailed attention.[2] In retrospect, such works take on the air of Parthian shots, loosed before the writer quit England for all time.

Throughout the next few years, the course of Swift's poetic career divides into two streams. This split is expressed in the layout of the standard edition of his *Poems.* Harold Williams opted to print the main series of "Miscellaneous Poems" from 1724 to 1736 in Volume II, along with the items relating to Stella and Vanessa. The pieces concerning Wood's Halfpence had gone into Volume I, while the editor consigned to the third volume "Irish Politics, 1724–1737," "Poems relating to Market Hill," and "Riddles by Swift and his Friends." At first sight such a breakdown may look arbitrary, but it is eminently justified by the tone, texture, and themes of the respective groups. Little of the "Irish" material printed here displays great intensity, until the final crushing blows of "The Legion Club" in 1736, when Swift delivered his last great pronouncement on affairs of state. The Market Hill group contains some characteristic works of great interest, but they belong essentially to a mode of social satire, as with the Horatian comedy of "The Grand Question Debated." None of these poems, excepting again "The Legion Club," displays a scintilla of the compact force exhibited by Swift's prose writings on the Irish scene, whether in *The Drapier's Letters* or *A Modest Proposal.* They carry an impression of the local, the provincial, the journalistic, even the trivial: it is as though the rhetoric admits that Dublin is a place of minor importance fit for minor poetry, and the second city merits only secondary work.

By contrast, the group dealing with English affairs contains some of Swift's most considerable achievements in verse. Some would argue that works such as "Verses on the Death of Dr. Swift," "A Libel on Dr. Delany," "On Poetry: A Rapsody," and "An Epistle to a Lady" embody his most effective writing, from any stage in his poetic career. Yet they represent a paradoxical situation we generally ignore. Thrown off the track by their confident mastery, we close our eyes to their strangely belated quality. In fact, these poems have a number of features in common. They largely concern matters which for the most part (1) relate much more directly to

England than to Ireland; (2) go back many years in personal and political terms; (3) involve persons and events often unconnected with Swift; (4) take up the quarrels of others, Pope especially; (5) echo the accents of *The Dunciad*, which first appeared not long after the second trip to England; and (6) appeal to an implicit audience in London, rather than in Dublin. All these aspects of the poetry may find ready explanations, from a literary or psychological standpoint. The trouble is that, if so, nobody has done the explaining.

Most of these items combine allusions to the political scene with vignettes from the world of letters. This applies also to pieces such as "Directions for a Birth-day Song," arguably Swift's first mature poem on politics, or "To Mr. Gay." Even among the very different set of so called "excremental" poems, written in this period, the presumed locale, where it can be determined, appears to lie across the water from Dublin. "A Beautiful Young Nymph Going to Bed" openly announces its heroine as "*Corinna*, Pride of *Drury-Lane*," and sets its action amid the familiar sites of Augustan satire – Covent Garden, Bridewell, the Fleet Ditch. "Cassinus and Peter" belongs in Cambridge, as squarely as Chaucer's "Reeve's Tale." Even poems on Irish episodes, published in Ireland, carry English freight: we need think only of "An excellent New Ballad: or, The true *En*[*gli*]*sh* D[ea]n to be hang'd for a R[a]pe" (1730). The title announces a key fact: Rev. Thomas Sawbridge was an English importee, and this makes it easier for Swift to effect a comparison with "brave Colonel *Chartres*" (l. 49). This alludes to the notorious Francis Charteris, the "rape-master" satirized by Pope, Arbuthnot, Hogarth, and Fielding, a Scotsman with close links to the Walpole administration. The final stanza of this poem takes a familiar line: "Our Church and our State dear *En*[*gla*]*nd* maintains" (l. 67); Swift never allows us to rest in the delusion that Hibernian matters stand by themselves. What do they know of Ireland, the text suggests, that only Ireland know?

II

It would not be going too far to say that Swift's major poems in the period, as just defined, evade Irish concerns. "Verses on the Death of Dr. Swift" represents only a partial exception. For the rest, these works fix their attention on England for their poetic material.

The tendency already manifests itself in "Directions for a Birth-day Song." Swift wrote it around October 30, 1729, marking the birthday of

George II. Loyal effusions were expected on such occasions, and the Dean's protégé, Matthew Pilkington, had geared himself up for the task. The letter of advice which Swift gave Pilkington broaches some of the most contentious issues of the day. It begins by alluding to the bad relations between the king and his children, especially Frederick, Prince of Wales. Throughout the 1730s, the opposition to Walpole tried to drive a wedge between father and son, and unrealistically cast Frederick as a patriot king in waiting. The poet tells his supposed pupil to present the monarch as a victorious soldier, dealing out blows like Jove's thunder on the enemy. This stale conceit, beloved of poetasters, most directly recalled the praise Addison's *Campaign* had heaped on Marlborough. This eulogy of the duke served as the embodiment of everything that Swift reviled and everything he had tried to counter with his polemical writing at the time of the Harley administration – a period he could now recall only with a wistful sense of loss. There is a problem, the "director" admits, because Britain has enjoyed peace for fifteen years. Even the press, ready to stretch the truth in the interests of the great, can find no war on the horizon: "Nor London Journals, nor the Post-men / Tho fond of warlike Lyes as most men" (ll. 53–4). The king must be shown as Apollo, just as "Robin Walpole is Mecaenas [*sic*]" (l. 60). Further implausible compliments are suggested, based on the needs of the would-be panegyrist: "Your Int'rest lyes to learn the knack / Of whitening what before was black" (ll. 115–16). Exactly the same rhetorical gestures turn up at the end of Pope's *Epistle to Augustus* (1737): no surprise, because the two men are writing about precisely the same thing.

Commentators have long recognized Swift's target as Laurence Eusden, poet laureate since 1718, whose function had been to bring out the yearly odes until he died on September 27, 1730. Most likely Swift had not yet heard this news, when he wrote the "Directions" about a month later.[3] In any case Colley Cibber, appointed to succeed on December 3, gratefully took on the role of supplying vapid celebratory poems to order. Eusden had done nothing at all to offend Swift personally; but *The Dunciad* had greatly enhanced his suitability as an object of satire. In the first version of the poem, of course, Pope cast Lewis Theobald as laureate, to be succeeded by Colley Cibber in the revised version more than a decade later. However, Eusden does not escape all attention: in the new Saturnian dispensation, "Beneath his reign, shall Eusden wear the bays, / Cibber preside Lord-Chancellor of Plays" (*Dunciad Variorum*, bk. 3, ll. 319–20).[4] A long note to this passage draws out some of Eusden's failings, with the blank judgment, "Mr. *Eusden* was made Laureate for the same reason that Mr. *Tibbald* was made *Hero* of This Poem, because there was *no better to be had*" (bk. 3, l. 319, n.). Other damaging references occur in the text: for example, the Goddess of Dulness saw "Eusden eke out Blackmore's endless line" (bk. 1, l. 102). In the *Epistle to Arbuthnot* Pope would once more find room for Eusden, as "a Parson, much be-mused in Beer" (l. 15). But earlier than this the laureate had earned a mention in chapter IX of *Peri Bathous* (1728): "Who sees not that [Eusden] was the poetical son of . . . Blackmore?"[5] He turned up in Pope's correspondence, as the embodiment of the second-rate, even before he gained official approval, for Pope wrote to Gay in 1716, "Poor Poetry! the little that's left of it here longs to cross the Seas, and leave Eusden in full and peaceable Possession of the British Laurel."[6] A strong probability exists that Pope's references had alerted Swift to the potential offered up by the hapless laureate.

We do not have to look far in Eusden's official verse to see the worst presentiments of the *Directions* realized. Swift's spokesman refers disparagingly to inferior fellows such as "Julius, or the Youth of Pella" who had done a little conquering in their time. In 1721 Eusden had built one of his odes for George I around the idea that the king rivaled the greatest figures in history, especially (and recurrently) Julius Caesar: "Thy Equal in no future Age shall rise: / One *Caesar* rule the Earth, one *Jove* the Skies!"[7] In his *Epistle to Walpole* (1726), Eusden invokes the poets at the court of Augustus, adding, "Those made *Maecenas*, not *Maecenas* those: / But we, their weak descendants, wisely chuse / A WALPOLE's Name to dignify the Muse."[8] Similarly, the poem he addressed to the Prince of Wales in 1729 dilated on his subject's early promise, his war-like disposition, and his personal charms, all matters which appear in Swift's sneering lines on "his little Highness Freddy" (l. 187). Eusden has this:

> An inborn Sweetness, and majestic Grace
> Form a blest Mixture, and compose thy Face:
> Thy Face in Paint, or rich Intaglios spy'd,
> What royal Nymph but glows to be a Bride?[9]

Swift manages to give the same idea a very different feel:

> With so much beauty, shew me any maid
> That could refuse this charming Ganymede,
> Where Majesty with Sweetness vyes. (ll. 189–91)

Later in his poem Swift advises the aspirant poet to celebrate the queen, mainly it seems because of the harmony of the syllables making up her name, compared to the rough Teutonic sound of names like George, Brunswick, and Hesse Darmstedt:

> May Caroline continue long.
> For ever fair and young – in Song.
> What tho the royal Carcase must
> Squeez'd in a Coffin turn to dust;
> Those Elements her name compose
> Like Atoms are exempt from blows. (ll. 233–8)

Eusden had already found occasion to trumpet forth the name: " 'Tis CAROLINA all their Hopes destroys, / The fruitful Mother of our Joys!"[10] Compare the words of Venus in an earlier poem: "Not ev'n *Augustus* dares to disobey, / His *Carolina's* Looks confirm my Sway."[11] Pope took the hint in his first imitation of Horace, that of the first satire of the second book (1733): "Let *Carolina* smooth the tuneful Lay" (l. 30).

Clearly Swift had kept a close eye on the topics found in these laureate effusions, and on their particular diction. He even incorporated some localized references to "Doctor Clark," that is the theologian Samuel Clarke, who loomed much larger in the capital than in Ireland; and to "Minheer Hendel." It would be another decade before the composer took *Messiah* over to Dublin, and found the Dean of St. Patrick's unwilling to allow the vicars choral to "assist at a club of idlers in Fishamble Street" to perform *Esther*. At this date Swift got his information on the musical world from the contacts that his London friends, Arbuthnot, Gay, and Peterborough especially, maintained with the world of opera. All in all, the "Directions" show that he identified some of the more crass features of contemporary writing with the Whitehall-based mafia. No hint emerges that anyone on the Irish side of the channel commits equivalent solecisms.

Dating from just a few months later, "A Libel on D[r.] D[elany]" (1730) had its origins in an exchange involving Swift's friend Patrick Delany, who was seeking the patronage of the Lord Lieutenant, and who had cited purely Irish instances in his petition. However, the sequel transfers its action across the sea, on the grounds presumably that "*E[ngland]* is our Master." To demonstrate the folly of chasing preferment from the great, Swift launches into a series of brief life-studies, devoted respectively to Congreve, Steele, Gay, Addison, and Pope. None of these relate to the experience of Ireland, where Delany's interests lay, even though Congreve and Steele had Irish roots. Yet again a major aim of this sequence seems to be to remind the world (and perhaps Swift himself) of the network of friends he had established in the literary world – the London literary world, of course. Writing to Pope on February 6, 1730, he remarked elliptically, "You will see 18 lines relating to your self, in the most whimsical paper that ever was writ, and which was never intended for the publick."[12] The lines embody a characteristic tribute, worthy to set aside the ten verses Pope had placed at the head of *The Dunciad*:

> Hail! Happy *Pope*, whose gen'rous Mind,
> Detesting all the Statesmen kind,
> Contemning *Courts*, at *Courts* unseen,
> Refus'd the Visits of a Queen . . .
> A Genius fit all Stations fit,
> Whose meanest Talent is his Wit:
> His Heart too great, though Fortune little,
> To lick a *Rascal Statesman*'s Spittle. (ll. 71–82)

The story that Pope left home to avoid a visit by the queen appears to have no foundation. But there is no mistaking the fervor of Swift's address, and his desire to enlist his friend as an example to other writers, as he "sits aloft on *Pindus* Head, / Despising *Slaves* that *cringe* for Bread" (ll. 87–8).

A year later, Swift returned to similar themes in his verses "To Mr. Gay on his being Steward to the Duke of Queensberry" (1731). It mattered little that the rumor Swift had heard about his friend proved to be untrue. The poem begins with Gay's unsuccessful efforts to obtain a worthwhile post at court, before his supposed appointment by the Duke. It modulates into a consideration of the nature of stewardship, reviling the rapacious Peter Walter (land-agent, attorney, marriage-broker, and political facto-tum), "that Rogue of *genuine ministerial* Kind" (l. 102). However, Swift's real target is the great "manager" of the nation, Robert Walpole. Two of Christ's parables underlie the entire poem: first, that of the faithful steward (Matthew 24:45–51; Luke 12:41–8), and second, that of the unjust steward (Luke 16:1–13). Swift takes a phrase "*th' unrighteous Mammon*" (l. 73) from the latter, and comes close to echoing its conclusion, "No servant can serve two masters . . . Ye cannot serve God and Mammon." The implicit message is that Walpole deserves the fate of the evil servant, who in the end "shall receive many lashes." Again Swift writes with an apparent first-hand knowledge of affairs – something which his blunder about Gay's appointment belies. Rhetorically, it is a poetry which strives to seem written on the spot.[13]

"Verses on the Death of Dr. Swift" (written *c.* 1731) announces its subject at the outset, in paraphrasing La Rochefoucauld: "In all Distresses of our Friends / We first consult our private Ends" (ll. 7–8). Thus friendship will lie at the heart of the poem. Readers might naturally anticipate that this would involve some of Swift's Dublin acquaintances – if not the shopkeepers and craftsmen with whom he could exchange *craic* in the environs of his plot of ground at Naboth's Vineyard, then at least some acknowledged comrades in his "adopted" country – Dan Jackson or Robert Grattan, say, among his boon companions in the 1720s, most of whom were fellow graduates of Trinity College. We might look for newer contacts such as Laetitia and Matthew Pilkington, and it would have been apt if Swift had chosen to recognize Lady Acheson, whose estate at Market Hill gave him a retreat and a stimulus to verse-making. His old ally Anthony Raymond had died in 1726, but he still had friends with a scholarly and literary bent, notably his ecclesiastical colleague Patrick Delany and the schoolmaster Thomas Sheridan. None of these warrants a single couplet in the "Verses."

Some might argue that this fact derives from the element of auto-biography or pseudo-autobiography pervading the work. It is true that much of the most deeply felt writing concerns the time when Swift enjoyed his closest relation with power, during the years of the Harley administration:

> And, oh! How short are human Schemes!
> Here ended all our golden Dreams.
> What St. John's Skill in State Affairs,
> What Ormond's *Valour*, Oxford's Cares,
> To save their sinking Country lent,
> Was all destroy'd by one Event. (ll. 371–6)

The one event, of course, means the loss of "that precious Life" (l. 377), the death of Queen Anne. This remains the key datum in Swift's account of recent history, and in his own curriculum vitae. Oxford had died long before, but Bolingbroke remained a thorn in Walpole's side and had seen his exile reversed. Could Swift perhaps hold out the same hopes, if not for Ormond (an unregenerate Jacobite, who dragged out the 1730s in Avignon, plotting an unlikely invasion), then for himself? In any case, the poet's selective memory leaves room only for a tiny

group, consisting of an inner metropolitan circle. When the news comes
of Swift's death:

> Here shift the Scene, to represent
> How those I love, my Death lament.
> Poor POPE will grieve a Month; and GAY
> And ARBUTHNOTT a Day.
> ST. JOHN himself will scarce forbear,
> To bite his Pen, and drop a tear.
> The rest will give a Shrug and cry,
> I'm sorry; but we all must dye. (ll. 205–12)

The lines have become so familiar that we miss the oddity. Swift mentions no other response by an individual: his "female Friends" (l. 225) are
parceled together in unheeding chatter while they shuffle their cards.
Otherwise, we hear only of "The rest" (l. 211). In a poem on friendship,
only four persons merit a name when Swift considers the moment of his
dissolution. None of them was Irish.

A few lines earlier, Swift had imagined the immediate response of
another group, outside "those I love" (l. 206). They encompass a few
privileged individuals – privileged in various ways. We begin the roll-call
at court, with Henrietta Howard (now Lady Suffolk) and the queen. The
verse paragraph following enacts a telling conjunction, that of Colonel
Charteris and Robert Walpole. And then a more surprising nominee:

> Now *Curl* his Shop from Rubbish drains;
> Three genuine Tomes of *Swift's* Remains.
> And then to make them pass the glibber,
> Revis'd by *Tibbalds, Moore,* and *Cibber.*
> He'll treat me as he does my Betters,
> Publish my Will, my Life, my Letters.
> Revive the Libels born to dye;
> Which POPE must bear, as well as I. (ll. 197–204)

The notes here make the point even more strongly:

Curl hath been the most infamous Bookseller of any Age or Country: His
Character in Part may be found in Mr. POPE's Dunciad. He published three
Volumes all charged on the Dean, who never writ three Pages of them: he hath
used many of the Dean's Friends in almost as vile a Manner. (l. 197, n. 5)

In a moment we shall return to Curll, but first we need to look at the next
note, referring to the fourth line in the passage quoted:

Three stupid Verse Writers in London, the last to the Shame of the Court, and
the highest Disgrace to Wit and Learning, was made Laureat. *Moore,* commonly

called *Jemmy Moore*, son of *Arthur Moore*, whose Father was Jaylor of *Monaghan* in *Ireland*. See the Character of *Jemmy Moore* and *Tibbalds, Theobald* in the Dunciad. (l. 200, n. 1)

It is salutary to remind ourselves that Swift had absolutely no bone to pick with any of these men. The only vestigial contact they had with Ireland is the one Swift specified, relating to Moore's grandfather. As for the story of Arthur Moore's roots, this may be true, and he seems to have begun life as a groom. But he had come to England by the early 1680s. Swift knew him as a venal politician, perhaps the least respected member of Harley's administration. A thoroughgoing City man, he would incur Swift's distrust, and he did as much as anyone to blight the reputation of the South Sea Company in its troubled opening years.[14] As for James Moore Smythe, not a shred of evidence survives to link him with Swift. Likewise with Cibber and Theobald: these quarrels existed at one remove, under the instigation of *The Dunciad* – as the phrasing of the note gives away.

What of Edmund Curll? Swift could find plenty to complain about here. Curll had produced some pirated versions of his work, including a fraudulent edition of *Miscellanies* in 1711. He had attributed a number of bogus items to the Dean (although he was far from alone in this), such as Sheridan's *Ars Pun-ica*. The trouble was that genuine items, often of an embarrassing nature, tended to inveigle themselves into the phony collections. In 1726 Curll's *Miscellanea* compounded these insults, even if by his date there were few "new" misdemeanors, just repeat offenses. But Swift had mostly kept quiet about his feelings on this score, excepting a few barbed references in his correspondence. Curll only begins to figure in his printed output from the time of the trips to England. For example, "Advice to the Grub-street Verse Writers" (1726) suggests that starving poetasters ought to get their works printed by Curll with wide margins. They should then lend these to Pope, and recall them once he has annotated them with his own verse drafts. After this, "Sell them to *Curl* for Fifty Pound, / And swear they are your own" (ll. 19–20). Suddenly Curll achieves much greater prominence in the "Verses," when Swift added a further note to the one already quoted. This supplies biographic information and plainly draws on facts cited in the notes to *The Dunciad*. We do not have to seek far for a reason: Curll had become identified above all by his struggles with Pope, and had figured extensively in the latter's work – three prose pamphlets, starting in 1716, and a starring role in the great mock-epic in 1728. In short, Pope had already created the image of Curll that has survived until the present day. We may justifiably wonder whether Swift would have bothered to rake up his old troubles with the bookseller, unless his friend had imparted to Curll this mythological resonance within the culture of the day.

Another publisher occupies center stage: Bernard Lintot, whose stock proves incapable of supplying any works by Swift, just a year after the Dean's supposed death. By now it should occasion little surprise to discover that Lintot had never had any close involvement with Swift, who employed English publishers like Benjamin Tooke, John Morphew (a "trade" publisher, or distributor), and Benjamin Motte. One overwhelming reason presents itself for the decision to use Lintot so prominently in the "Verses," where he has a speech of over forty lines. He served as Pope's main outlet from 1712, when he issued the first version of *The Rape of the Lock* in his miscellany, until the later volumes of the *Odyssey* appeared in 1726. Arguably, Lintot had as much to do with Pope's rise to independence, financial and literary, as anyone. However, the two men had drifted apart over the years, and Pope ultimately managed to forge "a completely new relationship with the book trade, one in which the author takes charge, choosing his own printer and publisher and directing operations himself."[15] We could guess that a break with Pope had occurred from the undignified antics Lintot is made to perform in the second book of *The Dunciad*, where he runs a grotesque foot-race through the mire of Fleet Street with none other than Curll – a form of satiric derogation in itself. Many less respectable booksellers plied their trade in London, and also in Dublin. Swift could have chosen such individuals to do the necessary business in the "Verses." He opted rather to employ Lintot, and this can only have been because of the notoriety the publisher had acquired through the treatment he received at the hands of Pope. The Faulkner edition has a note, "Bernard Lintot. A Bookseller in London. *Vide* Mr. Pope's *Dunciad*." But as far as Swift went, Lintot had lived a blameless life.

Numerous allusions confirm the fact that the imagined milieu of the "Verses" lies, if not within the sound of Bow Bells, then certainly within the bills of mortality that defined the bounds of the capital. In his speech Lintot mentions the bookshops of Duck Lane, not far from Smithfield market. He alludes to "*Colley Cibber*'s Birth-day Poem," and to a poem on the queen by Stephen Duck (ll. 270–2). Swift had already written a quibbling epigram "On Stephen Duck, the Thresher, and favourite Poet" (1730): this despite the fact that the thresher poet had surfaced only after Swift last visited England. Significantly, though, Pope had tangled with Duck by the time the "Verses" were written. Subsequently Lintot goes on to mention the eccentric "orations" of the preacher John Henley, as well as the tracts of Thomas Woolston, a controversial figure who had become even more notorious as a result of his trial for blasphemy in 1729 (he appears among official documents on the same charge sheet as Curll). The next scene is set at a meeting of "A Club assembled at the *Rose*" (l. 300). Now Dublin had such a tavern, situated in Castle Street, and noted at this time for political clubs. But the surrounding context makes it clear that Swift has in mind the most famous establishment with this name, which stood on the corner of Brydges Street and Russell Street, just across from Drury Lane theatre. In the next paragraph we again encounter Colonel Charteris, on whom Swift very likely never set eyes. These passages lead up to the first genuinely Irish segment of the poem, describing the affair of Wood's Halfpence, and Swift's triumph in the role of Drapier. It includes the celebrated line, "Fair LIBERTY was all his Cry" (l. 347). But the interval does not last long: within a few lines we come to the section on Queen Anne's ministers, quoted earlier.

So we approach the conclusion of the "Verses," with its famous self-panegyric of the Dean. Here the references to Ireland grow more numerous and more explicit: they include an allusion to the sins of the Dublin parliament, and a final bitter comment on Swift's decision to leave his money to found St. Patrick's Hospital for mental patients. Even at this point, though, the protagonist leaves us in no doubt how we should regard his situation. In Ireland his friendships were "to few confin'd," as opposed to the warm relationships he had formerly enjoyed across the sea:

> In Exile with a steady Heart,
> He spent his Life's declining Part;
> Where, Folly, Pride, and Faction sway,
> Remote from ST. JOHN, POPE, and GAY. (ll. 431–4)

The word "remote" points to a trope of absence which runs through the whole text. Amongst its varied components, the poem offers a drama of enforced isolation.

IV

The "Epistle to a Lady," first published in 1733, adopts a less immediately personal approach than the other Market Hill items.[16] It begins with a speech in the voice of Anne Acheson (ll. 11–92), requesting Swift to abjure "That same paultry *Burlesque* Stile" he had previously adopted (l. 50). He replies with a kind of *nolo contendere* plea, admitting some of the charges she had made, but professing his inability to praise her in the heroic style she had allegedly desired.

Gradually the focus of attention shifts from Swift's elective affinities as a poet to the topics where he feels most at home in his native satiric vein – "Wicked Ministers of State" and "the Vices of a Court" (ll. 143 and 147). He again berates Walpole (a blank disguises the name in the original printing, but it is identifiable from the rhyme words "all pull"). His urge, like that of Demosthenes, is "in a Jest [to] spend his Rage" (l. 168). The more serious business of political critique can be left to others:

> Leave to D'ANVERS and his Mate,
> Maxims wise, to rule the State.
> POULTNEY deep, accomplish'd ST. JOHNS,
> Scourge the Villains with a Vengeance. (ll. 173–6)

Nicholas Amhurst had initiated the *Craftsman* in late 1726, under the pseudonym of Caleb D'Anvers. This opposition journal was thus a product of the period when Swift twice visited England and renewed acquaintance with his old friend Henry St. John, Viscount Bolingbroke. Briefly interrupted by Lady Acheson, the narrator launches into an even more direct assault on the leaders of the nation:

> If I treat you like —[a crowned head]
> You have cheap enough compounded.
> Can you put in higher Claims,
> Than the Owners of *St. J*[ame]*s*.
> You are not so great a Grievance
> As the Hirelings of *St.St*[ephen']*s*.
> You are of a lower Class
> Than my Friend Sir *R*[obert] *Br*[as]*s*. (ll. 239–46)

The royal court, the two houses of parliament, the prime minister himself – all face indictment.

"On Poetry: A Rapsody" (1733) stands alone, as the most sustained review of literary issues that Swift ever attempted in verse. Other poems include brief discourses on particular aspects of writing: and a few works, such as "Directions for a Birth-day Song," explore (often through parody) stylistic and generic questions. Among the early odes, we find in the poem addressed "To Congreve" a somewhat woolly and diffuse picture of the writer's condition. However, only the "Rapsody" provides a wide-ranging survey of the nature of authorship in the contemporary world.

Predictably, the author restricts the scope of his work to the world of letters as experienced in London. We soon hear of the sum "paid to the Poet Laureat, which Place was given to one *Cibber*, a Player," as a footnote has it (l. 54, n.) The post is "For ever fixt by Right Divine / . . . on *Grubstreet* Line" (ll. 57–8). We realize today that Dublin possessed its own Grub Street: a variety of writers worked for money in the city, some highly talented and some less so. Swift knew that well enough, and at times engaged with some of the lesser lights. But for the purposes of the poem, he ignores this fact, and limits his examples to the archetypal dunces of the original Grub Street. Once more Lintot serves as the designated bookseller to whom the hack author must send his work (ll. 105–16). After publication the scribbler should show himself at Will's, the famous literary haunt on the corner of Bow Street and Russell Street – although the coffee-house had attained its greatest prominence in the days of Dryden and of Swift's own earlier sojourn in London.

One passage, halfway through the "Rapsody," illustrates just how localized a focus the poet employs:

> Our Poets (you can never want 'em,
> Spread thro' *Augusta Trinobantum*)
> Computing by their Pecks of Coals,
> Amount to just Nine thousand Souls.
> These o'er their proper Districts govern,
> Of Wit and Humour, Judges sov'reign.
> In ev'ry Street a City-bard
> Rules, like an Alderman his Ward,
> His indisputed Rights extend
> Thro' all the Lane, from End to End. (ll. 279–88)

Here Swift reduces the province of letters to a few streets in a handful of precincts, charted by some municipal surveyor or political arithmetician. The rival bards contend for preeminence:

> Some famed for Numbers soft and smooth,
> By Lovers spoke in *Punch's* Booth.
> And some as justly Fame extols
> For lofty Lines in *Smithfield* Drols.
> *Bavius* in *Wapping* gains Renown,
> And *Mævius* reigns o'er *Kentish-Town*:
> *Tigellius* plac'd in *Phœbus'* Car,
> From *Ludgate* shines to *Temple-bar*. (ll. 297–304)

In this sequence Swift applies the names of Roman poetasters to a set of unknown English scribblers, dispersed around some of the less salubrious corners of the city. It is as though the Palio had been transferred from Siena to the streets to London, with a vigorous contest between the different wards. The last line quoted shows that Swift had paid close attention to the movements of the dunces, as Pope described them.

In the second half of the poem, Swift further anatomizes the ranks of dullness. The traditional line of descent incorporates Richard Flecknoe, Sir Robert Howard, and finally Sir Richard Blackmore. A casually dismissive paragraph (ll. 393–404) scalds Welsted, Fielding, Concanen, and "smart JEMMY MOOR" (l. 399) – James Moore Smythe, again. With the dubious exception of Concanen, these men had absolutely no links with Swift. They were Pope's enemies, and *The Dunciad* had given them almost all the literary notoriety they possessed. Equally, the political references toward the end of the poem fix on the usual targets – Walpole, the king and queen, the Prince of Wales ("Our eldest Hope, divine *Iülus*," l. 429). The text is littered with words familiar to the metropolitan world – "a *Statesman*, or a South-Sea *Jobber*" (l. 162); "A Duchess, or a Suburb-Wench" (l. 166); "Wise *Dennis*" (l. 250); "Great Poet of the *Hollow-Tree*" (an MP and poetaster, William Grimston, l. 376); and "*Woolston*" (l. 494). For the heroes of this piece, we must look to the "*Popes* and *Youngs* and *Gays*" (l. 467). Swift could have written the "Rapsody" if he had never set foot outside London.

v

It is easy to find reasons why Swift might have concentrated so heavily on England in his major poems of this period. But the emphasis remains striking, and the reasons will not explain everything away. We could argue that Swift was simply being realistic, in accepting the fact that the real center of power lay in London. Yet the Irish parliament, with its panoply of Anglo-Irish functionaries in administrative and legal roles, generated a distinct politics in Dublin, and Swift showed himself ready enough elsewhere to dabble in these domestic matters. "Hibernian Politicks, O Swift, thy doom," Pope had mourned (*Dunciad*, bk. 3, l. 327). The separate status of the Church of Ireland gave rise to specific ecclesiastical controversies, into which the Dean of St. Patrick's energetically threw himself. We might claim that London dominated the world of letters: but Dublin had a thriving book trade, not wholly dependent on the products of English publishing houses. If we observe, fairly enough, that Swift aimed to generalize his insights about politics and literature, this does not fully account for the wholesale evasion of local issues in the "Rapsody."

Of course, he naturally looked back to his days in the sun, and wistfully recalled his deep engagement with national affairs during "the gentle Reign of My Queen *Anne*", as Pope indulgently put it (*First Ode of the Fourth Book of Horace*, l. 4). Swift valued his friendship with some of the greatest writers of the age. But the Scriblerus group had long withered away: with Parnell dead by 1718, Lord Oxford by 1724, then Gay in 1732, and Arbuthnot in 1735. Efforts to revive the club had failed, and now Pope alone kept the flame alive. By the time Swift wrote his "Rapsody," the Scriblerian enterprise had become a distant dream. Of course, offshoots of its project to satirize abuses of learning had continued to appear, with *Peri Bathous*, *The Dunciad* – and not least *Gulliver's Travels*. Self-evidently, Pope's great mock-epic had mightily impressed Swift, with its conspicuous tribute to one labeled "Dean, Drapier, Bickersttaff, or Gulliver" (*Dunciad*, bk. 1, l. 18). We might feel sometimes that Swift was *too* impressed by Pope, too ready to grant primacy to his friend ("In POPE I cannot read a Line, / But with a Sigh, I wish it mine", "Verses on the Death of Dr. Swift," ll. 47–8). Perhaps he did so not just because he respected Pope's talents so much, but also because he envied the other man's favored situation on the edge of London and on the fringe of the political establishment.

It seems reasonable to seek out a deeper psychological pattern underlying the themes and methods Swift used in these poems – deeper urges than the obvious desire to reach a wide audience and the ambition to speak for more than a single nation. Somehow the inner life of the poetry springs from a compulsive desire to belong once again to the inner circle. The need Swift felt to swerve from Irish concerns has its roots in a refusal to accept the limitations of his condition. Possibly the stages of recovery mentioned earlier had stalled, and he had reverted to a state of denial. To write in his most powerful vein required him to erase the present and the recent past, and insinuate himself once more into the metropolitan spotlight that had once picked him out. If that meant borrowing Pope's quarrels and Pope's victims, so be it. The nature of exile, after all, lies in more than displacement itself: it implies an awareness of difference, of change, and at some level of loss. Swift confessedly looked on himself as an exile, and the greatest of his later poems expresses this feeling, both in the topics they address and in the matters to which they resolutely decline all attendance.

NOTES

1 This and all citations of Swift's poetry derive from *The Poems of Jonathan Swift*, ed. Harold Williams, 2nd edn., 3 vols. (Oxford: Clarendon, 1958).

2 A lesser product of these visits was "Dr. Sw – to Mr. P—e, While he was writing the *Dunciad*," a title which reflects Swift's willingness to make his own poems subservient to Pope's schedule.

3 "Pope evidently did not know that the Rev. Laurence Eusden, called here 'a drunken sot,' had died on 27 Sept. There may have been rumours to that

effect, but the earliest direct statement of his death in Lincolnshire noted is in *The Universal Spectator*, Oct. 31, 1730. *The Grub-street Journal*, 15 Oct., retailing a rumour from *The Daily Journal* that Stephen Duck will succeed as laureate, comments, 'I wonder at this article, since the bodily life of ... Eusden is at present in no danger' " (note on Pope to Gay, October 23, 1730, *Correspondence of Alexander Pope*, ed. George Sherburn, 5 vols. [Oxford: Clarendon Press, 1956], vol. III, p. 143).

4 This and all subsequent citations of Pope's poetry derive from the *Twickenham Edition of the Poems of Alexander Pope*, ed. John Butt *et al.*, 11 vols. (London: Methuen, 1939–69).

5 *The Prose Works of Alexander Pope*, ed. Rosemary Cowler, 2 vols. (Oxford: Basil Blackwell, 1986), vol. II, p. 203.

6 Pope, *Correspondence*, vol. I, p. 347.

7 Laurence Eusden, *An Ode for the Birthday, MDCCXXI. As it was sung before His Majesty* (London, 1721), p. 1.

8 Laurence Eusden, *An Epistle to the Noble, and Right Honourable Sir Robert Walpole* (London, 1726), pp. 6–7.

9 Laurence Eusden, *A Poem humbly inscribed to His Royal Highness Prince Frederic, on his Safe Arrival in Great Britain, and on his being created Prince of Wales* (London, 1729), p. 7.

10 Laurence Eusden, *The Ode for the Birth-day, MDCCXXIII. in English and Latin* (Cambridge, 1723), p. 6.

11 Laurence Eusden, *Poem on the Marriage of His Grace the Duke of Newcastle to the Right Honourable the Lady Henrietta Godolphin* (London, 1717), p. 6.

12 Jonathan Swift, *Correspondence*, ed. Harold Williams, corrected edn., 5 vols. (Oxford: Clarendon Press, 1965), vol. III, p. 278.

13 Around the same time Swift composed his verses "On Mr. *P*[*ultene*]*y* being put out of the Council," dealing with another little local difficulty in Walpole's domestic management. Soon afterwards came a short satirical "Character" of the prime minister, in a rapid triple meter uncharacteristic of Swift. The poem is accepted by Williams (Swift, *Poems*, vol. II, pp. 539–40) and the bulk of the evidence supports the ascription.

14 On Arthur Moore (*c.* 1666–1730), see the detailed account in *The House of Commons 1690–1715*, ed. Eveline Cruickshanks, Stuart Handley, and D. W. Hayton, 5 vols. (Cambridge: Cambridge University Press, for the History of Parliament Trust, 2002), vol. IV, pp. 905–15. He had died in much reduced circumstances about a year before Swift wrote the passage on his son.

15 David Foxon, *Pope and the Early Eighteenth-Century Book Trade*, ed. James McLaverty (Oxford: Clarendon, 1991), p. 102.

16 The poem may have been begun as early as 1728, although no clear evidence exists to show that it goes back this far. Addressed to Lady Acheson, it grew out of the Market Hill group of poems, and a few turns of phrase recall the earlier manner of writing. When Swift refers to "modern Dames" at line 67 (the epithet is italicized in Faulkner's edition) he obviously intends a sly recollection of *The Journal of a Modern Lady* (1729).

CHAPTER 9

"Verses on the Death of Dr. Swift": the interest of cuts and gaps

Howard Erskine-Hill

I

The circumstances by which this well-known poem of Swift came into print are highly unusual and serve to give the modern reader a good sense of what was regarded, in the 1730s, as acceptable, as dangerous, or as personally reprehensible.[1] In the early twenty-first century, when many readers have an easy and indulgent attitude towards eighteenth-century satire – in so far as they have an attitude to it at all – it is well worth rehearsing the strange twists and turns which attended the print publication of this famous poem.

First, Swift, writing to John Gay on December 1, 1731, says he has been "severall months writing near five hundred lines on a pleasant Subject, onely to tell what my friends and enemyes will say on me after I am dead. I shall finish it soon . . ."[2] In April 1733, J. Roberts published a poem, in London, entitled "The Life and Genuine Character of Doctor Swift. Written by Himself." It was dedicated to "Alexander Pope, Esq"; dated "Apr. 1 1733" and signed "L. M.," which Sir Harold Williams takes to be a joking reference to Matthew Pilkington, "Little Matthew," or, perhaps, "Laeticia Pilkington."[3] It is now thought that Swift himself may have written this ironical dedication. The poem itself, once considered spurious, is in twentieth-century scholarship generally regarded as genuine, and was, almost certainly, a try-on by Swift, to see how his near-500-line verse life – though it was nothing like so violent and dangerous as "Verses" – might take with the London readership of printed poems, and in this case by a famous name, though, as Swift professed to think, one now out of fashion. Williams notes that Mrs. Pilkington, the fifth Lord Orrery, and Faulkner (the publisher of the full-length "Verses" in 1739) all believed that "The Life and Genuine Character" was by Swift himself, and, for reasons which will appear, that Pope agreed, or at least "strongly suspected" Swiftian authorship.[4]

II

There now comes a remarkable episode. William King, the discreet but devoted Jacobite Principal of St. Mary Hall, Oxford, traveled to Ireland on legal and family business, in 1734, and became acquainted with Swift. Swift evidently entrusted to King a complete MS of "Verses." This is perhaps a surprising decision by Swift. His English friends – Arbuthnot, Pope, Bolingbroke, above all – might have been his first resort if he felt in need of advice about the literary merit, or the political dangerousness, of the poem. There may, however, be a pragmatic explanation. King, whom Swift seemed to like, was then in Dublin preparing to return to England. Neither Swift nor Pope trusted the English mails – indeed they joked in their letters about what Walpole's agents would find when their letters were opened, in search of conspiracy or treason.[5] Swift seems to have taken to King, and trusted him as a safe courier.

Further, King was already, and would in due course be still further, a distinguished Latin poet. The first two books of his Latin mock-heroic poem, *The Toast*, had been published in 1732.[6] King's Jacobitism may also, in some degree, have inclined Swift towards him. Swift himself, I dare say, was no committed Jacobite. But he was loyal to his old friends who had become Jacobite, albeit some transiently. The Duke of Ormond, who went into exile in the service of King James III after 1714, is honored in "Verses." Robert Harley, Earl of Oxford, also honored in "Verses," was in the Tower for some time, but eventually released. He intrigued on behalf of the exiled dynasty while imprisoned. Henry St. John, Viscount Bolingbroke, as is well known, was Secretary of State to King James during the 1715 Rebellion, but afterwards pulled out and purchased his reprieve. These are all different cases – but Swift remained loyal to all three. Swift probably felt some sympathy for King's position. There is a final consideration. King knew the political/Jacobite playing field in England pretty well. Swift himself may by this time have been beyond caring whether he got himself into more political trouble, but he is unlikely to have been unconcerned about getting other and more vulnerable people into difficulty. King's sensitive and up-to-date advice would be helpful here.

King then returned to England with the MS "Verses," nearly 500 lines, in his luggage. Leisurely, then, over the years, he appears to have consulted various people, but all we know is that Pope was consulted and Lord Orrery seems to have seen the MS. It would be surprising if Arbuthnot were not consulted, though he was, in these years, much concerned with the illness and death of his son.[7] "Verses" was eventually published in 1739 from Charles Bathurst. Swift's MS was, however, radically revised and reduced. The more dangerous parts of Swift's poem are asterisked or cut, and much that is cut is not quite perfectly filled out by passages from "The Life and Genuine Character," as has long ago been demonstrated.[8] King was evidently eager that Swift should be pleased at the apparently good reception accorded to the cut-down poem. When, however, it became clear to King that a version of Swift's MS had been published by Faulkner, Swift's Dublin publisher, and had thereafter begun to circulate in print in London, he is likely to have realized that Swift was offended, if not, perhaps, enraged. King, however, is explicit on his having consulted Pope about the revisions, and says the cuts were made in deference to Swift's English friends.[9] Thus far, we have only King's and Pope's reactions to Swift's MS. It is not absolutely clear that Pope is writing about Swift's MS to Lord Orrery on September 25, 1738, but it is probable:

I return the Verses you favor me with, the latter part of which is inferior to the beginning, the Character too dry, as well as too Vain in some respects, and in one or two particulars, not true.[10]

It was of course the "latter part" of Swift's MS which was censored and replaced by King and Pope. By "dry" Pope may have meant that he wanted more shading, more complexity. King himself picks up the question of vanity and that of literal truth. It certainly seems that King and Pope had been in consultation; the only odd thing is that Orrery should have sent Pope Swift's verses so late as 1738. But perhaps Orrery had been deliberately kept out of the loop until a late stage. He was, after all, a tepid correspondent of James III and son of the fourth Earl, a careful (and fortunate) survivor of the Jacobite Plot of 1723.[11]

    King was a candid and expansive correspondent on the subject of the revision of the MS of Swift's "Verses." To Swift himself, on January 23, 1738/9, King writes a full, frank, and apologetic letter:

That part of the poem which mentions the death of queen *Anne*, and so well describes the designs of the ministry, which succeeded upon the accession of the late king, I would likewise willingly have published, if I could have done it with safety: but I don't know whether the present worthy set of ministers would not have construed this passage into high treason, by aid of the doctrine of innuendos: at least a lawyer, whom I consulted on this occasion, gave me some reason to imagine this might be the case. I am in truth more cautious than I used to be, well knowing that my superiors look on me at present with a very evil eye, as I am the reputed author of the *Latin* poem I have sent you by the same gentleman [*Miltonis Epistola ad*

Pollionem, 1738] . . . for although that piece has escaped the state inquisition, by being written in a language that is at present not very well understood at court, and might perhaps need consult the attorney-general to explain, yet the scope of the poem and principal characters being well understood, the author hereafter expects no money, if he gives his enemies any grounds to attack him.[12]

This letter, not always quoted by those who have recently discussed the different printed versions of " 'Verses," makes a good deal pretty clear. Eighteenth-century readers of printed poems which alluded to living individuals were of course well used to filling in blanks and asterisks with the right proper names, and this practice is to be found necessary in both the Bathurst and the Faulkner versions of "Verses." The dashes, asterisks, cuts, and replacements found in the King/Pope Bathurst version go far beyond this well-known practice. While it is probably right to say that Swift loved to keep his readership guessing, and did so still in the Faulkner edition, the asterisks, cuts, and replacements in the Bathurst edition were motivated by political fear alone.[13] In this light Pope's idea that the latter part of Swift's poem might be "too dry, as well as too Vain," and King's fear "that the latter part of the poem might be thought by the public a little vain, if so much were said by himself of himself" may be thought, though possibly sincere critical reservations, really a cover for the fact that Swift's MS was too bold for them to dare to print.

III

At the same time, the King/Pope Bathurst edition of Swift's poem should not be derided. It is at least an intelligent compromise and a considerable advance upon Swift's try-on poem, "The Life and Genuine Character." It includes, ostentatiously asterisked indeed, the first allusion to the quite well-known episode of Swift's audience of the Princess Caroline, wife of the Hanoverian Prince of Wales, and of her broken promise to send Swift medals (more of this episode anon). Swift, in his deadly account of how other people would react to the news of his death, set the Countess of Suffolk and Caroline, now queen, at the head of his list of named individuals:

> From Dublin soon to London spread,
> 'Tis told at Court, the Dean is dead.
> And Lady _____ in the Spleen
> Runs laughing up to tell ***.
> ** so gracious, mild and good
> Cries, "Is he gone: 'tis time he shou'd."[14]

There follow six lines of asterisks and stars: an unusual typographical effect. Of this, King wrote to Swift: "There are some lines, indeed, which I omitted with a very ill will, and for no other reason but because I durst not insert them, I mean the story of the medals: however, that incident is pretty well known, and care has been taken that almost every reader may be able to supply the blanks." All this had been briefly alluded to in "The Life and Genuine Character," enigmatically disguised but still printing the word "Medals," and still further disguised by Swift in an un-Swiftian triplet.[15]

More may be said in favor of the expurgated Bathurst version. It includes the great crux of Swift's longer poem:

> The Time is not remote, when I
> Must by the Course of Nature dye...[16]

That, I venture to think, is the *fons et origo* of the whole original poem, slightly prefigured in "The Life and Genuine Character of Doctor Swift" (ll. 68–9).[17] Then, the Bathurst version includes the ladies' card-game after Swift's death, reminiscent as it is of Pope's game of ombre in *The Rape of the Lock* (1714). This is not done in the subtly allusive Popeian way, but in a way that is plainer and more Swiftian – yet, as in Pope, political allusions are still in place: "(I wish I knew what King to call.)..."[18] Further, the discussion of the dead Dean at "A Club assembled at the Rose" (a London tavern) is there in Bathurst, and gave King and Pope their idea of replacing Swift's long, defiant, final monologue, with a discussion of the dead Dean among several different voices, some hostile, some favorable. While the Rose tavern is not specified in "The Life and Genuine Character," that poem did give King and Pope a precedent in concluding with a discussion rather than a speech by Swift (albeit under the guise of a slight *persona*) "by himself of himself."

So much may be said in defense of the Bathurst version of "Verses," and we may conclude that if, in "The Life and Genuine Character," Swift had wished to draw his London readers into a knowing guessing game, King and Pope kept up the sport. Further, a good deal more of Swift's MS, some of it of the greatest importance, now came into print.

But of course, for anyone who had seen the complete MS and for Swift who wrote it, there were huge losses. Where is, for example, "Fair LIBERTY! was all his Cry;... / For her he boldly stood alone" (ll. 347, 349). Nowhere. As D. W. Jefferson wrote, in a 1971 volume edited by Claude Rawson, "for one moment, virtually in a single line, the poem soars and achieves great beauty... 'Fair LIBERTY was all his Cry.'"[19] One may add that in these famous lines Swift doesn't only soar to beauty. He shows courage.

Sometimes courage entails candor. If your friends and allies are in defeat, if all you have hoped for has come crashing down, you might keep a straight face and make quiet moves to survive the catastrophe. Quite possibly this was Swift's first *politique* response to what we might designate the Hanoverian revolution of 1714. Indeed he appears to have maintained this front in public for at least twelve years, if we except *The Drapier's Letters* (1724), and played the part of a pragmatic survivor. No doubt he was torn between strongly surviving ambition, on the one hand, and political and religious values now deep-rooted in his mentality. When he came to draft "Verses" Swift may have given up his ambition. At all events he comes clean about his reactions to 1714 in the long passage beginning "And, oh! how short are human Schemes!" (l. 371), which culminates in the lines:

> With Horror, Grief, Despair the Dean
> Beheld the dire destructive Scene:
> His Friends in Exile, or the Tower,
> Himself within the Frown of Power. (ll. 391–4)

This political narrative is of course part of the long concluding address in which Swift dramatizes his own self-defense. If that were to be held back then of course these climactic passages, and much else, had to be held back too. Among the rest was Swift's scathing attack on the Irish Parliament, lacking the imaginative power of the passages quoted above, but quite sufficient to have got Swift, his publisher, and anyone else involved, into serious trouble. No notes had been included in the Bathurst edition. They were included in the Faulkner edition, and almost amount to an additional narrative of Swift's life in prose. But, like much of "Verses" in Faulkner, many of the notes were subjected to cuts.[20]

IV

While the Bathurst edition of "Verses" survived remarkably long in editions and anthologies, nobody now doubts that Faulkner's Dublin edition is nearer to what Swift wanted. But Faulkner too printed with cuts and asterisks, as S. E. Karian notes, and modern readers of Swift's poem must appreciate that the best modern texts are based on the admirable and widely researched reconstruction by Sir Harold Williams in *The Poems of Jonathan Swift* (1937).[21] Nobody can be but grateful for

Williams's reconstruction. But, as Karian observes, nobody wishing to read Swift's poem as it was during Swift's lifetime, or even long after, could have read in print anything like Williams's reconstructed text. We now have the names and the lines. The eighteenth-century reader was still guessing, though for the most part, probably, in an intelligent and informed way.

With all this substructure of publishing history before us, most of it well known but essential to rehearse, we may now turn to the Faulkner-based versions of "Verses" for a critical overview. Modern criticism of "Verses," taking too seriously, perhaps, Pope's evident view that the poem is uneven, has tended to evaluate it in a somewhat cherry-picking way. The late Irvin Ehrenpreis, in volume III of his biography, singles out the lines on the grief of Pope, Gay, and Arbuthnot at Swift's death as one of the best things, and then the ladies' card-playing at quadrille. He avers that "the superiority of the *Verses* to the *Life* demonstrates again that for Swift the total structure of a poem . . . does less to establish its merits than the separate things within it."[22] On the other hand, Swift's resistance to the Bathurst cuts and infillings suggests that he did not think that "Verses" was just a loosely linked chain of good things. Above all, he wanted to keep the long, aggressive, confessional conclusion.

This suggests, at least, that Swift thought "Verses" had a coherent trajectory. It moves, inexorably, from Rochefoucault's somewhat secular generalizations about the prevalence of self-love over friendship or respect, to the particular case of Swift, before and after his anticipated death. This move is then from general to personal, but as Swift introduces his own life he does not forget the opening maxims, which are now given substance and edge by the individual example. As Swift's narrative passes through the event of his own imagined death the maxims gather a satirical color. The matter of reputation and memory now comes to the fore. This theme strongly and dramatically (for those who could interpret the asterisks) emerges in the episode of Princess Caroline, Swift, and the medals. It carries on, going down the hierarchy, with comments by Sir Robert Walpole and Francis Charteris, touches on the varying grief of Pope, Gay, Arbuthnot, and Bolingbroke, comes to the ladies' comments on Swift's death at the game at quadrille, coming then to the truly mortifying episode of the visit of the plainly out-of-fashion "Country Squire" to Lintot's bookshop to enquire for "SWIFT in Verse and Prose." The shop has no Swift, though otherwise filled with fashionable materials. Then comes the "Club assembled at the *Rose*" (l. 300) where the "indifferent" and "impartial" supporter, or *persona* of Swift himself, takes up the defense, abandoned apparently by the world, and commands the long final passage of the poem.

It may well be seen, and indeed heard, what a remarkable sequence of voices composes Swift's poem. The generalizing maxims of Rochefoucault give way to Swift's personal narrative of his probable future, but just before his expected death two anonymous voices – " 'How is the Dean? He's just alive'" (l. 148) – herald a positive crowd of voices, named and unnamed, which compose the world's ingratitude to or careless neglect of Swift's fierce and proud egoism. His defending *persona* then takes over the poem, concluding it with a characteristically Swiftian black joke: the bequest for a madhouse to a kingdom which certainly needed one. So much for the dramatic and eloquent trajectory of Swift's poem.

We may now take a second and closer look at three of the more salient passages in Swift's poem. The first is what King called "the story of the medals": Swift and the Princess Caroline. When Swift revisited England in 1726 the princess was evidently curious to meet him. She sent him several invitations, no doubt shading into polite commands, which, doubtless out of pride and suspicion, Swift at first ignored. At length he obeyed and apparently found her gracious. On his return to Ireland he sent, through Mrs. Howard, later Countess of Suffolk, a small sample of Irish poplin, which he intended Mrs. Howard should show the princess. The princess admired it, and sent through Mrs. Howard a generous order, of course promising to pay for it. Swift was proud and refused payment – only would he accept a gift of a medal, or medals, from the princess, which had been apparently been suggested by her before the Irish poplin was shown her or ordered. But, for whatever reason, the medals were never sent.[23]

Swift had had two motives in all this. Proud as he was, he hoped for the patronage of the princess to secure him what, after the 1726 visit, he despaired of getting from Walpole, an English preferment. Then he hoped that a commission from the princess would help popularize Irish textiles. Swift seems to have thought well of the princess until November 1730, when a letter to Gay marked his change of heart.[24]

What were the medals the princess had seemed to promise? Were they ancient medals, such as Pope had written about in his epistle *To Addison*? If so enquiry is pretty hopeless, the scope is so large, and the content of the princess's talk with Swift unrecorded. There is, however, another possibility. A medallic war was being waged between the exiled Stuart kings and the *de facto* Hanoverian line. William King, in 1720/1, had shown Hearne the beautiful medal by Otto Hamerani which celebrated

Princess Clementina Sobieska's escape from Innsbruck to become the bride of James III in Italy. Part of the legend ran: "Fortunam. Causamque. Sequor. MDCCXIX."[25] Subsequently the exiled Stuart court ordered medals to be struck to mark the births of the two royal princes, Charles Edward (1720) and Henry Benedict (1724).[26] Did the princess promise to give Swift – a significant political figure with a suspicious past from a Hanoverian point of view – medals promoting the new Hanoverian dynasty? It would have been a delicate gesture, and perhaps worthy of Caroline at her best. Swift would not have been required to sign up to the new regime, but acceptance of Hanoverian medals by Swift would have been a graceful signal.

If so – and of course this is still all hypothesis – there are several Hanoverian medals which the princess might have had in mind. The medal struck by George I after the 1715 Rebellion, called the Act of Grace and bearing the legend "Clementia Augusti," might have encouraged a supposedly disaffected political writer. The medal of the Princess Caroline, 1718, bearing the legend "*Rosa sine spina*" (the rose without a thorn), is another good possibility.[27] What may further support the hypothesis that the princess had been promising (and forgetting, or having second thoughts about) Hanoverian medals is the letter from Swift to Mrs. Howard, November 21, 1730, in which he now writes: "I will receive no medal from Her Majesty [i.e. Caroline, now queen]" but would accept a half-length portrait of her "drawn by Jervas; and if he takes it from another original; the Queen shall sit at least twice for him to touch it up."[28] Swift, on the brink of bitter disappointment, was here raising the stakes. An image of Caroline seemed still in question. Portraits of royalty were potent symbols. Mrs. Charles Caesar cherished a well-concealed portrait of James III. Swift might have boasted one of Queen Caroline. It is likely, however, that Walpole, or even George II, advised Caroline to give up the idea. Swift's riposte to all this, completed by 1734 if not earlier, is a savage counter-attack:

> "He's dead you say; why let him rot;
> I'm glad the Medals were forgot.
> I promis'd them, I own; but when?
> I only was the Princess then;
> But now as Consort of the King,
> You know 'tis quite a different Thing." (ll. 183–8)

So much for the good faith of crowned royalty. No wonder it had to be asterisked.

V

I want now to touch again briefly on the episode of the "Country Squire" at Lintot's bookshop, enquiring after Swift's works:

> Says *Lintot*, "I have heard the Name." (l. 255)

Can there be a more exquisite piece of self-humiliation in all English poetry? The bookshop is innocent of any Swift, but Lintot gives a long list of the currently fashionable and acceptable, predictable enough. This ends, however, with Swift's ironical polemic against "*Wolston's* Tracts" (ll. 281–98). Swift may have had two writers in mind, Thomas Woolston (1670–1733) and William Wollaston (1660–1724), each an extreme theological free-thinker. King may have suspected that Swift confused the two,[29] but recent scholarship has argued tenaciously for Woolston. There is a third possibility, that "Wolston" is a satiric compound figure, the similarity of name and viewpoint indicating not just one shocking example, but a dismaying trend. Lintot's enthusiastic summary says it all:

> "He doth an Honour to his Gown,
> By bravely running *Priest-craft* down:
> He shews, as sure as God's in *Gloc'ster*,
> That *Jesus* was a Grand Imposter:
> That all his Miracles were Cheats,
> Perform'd as Juglers do their Feats:
> The Church had never such a Writer:
> A Shame, he hath not got a Mitre!" (ll. 291–8)

The shades of Swift's *Argument against Abolishing Christianity* (1708) seem to gather about these lines. The Church, with all its promotions and preferments, is of course indispensable. But surely the Church might be kept up without the subtle and demanding Christian creed? At all events, these lines, spoken by Lintot, are here in "Verses" to warn of a most fundamental sell-out – not just a literary distinction, or political bravery, or loyalty to the crown, but of the extraordinary example of Christ as formulated finally by Athanasius in its full physical and metaphysical complexity. Lintot's encomium alerts us to an otherwise understated Christian vein in "Verses" and may suggest that the trajectory of Swift's poem crosses, transiently perhaps, the well-known territory of the Christian *ars moriendi* tradition. Preparation for death and the making of a good death are at the heart of this teaching and literature, and we may want to look at Swift's text in this light. Swift, I would argue, does not conform to its exemplary approaches, but, equally, he does not ignore them. His first announcement of the subject of death seems to me dignified, plain, understated, and secular: "The Time is not remote, when I / Must by the Course of Nature dye" (ll. 73–4). The death has of course been flagged up in the title of "Verses." When the Dean is "just alive," "Now the departing Prayer is read" (ll. 148–9). In fact there is in the Book of Common Prayer of the Church of England no prayer specifically so designated: it is likely that the prayer, taken from St. John 5:24, in the Service for the Visitation of the Sick, is intended. Jeremy Taylor, in his *Rule and Exercises of Holy Dying* (1650–1), includes several such prayers for the sick who pass through death to life, at the end of his chapter on the visitation of the sick.[30]

There are further reminders of the *ars moriendi* tradition. Thus: " 'O, may we all for Death prepare!' " (l. 153). That this line is a mere mantra, a fossil in the stone, is shown by the rest of the couplet: " 'What has he left? And who's his Heir?' " (l. 154). This does not mean, however, that the first line does not convey something important to the reader. A similar effect is to be observed in the ladies' game at quadrille:

> "The Dean is dead, (*and what is Trumps?*)
> Then Lord have Mercy on his Soul.
> (Ladies I'll venture for the *Vole.*)" (ll. 228–30)

Such collocations tell the reader that Swift thinks piety has become auto-matic, and thus remind of what has been lost in such automatic piety.

Jeremy Taylor, royalist in the mid-seventeenth-century civil war, was after the Restoration Bishop of Down and Connor, later of Dromore, in Ireland. According to Faulkner's catalogue of Swift's library Swift owned six of Taylor's works, including his *Sermons* (1651), but not including the *Holy Living and Holy Dying*.[31] It is most improbable that Swift did not know this best-selling religious classic by an episcopalian Irish bishop. It was not among Swift's more learned books, perhaps, because he used it in his regular devotions. It is not my purpose here to argue for verbal debts on Swift's part to Taylor's *Holy Dying* but, rather, that to read "Verses" against a background of Taylor throws into relief some ways in which Swift remains loyal to Taylor's tradition, and some ways in which he makes a new *démarche*.

Taylor opens *Holy Dying* on a strikingly satirical note. He is not, of course irreligious, but he writes about humanity rather with scorn than with love:

A Man is a bubble. . .All the world is a Storm, and Men rise up in their several generations like Bubbles descending, *a Jove pluvio*, from God and the dew of Heaven, from a tear and drop of Man, from Nature and Providence: and some of these instantly sink into the deluge of their first parent, and are hidden in a sheet of water, having had no other business in the world, but to be born, that they might be able to die: others float up and down two or three turns, and suddenly disappear, and give their place to others: and they that live longest upon the face of the waters are in perpetual motion, restless and uneasie, and being crushed with a great drop of cloud sink into flatness and a froth; the change not being great, it being hardly possible it should be more a nothing than it was before. So is every man: He is born in vanity and sin.[32]

While Taylor is writing about the whole human condition, the restless, ambitious, hopeless expectations of talented people in turbulent times are well represented here. Swift never found, as Taylor did after 1660, a revolution which threw him into a bishopric. Taylor, however, did not foresee the change of state when he wrote the first paragraph of *Holy Dying*. A few other precepts from Taylor may briefly be recited here. *"He that would willingly be fearless of Death must learn to despise the world;* He must neither love anything passionately, nor be proud of any circumstance of his life."[33] Again: "That a man cannot think too meanly of himself, but very easily he may think too high."[34] Such advice might have been valuable to Swift. Very likely he knew that it was. But something rebellious and complex prompted him to a divergent projection of his own death.

Here we may recall two cases of the deaths of famous intellectuals, one earlier, and one later, than the date of the composition of Swift's poem. First, there is the case of Addison on his deathbed, as recounted by Samuel Johnson in *The Lives of the Poets*. Johnson did justice to Addison's literary talent, but probably did not much admire his personal or political life. At all events, when Addison knew he was dying, he sent for his stepson, the young Earl of Warwick, whom he had often and unsuccessfully reproved for "his irregular life, and perhaps [for his] loose opinions." "I have sent for you," said Addison, "that you may see how a Christian can die."[35] One doesn't find much of that note in Swift's account of his own anticipated death. Then there is the case of Voltaire, as brilliantly set forth by John McManners. Voltaire wished his death to be conventional in all outward forms. He wished to die and be buried according to the religious procedures and forms of his native France, and took a good deal of care to make sure that this could not be challenged in law. There was, however, one thing his confessor, the abbé Gaultier, kept asking. Gaultier passed over Voltaire's failure to disavow his writings, and did not press him to acknowledge Revelation. McManners remarks that Voltaire was a Catholic but not a Christian. After many courteous evasions on Voltaire's part, the abbé asked Voltaire, on his very deathbed: "do you recognize the divinity of Jesus Christ?" Voltaire's reply, so compassionately recounted by

McManners, was: "Laissez-moi mourir en paix."[36] What can we think of Swift in the light of Taylor, Addison, and Voltaire?

First, it is quite likely that Swift, in his blackest moments, thought that his own life, at least, had been "*a bubble*": a cheat; the metaphor had a long, special life in the earlier eighteenth century. Taylor advocated humility, but humility came to Swift in special, complicated ways. Then there was the question of "vanity" which even his friend King felt evident in the long conclusion of Swift's poem. I shall suggest that, as Swift reviewed his life and anticipated his death, humility and vanity needed one another. Then there is the example of Addison. Addison may have been sincere in his bit of pious play-acting. One may feel a bit suspicious, but one cannot judge. One thing is sure: when Swift in "Verses" anticipated his own death he expressed not even the merest hope, as many might have done, that he would display such an exemplary example. And then Voltaire. Of course to compare a modern historian's account of the death of an eighteenth-century intellectual with an earlier eighteenth-century intellectual's poetic vision of his own death is a hazardous matter. Still, one thing seems clear: Swift does not seem to evade the notion that Jesus was divine. At least he affirms, by the reverse of his irony against Lintot, that all Jesus' miracles were the real thing, and nothing else in "Verses," so far as I can see, pulls Swift away from this crux.

VI

We must now return, for the last time, to the long concluding passage of "Verses," censored by Pope and King. Pope and King are not, I think, entirely to blame. By the time the Bathurst edition of "Verses" had been published, in 1739, both Pope and King – King in the faint disguise of Latin, Pope in plain English – had attacked Walpole and the England of the 1730s. Their political caution was understandable; neither writer was a coward. But what may have been galling to Swift is that his own invocation to "LIBERTY" in "Verses," so long withheld and finally denied print by Pope and King, may have been the inspiration for King's and Pope's courageous attacks upon the times.

It is reflections of this kind which pull one back to the notion of Swift's radically different and highly individualized *ars moriendi* in "Verses." To say that you are nothing, a mere bubble on the stormy seas of life, by comparison with the love of God and the heroic passion of Christ upon the cross for the sake of mankind is one thing, and unlikely to have been denied by Swift. But to deny that he had genius, that he had achieved some remarkable things with his political pen, surely would be, almost, to be guilty of the automatic mantra of "O, may we all for Death prepare!" (l. 153). Swift's *ars moriendi*, in so far as the term may be tentatively applied, would not accept a blanket condemnation of the vanity of mankind (including, of course, himself) but would accept talent having been bestowed (remember the New Testament parable of the talents) and would acknowledge that, on one or two occasions, even in defeat and disappointment, the talent had been well used. Swift is, however, most impressive when he admits defeat. Leading up to the lines already quoted (ll. 391–4) are others, extraordinary to have been intended for print in the 1730s:

> "AND, oh. how short are human Schemes!
> Here ended all our golden Dreams.
> What ST. JOHN's Skill in State Affairs,
> What ORMOND's *Valour*, OXFORD's Cares,
> To save their sinking Country lent,
> Was all destroy'd by one Event.
> Too soon that precious Life was ended,
> On which alone, our Weal depended.
> When up a dangerous Faction starts,
> With Wrath and Vengeance in their Hearts:
> By solemn League and Cov'nant bound,
> To ruin, slaughter, and confound;
> To turn Religion to a Fable,
> And make the Government a *Babel*:
> Pervert the Law, disgrace the Gown,
> Corrupt the Senate, rob the Crown;
> To sacrifice old *England*'s Glory,
> And make her infamous in Story.
> When such a Tempest shook the Land,
> How could unguarded Virtue stand?" (ll. 311–90)

We must still remember Faulkner's (and perhaps Swift's) cuts. In this passage "Senate," "Crown," and "*England*" are blanked by dashes, as is most of Swift's explanatory and historical footnote. A poet expressing bitter political disappointment still had to keep up his guard, as did his publisher. There is then something remarkable that a poem so fraught with knowledge of the vanity of human wishes should still have originally censored itself in print. But "Verses on the Death of Dr. Swift" is not only a great but (so far as I know) a unique poem. "*A Man is a bubble*. . . All the world is a Storm." Swift's poem well exemplifies Taylor's generalized piety in his *Holy Dying*. Swift's *ars moriendi*, however, is personal and dramatic, rather than pious and universal. His Christian affirmations are made with so much sarcasm and grief that it is too easy for the modern reader simply to categorize them as satire. Swift, talented, proud, ambitious – perhaps it is right to remember Wolsley in Johnson's *The Vanity of Human Wishes* – made his holy dying penitence in two new ways. First, he did not write a poem which absorbed himself into the generality of mankind, bubbled, cheated, vain, misled. Was he vain, as King evidently thought? Or did he know that, as in the parable of the talents (Luke 19:12–26), it would be no true humility to abjure what God had given him? Swift's *ars moriendi* – and I think it truly falls, theologically speaking, between Taylor and Voltaire – is so remarkable because he abases his proud and aggressive spirit. He acknowledges that, talented and remarkable as he was, the revolution of 1714 had defeated him and had, as it were, left him to perish on the shore. He acknowledges that, despite the talents God gave him, of which he was proud (sometimes, perhaps, according to King, vain), he had failed. He acknowledges that he will not be remembered. He admits that even his famous political and literary victory in his *Drapier's Letters* will be unloaded onto the second-hand bookseller in Duck Lane. He will be forgotten, he thinks. This is no insignificant act of humility. One may also note that *A Tale of a Tub* and *Gulliver's Travels*, which Swift almost certainly thought his greatest works, are not mentioned in "Verses." The penitence of his *ars moriendi*, unusual as it is, is to confront and dramatize a vision in which for all his talent, all his opportunities, he would be quite forgotten.

NOTES

1   The present essay has been written as a companion-piece to an earlier essay on the verse of Swift, "Swift's 'Knack at Rhyme'," in *Sustaining Literature: Essays on Literature, History, and Culture, 1500–1800, Commemorating the Life and Work of Simon Varey*, ed. Greg Clingham (Cranbury, NJ: Associated University Presses, 2007), pp. 137–52. My subtitle acknowledges the recent work of Stephen E. Karian, "Reading the Material Text of Swift's 'Verses on the Death of Dr. Swift'," *Studies in English Literature*, 41 (2006), 515–41. My argument tends to a different goal from his, but I have profited greatly from his work. I also wish to acknowledge the valuable advice of Professor Jonathan Clark, Professor Richard McCabe, Dr. Valerie Rumbold, Mr. Richard Sharp, and Professor David Womersley.

2   *Correspondence of Jonathan Swift*, ed. Harold Williams, 5 vols. (Oxford: Clarendon Press, 1965), vol. II, p. 506.

3   *The Poems of Jonathan Swift*, 2nd edn., ed. Harold Williams, 3 vols. (Oxford: Oxford University Press, 1958), vol. II, p. 571. All subsequent citations of Swift's poetry derive from this edition. I draw my quotations from Williams,

rather than the good recent edition of Pat Rogers, so as to preserve the Swift/Faulkner "accidentals."

4 *Poems of Jonathan Swift*, vol. II, pp. 542–3.

5 Swift, *Correspondence*, vol. III, p. 418. See also *The Correspondence of Alexander Pope*, ed. George Sherburn, 5 vols. (Oxford: Clarendon Press, 1956), vol. III, pp. 432–3; vol. IV, p. 456.

6 David Greenwood, *William King: Tory and Jacobite* (Oxford: Clarendon Press, 1964), p. 50.

7 Swift, *Correspondence*, vol. V, pp. 136–7; Sherburn, *Correspondence of Pope*, vol. IV, p. 130 (Pope to Lord Orrery, September 25, 1738).

8 *Poems of Jonathan Swift*, vol. II, pp. 541, 551–2.

9 Swift, *Correspondence*, vol. V, pp. 136–7.

10 Sherburn, *Correspondence of Pope*, vol. IV, p. 130

11 Orrery's correspondence with the exiled court is plentifully found in the Royal Archives (Stuart MSS), Windsor Castle, in which each volume is prefaced by a list of chief correspondents. For Orrery's father, the fourth Earl, see Eveline Cruikshanks and Howard Erskine-Hill, *The Atterbury Plot* (Basingstoke: Palgrave, 2004), in which he is well indexed.

12 Swift, *Correspondence*, vol. V, pp. 135–6.

13 As appears from the letter just cited.

14 "Verses on the Death of Dr. Swift. Written by Himself: Nov. 1731." (London: Printed for C. Bathurst...MDCCXXXIX), p. 9. Hereafter referred to as "Bathurst Verses." See also Swift, *Correspondence*, vol. V, p. 135.

15 *Poems of Jonathan Swift*, vol. II, p. 547. See ll. 90–2.

16 "Bathurst Verses," p. 4.

17 It is less well expressed in the Bathurst edition.

18 "Bathurst Verses," p. 11.

19 D. W. Jefferson, "The Poetry of Age," in *Focus: Swift*, ed. Claude Rawson (London: Sphere, 1971), p. 133.

20 As Karian points out in "Reading the Material Text," p. 522. See also *Poems of Jonathan Swift*, vol. II, pp. 552–3.

21 *Poems of Jonathan Swift*, vol. II, pp. 551–72.

22 Irvin Ehrenpreis, *Swift: The Man, His Works, and the Age* (London: Methuen, 1983), p. 713.

23 See *Poems of Jonathan Swift*, vol. II, p. 559, for Swift's (reconstructed) footnote account of this episode, asterisked in Faulkner's earlier editions.

24 Swift, *Correspondence*, vol. III, p. 418.

25 Greenwood, *William King*, pp. 21–2.

26 See Noel Woolf, *The Medallic Record of the Jacobite Movement* (London: Spink, 1988), item 43, p. 87. This medal was struck at the end of 1731. See too Woolf, *Medallic Record*, item 46 1a and 1b, p. 89. This latter medal was probably struck in 1737.

27 Edward Hawkins, *Medallic Illustrations of the History of Great Britain and Ireland*, 2 vols. (London, 1885), vol. II, item 36 and item 47. See also Woolf, *Medallic Record*, item 34, 1a, p. 75.

28 Swift, *Correspondence*, vol. III, p. 423.
29 Swift, *Correspondence*, vol. V, p. 140 (King to Mrs. Whiteway, March 6, 1738/
   9). See Pat Rogers (ed.), *The Poems of Jonathan Swift* (New Haven and
   London: Yale University Press, 1983), p. 853.
30 Jeremy Taylor, *The Rule and Exercises of Holy Dying*, 13th edn. (London,
   1682), chapter 5, pp. 439–41. 1682 was not, perhaps, an unreasonable date for
   the precocious young Swift, though he could have found this famous work
   almost anywhere.
31 Faulkner's *A Catalogue of Books, the Library of the late Rev. Dr. Swift* (Dublin,
   1745).
32 Taylor, *Holy Dying*, p. 1.
33 Taylor, *Holy Dying*, p. 103.
34 Taylor, *Holy Dying*, p. 231.
35 Samuel Johnson, *The Lives of the Most Eminent English Poets*, ed. Roger
   Lonsdale, 4 vols. (Oxford: Clarendon Press, 2006), vol. III, pp. 19, 261, n. 101,
   and see Horace Walpole's skeptical remarks.
36 John McManners, *Death and the Enlightenment* (Oxford: Clarendon Press,
   1981), pp. 266–9.

CHAPTER 10

Naming and shaming in the poetry of Pope and Swift, 1726–1745

James McLaverty

The relationship between Swift and Pope developed from the warmest friendship during Swift's visit to England in the spring and summer of 1726 to an alliance speckled with antagonism in the 1730s, an antagonism somewhat veiled by the publication of their correspondence as a record of enduring friendship in 1741. Representative of a tendency to disagree on fundamental issues of authorship is their attitude to naming in satire.[1] By the late 1730s Pope had developed a clear point of view, best represented by Dialogue II, *One Thousand Seven Hundred and Thirty Eight* (later called the *Epilogue to the Satires*), published on July 18, 1738. In the Dialogue, Pope's friend makes the case against naming, only to find it sharply rejected:

> *F.* Yet none but you by Name the Guilty lash;
> Ev'n *Guthry* saves half *Newgate* by a Dash.
> Spare then the Person, and expose the Vice.
> *P.* How Sir! Not damn the Sharper, but the Dice? (ll. 10–13)[2]

Guthry, as Pope explains in a note, was the Ordinary of Newgate, who published the memoirs of malefactors. Pope's punishments, as he explains in a famous passage in this poem, are comparable to those of the law:

> Yes, I am proud; I must be proud to see
> Men not afraid of God, afraid of me:
> Safe from the Bar, the Pulpit, and the Throne,
> Yet touch'd and sham'd by *Ridicule* alone. (ll. 208–11)

The corrective nature of such satire is dependent on the naming, or at least the identification, of its victim.

A view counterbalancing Pope's, though one much more equivocal in status than any position adopted by "P." in one of Pope's dialogues, is to be found in Swift's "Verses on the Death of Dr. Swift," which Swift seems to have sent off for publication late in 1738. At the end of the poem an "impartial" speaker at the Rose Tavern draws a character of the Dean. The reliability of the speaker and the nature of any irony present in the portrait are problematic, but, as the speaker moves towards the conclusion of his panegyric, a clear evaluation of Swift's satiric practice is put forward:

> "PERHAPS I may allow the Dean
> Had too much Satyr in his Vein;
> And seem'd determin'd not to starve it,
> Because no Age could more deserve it.
> Yet, Malice never was his Aim;
> He lash'd the Vice but spar'd the Name.
> No Individual could resent,
> Where Thousands equally were meant." (ll. 455–62)[3]

The advocacy of general satire is followed by other customary defences that are also problematic in relation to Swift (only remediable faults are criticized; ugliness and stupidity are mocked only when they are accompanied by affectation), but it is the claim that Swift had "spar'd the Name" that stands out and disturbed his contemporaries, including Pope. Swift had originally sent his poem to be published in London by Dr. William King, Principal of St. Mary Hall, Oxford, who, in consultation with Pope, had made many excisions and insertions. One of the excisions was this section. Writing to Swift's cousin Martha Whiteway, King explained that the lines "might be liable to some objection, and were not, strictly speaking, a just part of his character; because several persons have been lashed by name, a *Bettesworth*, and in this poem, *Charteris* and *Whitshed*, and for my part, I do not think, or ever shall think, that it is an imputation on a satirist to lash an infamous fellow by name."[4] But Swift was clearly unmoved by such reflections; when he speedily reprinted the poem through the services of William Faulkner in Dublin, the lines were restored. Although it is important to leave room for a playfulness in Swift's presentation of his Rose Tavern eulogist, I suspect he wished to endorse what was said. In 1726 he and Pope had shared a negative view of the role of naming in satire, but they responded to the social and political pressures on their writing in the following years in different ways. Pope had changed his mind and gone over to the other side; Swift had retained his position but with complex reservations. In this essay I want to trace these developments with special regard to the volumes of *Works* they produced in 1735, which raised acutely the difficulty of what they, in their own names, were prepared to say about named others.

SWIFT–POPE *MISCELLANIES*

The four volumes of Swift–Pope *Miscellanies* (1727–32) that emerged
from collaboration in the summer of 1726 have a preface that focuses on
the issue of naming. The publication of the volumes is justified, the
authors say, because a number of pieces have slipped into print without
their permission, and the printing of these pieces has led to others being
attributed to them: that is, to their own names being used improperly.
The pieces that they have written will, therefore, be acknowledged by
publication in this volume, but a problem they face is the treatment of the
people they have satirized:

We are sorry for the Satire interspersed in some of these Pieces, upon a few People,
from whom the highest Provocations have been received, and who by their
Conduct since have shewn that they have not yet forgiven us the Wrong They did.
It is a very unlucky Circumstance, to be obliged to retaliate the Injuries of such
Authors, whose Works are so soon forgotten, that we are in danger already of
appearing the first Aggressors. It is to be lamented, that *Virgil* let pass a Line, which
told Posterity he had two Enemies called *Bavius* and *Mævius*. The wisest Way is
not once to name them, but (as the Madman advised the Gentleman, who told
him he wore a Sword to kill his Enemies) *to let them alone, and they will die of
themselves.* And according to this Rule we have acted throughout all those Writings
which we design'd for the Press: But in these, the Publication whereof was not
owing to our Folly but that of others, the Omission of the Names was not in our
Power . . . In regard to two Persons only, we wish our Raillery, though ever so
tender, or Resentment, though ever so just, had not been indulged. We speak of
Sir *John Vanbrugh*, who was a Man of Wit, and of Honour; and of Mr. *Addison*,
whose Name deserves all Respect from every Lover of Learning.[5]

It is reasonable to assume that on such an important matter there was
agreement between Pope and Swift, though I suspect Pope was responsible
for the actual drafting. For the time being we are presented with something
like solid ground. As a general principle, personal satire is allowable because
some people are unworthy (unlike Vanbrugh and Addison) and they are
also aggressors. But naming is undesirable, even though illicit publication
has led to unintentional naming. You should not name people in your
deliberate and acknowledged publications. The "Rule," which has been
observed in writings designed for the press, is to leave the offenders
unnamed. Even this rule leaves a large doubtful area for exploration. It is
permissible, presumably, to name someone in material moving only within
your own private circle, through manuscript circulation, because otherwise
the name could never escape. And the question left hanging in the air is:
What if you're publishing anonymously? What if your lines are published

because you leak them or are willing to have them leaked? And what if you stop short of direct naming by using a nickname, or a fictitious name, or a precise reference? The decision to single out Vanbrugh and Addison for regret suggests that two separate arguments may be blurred together in the passage, one from prudence and one from morality. It is imprudent to name fools and bad writers; it is wrong to name men of worth unfavorably. This distinction became important in the preparation of *The Dunciad*.

THE DUNCIAD

Swift, surprisingly in the light of his views so far, was concerned that *The Dunciad* should name its dunces. His position was consistent and unequivocal. In a letter to Gay of February 26, 1728, he asks, "Why does not Mr Pope publish his dullness, the rogues he mawles will dy of themselves in peace, and so will his friends, and so there will be neither punishment nor reward."[6] His sentiments echo, but with an inverted conclusion, the preface to the *Miscellanies* (enemies will die, even if you leave them alone), while the support for rewards and punishments chimes in with his support for such a system of justice in Lilliput.[7] A subsequent letter to Pope of July 16, 1728 shows he has been reflecting on the precise annotation required:

I have often run over the Dunciad in an Irish edition (I suppose full of faults) which a gentleman sent me. The notes I could wish to be very large, in what relates to the persons concern'd; for I have long observ'd that twenty miles from London no body understands hints, initial letters, or town-facts and passages; and in a few years not even those who live in London. I would have the names of those scriblers printed indexically at the beginning or end of the Poem, with an account of their works, for the reader to refer to. I would have all the Parodies (as they are call'd) referred to the author they imitate . . . How it passes in Dublin I know not yet; but I am sure it will be a great disadvantage to the poem, that the persons and facts will not be understood, till an explanation comes out, and a very full one. I imagine it is not to be published till towards winter, when folks begin to gather in town. Again I insist, you must have your Asterisks fill'd up with some real names of real Dunces.[8]

He later asks whether the commentator responsible for the new variorum edition should "take all the load of naming the dunces, their qualities, histories, and performances."[9] He shows no concern about the identification of particular dunces being imprudent or unethical. Pope, however, was concerned about an issue that was not raised in the *Miscellanies* preface; he was worried that his satire might open him up to legal action, and his attitude to naming in the poem was partly shaped by fear of the law of libel.

Pope's fears that *The Dunciad* would provoke and justify litigation are apparent from the history of its publication. The first edition was made to look as though it was an Irish publication (perhaps from the pen of Swift): "Dublin, Printed, London reprinted for A Dodd, 1728," and, when it came to the *Variorum* with the notes and indexes Swift had anticipated, Pope chose not to publish through his new bookseller, Lawton Gilliver, but to sell the copyright to Lords Oxford, Bathurst, and Burlington, who he anticipated would lie beyond the reach of libel actions.[10] He also had the *Variorum* checked by the lawyer Nicholas Fazakerley, later distinguished for his role in the *Craftsman* libel trial of 1731. As he wrote to Lord Burlington,

> The whole Question is only this: If there be any thing in these sheets . . . which an Action may be grounded upon? and if there be, which those things are? that Mr F. would mark or alter them in this Copy. . .Your Lordship needs not even name *me* as any way concern'd in that publication, which Mr F. will observe is guarded against by the manner in which it is publish'd . . .[11]

Pope draws attention to a desirable asymmetry in which he is not named but the dunces are, but, as the letter suggests, there were three matters he had to keep in mind if he was to avoid successful litigation. The first was whether the text was itself libellous: that would be decided by the judge. The jury would decide on the two other matters, and to those Pope and Swift always devoted much attention: "The jury could decide on only two major questions: whether or not the defendant had written, published, or sold the document in question, and whether or not the words in the alleged libel had the meaning assigned to them in the . . . information."[12]

By publishing anonymously, and by obscuring the issue of copyright, Pope had dealt with the first matter. The second was dealt with by obscuring the nature of reference in the poem and its apparatus, thus rendering the innuendoes uninterpretable.

An innuendo was "any word the referent for which was not immediately obvious when the word was taken out of context. Thus all pronouns and such phrases as 'the state' (*innuendo* England) or 'the minister' (*innuendo* Wapole) were regarded as innuendoes."[13] The first edition of *The Dunciad* was full of innuendoes, to the perplexity, Swift claimed, of Dublin's readers. "Tibbald," a nickname rather than a proper name, provided the protagonist, while "C—r," "Jo—n.," "O—l," and the like were used for the personages all through the poem. In his edition of Jonathan Richardson's marked-up copy of the first edition, David Vander Meulen analyzes this deliberate withholding of full naming: "In the manuscripts we see the basis for Pope's statement in 1729 that the names of the dunces were clapped in as they arose, how the nature of the appellations shifts (as Tryphon becomes identifiable as Tonson, for instance, in book 2), or how the use of initials and blanks reflects Pope's intention as it represents a calculated ambiguity after he has labelled the targets unmistakably in the drafts."[14] But though the authors were made for the poem, rather than the poem for the authors, and though the dramatis personae changed from time to time, Pope seemed to feel that the legal threats hovering over his poem released him from any sense of *Miscellanies*-style moral obligation, and he used the *Variorum* – the notes of various commentators releasing him from responsibility – to identify his dunces with much greater clarity than he had in the first edition. The "Index of Persons celebrated in this Poem," which might have been included at Swift's request, has only three out of eighty-five persons with blanks still in place, and in general the blanks are filled in, while the notes provide the offenses which have been committed. Pope is quite frank about his intentions in the Advertisement at the start of the *Variorum*:

It will be sufficient to say of this Edition, that the reader has here a much more correct and compleat copy of the DUNCIAD, than has hitherto appeared: I cannot answer but some mistakes may have slipt into it, but a vast number of others will be prevented, by the Names being now not only set at length, but justified by the authorities and reasons given. I make no doubt, the Author's own motive to use real rather than feign'd names, was his care to preserve the Innocent from any false Applications; whereas in the former editions which had no more than the Initial letters, he was made, by Keys printed here, to hurt the inoffensive; and (what was worse) to abuse his friends, by an impression at *Dublin* [italics reversed].[15]

Pope's motivation is justice, to innocent and guilty, and the reference to Dublin ties in his practice to the advice of his friend in the deanery.

A more thoroughgoing justification of the naming practice of the *Dunciad Variorum* emerged in a publication from the team of John Wright and Lawton Gilliver, Pope's own printer and bookseller, in 1730. Combined in a pamphlet were Walter Harte's "An Essay on Satire, Particularly on the Dunciad" and a translation of Boileau's "A Discourse on Satire, Arraigning Persons by Name." Boileau had figured largely in the *Variorum* as a poet to be compared with Pope, and the possibility arises that Pope himself was the translator of Boileau's essay or at least the inspirer of the translation, just as he had been of his protégé Harte's poem, every page of which had been corrected by his own hand. Harte, who sees satire as of equal dignity with epic, is strongly in favor of satiric attacks on individuals. The noble purpose of satire is

> To scourge the bad, th'unwary to reclaim,
> And make light flash upon the face of shame.[16]

As the prefixed summary of the poem says, "From the Practice of all the best Writers and Men in every Age and Nation, the *Moral Justice* of *Satire* in General, and of this Sort in Particular, is Vindicated. The *Necessity* of it is shewn in *this Age* more especially, and why bad Writers are at present the *most proper Objects of Satire*" [italics reversed].

That bad writing is a particularly appropriate object for personal satire seems agreed between Harte, Pope, Swift, and Boileau. Writers put themselves forward for criticism. Whatever the usual rules about personal attacks, they should be suspended for the consideration of writers. In his "Discourse" Boileau is quite clear that he has a right to name names:

I think I have shewn clearly enough, that without any prejudice either to one's Conscience or the Government, one may think bad Verses bad Verses, and have full right to be tir'd with reading a silly Book. But since these Gentlemen have spoken of the liberty I have taken of *Naming* them, as an Attempt unheard-of, and without Example, and since Examples can't well be put into Rhyme; 'tis proper to say one word to inform 'em of a thing of which they alone wou'd gladly be ignorant, and to make them know, that in comparison of all my brother Satirists, I have been a Poet of great Moderation.[17]

Boileau goes on to cite examples of naming from Lucilius, Horace, Persius, and Virgil. Juvenal looks like an exception because he takes his examples of great men from the previous age, but "as for the *Writers*, he never look'd for them further than his own time."[18] Harte and Boileau make explicit the argument present in Swift's letters and implicit in the apparatus of the *Dunciad Variorum*: in the case of bad writing, particular satire is desirable, an ethical imperative.

POPE'S WORKS 1735

The Dunciad remained anonymous. The question of how you should satirize in your own name and treat vices and follies, other than those in writing, remained open. The evidence suggests that in planning his *opus magnum* (the *Essay on Man* and supplementary essays) that was to accompany the *Dunciad* in a new volume of *Works* (finally published in

1735), Pope planned to use a system of fictional names and fused attacks. The plan may have drawn on advice from Fazakerley about how to handle innuendo. The trick was to avoid explicit naming, of course, but also to engage a plurality of reference, so that any passage might validly apply to a person other than a complainant. Such a satiric method explains, and invalidates, the debates about who was the object of particular satiric attacks. Atossa in *To a Lady* is both the Duchess of Marlborough and the Duchess of Buckingham and, because some details will fit the one but not the other, neither. Similarly Bufo in *To Arbuthnot* is both Halifax and Doddington, and the Dean in *To Burlington* who "never mentions Hell to ears polite" is both White Kennett and Knightly Chetwood.[19] *To Burlington* brings us to the case which threatened Pope's program and led to a change of policy: that of Timon. The furore around the identification of the Duke of Chandos as Timon showed the limitations of a skillful use of innuendo. Fused reference might save you in a court of law, but it was no protection against gossip and pamphlet attack.[20] Pope's frustration at the failure of his tactic is plain from his letter to Burlington of December 21, 1731, only a week after the poem's publication:

Either the whole Town then, or I, have lost our Senses; for nothing is so evident, to any one who can read the Language, either of English or Poetry, as that Character of Timon is collected from twenty different absurditys & Improprieties: & was never the Picture of any one Human Creature. The Argument is short. Either the Duke these folks would abuse, *did* all those things, or he *did not.* If he did, he would deserve to be laughd at with a Vengeance; and if he did *not,* then it's plain it cannot be the Duke: and the latter is really the case.[21]

Pope admits here, and in the letter to Burlington that he chose to prefix to the third edition of the poem, that Chandos was implicated in the satire, being one of the twenty satirized. It is a remarkably frank admission, and it is followed in the third edition by a suggested revision of the approach to naming in satire that was to be reflected in *To Bathurst* and also the Horatian imitations of the late 1730s:

I have learnt there are some who wou'd rather be *wicked* than *ridiculous*; and therefore it may be safer to attack *Vices* than *Follies.* I will leave my Betters in the quiet Possession of their *Idols*, their *Groves*, and their *High-Places*; and change my Subject from their *Pride* to their *Meanness*, from their *Vanities* to their *Miseries*: And as the only certain way to avoid Misconstruction, to lessen Offence, and not to multiply ill-natur'd Applications, I may probably in my next make use of *Real* Names and not of *Fictitious* Ones. [italics reversed][22]

Although some, including Johnson, have been inclined to mock Pope's minatory tone in this letter, he was as good as his word, and the subsequent *To Bathurst* named names and helped to shape the *Works* of 1735.[23]

Whereas the names in Pope's *Works* I (1717) were largely those of the poets who praised him in prefatory verse – the letter to Arabella Fermor at the start of the *Rape of the Lock* is an interesting exception – *Works* II is full of proper names. The attitude to naming adopted in the second Dialogue of *One Thousand Seven Hundred and Thirty Eight* is already in place within the *Works of Mr. Alexander Pope*. Pope says that he wanted to add notes to all the ethic epistles – something that might have changed our interpretations of the poems – but that the volume became too big, so in the endnotes he prints the notes that appeared in the original editions, with some editing. In particular the notes specify the histories of the villains of *To Bathurst*: John Ward of Hackney, Francis Chartres, William Colepepper, "Vultur" Hopkins, Japhet Crook, Denis Bond, John Blunt, and many others. As a counterbalance, these notes finally give the Man of Ross his personal name. The justification for the majority of naming lies in the vicious nature of the individuals and the failure of general satire in *To Burlington*. There are still, however, some exceptions to the general policy of naming. The law of libel is still potentially a problem. Peter Walter is criticized throughout these epistles, but Pope explicitly avoids an explanatory note on him, calling him "Waters": "this Gentleman's History must be deferr'd till his Death, when his Worth may be known more certainly."[24] Nevertheless an ambiguous note was added to line 125. Some major figures were still referred to by using fictitious names or nicknames. Most remarkably Lord Hervey, commonly Lord Fanny in Pope's poems of this period, is called Paris in the first edition of *To Arbuthnot* but Sporus, the name of the eunuch Nero had castrated and used as his wife, in the *Works*. Pope draws attention to the change in the apparatus, with an ironic note:

Sporus.] It was originally *Paris*, but that Name having been, as we conceive, the only reason that so contemptible a Character could be applied to a Noble and Beautiful Person, the Author changed it to this of *Sporus*, as a Name which has never yet been so mis-applied.[25]

If Pope thought Hervey had been responsible for the identification of Timon as Chandos, the play with recognition here is pointed.[26] Pope pretends to want to avoid the identification of his portrait with a nobleman; he, therefore, adds contempt even to the name so that there is no misapplication. The application to Hervey will nevertheless be made.

The tricks played with Addison's name are even more complicated than those played with Hervey's nickname. In the preface to the *Miscellanies* Pope and Swift say they regret the attack on Addison, but that it has already been published with his name included. In printing "Fragment of a Satire," later to be the Atticus portrait, in *Miscellanies*, they reduce the name to "A—n." In *Works* II Pope substitutes "Atticus" for "A—n" but extraordinarily leads into the portrait with the name while pointing to its omission in a note. After a section in which various members of Addison's circle are ridiculed, Pope concludes:

> How did they fume, and stamp, and roar, and chafe?
> And swear, not *Addison* himself was safe. (ll. 191–2)

He then continues "Peace to all such!" and proceeds with Addison's portrait. In the endnote he elaborates:

Atticus] It was a great Falshood which some of the Libels reported, that this Character was written after the Gentleman's death, which see refuted in the Testimonies prefix'd to the Dunciad. But the occasion of writing it was such, as he would not make publick in regard to his memory; and all that could further be done was to omit the Name, in the Editions of his Works.[27]

The ostensible purpose of the note is to draw attention to the poet's tenderness to the memory of the Gentleman, but for this section of the poem to work, we need to know who the Gentleman is; and so the name is put into the wrong place, only to be effectively relocated by the note. Pope's motivation in this maneuver is unclear. His reputation is probably of first concern, but "not Addison himself was safe" accommodates a sense that actually naming someone in an attack does him a damage that reference, however precise, does not. I suspect there lurks behind Pope's practice a sense of the magic of naming, the idea that naming exercises some power over the individual named and that Pope's setting aside that power is meritorious.[28]

SWIFT'S *WORKS* 1735

When Swift came to prepare his own poems for the second in the four volumes of his *Works* (1735), in collaboration, though he would have denied it, with the Dublin bookseller George Faulkner, questions of naming came to weigh heavily with him. The title-page of the *Works*, presenting the author as "*J.S.*, D.D. D.S.P.D." is itself equivocal, but a notable feature of these poems when they are compared with Pope's is the importance of ordinary naming. Because they are frequently occasioned by domestic incidents or by events in Swift's private or public life, the poems are peopled by figures with their everyday names: Frances Harris, Mary the cook-maid, Partridge the almanack-maker, the miser Mr. Demar, Sheridan, Delany, Sir Arthur [Acheson], Judge Boat, Judge Whitshed, and assorted butlers and gatekeepers. Sometimes a mythological name will appear (Harley as Atlas); sometimes a character may be created (Pethox the Great); and sometimes nicknames with a life outside the poetry will be used (Stella, Cadenus and Vanessa, George, Nim, Dan, Dean). Sometimes the poems will be built out of play on a personal name (Wood or Boat) or out of a libel on Delany. Politicians are also present, though sometimes without their vowels, and so are Swift's literary friends, Pope and Gay. Swift's instinct is to name freely and playfully, but the pressures of politics and of the responsibilities of compiling a *Works* led to some restraints. In particular Swift canceled some pages of the *Works* at a late stage, and an examination of the changes he made provides the best opportunity of throwing some light on his developing attitude to naming.

On August 30, 1734, Swift explained to Lord Oxford that there had been a delay in publication of the second volume of *Works*: "I have put the Man under some Difficultyes by ordering certain Things to be struck out after they were printed, which some friends had given him. This hath delayed his work, and as I hear, given him much trouble and difficulty to adjust. Farther I know not; for the whole affair is a great vexation to me."[29] This must be a case of reading the final page-proofs. There may have been a preliminary read-through of the material with Faulkner, but if so Swift missed the offensive material. Fortunately we know what the struck-out material was. There is a copy of volume II of the *Works* in the English Faculty Library at Oxford that has both the uncanceled sheets and the cancels, and this important discovery was announced and interpreted in an important article by the late Margaret Weedon, the Faculty Librarian.[30] The material affected by the cancellations falls into four sections: first, the poems omitted, in order to escape political controversy or, as I shall argue, to remove personal attacks; second, those poems that replaced them and must have been discovered with Swift's assistance; third, those poems that were retained but censored, again to escape political controversy and, I think, to remove personal attacks; and fourth, those that were incidentally reset. I shall concentrate on the omitted and censored.

There were four poems omitted: "To a Lady," "A Dialogue between Mad Mullinex and Timothy," "Traulus" (parts 1 and 2), and "Epigram on Fasting." The need to cancel "To a Lady" was obvious. The printer and bookseller of the London publication had been arrested in January 1734, and the poem was offensive to the government, largely, I suspect because of its references to the monarch ("Where a Monkey wore a Crown") rather than those to the first minister ("Sir R—t Brass").[31] This poem was omitted completely, but Swift took the opportunity of this excision to reconsider some of his other satiric attacks. "A Dialogue between Mad Mullinex and Timothy" had already been printed in *The Intelligencer* and *Miscellanies. The Third Volume. It is an attack on Richard Tighe, the Whig politician. Weedon suggests that Swift regretted the private injury and omitted the poem in accordance with the position on personal satire expressed in the "Verses." Tighe is not named, but he is clearly represented as "Timothy," and I think she is right. The poem has a political basis but its satire is personal. It could be said to have emerged without Swift's full consent, and he deemed it inappropriate in a *Works* by *J.S.*, D.D. D.S.P.D. "Traulus" is similarly an abusive attack on Joshua, Viscount Allen. It had already appeared on its own anonymously in 1730. I do not believe that Swift had changed his mind about Allen, but like "Mad Mullinex and Timothy" this poem is a flyting and inappropriate for a *Works*. The "Epigram" can be ignored for this purpose.

Of the poems censored the most interesting is "The Author upon Himself," first published here. The first couplet of the poem,

> By an † old red-Pate murd'ring Hag pursu'd,
> A crazy *Prelate, and a ¶ Royal Prude,

was heavily censored to produce:

> By an — — — pursu'd,
> A crazy *Prelate, and a ¶ Royal Prude.

A note identifying the pursuer as "*The late D—ss of S—t*" was removed, but the notes identifying the Prelate as "*Dr. Sharp, Archbishop of* York" and the Royal Prude as "*Her late M—*" were retained. The Duchess of Somerset had died in 1722. There could be no fear of libel here, and the attacks on Sharp and the queen are left in line 2. What must have been unacceptable to Swift was the viciousness of the attack on Somerset. So in the revision, she is completely removed. The name is deleted again at line 53, when she turns up as Madam Coningsmark, accused of murdering her husband. This time the result is a poetry even more marred by its omissions. The relevant couplet,

> Now, ¶ Madam *Coningsmark* her Vengeance vows
> On S—'s Reproaches for her murder'd Spouse

becomes

> Now, — — — her Vengeance vows
> On S—'s Reproaches for her — —

There can be little doubt that the change was in order to lash the vice but spare the name. In the same poem, however, Harley, because he is praised, can appear in full in line 28, whereas Walpole, already "*W _ le*" is reduced to "*W_*" in line 41. Doubtless the aim here is to decrease the interpretability of the innuendo.

A different approach is taken to a note on William Whitshed, which serves as an introduction to "An Excellent New Song." Whitshed had died in 1727, so again there was no problem with libel, and yet the attack is moderated. I present below first the uncanceled passage and then its cancel, with the changes emboldened:

> The Author having **writ** a Treatise, advising the
> People of Ireland to wear their own Manufactures;
> that infamous Wretch Whitshed prosecu**ted**
> Waters the Printer with so much Violence **and**
> **Injustice**, that he kept the **Jury Nine Hours**, and
> sent them away Eleven Times, **till out of meer**
> Weariness they were forced to give a special Verdict.

> The Author having **wrote** a Treatise, advising the
> People of Ireland to wear their own Manufactures,
> a Prosecution was set on foot against Waters the
> Printer thereof, which was carried on with so
> much Violence, that one Whitshed, then
> **Chief Justice**, thought proper, in a Manner the
> most extraordinary, to keep the **Grand-Jury above**
> **twelve Hours**, and to send them eleven times out
> of Court, until he had wearied them into a special
> Verdict.

Whitshed is no longer an "infamous wretch;" he is no longer responsible for the prosecution; there is no direct charge of injustice; the jury are no longer forced. (But the jury is kept longer.) One can imagine that in revisiting this note, Swift felt its inaccuracy amounted to unfairness. But Whitshed is still named and shamed; this is, after its revision, no longer a personal satirical attack; it is a complaint about injustice.[32]

Finally in "To Mr Gay" Swift takes advantage of the canceling process to diminish the attack on the prime minister by changing "*B – b*" to "*B –.*". Although the aim is to remove interpretable innuendo, I think Swift is also aiming at an increase in tact. He still intends to satirize Walpole, but he is going to do so expressing the maximum deference compatible with his satire. Similarly "STATESMAN" is changed to "ST*·*·*MAN" at line 32, and in line 52, following "The people with a sigh their taxes bring," "And cursing *B — b*, forget to bless the —" is changed to "And cursing *B — ,* forget to bless — ." Swift may be insulting the king and queen and their prime minister, but, after the attempt to prosecute "To a Lady," he is doing so politely, and with a respect for their power that leads him to avoid naming.

Whereas Pope's *Works* of 1735 show him adopting an aggressive policy on naming, on the grounds that "The fewer still you name you wound the more" (*First Satire of the Second Book of Horace*, l. 42), Swift's *Works* of the same year show him drawing back from naming for both personal and political reasons. Both poets produce instances of powerful personal satire, yet both are troubled about the appropriate limits of such satire. If, as I suspect, particular satire can be justified not by general rules but by the close examination of particular cases, their troubled and sometimes conflicting practices serve to show the seriousness of their approach to these problems.

NOTES

1 Lucid accounts of naming in satire are to be found in P. K. Elkin, *The Augustan Defence of Satire* (Oxford: Clarendon Press, 1973), chapter 7, and Gregory G. Colomb, *Designs on Truth: The Poetics of the Augustan Mock-Epic* (University Park, PA: Pennsylvania State University Press, 1992), chapter 3.

2 *Twickenham Edition of the Poems of Alexander Pope*, ed. John Butt *et al.*, 11 vols. (London: Methuen, 1939–69), vol. IV, pp. 313–14. All subsequent citations of Pope's poetry derive from this edition, cited as *Twickenham Pope*.

3 *The Poems of Jonathan Swift*, ed. Harold Williams, 3 vols. (Oxford: Oxford University Press, 1958), vol. II, p. 571. All subsequent citations of Swift's poetry derive from this edition.

4 *Correspondence of Jonathan Swift*, ed. Harold Williams, 5 vols. (Oxford: Clarendon Press, 1965), vol. V, p. 140. For an outstanding account of the blanks in the "Verses" themselves, see Stephen Karian, "Reading the Material Text of Swift's *Verses on the Death*," *Studies in English Literature, 1500–1900* 41 (2001), 514–44.

5 *The Prose Works of Alexander Pope*, ed. Rosemary Cowler (Hamden, CT: Archon Books, 1986), vol. II, pp. 90–1.

6 *The Correspondence of Jonathan Swift*, D.D., ed. David Woolley, 4 vols. (Frankfurt: Peter Lang, 1999–), vol. III, p. 162. All subsequent citations of Swift's correspondence derive from this work.

7 The ancient constitution of Lilliput provided rewards as well as punishments. See *Gulliver's Travels*, ed. Claude Rawson and Ian Higgins (Oxford: Oxford University Press, 2005), pp. 52–3. Swift was expecting to be rewarded in *The Dunciad* by the dedication that finally, after an irritating delay, appeared in the *Variorum*.

8 Swift, *Correspondence*, vol. III, p. 189.

9 Swift, *Correspondence*, vol. III, p. 189.

10 The manuscript, dated October 16, 1729, is BL MS Egerton 1951, f. 7.

11 *Correspondence of Alexander Pope*, ed. George Sherburn, 5 vols. (Oxford: Clarendon Press, 1956), vol. III, p. 4.

12 C. R. Kropf, "Libel and Satire in the Eighteenth Century," *Eighteenth-Century Studies* 8 (1974), 153–68 (p. 157).

13 Kropf, "Libel and Satire," p. 159. According to Kropf, on the same page, "an innuendo, of itself, could not be used to identify its referent," but by 1724 the practice had changed, as a reading of the *Craftsman* trials suggests. See Richard Reynolds, "Libels and Satires! Lawless Things Indeed!," *Eighteenth-Century Studies* 8 (1975), 475–7.

14 *Pope's Dunciad of 1728: A History and Facsimile*, ed. David L. Vander Meulen (Charlottesville and London: Bibliographical Society of the University of Virginia for The New York Public Library and the University of Virginia Press, 1991), p. 59. I am grateful to Valerie Rumbold for giving me access to her notes on identifications. Her Longman edition will make a full study of *Dunciad* naming feasible.

15 *Twickenham Pope*, vol. V, p. 8.

16 Walter Harte, *An Essay on Satire, Particularly on the Dunciad*, ed. Thomas B. Gilmore, Augustan Reprint Society, Publication no. 132 (Los Angeles: William Andrews Clark Memorial Library, 1968), pp. 24–5. See as well the helpful introduction to this volume.

17 In Harte, *An Essay on Satire*, p. 40.

18 In Harte, *An Essay on Satire*, p. 44.

19 See *Twickenham Pope*, vol. III. ii, pp. 159–64, vol. IV, p. 112, and vol. III. ii, p. 152.

20 See *Twickenham Pope*, vol. III. ii, pp. 170–4. For the range of attacks on Pope over this affair, see J. V. Guerinot, *Pamphlet Attacks on Alexander Pope, 1711–1744* (London: Methuen, 1969), pp. 205–17 and subsequently.

21 Pope, *Correspondence*, vol. III, p. 259.

22 *Twickenham Pope*, vol. III. ii, p. 132.

23 *Lives of the Most Eminent English Poets*, ed. Roger Lonsdale, 4 vols. (Oxford: Clarendon Press, 2006), vol. IV, pp. 35–6.

24 "Notes," in *Works* II (1735), p. 208.

25 *Twickenham Pope*, vol. IV, p. 117.

26 For relations between Pope and Hervey in relation to *To Burlington*, see the introduction to "A Letter to a Noble Lord," in *Prose Works* II, pp. 433–9.

27 *Twickenham Pope*, vol. IV, p. III.

28 Robert C. Elliott, *The Power of Satire: Magic, Ritual, Art* (Princeton: Princeton University Press, 1960), is excellent on this aspect of naming.

29 Swift, *Correspondence*, vol. III, p. 753.

30 Margaret Weedon, "An Uncancelled Copy of the First Collected Edition of Swift's Poems," *Library* 22 (1967), 44–56. This article helpfully summarizes the textual changes brought about by the cancellation.

31 John Fischer, "The Government's Response to Swift's An Epistle to a Lady," *Philosophical Quarterly* 65 (1986), 39–59.

32 Swift defends attacking Whitshed, even after his death, in his *Answer to a Paper Called a Memorial* (1728), a defense that develops into a justification of personal satire of villains (*Irish Tracts, 1728–1733*, ed. Herbert Davis (Oxford: Basil Blackwell, 1955), pp. 23–5).

PART III

Beyond Swift

CHAPTER 11

Pope and the evolution of social class

Nicholas Hudson

The writers we used to call "Augustan" – Swift, Gay, Pope – forged comparable satiric techniques in the face of similar social circumstances. All were authors of relatively modest social origins who reached success through the literary marketplace rather than noble patronage. They share some claim, indeed, to being the first wave of successful professional authors in the English language. But here, as well, lies a paradox. For the political and social ideology of these literary parvenus was notoriously conservative, and is often regarded as hostile to both the literary market-place and capitalism in general. This is a paradox that the following essay will examine, particularly in relation to Swift's great friend, Alexander Pope. I will be focusing on early eighteenth-century strategies of rhetoric and language, whose subtleties and complications have been explored with unparalleled subtlety and depth by Claude Rawson.

Pope's place within the evolving English class-system of the early eighteenth century has presented recent scholars with something of a problem. On the one hand, it would be difficult to think of a writer of his era so representative of the most aggressive, acquisitive, and socially ambitious wing of the English middle orders, the group that would eventually dub itself the "middle class" in the nineteenth century. He was born in the City of London, the son of a successful linen-merchant who began his life as an apprentice. Pope the younger made literature his trade, manipulating the publishing market with a ferocity that earned him a respectable fortune, but generally left those he bargained with feeling short-changed and litigious. Yet Pope evidently despised the capitalist world that nurtured him and enriched him. Pope's wealth was earned, ironically, from a mass of writing that seems to condemn writing for money, and which appears, at least, to celebrate a world of polite landed gentlemen exchanging poems and seeking no reward except the praise of judicious gentlemen of taste such as themselves. If one weighs merely the evidence of Pope's writing, then Brean Hammond's conclusion may well seem credible: "the character of Pope's ideology is that of a family-based Christian aristocrat or landed gentleman, implacably opposed to the élite of, as he believed, corrupt financiers, bankers and brokers who governed the country."[1]

This is not to claim that Hammond's assessment (which in fact seems broadly representative of recent scholarship) lacks evidence drawn from Pope's life. For Pope's capitalist and City patrimony is complicated by factors that link him with an older, more traditional ideology. He was a lifelong Catholic whose family was forced to leave London for the countryside near his spiritual landscape of Windsor Forest when he was in his early teens. He may even have been disposed to Jacobitism, though with an acknowledged lack of useful energy, especially in later life.[2] In much recent scholarship, therefore, we find Pope portrayed, in various interesting ways, as struggling between these two opposed forces in his poetry and his life. On the one hand, Pope is the ideological feudal gentleman who defends the "seigneurial ideal."[3] On the other hand, an increasing body of criticism seems to be hearing a capitalist cacophony behind the genteel music of his poetry. In his most recent work, Colin Nicholson finds Pope "yoking together," for comic effect, the opposite forces dividing Hanoverian England and his own character. The commodity theatre of *The Rape of the Lock*, Nicholson argues, abrades laughably across Pope's nostalgia for the pre-commodity world of Homer.[4] Nicholson's analysis is professedly indebted to John Barrell's compelling analysis of ideological contradiction in *Epistle to Bathurst*, a poem where Pope declaims with eloquent moralism about capitalist sins which, with strange significance, he also justifies as ineluctable natural forces.[5]

Neither Nicholson nor Barrell is quite talking about the problem of social hierarchy in Pope's poetry. Their interest is rather with Pope's relationship with capitalism – which, confusingly, recent scholars have tended virtually to equate with the stock-market, banking, and paper credit. As much as he may have disliked stock-jobbers and the funds, there is no evidence that the author of *Windsor Forest* hated commerce in real goods. Indeed, there can be no serious claim that Pope hated making money, even from so insubstantial and inedible a commodity as literature. Material analyses of Pope's ideology, for all their supposed realism, actually offer a kind of dodge from the difficult issues that his work really presents. For what really preoccupied Pope was, surely, not *how* money was made. Rather, his satire dwells on *who* was making the money – the intangible value of those who had risen, including himself, as the result of the expansion of the marketplace in all sorts of goods, including poetry.

While not uninterested in the social origins of those he either satirizes or praises, this self-made man could not, at least without hypocrisy, judge his contemporaries merely on the basis of whether their wealth was inherited or earned. Nor, as a Catholic prohibited from owning land, could Pope enlist himself in the ranks of the landed gentry. In fact, we will encounter numerous instances of Pope's harsh criticism of the old elite and his praise of those who had made their fortunes through trade or even the funds. (An instance of the latter is his friendship with John Barber, Mayor of London from 1732 to 1733, and a beneficiary of the South Sea Bubble.)[6] The abiding concern of Pope's satire was, instead, the regulation of standards for social authority – who, that is, should or should not have power and prestige in his society.

The familiar Marxist term for the structure regulating this judgment of social authority, "social class," is inadequate for at least two main reasons. First, Marx forged an inexorable connection between what – as I have just suggested – we must disjoin in our analysis of Pope. Marx derived ideology and his own idea of social division from forms of labor, as connected with prevailing modes of production. Almost everyone, however, will agree that the Marxist model is at least problematical when applied to Pope. While Pope made his money in the capitalist marketplace, a wide consensus indicates that he seems drawn ideologically towards the interests of an older elite of hereditary aristocrats and landed gentlemen. A second problem with "social class" is that this category can be applied only anachronistically to the age of Pope. While Marx adopted "social class" from the vocabulary of his own Victorian context, this term was not used in Pope's time, and has at best clumsy application to the social hierarchy characteristic of his society.[7] For Pope wrote just at the nexus of the clash between traditional standards of ranks or status and the considerable enrichment of England's upper-middle ranks. The merchants and traders of England, the people who would much later call themselves the "middle class" or "bourgeoisie," did not yet have a fully formed identity or a consistent set of distinctive social values. In fact, the nascent "bourgeoisie" was not so much in the process of overthrowing the old elite as appropriating its life-styles, its fashions, even its snobbery.

Here is a phenomenon that strikes me as having outstanding importance in eighteenth-century culture and literature: the widely parasitic nature of middle-rank values on an older, aristocratic set of values and fashions. For Pope, as I will argue, was entirely typical of his middle-rank origins and milieu in his appropriation of traditionally elite standards, both social and literary. He was typical even in his embarrassment with his own origins and his displays of animosity towards the commercialization of both society and literature. What other scholars have called a "contradiction" in Pope's work stemmed from his awareness that he could not rely on traditional sources of authority and prestige that remained, notwithstanding, the main reservoir of cultural capital in the England of the early eighteenth century.

The particular moment of Pope's writing, that is, gave rise to a particular mode of language, and to maneuvers, some conscious and some not quite so conscious, designed to accommodate social tensions inherent in his life and times. Rhetorical responses to complications of birth, rank, and manners in this age are illuminated in Claude Rawson's essay "Gentlemen and Dancing-Masters,"[8] to which I am much indebted, though his subjects are principally Fielding, Chesterfield, and Swift, rather than Pope. The lesson of Rawson's essay lies in the need to be sensitive to "ambiguity" and "oscillations of mood" characteristic of authors. There is nothing "systematic" about Pope's response to social rank: his approach changes from work to work and is always filled with ambiguity. The consistency of Pope's writing derives rather from his search for ways of belonging to a reconstituted social order that nonetheless remains reliant on older forms of prestige.

Examined through the lens of social criticism, eighteenth-century literature dwells on *surfaces*, confusions in the signs or insignia of rank and wealth. Wigs, swords, coats of arms, dancing, French, effete manners – these commodities were originally coined in an aristocratic mint. Yet these products were increasingly open for purchase by anyone with money in an expanding commercial economy. The comic disconnection of these signs from their traditional role as signifiers of a hereditary rank constitutes one of the main inspirations of Restoration and eighteenth-century social satire. This was the disjunction satirized most influentially in Molière's *Le bourgeois gentilhomme*, widely imitated in England. In Edward Ravencroft's *The Citizen turn'd Gentleman* (1672), one of the most popular plays of the Restoration,[9] Mr. Jorden translates his mercantile earnings into a suit of lacy clothes, dancing, and French lessons, and an assurance that he will one day dally at St. James's Palace. "Well, Sir, I have a sword too in my house;" he boasts to Sir Simon, with whom he is matching his daughter, "am a Gentleman, and may in time be a Knight."[10] In Ned Ward's *London Spy* (1699), a naïve country visitor is astonished to learn that the fashionable "gentlemen" he has just dined with include a sword-hilt maker, an apprentice wine-cooper, and a highwayman.[11] Ned Ward's London was also essentially the London of Gay's *The Beggar's Opera* (1728), where fashionable commodities and fashionable values circulate indiscriminately across the social spectrum, from Newgate to St. James, and back.

This collapse of traditional social insignia had, of course, an important literary dimension as well. The language of the old elite, the language of classicism, became the commercial popular medium of post-Revolution print culture aimed at readers who aspired to a reputation for "taste." As recently discussed by Abigail Williams, the most popular poems of the Restoration and the eighteenth century were not our present canonical productions of Swift, Gay, or Pope, but rather exercises in a high, even strained Latinism – Charles Montagu's breathlessly heroic *Epistle to Dorset* (1690), the epics of Sir Richard Blackmore, the Virgilian *Pastorals* (1708) of Ambrose Philips.[12] The notorious *querelle des anciens et des modernes* was not fought between those who upheld ancient models and those who did not. The real debate lay, rather, between those who slavishly imitated the classics and those who, in a display of gentlemanly nonchalance, showed their ability to expand in new ways on classical models. To the latter category Pope definitely belonged, for the literal dressing up in eighteenth-century society had an analogue in poetic "dress of thought." If the City beau and lady exposed their origins by trying too obviously to imitate the fashions of the old elite, the bad commercial poet wore the greaves of classical poetry with clunking incongruity. Pope donned classical dress too, but with an insouciance and ease that belied the fact he, as well, had *learned* the dance of gentility: "True Ease in Writing comes from Art, not Chance, / As those move easiest who have learn'd to dance" (*Essay on Criticism*, ll. 362–3).[13]

Implicit in the very form of Pope's classicism, that is, are constant comparisons with those who shared his modest origins and social aspirations. The full, nasty richness of *The Dunciad*, for example, comes to light only when the reader keeps in mind, as Pope's contemporaries certainly did, his own deep complicity with the people and the world he satirizes. As James Foxon tells us, this superficially "anti-City" poem marks the point where Pope moved with unprecedented energy toward the exploitation of the publishing marketplace that he seems to condemn.[14] He took full control over the poem, hiring a bookseller and printer he could be sure to manipulate, and fought a long and unsuccessful battle against none other than Bernard Lintot for profits from its sale. He returned dirt for dirt, scandal for scandal, and demonstrated his mastery of the strained heroism typical of commercial writing. The sarcasm and flaunting hypocrisy of *The Dunciad* was not lost on his targets, who loaded him, impotently, with charges of cruelty and venality.[15]

The message of this poem is surely the following: I have succeeded where you have not; I am rich, successful, and accepted by those who count – but you are not. In less aggressive ways, this role as the successful *arriviste* in fact infuses virtually all that Pope wrote. Pope's poetry displays him in arrangements of easy and witty camaraderie with Bolingbroke, Cobham, Bathurst, Burlington, and a succession of blue-blooded glitterati. On the other hand, Pope's dialogues with these men resist any confusion with cringing dedications to noble patrons: Pope's narrator is characteristically frank with his noble interlocutor, even cocky. As *The Dunciad* shows, Pope easily outstripped his competitors up the muddy path of Fleet Street. But he also brought an arguably City perspective into the homes of the nobility. Into the estates of his aristocratic friends, he imports a line of criticism of the corruption, uselessness, and vanity of the old elite most characteristic, in fact, of middle-rank literature.

Typical of that literature were conduct books aimed at training members of the aspiring middle ranks to join the ranks of "gentlemen," and reassuring this audience that inherited rank formed no essential part of true gentility. "It's a Madness to take the measure of our Deserts by the parts of our Forefathers," wrote William Darrell in *A Gentleman Instructed* (1704). What really counts is one's present virtue: "I value more an Innocent Ploughman, than a Vicious Prince, and prefer his Nobility who has built a great Fortune, upon Worth and Virtue, before his, who by Succession receives one."[16] In *The Man of Manners; or, the Plebeian Polish'd* (1735), the author denounces men of noble birth who are "all of a piece, *Clown* without, and *Coxcomb* within." True gentility is "acquired like other Arts, by Study and Application."[17] The same line of argument is advanced in Daniel Defoe's defense of upward mobility in *The Compleat Gentleman*:

The son of a mean person furnish'd from Heaven with an original fund of wealth, wit, sence, courage, virtue, and good humour, and set apart by a liberal education for the service of his country, that distinguishes himself by the greatest and best actions; is made acceptable and agreeable to all men by a life of glory and true fame; that hath the naturall beauties of his mind embellish'd and set off with a vast fund of learning and acquir'd knowledge; that has a clear head, a generous heart, a polite behaviour and, in a word, shews himself to be an accompish'd gentleman in every requisite article, that of birth and blood excepted.[18]

The hostility of these writers to those who pride themselves merely on noble blood, rather than virtue and accomplishment, is given exclamatory expression in *The Essay on Man* (1733–4):

> But by your father's worth if yours you rate,
> Count me those only who were good and great.
> Go! if your ancient, but ignoble blood
> Has crept thro' scoundrels ever since the flood,
> Go! And pretend your family is young;
> Nor own, your fathers have been fools so long.
> What can ennoble sots, or slaves, or cowards?
> Alas! not all the blood of all the HOWARDS. (IV, ll. 209–16)

If Pope values Bolingbroke in this poem, it is because St. John is wise and learned; if he admires Bathurst, it is because he uses his wealth usefully; if he shares candid opinions with Burlington, it is because this lord does not share the tasteless extravagances of his peers. Pope was not condemning the prestige of hereditary rank *per se*. But Defoe (who added the elegantly Norman "De" to his surname) also hastened to assure his audience that he valued birth: "All this is in favour of the *Gentry* and *Nobility* of the World, and to let you see that I am far from leveling the Clown and the Gentleman, the Great with the Mean and Base."[19] While in many ways the very embodiment of the middle-rank commercial author, Defoe wished not to dismantle the old elite, but to reform the social structure in ways that favored even low-born men of virtue, merit, and taste.

Notoriously, this was not a goal that Defoe pursued with much elegance as an author. That "Daniel" appears in *The Dunciad*, standing disgracefully in the stocks (I, 103), underlines both the stabbing snobbery of this satire and the coarseness of Defoe's literary life. Yet Pope's narrative pose of proud and meritorious independence from the nobility was essentially congenial to the ideals set out by Defoe and other writers promoting middle-rank advancement. Pope's assault on the sins of the old elite, and of those who pander grossly to the old elite, constitute a refrain that is, in fact, far more sustained that his criticisms of commerce and the City:

> Of all this *Servile Herd* the worst is He,
> That in *proud Dulness* joins with *Quality*,
> A constant Critic at the Great-man's Board,
> To *fetch* and *carry* Nonsense for my Lord. (*Essay on Criticism*, ll. 414–17)

Pope's persona – both genteel and independent, well-connected and candid – clearly had an immense appeal across the social spectrum of the age, as confirmed by his publishing success. This enjoyment cut across the boundaries of the hierarchy like the productions of no other eighteenth-century writer. As Samuel Johnson observed of *The Rape of the Lock*, "praises . . . have been accumulated on *The Rape of the Lock* by readers of every class, from the critick to the waiting-maid."[20] An important part of that appeal, as so well demonstrated by *The Rape of the Lock*, derived from Pope's peculiar combination of adoration for the elegance and wealth of the upper ranks with a proud assertion of his self-sufficiency: "I was not born for Courts or great Affairs, / I pay my Debts, believe, and say my Pray'rs" (*Epistle to Arbuthnot*, ll. 267–8). In other words, what Nicholson, Barrell, and others have called a comic tension in Pope's work might also be seen as a rhetorical self-positioning, a deliberate harnessing of the contradictions inherent in the middle ranks of the early eighteenth century. On the one hand, Pope certainly aspired to forms of prestige associated with the old order, whose traditional status he could not undermine without weakening his own claims to an elite reputation. On the other hand, Pope's willingness to assail the aristocracy, his assertions of independence and dignity despite his modest origins, imply a solidarity with middle-rank values and attitudes. Viewed in the light of this dilemma, so characteristic of the middle orders in his day, Pope's rhetorical strategies appear uniquely complex, subtle, and various.

As a younger man, Pope seemed to leap at opportunities to make peace between the City and the court, commerce and the land. Such an opportunity was presented by the Peace of Utrecht, subject of Pope's magnificent exercise in social reconciliation, *Windsor Forest* (1713). Whigs were well aware that this treaty with France, negotiated by the Tories, had considerable appeal in the City by securing new territories for Britain and making the seas safe again for trade. In a poem that outsold *Windsor Forest*, *A Poem to his Excellency the Lord Privy Seal, on the Prospect of Peace* (1713), Thomas Tickell made the best of this commercial appeal by portraying the Peace as a conquest over France, in the style of Williamite heroic verse like Charles Montagu's popular *Epistle to Dorset* (1690) or Blackmore's *Advice to the Poets* (1700). Tory poems on the same occasion, such as Bevill Higgons's *A Poem on the Glorious Peace of Utrecht* (1713), openly vaunt the interests of the City: "The Merchant now shall sail with every Breeze, / And fear no Danger, but from Winds and Seas."[21] Pope's approach is more subtle. On the one hand, as splendidly argued by Pat Rogers,[22] the poem is filled with the imagery of Jacobitism, and seems to raise hopes for an imminent Stuart succession to the ailing Queen Anne. But the poem also praises the benefits of the Peace to British trade and commerce. While never using the word "Merchant," Pope uses patriotic, even Jacobite imagery to laud the interests of the City. Bringing together the old and the new, reminders of English tradition and praise of the modern age, Pope uses the forest's oaks to stand for merchant vessels: "By our Oaks the precious Loads are born, / And Realms commanded which these trees adorn" (ll. 31–2). Similarly, like many a pastoral river, Father Thames orates majestically in the poem's concluding passage. Yet the Thames, a symbol of all that is abiding in English tradition, is also a metonym for the modern phenomenon of English trade. Father Thames's praise of commercial empire translates the language of London merchants into a nobler and more ancient key. In short, the *concordia discors* of *Windsor Forest* has a political and social implication: what "differs" but also "agrees" in the poem is not only the variegated landscape of the forest but also the landed and commercial interests, the old order and the rising commercial middle ranks.

Windsor Forest derives from an early stage in Pope's career, when he was just establishing his genteel credentials. As Pope became an older, more established poet – secure in his wealth and acceptance among the elite – he was evidently prepared to flaunt the social tensions that the early poems strive to smooth into harmony. In *The Dunciad*, as we have seen, Pope sharpens the disparity between his commercial provenance and his elite status into a satiric weapon against opponents unable to match him in either skill or success. But the same period also gave birth to *Epistle to Bathurst* (1733), his most direct meditation on capitalism and social mobility. This poem leaves Pope's own social position in a kind of limbo, and it rhetorically neutralizes moral certitude about the economic and social issues that it worries about. Such incertitude, as we will consider, was by no means disadvantageous to middle-rank ideals and aspirations.

The rhetorical framing of *Epistle to Bathurst* situates Pope ambiguously between the aristocratic interlocutor of the poem and the various City types that he describes. On the one hand, Bathurst himself seems – comically at odds with Pope's earnest monologue – disinterested in the theme of the poem. Evidently free himself from financial worries, Bathurst dismisses money as "a standing jest of Heav'n" (l. 4), a joke on both those who save and disperse their gold. Bathurst interjects, impatiently, twice more. His first interjection irritably dismisses Pope's ardent philosophical meditations on the difference between barter, gold, and credit: "What say you? 'Say? Why take it, Gold and all' " (l. 80). But Pope ploughs on, apparently sending Bathurst to sleep. Pope concludes the poem by telling the exhausted Bathurst a bedtime story, the Puritanical

fable of the rise and fall of a Cit named Balaam. "A knotty point!"
declames Pope, in full swing, "to which we now proceed. / But you are
tir'd – I'll tell a tale. 'Agreed' " (ll. 335–6). We might care about what
Pope has to say in this poem (as evidenced by a history of very earnest
criticism), but its noble interlocutor does not.

Pope has a similarly complicated relationship with his various portraits
of men who exemplify the proper and improper use of riches. Modern
criticism has tended to focus almost exclusively on figures drawn from the
worlds of commerce and finance, leaving the impression that the poem is
essentially about Pope's hostility to capitalism. But this impression is
exaggerated. Pope directs sustained satire at three personages who made
their money through trade and banking – Sir John Blunt, Sir John
Cutler, and Sir Balaam (possibly based on Thomas Pitt). But there is also
a long satirical portrait of the Duke of Buckingham, and he mentions
other wasteful and vicious members of the gentry such as the Earl of
Bristol ("Uxorio") and the Duke of Wharton. The Man of Ross, based on
John Kyrle, has been cited as the exemplar of Pope's "seigneurial ideal."[23]
But he is introduced specifically in contrast *not* to money-grubbing Cits
but rather to the "seigneurs," the old elite:

> Who starves by Nobles, or with Nobles eats?
> The Wretch that trusts them, and the Rogue that cheats.
> Is there a Lord, who knows a cheerful noon
> Without a Fiddler, Flatt'rer, or Buffoon? (ll. 236–40)

Pope keeps up this attack on the old elite for several lines before turning
to the Man of Ross: "But all praises why should Lords engross? / Rise,
honest Muse! sing the MAN OF ROSS" (ll. 249–50). As a representative
of the untitled and modestly endowed gentry, the Man of Ross represents
a kind of safe and conventional social center. Addison's Mr. Spectator, for
example, represents very much the same social grouping of the untitled and
only modestly wealthy landed gentry: "I was born to a small Hereditary
Estate, which according to the tradition of the Village where it lies, was
bounded by the same Hedges and Ditches in *William* the Conqueror's
Time that it is at present, and has been delivered down from Father to
Son whole and entire, without the Cross or Acquisition of a Single Field
or Meadow, during the Space of six hundred Years."[24] The economist
Josiah Tucker, who wrote one of the century's most energetic defenses of
English capitalism, similarly presented the middle gentry as a kind of
ideal of national respectability.[25] There is, in short, nothing particularly
provocative or conservative (much less "feudal" or "Jacobite") about Pope's

praise for this figure. The Man of Ross could not conceivably offend anyone at all, and this portrait by no means implied a hostility to the City or commerce.

In so far as Pope does concern himself directly with upwardly mobility and its commercial roots, his targets display moral scruples about the evil of wealth which seem, with odd significance, to echo Pope's own strictures. The following lines, for example, have been cited as evidence of Pope's intense discomfort with the erosion of social boundaries in modern England:[26]

> At length Corruption, like a gen'ral flood,
> (So long by watchful Ministers withstood)
> Shall deluge all; and Av'rice creeping on,
> Spread like a low-born mist, and blot the Sun;
> Statesman and Patriot ply alike the stocks,
> Peeress and Butler share alike the box, (ll. 137–42)

But these are not "Pope's" words. They are, rather, the gripings of a "wizard" who advised Blunt and provoked him to launch the South Sea scheme in order to "give thy Country peace" (l. 153). Blunt is a study of moral hypocrisy and self-justification, the blustering moralism of a man who condemned wealth and advancement on the one hand yet profited from financial scheming on the other. Much the same is true of the subsequent portraits of Sir John Cutler and Sir Balaam. Culter, though a merchant, sided with Tory interests, and was a generous financial supporter of the Stuarts, prospering under James II. Pope does not criticize Cutler for making money in the City. He sinned, rather, by neither feting the rich nor providing the kind of paternalistic hospitality traditionally expected of the lord of the manor (see ll. 179–98). Cutler appears again in the poem to moralize over the sad and impecunious end of the Duke of Buckingham (ll. 315–20), expounding a version of Pope's own message in the previous portrait: Pope bemoans Buckingham's heedless luxury, and so does Cutler. As in the portrait of Blunt, excessive moralizing over wealth seems itself to be problematic. For Cutler should have been more like Bathurst (in his implied boredom with Pope's own moralizing). This self-made man *should* have lived more like a generous and splendid man of the English gentry. He should have *risen*, Tory and gentleman, more fully and gracefully, spending more on his daughter's dowry, and at least hiring a decent doctor to attend his death-bed (see ll. 321–34).

The tailing portrait of Balaam is bedeviled by another set of narrative complications. As already indicated, it is a "tale" told to appease Lord

Bathurst, who is tired of Pope's philosophizing. It is, first, a Puritan tale worthy of John Bunyan: Balaam, "a plain good man" with frugal habits (ll. 341–2) provokes the envy of "The Dev'l" (l. 349), who crashes a ship on Balaam's Cornish coastline, initiating a fatal sequence of events. Two puddings a day start the slippery slide down to gambling, dancing, whoring, cheating, and the rest of the genteel vices of St. James's Court. Pope's tale of Balaam offers a version of Molière's *Le bourgeois gentil-homme*, but here Pope's irony is darker. Balaam's upwardly mobile folly concludes not with comic exposure but the noose; Pope's version of St. James's Palace really does seem diabolically corrupt. In other words, Pope draws simultaneously from two competing versions of the upwardly mobile man, one Puritan and one genteel. The Puritan tale of Christian misled by Satan cannot, clearly, be confused with the meaning of the poem. But this tale does, considerably, darken Molière's story of the ridiculous Cit, prancing about in lace and bad French. Balaam is funny, but not very.

Epistle to Bathurst ends abruptly, even jarringly, perhaps even waking up Lord Bathurst. He would have been awakened with the question of what, exactly, Pope means. And this question should perhaps also awaken us. It should seem quite obvious, first, that Pope's purpose was not to condemn the City *tout court* or to pledge allegiance to a defunct landed gentry. The narrator's relationship to both the aristocratic interlocutor and to the portraits of capitalist parvenus is equally difficult and ambivalent. Pope seems to be speaking a different kind of language from Lord Bathurst, more troubled and more serious. In fact, unlike Bathurst, Pope has something in common with the moralistic suspicion of wealth that, curiously, links the three main Cits of the poem, Blunt, Cutler, and Balaam. But these suspicions are in turn placed in "quotes," either through the invention of figures like the "wizard" or through the creation of a concluding "tale." Wealth, credit, luxury – all these features of his culture have a moral cost. Pope worries about this cost, especially in the poem's early sections. But he also seems aware that denouncing modern capitalism draws him into the circle of hypocritical moralists like his three citizens. For we can hardly take straight Pope's dour, even Puritanical, condemnation of gold and its paper extension, credit. "What Riches give us let us then enquire," he intones – and, in response to Bathurst's silence, answers himself: "Meat, Fire, and Cloaths. What more? Meat, Cloathes, and Fire" (ll. 81–2). What is "more," of course, is this poem itself, "a leaf, like Sibyl's" scattered "to and fro" (l. 75) for commercial transaction. As pointed out in recent scholarship, the poem itself represents a kind of paper credit, which we value as the words of "Mr. Pope" on the title page.[27]

We easily forgive Pope for his implied relationship with the world of credit, finance, and the City. And we forgive him for the reasons that he, rightly, believed his contemporaries should forgive him for: Pope *deserved* to be where he ended up. He writes so well, and he so seductively represents himself as a man of exemplary rationality and elegance. The touch of self-mockery in *Bathurst* is supremely elegant, for this disquisition before a bored but tolerant nobleman both flatters Bathurst and displays Pope's witty sense of place. In the earlier poems, these social messages are even more deeply coded. In contrast to Blackmore or Defoe, Pope knows what he should and should not say aloud. But the guard on Pope's social commentary began to relax somewhat in his later work. Personally, the older Pope had nothing more to prove, no more noble egos to soothe. Politically, an important segment of the old nobility, including many former Jacobites, was leaping on a populist bandwagon whose refrain trumpeted the need for national solidarity and the promotion of merit over wealth and self-interest.[28]

By the mid-1730s, the Opposition to Walpole increasingly presented itself as a movement devoted to national and popular interests. Lord Bolingbroke's *Remarks on the History England* (written *c.* 1735) offered one of the century's most vigorous defenses of the "ancient constitution," which J. G. A. Pocock has famously connected with Harrington's Republicanism and its later, predominantly Whig, legacy.[29] *The Idea of a Patriot King*, though sometimes presented as inspired by feudal and even Jacobite convictions, actually dwells with lengthy piety on the need to protect English trade and commerce. The parliamentary leader of the Opposition, Lord Chesterfield, took populist positions on the Gin Act, the Theatrical Licensing Act and other bills; outside the house, Chesterfield became renowned as a nobleman who promoted the interests of meritorious men of humble backgrounds.[30] To the aristocratic leaders of the Oppostion, street protests against Spanish depredations in the Caribbean during the late 1730s sounded like political music. In this cause, Pope himself set up a former footman, Robert Dodsley, as an Opposition bookseller. In 1738, Dodsley published "London," the first published poem of another low-born, commercial author, Samuel Johnson, who pronounced a resonant theme of Opposition literature at this time: "SLOW RISES WORTH, BY POVERTY DEPRESS'D."[31] Pope famously admired Johnson's poem, prophesying that its anonymous author would soon be "deterré."[32] Pope's own poetry of the same period reinforces the impression that he had fallen in strongly with the supposed cause of Patriots who proclaimed

that British society should be realigned along lines that respected merit
and virtue rather than merely rank. In his imitation of "The First Epistle
to the First Book of Horace" (1738), for example, he favorably compares
the Lord Mayor, Sir John Barnard, with the Duke of Kent ("Bug"):
"BARNARD, thou art a *Cit*, with all thy worth, / But wretched Bug, his
Honour, and so forth" (ll. 89–90). In the "Epilogue to the Satires" (1738),
Pope placed Barnard in the same class of worthy men as, of all people,
the Man of Ross: "I never (to my sorrow I declare), / Din'd with the
MAN OF ROSS or my LORD MAY'R" (II, ll. 99–100).

   Whatever may have been the real motives of Lord Bolingbroke or Lord
Chesterfield, whose sudden populism seems so opportunistic, one has to
feel that Pope really meant his expressions of solidarity with Dodsley,
Johnson, or Barnard. His late friendship with Ralph Allen, the low-born
entrepreneur later celebrated as Fielding's Mr. Allworthy, is marked with
a heartfelt enthusiasm that we never find in his support of the aristocracy
or the Stuarts:

God made this Man rich, to shame the Great, and wise, to humble the learned.
I envy none of you in Town the Honours you may have received at
Court . . . : I have past this Christmas with the Most Noble Man in England.[33]

The sense of identification with Allen is palpable: Pope was himself a man
of modest origins who became rich and, like Allen, successfully integrated
himself into noble circles. What differs between the Pope of *Windsor
Forest* and the Pope of this later period is the opportunity for frank
expression born of changes both in his personal life and the political
situation. As I have argued, much of Pope's earlier poetry negotiated in
complex and deft ways with a myriad range of conflicting factors connected with transformations in the traditional social order – Pope's own
lack of elite birth, his emulation of the elite, his proud independence
from noble patronage, the commercial source of his wealth, his caustic
one-upmanship among other commercial writers. In all these respects,
Pope seems so utterly typical of what would eventually call itself the
British "middle class."

   "Class" is our word, inherited from the nineteenth century. So let us
finally turn to the Victorians. Pope was not particularly a literary hero of
the Victorians. He was widely considered, in a striking twist of literary
history, platitudinous and philistine. The great bourgeois hero of the
nineteenth century was, rather, Shakespeare. "The Stratford Peasant," as
Thomas Carlyle called Shakespeare,[34] became for the Victorians an
archetype of the successfully upwardly mobile man, the poor boy who

achieved fame and fortune through sheer force of diligence combined with genius. It was precisely this myth of Shakespeare that Bernard Shaw assailed in his debunking of "bardolatry." According to Shaw, Shakespeare was not "a parvenu trying to cover his humble origin with a purchased coat of arms." Rather, "he was a gentleman resuming what he conceived to be his natural position."[35] Shaw's argument stemmed from his Fabian impatience with bourgeois self-satisfaction, but the gauntlet he throws with regard to Shakespeare's patrician outlook was less original than he made appear: in fact, Coleridge's assessment of Shakespeare as a "philosophical aristocrat" had been rehearsed in various forms by a series of commentators.[36] The notion that Shakespeare was a humble man who was somehow qualified by talent and temperament to belong to the nobility (who should have accepted him more fully) shaped the myth of the Bard of Avon as an inspirationally middle-class icon.

Pope helped to create this myth. In *Self-Help* (1859), a popular motivation guide for the upwardly mobile, Samuel Smiles quoted the preface to Pope's edition of Shakespeare at length before reaching his inspirational conclusion: "The greatest have not disdained to labour honestly and usefully for a living, though at the same time aiming after higher things ... Shakespeare was a successful manager of a theatre – perhaps priding himself more upon his practical qualities in that capacity than on his writing of plays and poetry."[37] Smiles's unapologetically bourgeois outlook should not, of course, be confused with Pope's, who wrote at a time when the "middle class" was itself early in gestation. Nonetheless, Pope had indeed portrayed Shakespeare as an author who wrote "to please the *Populace*" and who depended on "*Common Suffrage*" rather than aristocratic patronage. Pope connects Shakespeare's common origins and commercial aims with both the greatest virtues and the greatest faults of this author. Shakespeare's naturalness, his ability to capture the realities of life, reflected his need to appeal to an audience which could care less about the formal conventions of classical drama. But the same vulgar audience, Pope observed, promoted Shakespeare's willingness to descend to "mean buffoonery, vile ribaldry, and unmannerly jests of fools and clowns." In Pope's view, Shakespeare was rescued from total debasement by his essentially noble character. He was like "some Prince of a Romance in the disguise of a Shepherd or Peasant," and indeed fulfilled the full promise of his talent when he attracted the notice of a more courtly audience.[38]

To what extent did Pope identify personally with this beloved middle-class legend of Shakespeare's life? Looking back over Pope's career, I think that his identification with this story was substantial. This is not to deny that the differences between Pope and Shakespeare (in Pope's account of him) are important: Pope did not begin his career by stooping to the low taste of the City; he never quite thought of himself as a prince in disguise. On the other hand, Pope could parody "the mean buffoonery, vile ribaldry, and unmannerly jests of fools and clowns" with masterly exhibitionism, as *The Dunciad* shows. Similarly, everything in his work confirms his conviction that he *belonged* among the nobility by virtue of his talent, taste, and moral sense. But Pope never forgot that he was an exile, both religiously *and* socially, and this awareness, too, underlies everything he wrote. In subtle and various ways, Pope's satire negotiates between these contradictions inherent in his own life and the world he lived in. To read Pope as a great practitioner of a kind of literature characteristic of a nascent middle-rank perspective is by no means to diminish awareness of the complexity and richness of his writing. Such a reading is to take full measure of his complexity, and perhaps also of our own.

NOTES

1 Brean S. Hammond, *Pope* (Brighton: Harvester Press, 1986), p. 3.
2 Howard Erskine-Hill has presented a persuasive case for Pope's Jacobite sympathies in "Alexander Pope: The Political Poet in his Time," *Eighteenth-Century Studies* 15 (1982), 123–48. See also Douglas Brooks-Davies, *Pope's "Dunciad" and the Queen of the Night: A Study in Emotional Jacobitism* (Manchester: Manchester University Press, 1985), and Pat Rogers, *Pope and the Destiny of the Stuarts: History, Politics and Mythology in the Age of Queen Anne* (Oxford: Oxford University Press, 2005). But Erskine-Hill concludes by admitting that Pope "trimmed his sails" in his support for the Jacobites, and that we can only "infer" that he was "not utterly averse" to a Stuart restoration (p. 141). Pat Rogers presents *Windsor Forest* as a kind of last gasp for Pope's emotional Jacobitism, for he "probably felt that the sun had set on the Jacobites' hopes as far back as 1723" (p. 86).
3 Colin Nicholson, *Writing and the Rise of Finance: Capital Satires in the Early Eighteenth Century* (Cambridge: Cambridge University Press, 1994), p. 153. In this book, Nicholson appears to take a more unqualified position with regard to Pope's supposed anti-capitalism than he does in his more recent essay, cited below.
4 Colin Nicholson, "The Mercantile Bard: Commerce and Conflict in Pope," *Studies in the Literary Imagination* 38 (2005), 77–94.
5 John Barrell, "The Uses of Contradiction: Pope's 'Epistle to Bathurst'," in *Poetry, Language and Politics* (Manchester: Manchester University Press, 1988), pp. 79–99.

6 Though City-born and -raised, Barber was a Tory – and perhaps a Jacobite – who was associated with Pope's Tory circle. His former apprentice, John Wright, became Pope's printer at the time of the *Dunciad Variorum*. See the *DNB* entry for Barber, written by Nicholas Rogers.

7 While literary scholars have been rather slow to catch up with revisions to classic Marxist historiography, there is wide consensus among historians (including many Marxist historians) that the category of "class" cannot be applied to early eighteenth-century society with much accuracy. See Harold J. Perkin, *The Origins of Modern English Society, 1780–1800* (London: Routledge and Kegan Paul; Toronto: University of Toronto Press, 1969), pp. 176–217; Peter Laslett, *The World We Have Lost*, 2nd edn. (London: Methuen, 1971), p. 24; E. P. Thompson, "Eighteenth-century English Society: Class Struggle without Class?," *Social History* 3:2 (1978), 133–65; R. J. Morris, *Class and Class Consciousness in the Industrial Revolution, 1780–1850* (London and Basingstoke: Macmillan, 1979), pp. 12–20; Penelope J. Corfield, "Class by Name and Number in Eighteenth-Century Britain," in *Language, History and Class*, ed. Penelope J. Corfield (Oxford: Basil Blackwell, 1991), pp. 101–30; Jonathan Barry, introduction to *The Middling Sort of People: Culture, Society and Politics in England, 1550–1800*, ed. Jonathan Barry and Christopher Brooks (Houndmills and London: Macmillan, 1994), pp. 1–27; David Cannadine, *Class in Britain* (New Haven: Yale University Press, 1998), pp. 24–56.

8 See C. J. Rawson, "Gentlemen and Dancing-Masters," in *Henry Fielding and the Augustan Ideal under Stress* (London and Boston: Routledge and Kegan Paul, 1972), pp. 3–34.

9 This play was "staggeringly popular, performed more than thirty times in its first year" (Robert Hume, *The Development of English Drama in the Late Seventeenth Century* [Oxford: Clarendon Press, 1976], p. 276).

10 Edward Ravencroft, *The Citizen turn'd Gentleman* (London, 1672), p. 65.

11 See Ned Ward, *The London Spy*, ed. Paul Hyland (East Lansing, MI: Colleagues Press, 1993), pp. 14–15.

12 See Abigail Williams, *Poetry and the Creation of a Whig Literary Culture 1618–1714* (Oxford: Oxford University Press, 2005).

13 All references to Pope's poetry are from the *Twickenham Edition of the Poems of Alexander Pope*, ed. J. Butt *et al.*, 11 vols. (London, Methuen, 1939–69).

14 See James Foxon, *Pope and the Early Eighteenth-Century Book Trade*, ed. and rev. James McLaverty (Oxford: Clarendon Press, 1991), pp. 102–52.

15 See Foxon, *Pope and the Early Eighteenth-Century Book Trade*, p. 138.

16 William Darrell, *A Gentleman Instructed* (London, 1704), pp. 15–16.

17 Anon., *The Man of Manners: or, Plebeian Polish'd* (London, 1735), p. iv.

18 Daniel Defoe, *The Compleat Gentleman* (n.d.), ed. Kark D. Bülbring (London: David Nutt, 1890), p. 4.

19 Defoe, *The Compleat Gentleman*, p. 20.

20 Samuel Johnson, "Life of Pope," in *Lives of the Most Eminent English Poets*, 4 vols., ed. Roger Lonsdale (Oxford: Clarendon Press, 2006), vol. IV, p. 70.

21 Bevill Higgons, *A Poem on the Glorious Peace of Utrecht*, 2nd edn. (London, 1731), p. 14.

22 See Rogers, *Pope and the Destiny of the Stuarts*.

23 Nicholson, *Writing and the Rise of Finance*, p. 153.

24 *The Spectator*, ed. Donald F. Bond, 5 vols. (Oxford: Clarendon Press, 1965), no. 1, vol. I, pp. 1–2.

25 Tucker's important defense of trade was *A Brief Essay on the Advantages and Disadvantages which repeatedly attend France and Great Britain with regard to Trade* (London, 1749). But Tucker later presented the landed gentry as the bedrock of English values and respectability in a work whose long title summarizes the entire work: *An Humble Address and Earnest Appeal to those Respectable Personages in Great Britain and Ireland who, by their Great Permanent Interest in Landed Property, their Elevated Rank and Enlarged Views, are Ablest to Judge, and the Fittest to Decide, whether a Connection with, or a Separation from the Continental Colonies of America, be most for the National Advantage, and the Lasting Benefit of these Kingdoms* (Gloucester, 1775).

26 See Nicholson, *Writing and the Rise of Finance*, p. 151.

27 See Tom Jones, "Pope's *Epistle to Bathurst* and the Meaning of Finance," *Studies in English Literature* 44:3 (2004), 487–504. Jones focuses in particular on the comparable uncertainty of paper credit and the instability of words, as demonstrated by Pope's own vocabulary in the poem.

28 See Kathleen Wilson, *The Sense of the People: Politics, Culture, and Imperialism in England, 1715–1765* (Cambridge: Cambridge University Press, 1995), pp. 84–136. Wilson notes that even the Pretender started to sound populist.

29 See Henry St. John, Lord Bolingbroke, *Remarks on the History of England*, 3rd edn. (London, 1780), pp. 55–6; J. G. A. Pocock, *The Ancient Constitution and the Feudal Law: A Study of English Historical Thought in the Seventeenth Century* (Cambridge: Cambridge University Press, 1957).

30 See Nicholas Hudson, *Samuel Johnson and the Making of Modern England* (Cambridge: Cambridge University Press, 1993), pp. 95–6, 101–2; "Reassessing the Political Context of the *Dictionary*: Johnson and the 'Broad-bottom' Opposition," in *Anniversary Essays on Johnson's Dictionary*, ed. Jack Lynch and Anne McDermott (Cambridge: Cambridge University Press, 2005), pp. 63–7.

31 "London," l. 177, in *The Yale Edition of the Works of Samuel Johnson*, gen. eds. A. T. Hazen and J. H. Middendorf, 16 vols. (New Haven and London: Yale University Press, 1958–), vol. VI. Compare Johnson's line to Dodsley's frontispiece to *A Muse in Livery; or, the Footman's Miscellany* (London, 1732), p. i.

32 James Boswell, *Life of Johnson*, ed. G. B. Hill, rev. L. F. Powell, 6 vols. (Oxford: Clarendon Press, 1934–50), vol. I, p. 129.

33 Quoted in Maynard Mack, *Alexander Pope: A Life* (New Haven and London: Yale University Press, 1985), p. 765.

34 Thomas Carlyle, *The Hero as Poet* (1840), in D. Nichol Smith (ed.), *Shakespeare Criticism: A Selection 1632–1840* (London: Oxford University Press, 1946), p. 369.

35 Bernard Shaw, *Shaw on Shakespeare*, ed. Edwin Wilson (London: Cassel, 1961), p. 199.

36 Samuel Taylor Coleridge, *Coleridge's Shakespearian Criticism*, ed. Thomas Middleton Raysor, 2 vols. (London: Constable and Co., 1930), vol. II, p. 136. See also Edward Dowden, *Shakspere [sic]: A Critical Study of His Mind and Art* (1875; London: Routledge and Kegan Paul, 1957), p. 35; Frank Harris, *The Man Shakespeare and his Tragic Life Story* (London: Mitchell Kennersley, 1909), p. 397. Shaw was reacting specifically to Harris.

37 Samuel Smiles, *Self-Help: With Illustrations of Conduct and Perseverance* (London: John Murray, 1958), pp. 262–3.

38 See *The Prose Works of Alexander Pope*, ed. Rosemary Cowler, 2 vols. (Oxford: Basil Blackwell, 1986), vol. II, pp. 14–16.

CHAPTER 12

Fielding's satire and the jestbook tradition: the case of Lord Justice Page

Thomas Keymer

It cannot have helped the legal career that Fielding maintained alongside his career as a novelist that trigger-happy magistrates and self-serving judges were among his favorite satirical targets. One of his first stage comedies, *Rape upon Rape* (1730), features the memorable figure of Justice Squeezum, a lewd and brazen extortionist who suborns witnesses, packs juries, and runs a lucrative protection racket for bawdy houses. More than two decades later, *Amelia*, his last novel, involves scenes of blatant malfeasance by Justice Thrasher, a venal Westminster magistrate who (in a formula of mock approval that Fielding had been polishing since *Jonathan Wild*) "was never indifferent in a Cause, but when he could get nothing on either Side."[1] In the intervening years, miscarriages and abuses of justice by those charged with impartially administering the law are a recurrent theme of his satire.

Fielding's emphasis is typically on individual corruption, and he stops short of alleging that systematic or institutionalized injustice is inherent in the criminal code or the structure of law enforcement. Occasionally, however, particular cases suggest a bigger and bolder satirical thesis, as when Squeezum presents the justice system as designedly an instrument of social control. "The Laws are Turnpikes," he says, "only made to stop People who walk on Foot, and not to interrupt those who drive through them in their Coaches."[2] In this eloquent and very topical metaphor (popular protest against turnpikes had recently surged, to evident ministerial alarm),[3] legislation is enacted for the convenience and benefit of higher ranks at the expense of those below. In similar vein, a passage from *Joseph Andrews* on the generous scope for hanging established by Walpole's "Black Act" of 1723 targets the marked increase in the number of property crimes punishable by death that was a feature of the period's so-called "Bloody Code." In this case the magistrate involved, Justice Frolick, is merely unprincipled and capricious, but more sinister connotations surround the pettifogging attorney hired by Lady Booby, for whom the laws of the land are at the service of rank and wealth, and "are not so vulgar, to permit a mean Fellow to contend with one of your Ladyship's Fortune." At this lawyer's instigation, Joseph and Fanny are prosecuted under the Black Act for stealing a twig, and "if we had called it a young Tree they would have been both hanged."[4] This passage even supplies the epigraph to E. P. Thompson's classic study *Whigs and Hunters*, a work that trenchantly (if also somewhat hyperbolically) denounces eighteenth-century criminal law as a sanctimonious conspiracy of intimidation and terror, an apparatus created and used to shore up entrenched inequalities of wealth and power.[5]

Alongside *Amelia*'s hostile caricature of Justice Thrasher and Fielding's sideswipes against particular statutes in *Joseph Andrews* and elsewhere, the case examined in the present essay, Partridge's anecdote of a horse-stealing trial in *Tom Jones*, is less conspicuous and less often discussed. It concerns a real judge as opposed to a fictional magistrate,[6] occupies just part of a chapter, and exists at a double remove – interpolated within a larger interpolation, the Man of the Hill's tale in Book VIII – from the primary action of the novel. No less an authority than the hero himself thinks it an irrelevant digression, and tries to cut it short. Yet Partridge's tale from the assizes also has the structural function of a *mise en abyme*, with close thematic bearing on a work dominated throughout by legal or more broadly ethical questions about crime and punishment, mercy and severity, justice and judgment. It is important if only because of its uniqueness as a formal courtroom episode in a novel that otherwise, as John Allen Stevenson notes in the one sustained discussion of this passage in recent criticism, stages its scenes of judgment in informal settings.[7] Even in the immediate context of the Man of the Hill's narrative, the apparent digression is sharply to the point, providing a modern, Whiggish corollary to the most notorious instance of judicial misconduct in popular memory: the jeering brutality of Judge Jeffreys at the so-called "Bloody Assizes" of 1685, which the Man of the Hill has been lucky to escape following his youthful involvement in the Monmouth Rebellion, and which Fielding makes a point of reference in his political journalism. As well as denouncing Jeffreys for "the inhuman and unparallel'd Butchery committed in cold Blood, by his immediate Order, on *Monmouth's* conquer'd People in the West," Fielding's journalism elsewhere revives the old rumor that, in sorting the condemned from the reprieved, Jeffreys "put the Decision of their Guilt on Chance, and...determined which were the proper Objects of his Mercy, by the Casting of Dice."[8] A vicious compound of insouciance and intimidation, his conduct mirrors, on a genocidal scale, the smaller but no less lethal tyrannies of Partridge's courtroom bully.

Beyond these evident thematic links, Partridge's tale has much to tell us about the unpredictable energies of Fielding's satire, and in particular about its affinities with – even, to a discernible extent, its origins in – the disreputable and largely forgotten genre of the early modern jestbook. The significance of the tale has been obscured, however, by a chain of unexamined assumptions: first, that the trial described by Partridge actually took place; second, that this trial is factually reported rather than creatively reworked; third, that the whole episode is therefore somehow extraneous to the novel as a whole. The story has long been thought to derive from Fielding's memories as a rookie lawyer on the Western Circuit, and has been treated as interpretatively irrelevant, or so it would seem, because literally true: a chunk of journalism dropped into the text, based on the happenstance of a real-life incident, and of no interest to a criticism focused instead on imaginative, fictional patterns. Yet, as Stevenson rightly insists, Partridge's tale is "far too intricately plotted and tonally complex to consider as [narrowly] documentary,"[9] and further inspection strongly suggests that it is not documentary at all. This does not mean, however, that the episode lacks any origins outside Fielding's imagination, or that these origins have nothing to tell us about his creative practice. So far as the usual constraints of newspaper and archival survival permit, I demonstrate here that there is no historical basis for Partridge's anecdote, but plenty of evidence to suggest instead that Fielding reworked it from jestbook material. In this very different context – the context of popular literature as opposed to personal experience – the episode allows us, alongside similar passages in *Jonathan Wild*, *The Journal of a Voyage to Lisbon*, and other parts of *Tom Jones*, to recognize the jestbook tradition as a significant though underestimated force in Fielding's satire, and one bound up with some of its most wayward and disruptive impulses.

Like other elements of *Tom Jones*, including the hero's forgiveness of Enderson (the would-be highwayman of Book XII) and Black George (the pocket-book thief of Book VI), Partridge's tale is in marked tension with Fielding's strictures elsewhere against victims and witnesses who refuse, from misplaced tenderness, to assist in the prosecution of capital offenders.[10] The Man of the Hill has benefited in his youth (even before the Monmouth rising) from just such a refusal himself, and this prompts Partridge to describe the uneasy conscience of a friend, a farmer's son named Frank Bridle, who, following the theft of his father's horse, has apprehended the culprit and brought charges. The case comes to trial at the county assizes, and Bridle's testimony directly results in the conviction and execution of the alleged thief (whose guilt seems likely, but is never confirmed). After the hanging of this obviously ineffectual malefactor, Bridle finds his conscience, or perhaps his unconscious, miserably disturbed and haunted. In a clever reprise of the culminating joke from Fielding's early farce *Tom Thumb*,[11] he is even beaten up by the hanged man's ghost as he returns from a night at the alehouse; the bloodied body of a white-faced calf is found at the scene the next morning. Yet Bridle's predicament is poignant as well as absurd, and his experience is turned by Partridge into a solemn warning – albeit a warning he forgets when Enderson tries to rob him – about the psychological costs of bringing prosecution and bearing witness when hanging is the likely outcome. "He never was in the dark alone," Partridge reports of his conscience-stricken friend, "but he fancied he saw the Fellow's Spirit."[12]

The troubled recollections of Frank Bridle have much to do with the conduct of the trial, which violates eighteenth-century as well as modern expectations of due process. The presiding judge, whom Partridge identifies as a historical individual, the notoriously brutal and arbitrary Sir Francis Page (*c.* 1661–1741), allows the prosecutor to speak for half an hour, but refuses to hear a word from the prisoner's counsel. This is a significant over-ruling, for the old assumption that defendants should demonstrate innocence in their own unassisted voices had broken down by the 1730s, and judges were now routinely allowing defense counsel to cross-examine accusing witnesses.[13] Having been present himself at the trial, Partridge is disturbed by the imbalance of power in operation, with "my Lord, and the Court, and the Jury, and the Counsellors, and the Witnesses all upon one poor Man, and he too in Chains."[14] What disturbs Partridge most of all is the judge's technique of uniting those present against the defendant by making him the butt of malicious fun, a kind of comic scapegoat. When the hapless prisoner protests that he has "found," not stolen, the horse, Page rejoins in the following wise-cracking style:

"Ay!" answered the Judge, "thou art a lucky Fellow; I have travelled the Circuit these forty Years, and never found a Horse in my Life; but I'll tell thee what, Friend, thou wast more lucky than thou didst know of: For thou didst not only find a Horse; but a Halter too, I promise thee." To be sure I shall never forget the Word. Upon which every Body fell a laughing, as how could they help it.

Other jests follow, which Partridge forgets, and more merriment all around. Page's courtroom becomes a theater of cruelty, the sentence of death an occasion for judicial drolling and public derision. Only Partridge himself seems able to resist the infectious mood of the occasion, and then only in retrospect; the brutal pun on "halter" sears itself on his memory, together with a remorseful sense that the judge had made it "charming Sport to hear Trials upon Life and Death."[15]

The assumption that this anecdote in *Tom Jones* records an actual case is of long standing, and the callous quip is certainly in line with Page's reputation for delivering (as Pope puts it in one of several hostile lines) "Hard words or Hanging, if your Judge be *Page*."[16] The same individual is reviled by Johnson for conducting Richard Savage's celebrated murder trial of 1727 "with his usual Insolence and Severity," and Johnson quotes furious lines by Savage himself at this point. The lines in question (the source is a fragment of Savage's otherwise unpublished *An Epistle to Authors*) cast Page as a cynical, power-crazed bully, a smug exponent of judicial terror who gleefully laces his brutal sentences with "vile, buffoon Abuse."[17] In the years preceding the Savage affair, Page had already earned notoriety as a zealous enforcer of the Black Act in several showcase trials, and other contemporaries make similar allegations of arbitrary dealing and boorish spite. As John Butt reports with reference to Edmund Malone's manuscript notes for an edition of Pope: "Bishop Douglas of Salisbury told Malone that he had been present when a man was brought before Page for horse-stealing. As soon as the prisoner was led into court, Page remarked, 'A very ill-looking fellow; I have no doubt of his guilt.' The man was innocent, and was acquitted."[18] Salisbury is also the implied setting of the anecdote in *Tom Jones* (the felon is apprehended at a fair outside the city), and Page is known to have presided over the Western Circuit at the summer assizes of 1737 and 1739, before Fielding's legal career had been launched in earnest, but when he could conceivably have been present.[19] Wilbur Cross, F. Homes Dudden, and Donald Thomas are among the biographers of Fielding who treat the horse/halter anecdote as historical fact, and several modern editions of *Tom Jones* carry notes to the same effect. The assumption that Fielding was drawing on his own direct experience even creeps into the recent life of Page in the *Oxford Dictionary of National Biography*, which adds, perhaps by conflation with the story told by Bishop Douglas, that "at the original trial that Fielding had seen Page had in fact acquitted the prisoner."[20]

Yet none of these many sources cites hard evidence that the trial in question actually took place, and all depend directly or indirectly on a piece by J. Paul de Castro in a 1914 number of *Notes and Queries*. Here de Castro uses the past tense to clarify the relative roles of examining magistrate and presiding judge in the two-stage prosecution process described by Partridge: "Justice Willoughby committed the prisoner to take his trial, and bound over the witness (Francis Bridle) in a recognizance. The prisoner was tried, in fact, at Salisbury Assizes by Sir Francis Page."[21] This sounds like an assertion of historicity (the past tense, the "in fact"), as though de Castro had found court records naming Partridge's friend as a prosecuting witness. But he cites no documentary source at this point, and may well have been misunderstood. A habit of applying historic tenses to fictional plots is observable in other essays by the same scholar, and it seems clear in this particular context that his interjected "in fact" refers to nothing more substantial than a fact about the text: the relative roles assigned to Willoughby and Page in the anecdote itself, which had been muddled by a previous commentator in *Notes and Queries*, F. S. Dickson.

There, in any event, the trail goes cold. No "Francis Bridle" appears in the superb index of victims and witnesses of crime at the Wiltshire and Swindon Record Office,[22] and this is hardly surprising, since his name, pretty obviously, is not historically but thematically determined. Shaped by a story about nooses and bridles, and working also as a play on "free rein" (the free rein of the stolen horse, and of Frank's unbridled imagination), the name is no less artificial than that of Allworthy or Parson Supple. Nor does a matching case appear in the archive under other, less fanciful, names. Records from the Western Circuit are patchy for the years in question, but the best surviving source, the Gaol Book, records no case of horse theft at the Salisbury assizes in July 1737, a single acquittal in July 1738 (when judges other than Page presided), and a second case in August 1739, when William Brown was charged with stealing from William Smith a gelding worth £7.[23] No sentence is recorded in this second case, but since Brown had already been condemned to hang on a separate count of highway robbery, probably none was given: circuit judges operated on a tight schedule, and jurymen (with consequences famously alleged in *The Rape of the Lock*) had to get out and dine.[24] Extant copies of the *Salisbury Journal* record just two further cases of possible relevance, though without the detail that marks this newspaper's coverage of the highly charged spring assizes of 1739, when proceedings arising from the recent riot of Melksham weavers attracted national attention.[25] In the number for July 9, 1737 we learn that "last week was brought from *Ilchester*, and Committed to our County Gaol, *George Rawlings*, a Young Lad about Nineteen, for Horse-Stealing"; Rawlings's fate does not appear. At the summer assizes two years later,

among the prisoners acquitted was a possible candidate for Bishop
Douglas's story: "*William Parker*, for stealing one Yoke of Oxen, three
Heifers, and a Mare."[26]

All of this establishes that trials for horse-stealing did indeed come
before Page at Salisbury – which, given that one in every twenty property
crime indictments at mid-eighteenth-century rural assizes was for this
offense, is unsurprising enough.[27] But capital sentences at Salisbury in the
years at issue are recorded only in the more serious and violent cases of an
arsonist and two highwaymen.[28] No surviving source prior to de Castro's
ambiguous comment supports the assumption that Fielding's artful tale
about bridles and halters is founded in fact – just as nothing beyond mere
circumstantial possibility supports the assumption that he and Page ever
even coincided on the Western Circuit, from which Page at last retired
after the summer assizes of 1739, still almost a full year before Fielding
was called to the Bar. Page continued to hear trials elsewhere in his
decrepitude (his parting shot was reportedly to quip, in another anecdote
of dubious provenance, "you see, I keep hanging on, hanging on"),[29] but
there is no other evidence to suggest that he and Fielding ever crossed
paths in the remaining two years of Page's life.

There is, however, an alternative and much more plausible explanation
for Page's cameo appearance in *Tom Jones*, and for Partridge's tale of
Frank Bridle. For the vicious witticism about horses and halters that
Fielding places in Page's mouth has a pedigree reaching back in print for
more than a century. In general terms, its alliterative quality recalls a
more familiar hanging joke of the Walpole era, about carriages to court
and carts to the gallows, and Fielding uses this line in *The Author's Farce*:
"if you wou'd ride in your Coach, deserve to ride in a Cart."[30] There were
far closer precedents than this, however, for the horse/halter joke as it
appears in Partridge's tale. In Ben Jonson's *The Alchemist* (1616) – one of
the two plays to which Coleridge famously compares the perfection of
Tom Jones's plot – Face curses Subtle to the gallows with an insulting
quibble on "halter": "A horse draw you, and a halter, / You, and your flies
together."[31] The same play on the dual meaning of "halter" (a noose for
leading a horse or for hanging a man) is made in "The Oxford Expedition,"
a satirical ballad of 1689 by John Smith about a minor episode in the
Glorious Revolution. Here the protagonist of the poem rides on horseback with a gang of hired heavies, brutes who deserve to be hanged.
As Smith makes the point in his clumsy anapaests, it is the ruffian, not
his mount, who should be wearing the noose: "One's horse wore a
halter among all the rest, / Nor had the dull wight half the sense of his

beast, / And he of the two did deserve the rope best."[32] This verse satire found its way, via editions of *Poems on Affairs of State*, into a number of early eighteenth-century jestbooks, and there found its natural home. Later in the century, a similar exercise in gallows humor, rooted in the same pun, was to appear in several jestbooks of the next generation. As a compilation of 1778 reports: "Swift meeting a farmer with a black horse in a halter, said, 'Honest man, how can you use your horse so ill, to make him black in the face?' When the farmer replied, 'Ah, Maister! Had you looked as long through a halter as he has, you would be black in the face too.'"[33]

As this belated invocation of Swift suggests, eighteenth-century jests tended to congregate without much basis around figures known for their wit, or for some other quality relevant to the jest, much as George W. Bush has recently acted as a magnet for malapropism jokes. (In this case, the name of Swift flags the story as an Irish joke, but also points, in the farmer's reply, to a note of brutalized nonchalance that faintly recalls Swift's own satire.) Sir Francis Page, who as well as being coarse and severe was also the target of a long and effective smear campaign by Richard Savage's friends and fellow authors, came in for just such treatment in the literary culture of his day. Commenting with appropriate caution on a scathing *Dunciad* footnote, which represents Page as "always ready to hang any man, of which he was suffered to give a hundred miserable examples during a long life, even to his dotage," Valerie Rumbold observes that Page's name "was, perhaps undeservedly, a byword for brutality."[34] Savage himself, who had been sentenced to death by Page but reprieved by royal pardon, did everything he could to prolong this situation. Many of the apocryphal stories in circulation took their cue from Savage's vindictive lampoons, which stress Page's alleged reluctance ever to let considerations of mere justice stand in the way of a joke. "Ev'n *Innocence* itself must hang," as Savage rails against Page in "A Character"; "Must hang to please him, when of spleen possest: / Must hang to bring forth an abortive jest."[35]

The result was that Page acquired an infamy that was no doubt grounded in, but no less certainly an exaggeration of, his actual character and conduct. He became the ready handle for any exercise in black courtroom humor. Even E. P. Thompson – never one to think too generously of an eighteenth-century judge – cautions that some of the stories linked with his name are probably false.[36] Buried in the archives is evidence of a more complicated underlying reality, including a homicide case retrieved from Warwickshire assize records of the 1730s by the legal historian J. M. Beattie. On this occasion, Page directs a jury to convict

the accused prisoner of manslaughter (a lesser charge of criminally neg-
ligent, as opposed to intentional, homicide), but he is misunderstood or
ignored by the jurors, and a verdict of murder is returned. As Beattie
reports, "the judge (ironically in this case Mr. Justice Page, 'the Hanging
Judge,' who had a reputation for harshness) could only save this man
from the gallows by reprieving him and recommending him to the king
for a full pardon."[37] Unsurprisingly, one does not hear about this
counter-example from Savage and his supporters.

In surviving jestbooks, as opposed to formal satire and oral tradition,
Page is not a conspicuous figure by name, but other judges crop up as
sources of similarly nasty one-liners. As in the chortling courtroom
described in *Tom Jones*, moreover, the jestbook audience is invited to
relish, rather than, like Partridge, resist, the cruelty of the joke. A good
example is found in the 1721 edition of *Cambridge Jests*, where an attempt
by a condemned felon to charm his way to a commuted sentence is
crushed by more waggery from the bench:

> Sir *Nicholas Bacon* being appointed Judge for the Northern Circuit, was by a
> Malefactor mightily importuned to save his Life; but when nothing he could say
> did avail, he desir'd his Mercy on the account of Kindred: *Prethee*, said my Lord
> Judge, *how comes that in? Why, if it please you, my Lord, your Name is* Bacon, *and
> mine is* Hog, *and those two have ever been so near related, that they cannot be
> separated. I but*, replied Judge *Bacon, you and I cannot be Kindred, except you be
> hanged; for* Hog *is not* Bacon, *until it be hanged.*[38]

Labored and spiteful as this witticism now seems, it and others like it
seem to have appealed to the core readership of the jestbook genre, and
courtroom anecdotes became a standing feature of such works. Later
jestbooks associate ghoulish *bon mots* of just the same kind with Fielding's
sometime friend Sir Thomas Burnet, including one story in which Burnet
epigrammatically dismisses a felon's complaint that death is a dispro-
portionate punishment for stealing a horse. As Robert Baker writes in a
jestbook of the 1760s entitled *Witticisms and Strokes of Humour*, "*No,
Friend*, said the Judge: *you are not hang'd for stealing a Horse; but that
Horses may not be stolen.*"[39]

Readers of Fielding will recognize this languid riposte from its incorporation in a complex and volatile passage in *The Journal of a Voyage to
Lisbon*, where Fielding destabilizes his ostensible approval of Burnet's words
with sly ironic embellishments.[40] Exactly where the anecdote originates is
unclear: perhaps in a real flourish of extempore wit by Burnet, perhaps in
Fielding's authorial imagination, or perhaps in an undiscovered earlier

jestbook on which both *The Journal of a Voyage to Lisbon* and *Witticisms and Strokes of Humour* were surreptitiously drawing. The direction of the borrowing is of little importance. What matters here is Fielding's unmistakable closeness to the jestbook idiom, and in particular his uneasy relish for its characteristic brand of humor: a Hobbesian comedy of malice and triumph where exuberant cruelty and punitive humiliation are integral features, and jest is regularly a weapon inflicted on the disadvantaged – paupers, prisoners, cripples, and the like – by smirking authority figures.

Yet the attraction of the idiom is also accompanied in Fielding by a countervailing recoil. On one hand he enjoys, and invites readers to enjoy, a comedy of victimization in which knives are deftly twisted in wounds, insults are added to injuries, and targets are kicked when down. On the other he distances himself, with defensive irony, from the supercilious malice of the bullies and tormentors involved. His own version of the Burnet jest is mischievously expanded, with a stealthy intervention of his own that freezes the judge in mid-speech: " 'You are not to be hanged, Sir,' answered my ever-honoured and beloved friend, 'for stealing a horse, but you are to be hanged that horses may not be stolen.' " The timing is crucial here. By positioning his elaborate *inquit* exactly where he does, Fielding heightens the malicious suspense contrived by Burnet's own phrasing, which teases the felon with false hope of reprieve ("You are not to be hanged") and only then resolves itself into a smug lecture on deterrence. What adds to the cruelty in this case, given the usual practice of courts in the period (see above, n. 39), is the confidence a horse-thief might reasonably have had that he would indeed not be hanged. But it is above all the selection of honor and love as Burnet's special attributes, rather as Fielding elsewhere singles out for praise the benevolence of Blifil or the modesty of Laetitia Snap, that does the real damage. The incongruity is overwhelming, and removes the need for the more overt irony markers that characterize his account elsewhere of the exemplary mass hangings perpetrated by the prototype for both Burnet and Page, "the great Judge *Jeffries* (following I suppose the Opinion of *Plato*)."[41] At the very least, Fielding lavishes too much praise on Burnet here, of just the wrong kind and at just the wrong moment, not to grate on the ear. In a jarring extension of this passage, he then seems to switch his imaginative alignment, identifying no longer with his dubiously honorable, lovable friend, but instead with the hapless felon: "I was now, in the opinion of all men, dying of a complication of disorders."[42]

It is important in this context to recognize the ways in which, as Simon Dickie demonstrates in a path-breaking recent essay, the jestbook genre was moving commercially upmarket in the eighteenth century, with corresponding shifts in content and tone.[43] In their original guise as expressions of popular culture, crude chapbooks hawked by pedlars to peasant or artisan readers, jestbooks have been read as socially subversive works, celebratory of roguish insubordination and carnivalesque misrule, and this view still conditions assumptions about the genre as it developed.[44] The popular tradition certainly persisted in the eighteenth century, notably in the cheap compilations of droll antics and broad folk humor printed over several decades by the Dicey family. But jestbooks were now increasingly aimed at fashionable metropolitan consumers of higher rank. In publications of this more mainstream kind, elegant duodecimos priced at three or even five shillings, the boot was often on the other foot in terms of social hierarchy and the relations of comic power. Of growing prominence in the jestbooks of Fielding's lifetime was a scapegoating comedy in which violent pranks and malicious hoaxes inflicted by bucks and sparks on their social inferiors set the prevailing tone. Put-downs delivered to condemned felons were a verbal variant of this pattern, and in figures like Judge Burnet – notoriously a "Mohock" rake in his youth – the two kinds of bullying meet.[45] Typically, as the courtroom anecdotes are structured, the tormentor is the judge himself, named or unnamed; only rarely is he bested from the dock, and only rarely does reprieve follow, as though execution of the outwitted male-factor is necessary to complete the joke.

Fielding was publicly accused of plundering jestbooks in his fiction as early as 1751, when Robert Goadby alleged that some of Fitzpatrick's speeches in *Tom Jones* were plagiarized from the 1746 edition of *Cambridge Jests*, a compilation originally published in 1674.[46] The 1746 imprint does not survive, but Goadby's accusation looks very plausible, given that another anecdote in *Tom Jones*, the tale of Nell Gwyn's gruffly dignified footman in Book XI, is to be found in earlier surviving editions of *Cambridge Jests*, and that the twelve mock-proverbs in *Jonathan Wild* are lifted from one of the most popular of the new wave of jestbooks in Fielding's day, *Joe Miller's Jests* (1739).[47] It is only recently, however, that scholars have begun to track Fielding's use of compilations of this kind, perhaps because of a residual sense that these are unseemly sources for classic novels, unfit to appear alongside Homer and Virgil, or Tillotson and Barrow, in commentary and scholarly annotation. Yet Fielding's appropriations always involved creative transformation and imaginative surplus. Where jestbook sources are concerned, moreover, they display with unusual clarity one of the most distinctive tendencies of his satire, and one to which the criticism of Claude Rawson has attuned us over the past few decades: its habit of lurching unpredictably between competing positions and sets of values, without assimilating one to the other. In its original jestbook form, the Nell Gwyn anecdote works simply at the expense of the footman who, having misguidedly defended her honor with his fists, returns home bruised and bloodied, with torn clothes: "*Begone, you Rogue*, says she, *I shall have enough to do, to give you a new Livery for every one that calls me whore.*"[48] This put-down is repeated with relish in *Tom Jones*, but as well as tightening the wording and sharpening the pace of his source, Fielding also extends it, allowing the final word to the footman in a way that makes Gwyn's witty cynicism look, by comparison with his own dogged self-assertion, retrospectively ignoble: " 'You Blockhead,' replied Mrs. *Gwynn*, 'at this Rate you must fight every Day of your Life; why, you Fool, all the World knows it.' 'Do they?' cries the Fellow, in a muttering Voice, after he had shut the Coach Door, 'they shan't call me a Whore's Footman for all that.' "[49]

A similar double impulse emerges in Partridge's story, the most plausible identifiable source for which is not an actual sally of malevolent wit on Page's part but the following anecdote, traditionally associated with the legendary court fool John Scoggin, and first found in a Jacobean jestbook of 1613. The scene of this widely recycled jest is a confessional, where Scoggin is impersonating a priest; the version quoted here comes from an early eighteenth-century edition of *Oxford Jests*:

Another who came to him to be Confess'd, told him that he had stol'n a Halter. Well, said *Scoggin*, to steal a Halter, is no great matter. But, said the Fellow, there was a Horse tied at the end of it. Ay, marry, quoth *Scoggin*, there is something in that; there's difference between a Horse and a Halter: You must therefore restore the Owner the Horse, and when you have done that, come to me, and I'll absolve you for the Halter.[50]

Possibly Fielding was rewriting this relatively genial jest in dark colors in *Tom Jones*, converting Scoggin's amiable fake priest into a sneering, vindictive judge, and turning a flippant tale of confession and salvation into one of condemnation and death. Possibly he was reworking some other untraced variant of the horse/halter collocation from the jestbook tradition, this being an ephemeral genre with notoriously low rates of survival. What is clear, either way, is that in one form or another the joke was an established comic standby long before *Tom Jones*, and quite independently of Sir Francis Page. Page's tarnished reputation, however, gave Fielding the perfect peg on which to hang his elaborate development of the joke. It also gave him the opportunity to trump Pope's line about "Hard words or Hanging" with a narrative extension of the same allegation, in which Page inflicts both at once.

At the same time, the jest allowed Fielding to make the same characteristic move – the move William Empson famously called "double irony," and a move central to Rawson's reading of Fielding and Swift alike[51] – that makes the companion tale from the *Voyage to Lisbon* such an unstable, perplexing passage. While appropriating the "halter" punchline as a jest worth repeating, Fielding distances himself from Page's cruelty through Partridge's moralizing commentary – but then distances himself from the commentary as well by exposing Partridge as a superstitious fool, a believer in white-faced calves as avenging ghosts. While it is safe to conclude, then, that Fielding drew on an established line of jest when constructing this anecdote, it is far harder to locate a stable position from which he can be seen to weigh up his material and pass judgment. Just as in *Joseph Andrews* a jestbook-style comedy of cruelty is both repudiated and enlisted (infirmity and poverty should not be laughed at, the preface declares, yet the "Scene of Roasting" in which pranksters humiliate Adams solicits just such laughter),[52] so in *Tom Jones* Fielding has his cake and eats it. He incorporates an aggressive comedy that revels in persecution with elements of humane detachment that pull away from, without ever entirely negating, the underlying aggression.[53]

We continue to read Fielding's novels in a standard edition that, alongside its many virtues, presents *Tom Jones* as the work of an author steeped more in latitudinarian sermons than in disposable trash like *Scoggins Iestes* and its eighteenth-century descendants. As Rawson has influentially insisted, however, to do so is to risk missing the disruptive, counter-Augustan strain at the heart of Fielding's writing, which aligns it no less importantly with the wayward, amoral havoc of absurdist farce or the theater of cruelty.[54] It is now possible to see, in the accumulating evidence of Fielding's creative raids on the jestbook tradition, a significant new dimension of this alternative Fielding, and a new element in the mêlée of discourses that informs and energizes his satire. At least two anecdotes in *Tom Jones*, and probably also Fitzpatrick's Irish bulls, are developed from jestbook material, and these instances, with *Jonathan Wild*'s use of *Joe Miller's Jests* and the jestbook-style roasting in *Joseph Andrews*, suggest that scope exists for further identifications. Moreover, if the Burnet anecdote in *The Journal of a Voyage to Lisbon* did not originate in earlier jestbooks, it was certainly close enough to their uncompromising comic idiom to be absorbed in later examples, as though Fielding had become, through long acquaintance, a perfect mimic of the genre. As for Frank Bridle, haunted by halters, his case – his entirely, and brilliantly, fictional case – presents to us a Fielding whose satirical exposure of brutal power coexists with a tough-minded relish for brutal wit.

NOTES

1 Henry Fielding, *Amelia*, ed. Martin C. Battestin (Oxford: Clarendon Press, 1983), p. 21 (I. ii). Compare *Miscellanies*, ed. Bertrand A. Goldgar and Hugh Amory (Oxford: Clarendon Press, 1997), vol. III, p. 37 (I. xi), where Wild's good nature is such "that he never did a single Injury to Man or Woman, by which he himself did not expect to reap some Advantage"; this comic formula may originate in Dryden's satirical portrait of Slingsby Bethel ("Shimei"), who "never broke the sabbath but for gain" (*The Poems of John Dryden*, vol. I, *1649–81*, ed. Paul Hammond (London: Longman, 1995), p. 500 (*Absalom and Achitophel*, l. 588).

2 Henry Fielding, *Plays*, vol. I, *1728–31*, ed. Thomas Lockwood (Oxford: Clarendon Press, 2004), p. 447 (II. ii); Fielding later renamed this comedy *The Coffee-House Politician*, retaining his original subtitle, "The Justice Caught in His Own Trap."

3 See Andrew Charlesworth, Richard Sheldon, Adrian Randall, and David Walsh, "The Jack-a-Lent Riots and Opposition to Turnpikes in the Bristol Region in 1749," in Adrian J. Randall and Andrew Charlesworth (eds.), *Markets, Market Culture and Popular Protest in Eighteenth-Century Britain and Ireland* (Liverpool: Liverpool University Press, 1996), pp. 46–68. The rioting, above all a west-country phenomenon, began in 1727; it is a measure of its severity that turnpike destruction was made punishable by seven years' transportation for a second offense in 1728, seven years' transportation for a first offense in 1732, and hanging in 1735.

4 Henry Fielding, *Joseph Andrews*, ed. Martin C. Battestin (Oxford: Clarendon Press, 1967), pp. 285 (IV. iii), 290 (IV. v).

5 E. P. Thompson, *Whigs and Hunters: The Origin of the Black Act*, 2nd edn. (London: Peregrine, 1977), p. 13.

6 On the division of labor between magistrates (justices of the peace) and judges, see Norma Landau, *The Justices of the Peace, 1679–1760* (Berkeley: University of California Press, 1984), esp. pp. 209–65; on Fielding's own magistracy see Lance Bertelsen, *Henry Fielding at Work: Magistrate, Businessman, Writer* (New York: Palgrave, 2004), esp. pp. 11–34. Justices of the peace dealt locally with minor crimes and misdemeanors and held quarter sessions every three months to hear more serious cases, such as assault and petty larceny. In theory, quarter sessions had jurisdiction over all offenses except treason. But in practice, by Fielding's day, any case potentially involving the death penalty would be referred to the county assizes, a higher court where proceedings were conducted twice a year by traveling (circuit) judges.

7 John Allen Stevenson, *The Real History of Tom Jones* (New York: Palgrave Macmillan, 2005), pp. 103–24 (at p. 103); see also Stevenson's fine chapter on Black George and the Black Act, pp. 77–101, and, for a counter-argument to his overall thesis, my review of this study in the *TLS* for July 15, 2005.

8 Henry Fielding, *A Serious Address to the People of Great Britain* (1745), in *The True Patriot and Related Writings*, ed. W. B. Coley (Oxford: Clarendon Press, 1987), p. 7; Henry Fielding, *Contributions to The Champion and Related Writings*, ed. W. B. Coley (Oxford: Clarendon Press, 2003), p. 46 (December 6, 1739).

9 Stevenson, *Real History*, p. 110.

10 See especially *An Enquiry into the Causes of the Late Increase of Robbers*, ed. Malvin R. Zirker (Oxford: Clarendon Press, 1988), pp. 154–8. This paradox is central to the reading of the episode advanced by Stevenson, who argues from the *Enquiry* that Fielding "thinks that hanging, and plenty of it, is the right thing to do," and concludes from here that the brutal judge described by Partridge "is, quite consciously on Fielding's part, a version of at least part of the author himself" (*Real History*, pp. 120, 122). While reading *Tom Jones* with exemplary subtlety, Stevenson underestimates the *Enquiry* here, which does indeed use a rhetoric of severity, but for reasons inseparable from its designs on a specific and recalcitrant readership. It should not be forgotten that this treatise mounts a ground-breaking critique of public execution, without the humanitarian emphases we might now expect (the case is aimed at hard-nosed legislators, and pitched accordingly), but not without denouncing it as a shameful failure of public policy "that many Cart-loads of our Fellow-creatures are once in six Weeks carried to Slaughter" (*Enquiry*, p. 172). Fielding, like everyone in the period, endorsed the principle of capital punishment, but he disliked it in practice.

11 See the final scene of the farce, where Tom Thumb's death is followed by the murder of his ghost – thus prompting the famously stony-faced Swift to laugh, according to Laetitia Pilkington, on one of only two occasions in his entire life (*Plays*, vol. I, pp. 404, 370).

12 Henry Fielding, *The History of Tom Jones, A Foundling*, ed. Martin C. Battestin and Fredson Bowers (Oxford: Clarendon Press, 1975), p. 460 (VIII. xi).

13 On the emergent conventions of adversary procedure in the period, and in particular the growing involvement of defense counsel in the 1730s, see John H. Langbein, *The Origins of Adversary Criminal Trial* (Oxford: Oxford University Press, 2002), esp. pp. 106–77.

14 Fielding, *Tom Jones*, p. 459–60 (VIII. xi).

15 Fielding, *Tom Jones*, p. 459 (VIII. xi). Commenting on this phrase, Stevenson notes that in *Tom Jones* Fielding "uses both 'charm' and 'sport' elsewhere not only ironically but specifically as intensifiers of sadism" (*Real History*, p. 113).

16 Alexander Pope, *Imitations of Horace*, 2nd edn., ed. John Butt (London: Methuen, 1953), p. 13 (II. i. 82).

17 Samuel Johnson, *Life of Savage*, ed. Clarence Tracy (Oxford: Clarendon Press, 1971), pp. 34, 41 n. (quoting, in the footnote, a verse fragment about Page first published in the *Gentleman's Magazine* for September 1741 [8: 494] under the title "A Character").

18 Pope, *Imitations of Horace*, p. 376.
19 Fielding is known to have attended the summer assizes on the Western Circuit in 1740 and later years, and was at an unknown location outside London in summer 1739 (Martin C. Battestin with Ruthe R. Battestin, *Henry Fielding: A Life* [London: Routledge, 1989], pp. 272–3, 252). Page was not on the Western Circuit in summer 1736, 1738, 1740 and 1741; he died the following December.
20 A. A. Hanham, "Page, Sir Francis (1660/61?–1741)," in *ODNB*; see also Wilbur L. Cross, *The History of Henry Fielding*, 3 vols. (New Haven: Yale University Press, 1918), vol. II, p. 3; F. Homes Dudden, *Henry Fielding: His Life, Works, and Times* (Oxford: Clarendon Press, 1952), pp. 246–8; Donald Thomas, *Henry Fielding* (London: Weidenfeld and Nicolson, 1990), pp. 144–5; also editions of *Tom Jones* by Sheridan Baker, 2nd edn. (New York: Norton, 1995), p. 296 n., and by John Bender and Simon Stern, Oxford World's Classics (Oxford: Oxford University Press, 1996), p. 899. Battestin is more circumspect, noting only that the trial "would have taken place" in Salisbury (*Tom Jones*, p. 459 n.); likewise Stevenson, who notes that the assumption of historicity "should not overshadow the fact that the trial as Partridge recounts it – a quite perfect dramatic monologue – is far too intricately plotted and tonally complex to consider as in some way documentary in the rather narrow sense that de Castro implies. Fielding crafted this little episode with the greatest care" (Stevenson, *Real History*, p. 110).
21 J. Paul de Castro, "Fielding's *Tom Jones*: Its Geography," *Notes and Queries* 11th series 10 (September 26, 1914), 253.
22 I am grateful to Martyn Henderson of the Wiltshire and Swindon Record Office for checking the victim and witness index, an in-progress resource covering the period since 1728, on June 14, 2005.
23 I am grateful to William Keymer for working through the Western Circuit Gaol Book in the relevant years (The National Archives (PRO), ASSI 23/6). The principal record for the Western Circuit, the Assize Files, does not survive before 1803, and Depositions, Crown Minute Books, and Pleadings for this period are also lacking (J. P. M. Fowle, *Wiltshire Quarter Sessions and Assizes, 1736* [Devizes: Wiltshire Archaeological and Natural History Society, 1955], pp. lx–lxi). The Gaol Book reveals that several accused horse thieves were tried elsewhere on the Western Circuit by Page and his partner judge (Sir John Fortescue Acland in summer 1737, William Fortescue in summer 1739). Three of the accused were acquitted and five were sentenced to hanging, of whom two were respited for transportation. None of the names involved is relevant to *Tom Jones*, with the nice exception of "James Andrews, otherwise Henderson also Anderson" (acquitted at Exeter in 1739), who seems to have caused the clerk of the court exactly the problem caused for textual editors by Fielding's bungling highwayman (named variously in *Tom Jones* as "Anderson," "Enderson," and "Henderson").
24 Alexander Pope, *The Rape of the Lock and Other Poems*, 3rd edn., ed. Geoffrey Tillotson (London: Methuen, 1962), p. 168 (iii. 21–2).

25 See David McNeil, "The Spectacle of Protest and Punishment: Newspaper Coverage of the Melksham Weavers' Riot of 1738," *Media History* 7 (2001), 71–86.

26 *Salisbury Journal*, July 9, 1737 and August 14, 1739; I am grateful to Emma Jay for retrieving these cases from the complete run of the *Salisbury Journal* for 1736–9 held in the Beinecke Library at Yale. For the editorial principles governing reports of crimes and hangings in this newspaper, see C. Y. Ferdinand, *Benjamin Collins and the Provincial Newspaper Trade in the Eighteenth Century* (Oxford: Clarendon Press, 1997), pp. 159–60.

27 Peter King reports a figure of 5.0 percent from his analysis of Essex quarter sessions and assizes records, 1748–67: see his *Crime, Justice, and Discretion in England, 1740–1820* (Oxford: Clarendon Press, 2000), p. 137.

28 *Salisbury Journal*, August 1, 1737; *London Magazine* 8 (August 1739), 412.

29 Thompson, *Whigs and Hunters*, p. 223 n., citing William Hone's *Year Book* (1832), p. 614.

30 Fielding, *Plays*, vol. I, p. 235.

31 *The Complete Plays of Ben Jonson*, ed. G. A. Wilkes, 4 vols. (Oxford: Clarendon Press, 1982), vol. III, p. 242 (I. ii. 42–3).

32 George deF. Lord *et al.* (eds.), *Poems on Affairs of State: Augustan Satirical Verse, 1660–1714*, 7 vols. (New Haven: Yale University Press, 1963–75), vol. V, p. 67 (ll. 25–7).

33 *Aristophanes, Being a Classic Collection of True Attic Wit* (1778), p. 68; also in *Wit-A-La-Mode; or, Lord Chesterfield's Witticisms* (1778), p. 47, and several jestbooks of the 1780s. In practice, works of this kind were compiled from a common anecdotal stock, with extensive recycling, elaboration, and variation; favorite pranks and jokes recur across a variety of jestbooks, to be repeated in shifting order and wording, and with ongoing additions and subtractions, in successive editions of the most popular works. "The Oxford Expedition" reappears in Henry Playford's *Wit and Mirth; or, Pills to Purge Melancholy*, 2nd edn., 4 vols. (1707–9), vol. II, pp. 176–8, and in later editions of Tonson's *Miscellany*.

34 Alexander Pope, *The Dunciad in Four Books*, ed. Valerie Rumbold (Harlow: Longman, 1999), p. 277 (iv. 30 n.).

35 *Gentleman's Magazine* 11 (September 1741), 494, quoted by Clarence Tracy, *The Artificial Bastard: A Biography of Richard Savage* (Cambridge, MA: Harvard University Press, 1953), p. 86. Savage, it should be remembered, had killed a man.

36 Thompson, *Whigs and Hunters*, p. 223. It is worth noting that Thompson, a professional historian writing without knowledge of Fielding scholarship, automatically assumes that the *Tom Jones* anecdote is fictional, and that Page was simply, as Fielding constructed the tale, "the judge who came at once to his mind" (p. 211).

37 J. M. Beattie, *Crime and the Courts in England, 1660–1800* (Princeton: Princeton University Press, 1986), p. 96, citing Warwickshire assize records in The National Archives (PRO), SP 36/47, fo. 227.

38 *Cambridge Jests; or, Witty Alarums for Melancholy Spirits*, new edn. (1721), p. 15.
39 Robert Baker, *Witticisms and Strokes of Humour* (1766?), p. 50; also in *The Court and City Jester* (1770), p. 13, and *The Jovial Companion; or, Merry Jester* (1779), p. 37. In practice, sentences of hanging for horse thieves were normally commuted to transportation. Working from the unusually full records of Surrey assizes between 1663 and 1802, Beattie calculates that of 178 horse thieves sentenced to death, only 46, or 25.8 percent, were actually hanged (*Crime and the Courts*, p. 435). As King adds, this common crime could sometimes mean no more than being caught joyriding on a neighbor's horse, and judges generally took pains to distinguish casual offenders from organized rustling gangs (*Crime, Justice, and Discretion*, p. 214). For the record, the Western Circuit Gaol Book for summer 1737 and 1739 (when those hanged for horse-theft had also stolen additional goods: gold watches, bank notes, bills of exchange) suggests that Page's own practice was to respite for transportation when, as in Partridge's anecdote, nothing additional was stolen. Use of violence may also have been an aggravating criterion, and in practice those Page chose to hang were probably highwaymen.
40 Henry Fielding, *The Journal of a Voyage to Lisbon*, ed. Thomas Keymer (London: Penguin, 1996), p. 16.
41 Fielding, *Contributions to The Champion*, p. 46.
42 *Ibid.*, p. 16. This was a habitual, if perverse, identification. "If I am not hanged this Sessions, I know I shall ye next," James Harris reports Fielding as saying when his illness briefly abated in his last months (Clive T. Probyn, *The Sociable Humanist: The Life and Works of James Harris, 1709–1780* [Oxford: Clarendon Press, 1991], p. 313).
43 Simon Dickie, "Hilarity and Pitilessness in the Mid-Eighteenth Century: English Jestbook Humor," *Eighteenth-Century Studies* 37 (2003), 1–22.
44 Somewhat anachronistically, this approach dominates what is otherwise the best account of eighteenth-century jestbooks before Dickie's, Ronald Paulson's chapter "The Joke and *Joe Miller's Jests*," in his *Popular and Polite Art in the Age of Hogarth and Fielding* (Notre Dame: University of Notre Dame Press, 1979), pp. 64–84.
45 For the character of the historical Burnet, see Martin C. Battestin, *A Henry Fielding Companion* (Westport: Greenwood Press, 2000), p. 35; also the entry by David Lemmings in *ODNB*, which questions Burnet's "Mohock" reputation.
46 Ronald Paulson and Thomas Lockwood (eds.), *Henry Fielding: The Critical Heritage* (London: Routledge, 1969), p. 251.
47 Hollis Rinehart, "Fielding's Chapter 'Of Proverbs' (*Jonathan Wild*, Book 2, Chapter 12): Sources, Allusions, and Interpretations," *Modern Philology* 77 (1980), 291–6; Thomas Keymer, "*Tom Jones*, Nell Gwyn, and the Cambridge Jest Book," *Notes and Queries* 51 (2004), 408–9.
48 *Cambridge Jests*, p. 64.
49 Fielding, *Tom Jones*, pp. 604–5 (XI. viii).
50 William Hicks, *Oxford Jests*, 13th edn. (1720?), p. 133; also in the 12th (1720) and 14th (1740) editions, p. 133; see also, for the Jacobean version, *Scoggins*

Iestes (1613), p. 56. The three editions of *Oxford Jests* cited here also contain (on p. 17) an abbreviated version of the Bacon/Hog jest quoted above from *Cambridge Jests*.

51 William Empson, "*Tom Jones*," *Kenyon Review* 20 (1958), 217–49; see also, on double irony, Stevenson, *Real History*, p. 11; also Rawson's application to Swift of Empson's distinctions in *God, Gulliver, and Genocide: Barbarism and the European Imagination, 1492–1945* (Oxford: Oxford University Press, 2001), p. 16.

52 Fielding, *Joseph Andrews*, pp. 244–51 (III. vii). For affinities between the roasting scene and the jestbook tradition, see Simon Dickie, "*Joseph Andrews* and the Great Laughter Debate," *Studies in Eighteenth-Century Culture* 34 (2004), 271–332. Dickie reads the popularity of this scene among early readers as evidence of miscalculation by Fielding, who "seems careful to prevent readers from finding any of this amusing" (p. 272); however, Fielding's expressions of disdain for the pranksters cannot conceal his imaginative relish for the pranks themselves.

53 See also, in this context, Bertelsen's account of Fielding's comic strategies when reporting cases that had come before him as magistrate in the *Covent-Garden Journal*, a typical example of which "transforms a badly beaten woman into a kind of cartoon punching bag" (*Henry Fielding at Work*, p. 28); the effect that Bertelsen deplores here is precisely that of the jestbooks.

54 See, in particular, Claude Rawson, *Henry Fielding and the Augustan Ideal under Stress*, 2nd edn. (Atlantic Highlands, NJ: Humanities Press International, 1991). As Rawson puts it in his preface to the 1991 reprint, "one contribution of this book to later debate . . . lies in its emphasis on the 'darker' side of Fielding: on works in which both subject matter and outlook are at variance with the genial stereotype" (p. ix).

CHAPTER 13

Jane Austen: satirical historian

Peter Sabor

In a characteristically incisive introduction to Jane Austen's last completed novel, *Persuasion*, Claude Rawson makes a telling comparison
between Austen and Swift. Drawing attention to a passage in which Sir
Walter Elliot and Admiral Croft express genial condescension towards
each other, Rawson remarks:

On the surface, this seems like the kind of plague-on-both-houses irony which is
one of the virtuoso routines of Augustan satirical rhetoric, as in Swift's comment
on the violent inclinations of extremists of opposing factions: "And this is
Moderation, in the *modern* Sense of the Word; to which, speaking impartially,
the Bigots of both Parties are *equally* entituled."[1]

Rawson goes on to remark that Swift's "see-sawing reciprocities" are "also
present in Austen in a less ferocious but equally pointed form." Rawson
has shown us the ways in which Swift's satirical legacy extends to Austen
in what he calls her "mellowest novel," completed less than a year before
her death in July 1817. My concern here is primarily with the Austen of
the early 1790s, when there was nothing mellow about her writing and
when something of Swift's ferocity animated the sharpest of her youthful
productions.

Among Austen's first, and most enduring, objects of satire, was Oliver
Goldsmith, whose four-volume *History of England* was published in
August 1771, four years before her birth. Her response to this work took
several forms, including an extensive commentary in the margins of her
brother's copy of the book that she probably wrote in 1791. At about
the same time, she composed her own miniature history of England,
with illustrations by her sister Cassandra, as a parodic counterpart to
Goldsmith's work. Equally indebted to Goldsmith is the celebrated debate
on historical writing between Catherine Morland and Eleanor Tilney in
Northanger Abbey. Goldsmith's *History* also plays an intriguing role in
Mansfield Park, in which the unpleasant Bertram daughters, Julia and

Maria, have soaked up its contents like sponges, while Fanny Price and her sister Susan prove to be impervious to its attractions.

Austen's marginal commentary on Goldsmith first became known in 1920, when Mary Augusta Austen-Leigh, then aged eighty-two, published a memoir entitled *Personal Aspects of Jane Austen*, dedicated "to all true lovers of Jane Austen and her Works."[2] The daughter of Austen's favorite nephew, James Edward Austen-Leigh, Mary Augusta was certainly a true lover herself, and her book contains some significant material. Aged seven when Cassandra Austen died in 1845, Mary Augusta provides some vivid recollections of Austen's sister, as well as some feeble Austen family charades, including three by Jane. More important, she inherited a hoard of Austen papers passed down from James Austen to his son James Edward Austen-Leigh and thence to herself and her brother William. This archive included James's copy of Goldsmith's *History of England*.

Some other marginalia by Jane Austen have survived, including the mock-marriages she arranged for herself, at the age of fourteen, on printed pages of the marriage register at Steventon Church, but her remarks on Goldsmith's *History* are by far the most extensive. They are undated, but Mary Augusta Austen-Leigh's conjecture "from the nature of the remarks" that Austen wrote them at the age of twelve or thirteen is probably mistaken.[3] She completed her own miniature "History of England" on November 26, 1791, three weeks before her sixteenth birthday, and she might well have been writing in the margins of her brother's Goldsmith shortly before she turned to her own parodic history. In *Personal Aspects of Jane Austen*, Austen-Leigh provides ten examples of Austen's marginal commentary. Several of these remarks are fiercely pro-Stuart, Tory, and Jacobite, but since Austen-Leigh seldom quotes the passages by Goldsmith to which they respond, they cannot be fully understood in her transcription. Happily, Austen's four-volume Goldsmith survives, still in the possession of the Austen-Leigh family. The four volumes, well preserved in contemporary calf, provide a direct link to Austen's childhood. Since they have always been in the family's possession, their only known readers have been James Austen, Jane Austen, and a succession of Austen-Leighs. Someone, probably either Cassandra or Jane herself, has colored in the portraits of monarchs that stand at the head of each chapter: a device echoed in the medallion portraits that illustrate Austen's "History of England." The annotations, most in Austen's hand, are partly in ink and partly in badly faded pencil, but most are still legible.

Austen's annotations, over one hundred in all, are confined almost entirely to the third and fourth volumes of Goldsmith's *History*. On the flyleaf of the first volume, beneath her brother James's signature, Austen drew up a short list of major historical events up to the accession of King Stephen in 1135. A few passages in volume one are marked by dates, presumably, as David Gilson suggests, those on which they were first read,[4] and some obvious misprints are corrected, but there is only one marginal comment in the first two volumes: the single word "wretches" beside Goldsmith's account of the death of the two young princes at the hand of Richard III (p. 319).[5] In her "History of England" Austen presents the counter-argument for Richard's innocence of the princes' murder, following the revisionist line taken by Horace Walpole in his *Historic Doubts on the Life and Reign of Richard III* (1768), but she chose not to take issue with Goldsmith's version here.

In writing the word "wretches," however, Austen was already distancing herself from Goldsmith's avowed aim of narrating the history of England in a detached, impartial fashion. Even in *The Vicar of Wakefield*, the narrator claims, at the outset, to "profess with the veracity of a historian" that no one had ever found fault with his family's celebrated gooseberry wine.[6] And in the preface to his *History of England*, Goldsmith develops this idea of historical objectivity. Describing his work as an abridgement of previous histories of England – by Rapin-Thoyras, Thomas Carte, Smollett, and Hume – Goldsmith declares that his work contains "a plain unaffected narrative of facts, with just ornament enough to keep the attention awake, and with reflection barely sufficient to set the reader upon thinking." His sources, he continues, are "only . . . those authors which are best known, and those facts only have been selected, which are allowed on all hands to be true." In his concluding paragraph, he concedes that "in a country like ours, where mutual contention contributes to the security of the constitution, it will be impossible for an historian, who attempts to have any opinion, to satisfy all parties." He has, however, attempted to steer just such a middle course: "I have neither allured the vanity of the great by flattery, nor satisfied the malignity of the vulgar by scandal," and "as I have endeavoured to get an honest reputation by liberal pursuits, it is hoped the reader will admit my impartiality."[7]

Goldsmith's positivism, his insistence on the firm distinction between verifiable facts and merely ornamental opinion, emerges in his many historical writings, which include a well-received history of ancient Rome (1769) and a posthumously published history of Greece (1774). In a 1757 review of Smollett's *Compleat History of England*, he makes a similar distinction between "*Truth*," which "should be the main object of the Historian's pursuit," and "*Elegance*," which "is only its ornament."[8]

Intriguingly, Samuel Johnson supported Goldsmith's position. In a conversation recorded by Boswell, Johnson insists that as a historian Goldsmith "stands in the first class" and that his *Roman History* is superior to that of William Robertson, which "is not history, it is imagination . . . You must look upon Robertson's work as romance, and try it by that standard. History it is not."[9]

Johnson, however, at least for the purposes of disagreeing with Boswell, overlooked the imaginative component of Goldsmith's historical writings. Goldsmith's synthesis of the Whiggish Rapin, as translated by Nicholas Tindal, together with the more congenially Tory Smollett and Hume, inevitably created some startling inconsistencies in his narrative that Austen was quick to recognize. And Goldsmith did more than merely abridge his principal source; in editing Hume, he made his prose more like that of fiction. Austen found his pretensions of impartiality bogus. There are, in her view, no facts "allowed on all hands to be true" but only partial opinions, which honest historians will readily admit to holding.

Austen's dispute with Goldsmith begins with his chapters on the Civil War. For all his claims of objectivity, it is clear that Goldsmith favors the royalist over the parliamentary cause; the problem for Austen is that this preference is tepid and hedged with qualifications. Goldsmith displays considerable sympathy for the sufferings of Charles I, but his refusal to condemn Cromwell outright makes him far too non-partisan for Austen's taste. When Goldsmith writes that the parliamentarians "had the wishes of all the most active members of the nation," Austen responds indignantly: "Shame to such Members" (p. 319). Beside Goldsmith's remarks on the parliamentarian John Hampden and the royalist Lord Falkland, she writes: "The *last* was indeed a great & noble Man" (p. 320). Reading Goldsmith's account of the superior numbers and weapons of the parliamentary forces, Austen exclaims "What a pity!" (p. 321).

Many more marginalia on the Civil War and Commonwealth sections of Goldsmith's history follow. When Goldsmith observes that Cromwell "being the son of a second brother . . . inherited a very small paternal fortune," Austen exclaims: "And that was more than he deserved" (p. 321). Beside Goldsmith's remark on the courage of Lady Fairfax in condemning the parliamentary proceedings against Charles I, Austen writes "Charming Woman!" (p. 321). A comment by Goldsmith on Charles's valor in the face of his impending execution is glossed: "Such was the fortitude of the Stuarts when harassed and accused!" (p. 322). Goldsmith quotes the reputed words of one of Charles's executioners, who, holding the king's head aloft, exclaimed "This is the head of a traitor." In the margin, Austen replies: "or rather the hand of a traitor who held it" (p. 322). Most of Austen's observations on the Civil War reinforce Goldsmith's mildly pro-Stuart stance, but on occasion she rebukes him for complicity with Cromwell's party. An account of Cromwell's military conduct in Ireland provokes an indignant "Detestable monster!" (p. 323). Similarly, when Goldsmith claims that in an encounter with Scottish royalists, Cromwell "did not lose above forty men in all," Austen interjects "It is a pity there were not forty *one*" (p. 324), the forty-first presumably being Cromwell himself.

Austen's own "History of England" ends with the execution of Charles I, but Goldsmith's extends to the reign of George II, and Austen's commentary on his work continues to its conclusion. Her impatience with Goldsmith's attempts at impartiality is obvious throughout his chapter on the reign of Charles II. Recounting a naval battle between the Dutch and the English fleets, Goldsmith observes delicately that "the loss sustained by the two maritime powers was nearly equal; but the French suffered very little, not having entered into the heat of the engagement." Austen declares abruptly, "what cowards" (pp. 326–7). When the queen herself is accused by Titus Oates of being a Catholic, Goldsmith quotes, without commenting on, Charles's response: "I will not suffer an innocent woman to be abused." Austen takes his side with a firm "that's right" in the margin (p. 328). When Goldsmith describes John Hampden as "grandson to the great man of that name," Austen responds "for great read vile" (p. 328). And when Goldsmith writes that Lord Howard, one of the conspirators against Charles II, "was taken concealed in a chimney," Austen exclaims with relish, "how dirty he must have been" (p. 328).

Goldsmith's chapters on Charles's successor, his brother James II, which open volume four of the *History*, are colored by his own aversion to James's Catholic faith. In her "History of England," in contrast, Austen declares herself "partial to the roman catholic religion" (p. 186). For her, James's Catholicism is secondary to the fact that he is a Stuart, and thus the rightful heir to the throne. She wastes no time in revealing her sympathy, writing "Poor Man!" just below the medallion portrait of the king at the head of the chapter (p. 329). Austen repeatedly calls into question Goldsmith's judgments of James II and his reign. In an exculpatory passage on the Duke of Monmouth's rebellion, Goldsmith terms him "the darling of the English people...brave, sincere, and good natured, open to flattery and by that seduced into an enterprize, which exceded his capacity." Austen dismisses such sentiments with the sardonic phrase "Sweet Man!" (p. 329). Goldsmith terms an address to James from the Protestant bishops "modest." Austen retorts "*Modest*! It would have been *impudent* had it been from Catholics I suppose" (p. 331). Goldsmith writes that though the king's efforts to establish Catholicism in England made him "odious to every class of his subjects, he still resolved to persist; for it was a part of his character, that those measures he once embraced he always persevered in pursuing." Austen responds: "And if he thought those measures right, he could not be blamed for persisting in them" (p. 331). Goldsmith records a rumor that James's son, James Edward, was a foundling, "brought to the queen's apartment in a warming-pan," and adds: "But so great was this monarch's pride, that he scorned to take any precautions to refute the calumny." Austen responds, acerbically, "It would have been beneath him to refute such nonsense" (p. 332).

The counterpart to Austen's instinctive support for James II is her violent aversion to his son-in-law, William III. When his name first appears in Goldsmith's history, Austen immediately labels him "A Villain" (p. 332). In Goldsmith's version of the events of 1688, James is blind to the imminent invasion: "secure in the piety of his intentions, [he] thought nothing could injure his schemes calculated to promote the cause of heaven." For Austen, such devotion is rather a sign of James's moral probity: "Since he acted upon *such* motives he ought to be praised" (p. 333). Although convinced of the justice of James's cause, she can be satirical at the expense of his religion. Thus when Goldsmith writes that the king "appointed the pope one of the sponsors" at the baptism of his infant son, Austen muses in the margin: "I wonder whether his Holiness gave the Nurse the accustomed fee" (p. 333).

Austen's pro-Stuart and pro-Tory fervor culminates in her remarks on Goldsmith's chapter on Queen Anne and her Tory ministry. Whereas Goldsmith, despite his own Tory bias, attempts to treat Whigs and Tories evenhandedly, Austen repeatedly rebukes him for letting off the Whigs too lightly. In a characteristically measured remark, Goldsmith writes that "Through the course of the English history, France seems to have been the peculiar object of the hatred of the Whigs; and a constitutional war with that country, seems to have been their aim." Austen impatiently adds "& without any reason" (p. 335). When Goldsmith describes a piece of statesmanship by Queen Anne, without giving her any special credit for her skills, Austen interjects "This proves Anne to have been a sensible & a well-bred Woman" (p. 336). When Goldsmith mentions an anti-Jacobite pamphlet by Richard Steele, entitled *The Crisis*, Austen writes, "It is a pity that he had not been better employed" (p. 336). Much later in the *History*, when Goldsmith makes a passing reference to the Treaty of Utrecht, Austen declares "That was a good Treaty" (p. 345), thus insisting that a measure taken by Anne's Tory government should be duly praised. Goldsmith's cautious summation on the House of Stuart, at the end of his chapter on Anne, elicits some of Austen's strongest rhetoric. At first, she contents herself with tinkering with the text. Where Goldsmith writes of the Stuarts' "misfortunes and misconducts," Austen strikes out the last two words, and follows this up with the interjections "a lie" and "another" in response to Goldsmith's musings on their putative cowardice. Then, refusing to let Goldsmith have the last word, she adds a sentence of her own that begins by mimicking his sentence-structure, but turns it to her own ends: "A Family, who were always illused, Betrayed or Neglected, Whose Virtues are seldom allowed while their Errors are never forgotten." James Edward Austen-Leigh, the book's next owner, seconds this declaration with one of his own: "Bravo Aunt Jane just my opinion of the Case" (p. 337).

In the light of recent claims for the Jacobitical tendencies of Pope, Samuel Richardson, Samuel Johnson, and other eighteenth-century authors, Austen's overtly Jacobite sympathies in her marginalia on Goldsmith's chapters on George I and George II make fascinating reading. Goldsmith's contempt for the Old Pretender, James Edward Stuart, is obvious: "This unfortunate man, seemed to possess all the qualities of his father; his pride, his want of perseverance, and his attachment to the catholic religion. He was but a poor leader, therefore, to conduct so desperate a cause; and in fact, all the sensible part of the kingdom had forsaken it as irretrievable." In a spirited response, Austen declares: "Sensible. Oh! Dr Goldsmith. Thou art as partial an Historian as myself!" (p. 337). Alluding to the preface to Goldsmith's history, in which he hopes that "the reader will admit my impartiality," Austen underscores her belief that such a stance is doomed to failure. The title-page of her own "History of England" ascribes the work to "a partial, prejudiced, & ignorant Historian": partiality, for Austen, should be acknowledged, not concealed.

Although Goldsmith's concluding chapters are generally hostile to Whigs and favorably disposed towards Tories, Austen is likely to pounce on any remark critical of the latter. George I's accession, Goldsmith states, was marked by no public outcry, and "no rational measures were ever taken to obstruct his exaltation." Austen responds: "Oh no certainly no *rational* Measures *could* be taken by *Tories*!" (p. 338). When Goldsmith, conversely, criticizes Whigs for their hypocritical invocation of "Liberty," Austen cheers him on from the margins: "Yes, This is always the Liberty of Whigs & Republicans" (p. 338). In another comment disparaging the Whigs, Goldsmith observes: "It is, indeed, very remarkable that all the severe and most restrictive laws were enacted by that party that are continually stunning mankind with a cry of freedom." Austen addresses him with astonishingly precocious gravity: "My dear Dr G – I have lived long enough in the World to know that it is always so!" (p. 340).

Among Austen's heroes, in addition to the whole House of Stuart, are the Tory politicians Henry St. John, Viscount Bolingbroke, and Robert Harley, Earl of Oxford, both accused of plotting to restore the Pretender. When Goldsmith recounts Bolingbroke's flight abroad, Austen speeds him on his way with a "Well done my Lord" (p. 339). Addressing Lord Coningsby, who impeached Oxford in the House of Commons, Austen declares "More shame for you" (p. 339). And when Oxford speaks out in his own defense, concluding with the words "God's will be done," Austen exclaims in admiration: "Nobly said! Spoken like a Tory!" (p. 339).[10] Austen turns her attention to Robert Walpole when Goldsmith commends his scheme for reducing the national debt. "It is a pity," Austen notes dryly, "that a *Whig* should have been of such use to his Country" (p. 342). Summing up the reign of George I, Goldsmith declares circumspectly that "whatever was good or great in the reign of this monarch ought to be ascribed chiefly to himself; wherever he deviated he might have been misled by a ministry, always partial, sometimes corrupt." Austen accentuates the contrast between king and government by changing a single word: in her version, the Whig ministry is "always partial, always corrupt" (p. 343).

Goldsmith's account of the Jacobite uprising of 1745 produces, not surprisingly, another flurry of comments by Austen. The Old Pretender, James Edward, and the Young Pretender, Charles Edward Stuart, had, Goldsmith states, "long been the dupes of France." Austen sees them not as dupes but as long-suffering victims, "Not only ill used by the french but by everyone" (p. 347). "Fortune," Goldsmith writes of Charles Edward, "which ever persecuted his family, seemed no way more favourable to him." Here Austen, for once in full agreement, declares "Too true!" (pp. 347–8). Charles Edward's arrival in Scotland, in Goldsmith's view, "awakened the fears of the pusilanimous, the ardour of the brave, and the pity of the wise." Austen alters the sentence to her own liking, adding "And the good wishes of the Just" (pp. 348–9). When Charles Edward defeats the king's forces at Preston Pans, Austen exclaims "Delightful" (p. 348). Austen engages more fully with Goldsmith when he attempts, as usual, to deliver a balanced verdict on Charles Edward's misfortunes. "To the good and the brave," he writes sententiously, "subsequent distress often atones for former guilt; and while reason would speak for punishment, our hearts plead for mercy." Austen responds that "with the Just, Reason would not *have* plead for punishment" (p. 350): the just did not include Goldsmith.

Goldsmith's remarks on one of Charles Edward's supporters, "Sheridan, an Irish adventurer," elicit an intriguing aside by Austen: "It is a pity that his namesake is not equally praiseworthy" (pp. 349–50). The allusion is probably to Richard Brinsley Sheridan's role as a leader of the impeachment campaign against Warren Hastings, the former Governor-General of British India and a favorite of Austen and her family, which was taking place while Austen was writing her commentary. There follows a trail of observations on the defeated Jacobites and their chief. Goldsmith quotes the supposed words of James Edward when he sought refuge in the house of a foe: "I know your present attachment to my adversaries, but I believe you have sufficient honour not to abuse my confidence, or to take advantage of my distressed situation." While Goldsmith merely reports, an admiring Austen declares "Who but a Stuart could have so spoken" (p. 350). Among the most impassioned of Austen's often passionate marginalia is her reaction to the execution of one of Charles Edward's Scottish allies, Lord Balmerino. In Goldsmith's account, Balmerino "gloried in the cause for which he fell," and just before his death "cried out aloud, 'God bless king James!'" Austen writes in the margin: "Dear Balmerino! I cannot express what I feel for you" (p. 350). Austen's Jacobitism, of course, is of the 1790s, not of the 1740s, and as such is primarily an affectation of romantic nostalgia, akin to what Elinor Dashwood, in *Sense and Sensibility*, tartly terms her sister's "passion for dead leaves" (p. 101). Marianne Dashwood, hardly older, at seventeen, than the author of "The History of England," is also the Austen heroine who declares, "I love to be reminded of the past" (p. 107).

Austen's "History of England," with its thirteen water-color medallion portraits of monarchs in comically anachronistic and inappropriate costumes, painted by Cassandra, is often regarded as a typical piece of sparkling juvenile nonsense. First published only in 1922, it must have helped inspire Sellar and Yeatman's 1930 bestseller, *1066 and All That*, with its famous dictum, "History is not what you thought. *It is what you can remember.*"[11] Like Sellar and Yeatman, however, Austen was making a serious point in her apparently frivolous work. Having read through and annotated the 1,800 pages of Goldsmith's narrative, she collaborated with Cassandra on a miniature response, which begins in 1399 with the accession of Henry IV and ends abruptly with the execution of Charles I.

They produced a wildly arbitrary and bigoted narrative that insists on its right to be as selective and partisan as it pleases.

Austen wastes no time in demonstrating that her "History" is, as announced on its title-page, the work of "a partial, prejudiced, and ignorant Historian." The first two chapters amply display ignorance by referring readers to Shakespeare's *Henry IV* and *Henry V* for information on those monarchs and their reigns, while partiality and prejudice predominate in chapter 3, on Henry VI. Here Austen declares in favor of the Yorkists and reiterates her aims: "I shall not be very diffuse in this [History], meaning by it only to vent my Spleen *against*, and shew my Hatred *to* all those people whose parties or principles do not suit with mine, and not to give information" (178). In her chapter on Edward IV, Austen plays with Goldsmith's remark that the king's "best qualities were courage and beauty; his bad, a combination of all the vices."[12] In her version, we are told that "This Monarch was famous only for his Beauty and his Courage, of which the Picture we have here given of him, and his undaunted Behaviour in marrying one Woman while he was engaged to another, are sufficient proofs" (p. 178). Adding to the joke is Cassandra's portrait of Edward, which, with its protruding lips, turned-up nose, and staring eyes, makes him perhaps the least attractive of all the monarchs. He is dressed like an eighteenth-century country bumpkin, rather than a fifteenth-century king.

The contrast between Goldsmith's and Austen's approach to narrating history is exemplified by her chapter on Richard III, who, she declares, "has been in general very severely treated by Historians, but as he was a *York*, I am rather inclined to suppose him a very respectable Man" (p. 179). As well as revealing that her biases will determine her judgments, rather than her judgments keeping her biases in check, Austen also diverges from Goldsmith in contemplating, however briefly, two con-tradictory accounts of Richard's actions: "It has indeed been confidently asserted that he killed his two Nephews & his Wife, but it has also been declared that he did *not* kill his two Nephews, which I am inclined to beleive true" (p. 179). Providing no explanation for her belief, other than Richard's being a York, Austen now launches into a bizarre homosexual fantasy: "it may also be affirmed that [Richard] did not kill his Wife, for if Perkin Warbeck was really the Duke of York, why might not Lambert Simnel be the Widow of Richard." There are also homosexual jokes swirling through the chapter on James I, such as a pun on James's "keener penetration" in his male friendships.[13] There is nothing innocent about Austen's charade on James's Scottish favorite Robert Carr, likened to a carpet, and derided as a "pet," by the tag that "you tread on my whole" (p. 187).

As early as the reign of Henry VII, Austen already has her beloved Stuarts in sight. For Goldsmith, Henry, as founder of the House of Tudor, is the greatest of all English monarchs. For Austen, in contrast, Henry is of importance merely for giving birth to a daughter, Margaret, who "had the happiness of being grandmother to one of the first Characters in the World" (p. 180): Mary Queen of Scots. Part of Austen's aim is to feminize conventional versions of English history, deflecting attention away from powerful male monarchs while drawing a large number of women into her narrative. Nearly half of her characters are women, and half of her narrative, as Christopher Kent observes, is devoted to their actions.[14] Cassandra likewise helps redress the imbalance between male and female monarchs: omitting the portrait of Edward V and instead inserting one of Mary Queen of Scots, uncalled for by a history devoted specifically to English monarchs but a complement to Austen's repeated panegyrics on the Scottish queen. Cassandra's Mary is youthful, beautiful, and dressed in the style of the 1780s. She is the heroine of the "History," and Austen finds ingenious ways of bringing her into the narrative on the most unlikely occasions. Lady Jane Grey, for example, is described as an "amiable young woman," but, more important, she was "inferior to her lovely Cousin the Queen of Scots" (p. 180). Henry VIII's fifth wife, Katharine Howard, was probably innocent of the crimes of which she was accused, merely because "she was a relation of that noble Duke of Norfolk who was so warm in the Queen of Scotland's cause" (p. 181). The Duke of Somerset, beheaded while Protector during the brief reign of Edward VI, is given proleptic consolation: "he might with reason have been proud, had he known that such was the death of Mary Queen of Scotland" (p. 182). Queen Elizabeth, whose reign had been judiciously evaluated by Goldsmith, is inevitably a villain in Austen's narrative, since Mary's death at Fotheringay Castle is held to her account. Cassandra's portrait of Elizabeth caricatures her in both appearance and dress. Her profile – long, hooked nose and absurdly pointing chin – as well as her extravagantly ornate hairstyle and garishly colored costume turns the queen into a crone. And although Austen warns her readers at the outset that "There will be very few Dates in this History," she makes sure to write out in full the day and the date of Mary's execution, Wednesday 8 February, 1586 (pp. 176, 185).

Austen devotes more space to Mary Queen of Scots than to any other figure in her "History," but the queen has a significance that goes beyond her sex. As the mother of James I, Mary also stands at the head of the house of Stuart. James himself is of only minor interest to Austen, and it is significant that she writes no marginal commentary in the relevant chapters of Goldsmith's text. But Charles I, the subject of her final chapter, is a worthy figure in the Stuart line. Austen begins her chapter on Charles by arguing, with wonderfully circular reasoning, that "This amiable Monarch seems born to have suffered Misfortunes equal to those of his lovely Grandmother; Misfortunes which he could not deserve since he was her descendant" (p. 187). In demonstrating Mary's innocence, and in proving Queen Elizabeth's guilt, Austen has, she declares, accomplished her goal. There is no need to dwell on the Civil War, as she had in her commentary on Goldsmith's *History*, since Charles's parentage preempts rational debate about his virtues. "With one argument," Austen concludes, "I am certain of satisfying every sensible and well disposed person whose opinions have been properly guided by a good Education – and this Argument is that he was a **Stuart**" (p. 189).

Repelled by Goldsmith's smug boasts of impartiality, Austen sought a cause to champion and found it readily to hand in the Stuarts. Her underlying goal was to demonstrate that claims to write historical narrative in a transparent, apolitical, ungendered fashion are inevitably false. The most revealing of her marginalia to Goldsmith's *History* is perhaps that in which she addresses the author: "Oh! Dr Goldsmith. Thou art as partial an Historian as myself!" (p. 337). Goldsmith, after all, was also a novelist, and the suggestion here is that novel- and history-writing have more in common than Goldsmith was prepared to concede.

In 1798, seven years after completing her "History of England," Austen was at work on the first draft of *Northanger Abbey*, then entitled "Susan." Here, in the famous passage justifying novel-writing, the narrator contrasts "the abilities of the nine-hundredth abridger of the History of England" with those of the novelist, whose performances "have only genius, wit, and taste to recommend them."[15] The abridger in question is surely Goldsmith, author of both a history of England that, despite its considerable bulk, proclaims itself as an abridgment, and an extremely popular one-volume condensed version, published shortly after his death in 1774. In another celebrated passage, a conversation between the heroine, Catherine Morland, and her better-read friend, Eleanor Tilney, Austen takes up the debate on historical writing again. Catherine declares bluntly that "history, real solemn history, I cannot be interested in." It vexes and wearies her:

The quarrels of popes and kings, with wars or pestilences, in every page; the men all so good for nothing, and hardly any women at all – it is very tiresome: and yet I often think it odd that it should be so dull, for a great deal of it must be invention.[16]

Eleanor's thoughtful reply has received less attention than it deserves. Fond of history, she is, she declares, "very well contented to take the false with the true." Unlike Catherine, she appreciates the historian's imagination, and responds to historical writing as she would to a novel or a dramatic work: "If a speech be well drawn up, I read it with pleasure, by whomsoever it may be made – and probably with much greater, if the production of Mr. Hume or Mr. Robertson, than if the genuine words of Caractacus, Agricola, or Alfred the Great."[17] Tellingly, she cites Hume and William Robertson as her favorite historians, not Goldsmith, who prides himself on not inventing anything. In her reply, Catherine concedes that history-writing seems to have its merits, but still complains of authors who take "so much trouble in filling great volumes, which, as I used to think, nobody would willingly ever look into, to be labouring only for the torment of little boys and girls." Goldsmith's four "great volumes," as well as the young girl who read and annotated them at Steventon, are surely on Austen's mind here. She was probably also reading Hume at the time: her copy of Hume's *History of England*, now at the Beinecke Library, Yale, bears the date 1797 beneath her inscription.[18]

Austen was still dwelling on Goldsmith in 1811, when she began writing *Mansfield Park*. When ten-year-old Fanny Price arrives at Mansfield, her slightly older cousins, Maria and Julia Bertram, are at once struck by her ignorance. One of her striking deficiencies is that she seems to have no knowledge of Goldsmith's *History*, which her cousins have thoroughly digested: "How long ago it is, aunt, since we used to repeat the chronological order of the kings of England, with the dates of their accession, and most of the principal events of their reigns!"[19] At about the same age as Maria and Julia, Austen herself had mastered the chronological order of the kings of England, as the flyleaf of volume one of her Goldsmith reveals. Beginning with "Caesar landed," she continues with entries such as "Alfred beat out the Danes, 876," "William Rufus came to the Throne, 1067," and "Stephen ditto, 1135" (pp. 318–19). That Fanny Price, too, becomes familiar with Goldsmith is apparent near the end of the novel, when she acts as tutor to her younger sister Susan. For Susan, we are told, Fanny's "explanations and remarks were a most important addition to every essay, or every chapter of history. What Fanny told her of former times, dwelt more on her mind than the pages of Goldsmith; and she paid her sister the compliment of preferring her style to that of any printed author."[20] For Maria and Julia, history is merely a matter of reciting key dates; for Fanny and Susan, in contrast, as for Austen in her teens, it is the capacity of historians to make sense of the past that makes their works worth reading.

Goldsmith as historian plays no part in Austen's final novels, but in *Emma* she turns her attention to his fiction. In November 1815, Austen received a letter from a new acquaintance, James Stanier Clarke, the Prince Regent's librarian, with whom she had recently spent a day at Carlton House. Responding to an enquiry from Austen, Clarke informed her: "It is certainly not *incumbent* on you to dedicate your work now in the Press to his Royal Highness; but if you wish to do the Regent that honour either now or at any future period, I am happy to send you that permission which need not require any more trouble or solicitation on your part."[21] The "work now in the Press" was *Emma*, which duly appeared, in late December, with a brief dedication to the Prince, an early admirer of Austen's novels. (Her presentation copy remains in the Royal Library, Windsor Castle.) Clarke's letter continues with some unsolicited advice: a suggestion that Austen "delineate in some future Work the Habits of Life and Character and enthusiasm of a Clergyman – who should pass his time between the metropolis & the Country." "Neither Goldsmith," Clarke declared, "nor La Fontaine in his Tableau de Famille – have... quite delineated an English clergyman, at least of the present day – Fond of, & entirely engaged in Literature – no man's Enemy but his own."

Austen's dual response to this wonderfully self-important epistle is well known: first a letter to Clarke, in which she terms herself "the most unlearned, & uninformed Female who ever dared to be an Authoress," and then her burlesque "Plan of a Novel," featuring a clergyman "of a very literary turn, an Enthusiast in Literature, nobody's Enemy but his own."[22] Clarke had borrowed the latter phrase from Fielding's *Tom Jones*, and Austen deftly weaves it into her zany synopsis. Having retired to remotest Kamschatka, her clergyman "expires in a fine burst of Literary Enthusiasm." This is clearly not what the Prince's librarian had in mind.

In his November letter, the first of several attempts to furnish Austen with subjects for her novels, Clarke had alluded to Goldsmith's *The Vicar of Wakefield* (1766), suggesting, in effect, that it was valuable in its time, but that Austen might write a version "of the present day."[23] It is not, I believe, coincidental that the only allusions to *The Vicar of Wakefield* in Austen's published novels occur in *Emma*, published on December 23, 1815, five weeks after she received Clarke's proposal. During that period she was busy correcting proofs, as she mentions in several letters to her sister Cassandra, and making final alterations and additions. One such addition might have been to a passage in which Harriet Smith tells Emma about her suitor Robert Martin's preferred reading. His favorites, we hear, are "Agricultural Reports and some other books," which he reads to himself, and Vicesimus Knox's popular compilation, *Elegant Extracts*, from which he declaims anthology pieces to entertain Harriet. In addition, she declares proudly, in what could be a late insertion, "he has read the Vicar of Wakefield." Goldsmith's novel is, it seems, the only prose fiction that the distinctly non-literary Robert Martin has ever managed to get through. He certainly has no acquaintance with the Gothic: Harriet has sounded him on Ann Radcliffe's *The Romance of the Forest* and on Regina Roche's *The Children of the Abbey*, but "he had never heard of such books before I mentioned them."[24]

Austen returns to Goldsmith's novel when the narrator wittily recounts the death of the unpleasant Mrs. Churchill: "Goldsmith tells us, that when lovely woman stoops to folly, she has nothing to do but to die; and when she stoops to be disagreeable, it is equally to be recommended as a clearer of ill-fame. Mrs. Churchill, after being disliked at least twenty-five years, was now spoken of with compassionate allowances."[25] The allusion is to a languid poem read aloud to the Vicar by his daughter Olivia, "in a manner so exquisitely pathetic as moved me":

> When lovely woman stoops to folly,
> And finds too late that men betray,
> What charms can sooth her melancholy,
> What art can wash her guilt away?
> The only art her guilt to cover,
> To hide her shame from every eye,
> To give repentance to her lover,
> And wring his bosom – is to die.[26]

Austen will have none of the strikingly anti-feminist sentiments of Goldsmith's poem, which the vicar finds so exquisitely pleasing. She might have added the brief passage to *Emma* at proof stage, inspired to do so by Clarke's well-intentioned but rebarbative suggestion that she write a novel along the lines of *The Vicar of Wakefield*. Had the Prince Regent's librarian known of Austen's long-standing hostility to Goldsmith, of her antipathy to sentimental fiction, and of her place in the satirical tradition, he might have been more circumspect with his advice.

NOTES

1 Claude Rawson, "Introduction," in Jane Austen, *Persuasion*, ed. John Davie (Oxford: Oxford University Press, 1990), pp. xxii–xxiii.
2 Mary Augusta Austen-Leigh, *Personal Aspects of Jane Austen* (London: John Murray, 1920).

3 Austen-Leigh, *Personal Aspects*, p. 26.
4 David Gilson, *A Bibliography of Jane Austen* (Oxford: Clarendon Press, 1985), p. 441.
5 Appendix B, "Marginalia in Oliver Goldsmith's *The History of England*," in Jane Austen, *Juvenilia*, ed. Peter Sabor (Cambridge: Cambridge University Press, 2006), p. 319. All parenthetical references in the text derive from this edition.
6 Oliver Goldsmith, *The Vicar of Wakefield*, ed. Arthur Friedman (London: Oxford University Press, 1974), p. 9.
7 *Collected Works of Oliver Goldsmith*, ed. Arthur Friedman (Oxford: Clarendon Press, 1966), vol. V, pp. 338–40.
8 *Monthly Review*, May 1757, in *Collected Works*, vol. I, p. 45.
9 James Boswell, *Life of Johnson*, ed. George Birkbeck Hill, rev. L. F. Powell, 5 vols. (Oxford: Clarendon Press, 1934–51), vol. II, pp. 236–37 (April 30, 1773).
10 Austen-Leigh quotes this memorable line, but wrongly supposes that it glosses a speech by the prime minister, Robert Walpole; her suggestion that Austen is being "slightly ironical" is thus oddly misplaced (*Personal Aspects*, p. 27).
11 W. C. Sellar and R. J. Yeatman, *1066 and All That* (London: Methuen, 1930), p. vii.
12 Oliver Goldsmith, *History of England* (London, 1761), vol. II, p. 250.
13 Christopher Kent observes that Austen "cannot resist going farther than either Goldsmith or Hume in discussing James I's partiality for handsome young men," and notes the play on "penetration" ("Learning History with, and from, Jane Austen," in *Jane Austen's Beginnings: The Juvenilia and Lady Susan*, ed. J. David Grey [Ann Arbor: UMI Research Press, 1989], pp. 59–72 (p. 67).
14 Kent, "Learning History," p. 67.
15 Jane Austen, *Northanger Abbey*, ed. Barbara Benedict and Deirdre Le Faye (Cambridge: Cambridge University Press, 2006), p. 31.
16 Austen *Northanger Abbey*, p. 110.
17 Austen *Northanger Abbey*, p. 110.
18 See Gilson, *Bibliography*, p. 442.
19 Jane Austen, *Mansfield Park*, ed. John Wiltshire (Cambridge: Cambridge University Press, 2005), p. 21.
20 Austen, *Mansfield Park*, p. 485.
21 Clarke to Austen, November 15, 1815, in *Jane Austen's Letters*, ed. Deirdre Le Faye (Oxford: Oxford University Press, 1995), p. 296.
22 Austen to Clarke, December 11, 1815, in *Letters*, p. 306; "Plan of a Novel," in *The Works of Jane Austen*, ed. R. W. Chapman (London: Oxford University Press, 1975), vol. VI, p. 429.
23 Austen, *Letters*, p. 296.
24 Jane Austen, *Emma*, ed. Richard Cronin and Dorothy McMillan (Cambridge: Cambridge University Press, 2005), p. 28.
25 Austen, *Emma*, p. 422.
26 Goldsmith, *Vicar of Wakefield*, p. 133.

CHAPTER 14

Austen's voices

Jenny Davidson

To speak or write of the first-person voice or third-person narration is to borrow what was for a long time a mostly technical vocabulary associated with the study of grammar for purposes more literary than linguistic. The *Oxford English Dictionary*'s earliest citation of the phrase "first person narratives" dates only to 1907, though the notion had surely been available to writers many years previously: the dictionary's editors provide a 1719 citation from Defoe's *Farther Adventures of Robinson Crusoe* in which Crusoe states, "I shall no longer trouble the Story with a Relation in the first Person, which will put me to the Expence of ten Thousand *said I's*, and *said he's*, and he *told me's*, and I *told him's*, and the like, but I shall collect the Facts Historically, as near as I can gather them out of my Memory from what they related to me, and from what I met with in my conversing with them and with the Place."[1] This language suggests that first-person narration carries along with it a notion of the circumstantial, a reliance on particular detail that might be better avoided (Crusoe admits) in so far as it entails a dependence on the annoying verbal tics of reported speech – as opposed to the historical collection and collation of facts, a task he will execute (says Crusoe in the next paragraph) as "succinctly" and "intelligibly as [he] can."

The allure of certain novels lies irresistibly in the first-person voices in which they are narrated: *David Copperfield*, *Moby-Dick* and *The Catcher in the Rye* would be transformed, perhaps almost beyond recognition, were they to be recast in the voice of a third-person narrator.[2] Similarly the lofty, all-knowing tones adopted by the omniscient narrators of a Henry Fielding or a George Eliot contribute some essential rather than merely eleemosynary property to their novels. The *Pamela–Shamela* controversy of the 1740s can be thought of as a head-to-head confrontation between a first-person "writing to the moment" associated particularly with the novel of letters (Richardson) and a magisterial or at least managerial third-person voice (associated with Fielding) whose condition of knowing approaches omniscience and whose ability to select and sum up is dizzyingly foregrounded even at the partial expense of what Ian Watt called the "premise, or primary convention" of realism, "that the novel is a full and authentic report of human experience."[3] The story Watt tells about the novel depends on the notion that Austen's writing constitutes a coming-together of these two distinct strands of English fiction: a conclusion that is difficult to dispute, though it may admit of further clarification (this chapter's modest task). Both Richardson and Fielding flirt with the attractions of empirical observation on the one hand and the subjectivity of individual minds on the other, and Michael McKeon has traced a dialectic in which Fielding's later fictions increasingly hew (against the grain of his early polemical position) to an ideal of documentary veracity, while the Richardsonian letter "becomes a passport not to the objectivity of sense impressions but to the subjectivity of mind" wherein "the exhaustiveness of the protagonist's reflections is justified not by the fact that she really made them, but because they are her very own."[4] The radical skepticism we tend to associate with Fielding's highly self-reflexive fictions, in other words, also colors aspects of Richardsonian "writing to the moment," ruling out the possibility of identifying either historicity or subjectivity as inhering chiefly in one or the other of the first- and third-person voices.

Outside of the unpublished juvenilia, all of Austen's major fictions feature an authorial persona which occasionally makes pronouncements in the first person but would more aptly be described as a third-person narrator, perhaps an omniscient one – a strategy that aligns her with Fielding rather than Richardson. "In both Austen and Fielding," Claude Rawson observes in a perceptive essay on *Persuasion*, "the impression emerges not of an actual conversation faithfully recorded by a self-effacing narrator, but of a stylised anecdotal performance, bringing out the preposterous and the comically habitual, knowingly aware that the usual sentiments were uttered in the usual phrases."[5] Elsewhere in the same piece, Rawson suggests that Austen's "admiration for Richardson and her reservations about Fielding were both dominated by moral, rather than technical, considerations," with Fielding providing "the model for... management" by a "knowing narrator" in a way that Richardson does not.[6] Yet in spite of deep temperamental affinities with Fielding that are most clearly expressed in the narrative voice of her novels, Austen was strongly drawn in her early writings both to the epistolary format itself (associated with Richardson) and to radical experimentation with the first-person voice that can perhaps most profitably be considered in the context not of Fielding, say, or even of Sterne, but rather of Swift's demented first-person narrators.

This brings us to the crux of my essay. What are the essential characteristics of the Austenian narrator, supposing we allow there to be such a thing? More particularly, is it possible to discern the narrator's personal properties, or does the Austenian narrator have no such thing as personal properties? D. A. Miller has recently located "the staring paradox of Austen's narration" in the notion that it denies the claims of the person; it is "at once utterly exempt from the social necessities that govern the narrated world, and intimately acquainted with them down to their most subtle psychic effects on character," he says, observing elsewhere that "the secret dependency of perfection on imperfection, of narration on character, seems motivated less by a desire to affirm the superiority of the narrative voice, than by the endless fascination of that voice with the thing that it has forgone in order to speak."[7] In this view, style must be sacrificed (by Elizabeth Bennet, for instance) for the sake of self-realization in marriage, a trade-off whose sharp pathos Miller rather relishes.

It seems to me, on the basis of recent and rewarding classroom experience, that no single more inflammatory notion can be introduced into a discussion of Austen's fiction than this. Is the Austenian narrator a creature of properties or a profoundly depersonalized entity of the sort Miller describes? The question itself may well seem unanswerable, but one way of getting better traction on that slippery thing called voice involves going back to Austen's early unpublished writings, with their clear indebtedness not just to the eighteenth-century novel but to eighteenth-century satire and more particularly to Swift's remarkably unstable first-person voices. The authors (and they are certainly all authors as well as simply narrators) of *A Tale of a Tub*, *Gulliver's Travels*, and *A Modest Proposal*, to take the three most obvious examples, allow Swift to explore first-person voices that go well beyond the conventionally understood limits of personal identity, with its criteria of coherence and consistency. Though he is surely the most straightforward or "embodied" of these three narrators, Gulliver's letter prefatory to the *Travels* contains a mutually exclusive set of pronouns in conflict with one another: "I must freely confess," he writes to his cousin, "that since my last Return, some Corruptions of my *Yahoo* Nature have revived in me by conversing with a few of your Species, and particularly those of mine own Family, by an unavoidable Necessity; else I should never have attempted so absurd a Project as that of reforming the *Yahoo* Race in this Kingdom; but I have now done with all such visionary Schemes for ever."[8] Gulliver's "I" disintegrates under the pressure of Yahoodom, and his reforming project is one casualty of the debilitating contradiction between the wishful attribution "your Species," which allows Gulliver to think of himself as an honorary Houyhnhnm, and the more damaging admission concerning his membership in a Yahoo set titled "mine own Family."

With some notable exceptions, Austen criticism tends to overemphasize the very real importance of fictional first- and third-person precursors at the expense of other eighteenth-century experiments with voice, particularly those satires that do not fall under the rubric of prose fiction. This is not to say that the novelistic contexts don't matter. They do, a great deal. One special property appertaining to several of Austen's novels lies in their conjectural pre-history as epistolary novels. Brian Southam has laid out the evidence in support of Austen's having written early epistolary drafts of *Pride and Prejudice* (initially titled *First Impressions*, and according to Cassandra Austen begun in October 1796 and finished in August 1797) and *Sense and Sensibility* (begun in November 1797, but "I am sure" – Cassandra noted in a later memorandum – "something of the same story & characters had been written earlier & called Elinor & Marianne").[9] In the absence of either of these manuscripts, any discussion of the nature of Austen's preference for the third-person over the epistolary mode remains highly speculative, but Austen's thinking-through of the relationship between first- and third-person voices is obviously indebted not just to the long shadow of the Richardson–Fielding contretemps but also to more recent developments in the English novel. Gary Kelly has explored the implications of Austen's use of a third-person narrative voice that is loosely anti-Jacobin in its political and stylistic associations, and he suggests in particular (though he may here overstate the omniscient properties of Austen's narrators, just as "omniscient" hardly seems an appropriate term for the shifting authorial personae of *Tom Jones*) that "in causing her novel's central consciousness, a potential first-person narrator, to be absorbed into the third-person omniscient narrator, Austen has effectively merged the favorite narrative mode of the English Jacobin and Sentimental novelists into that of their adversaries."[10] Novels composed in letters can take more or less advantage of epistolarity; Burney's *Evelina*, for instance, is essentially a first-person narration poured into an epistolary mold (the letter from "Lord Orville" which causes the title character such grief may be structurally echoed in the letter Willoughby's fiancée forces him to pen to Marianne Dashwood in *Sense and Sensibility*), and Burney's three subsequent novels are all narrated in the third person. The letterness, as it were, of Richardson's novels is rather more profound: in *Pamela*, both the fact of Pamela's writing and the actual material letters she writes play an essential part in the story, and the relatively monologic aspect of this version of epistolary fiction would give way in Richardson's next major novel to a structure and plot that allowed for additional significant letter-writers (with all the additional advantages of voice and perspective such a choice entails).

All this is to say that Austen's fictions reveal a striking and highly productive tension between the first- and third-person voices, one symptom of which is the prominence of the technique that would later come to be called free indirect style. Again, I will borrow Rawson's apt definition (he prefers the term "free indirect speech") from the essay on *Persuasion*: this mode, he says, "combines the ostensibly factual reporting of speech and thought with complex and shifting intimations of judgmental perspective: of the attitudes and point of view, for instance, not only of a first- or second-hand reporter, or of a narrator (whether 'personalized' or 'authorial'), but also of participants in the reported conversation, and even those of a notional reader."[11] Rather than considering the techniques associated with free indirect style, I want to pursue a set of questions raised by that mode about the relationship between a character's thoughts – his or her internal voice – and the voice of the narrator. What sorts of agreement or alignment exist between the narrative voice and individual characters' assertions or opinions as they are filtered by that voice? What happens when the narrator seems to be at odds with the judgments made by a sympathetic main character, and what can such instances of disagreement tell us about Austen's narrators?

Austen's most extensive experimentation with contrasts or disparities between a female protagonist's point of view and the narrator's can be found in *Pride and Prejudice*, a novel punctuated by two distinct but (I will argue) related phenomena: a locally unsettling ironic use of free indirect style and a more metaphysically unsettling use of irony whereby Austen establishes an inverse relationship between a character's attractiveness or appeal to readerly sympathies and the correctness (either factual or moral) of her ethical or political assessments. It should not be particularly controversial to observe that *Pride and Prejudice*'s chief satirist is Mr. Bennet, and that both Elizabeth Bennet and the narrator at times seem to piggyback on that character's peculiar breed of ironic detachment. Early in the novel, when Jane asks for the carriage to take her to Netherfield, Mrs. Bennet responds, "No, my dear, you had better go on horseback, because it seems likely to rain; and then you must stay all night."[12] Because the horses are engaged, Jane is indeed "obliged to go on horseback," and so Mrs. Bennet is "delighted" when it rains hard: " 'This was a lucky idea of mine, indeed!' said Mrs. Bennet, more than once, as if the credit of making it rain were all her own. Till the next morning, however, she was not aware of all the felicity of her contrivance," – Jane having indeed developed a bad cold. The irony implicit in the narrator's obtrusive observation beginning "as if. . ." and the suspiciously elevated diction of "all the felicity of her contrivance" clearly anticipate a satirical remark uttered shortly afterwards by Mr. Bennet himself at the breakfast table: "Well, my dear," he tells his wife, "if your daughter should have a dangerous fit of illness, if she should die, it would be a comfort to know that it was all in pursuit of Mr. Bingley, and under your orders" (I. vii. 23). At other times, the ironic judgment seems to migrate into the narrative voice by way of Elizabeth Bennet's own imagination or intellect: following Elizabeth's relation to Jane of the initial encounter she has observed between Wickham and Darcy, for instance, the narrator concludes that "though Jane would have defended either or both, had they appeared to be wrong, she could no more explain such behaviour than her sister."[13] This is not classic free indirect style – the insight may well be Elizabeth's, but the link between the phrase itself and the person is not quite strong enough for the language to be categorized as such – and the diction, with its indebtedness to the formal grammatical patterns of eighteenth-century paradox, together with the mildly satirical insight into Jane's ludicrously generous cast of thought, might lead the reader to hear something like the narrator's own voice.

Strikingly, the narrator of *Pride and Prejudice* is capable of homing in (at least occasionally) on the private thoughts of characters whose minds are opaque to both Bennet ironists, father and daughter. The following sentence concerns Darcy's early interest in Elizabeth: "He really believed, that were it not for the inferiority of her connections, he should be in some danger" (I. x. 38). There is no witty phrasing here, nothing along the lines of the "either or both" formulation of my previous example, but the word "really" introduces a non-specific ironic effect, as though Darcy's own thought (again, this may not be a classic example of indirect style as it includes the tag "believed") has been transposed into the third person while retaining the self-deprecating and lightly ironized diction we might suppose Mr. Darcy to adopt when he is alone with his own thoughts. (We do not imagine him uttering these words to any actual living, breathing member of the group at Netherfield.)

Elizabeth Bennet herself is scarcely spared the kinds of irony that arise in the gap between a character's self-understanding and the narrator's assessment, and *Pride and Prejudice* offers a series of challenges to what might otherwise be the reader's unquestioning alignment or identification with such an attractive character. A test set by many of Austen's novels, to borrow another phrase from Gary Kelly, "involves tempting the reader to sympathize too much with the heroine," and the temptation is in this case particularly acute.[14] Taking a strong dislike to the aristocratic Darcy, Elizabeth chooses to affiliate herself instead with Wickham, son of the older Mr. Darcy's steward, and her own prejudices about property clearly form part of this judgment: she likes Wickham not just because of his looks and charm but because she takes him to be a kind of class underdog, a visible instance of the abuses of aristocratic privilege and an actual, real-life victim of Darcy's pride. Wickham plays on this tendency in Elizabeth when he says, speaking of himself and Darcy, "We were born in the same parish, within the same park, the greatest part of our youth was passed together; inmates of the same house, sharing the same amusements, objects of the same parental care. *My* father began life in the profession which your uncle, Mr. Philips, appears to do so much credit to – but he gave up every thing to be of use to the late Mr. Darcy, and devoted all his time to the care of the Pemberley property" (I. xvi. 61). What injustice could be greater? Brought up almost as a son, then brutally reminded of his real place in the social hierarchy, Wickham in one sense has his cake and eats it too, at least in terms of the appeal to Elizabeth's sympathies: his upbringing makes him indistinguishable from a Darcy, while his birth – the fact of his father being an attorney, in the same line of work as Elizabeth's uncle – allows him to claim middle-class solidarity.

The novel systematically tricks readers into aligning themselves with Elizabeth in her voicing of opinions that subsequent events will reveal to be grossly mistaken. At the ball at Netherfield, Miss Bingley intervenes to censure Elizabeth's favorable judgment of Wickham. Failing to understand Elizabeth's own class sympathies – or perhaps just affecting to misunderstand them with the real goal of rubbing them in – Miss Bingley assumes that Elizabeth must not have been told of Wickham's social origins:

"So, Miss Eliza, I hear you are quite delighted with George Wickham! Your sister has been talking to me about him, and asking me a thousand questions; and I find that the young man forgot to tell you, among his other communications, that he was the son of old Wickham, the late Mr. Darcy's steward. Let me recommend you, however, as a friend, not to give implicit confidence to all his assertions; for as to Mr. Darcy's using him ill, it is perfectly false; for, on the contrary, he has been always remarkably kind to him, though George Wickham has treated Mr. Darcy, in a most infamous manner. I do not know the particulars, but I know very well that Mr. Darcy is not in the least to blame, that he cannot bear to hear George Wickham mentioned, and that though my brother thought he could not well avoid including him in his invitation to the officers, he was excessively glad to find that he had taken himself out of the way. His coming into the country at all, is a most insolent thing indeed, and I wonder how he could presume to do it. I pity you, Miss Eliza, for this discovery of your favourite's guilt; but really considering his descent, one could not expect much better."

"His guilt and his descent appear by your account to be the same," said Elizabeth angrily; "for I have heard you accuse him of nothing worse than of being the son of Mr. Darcy's steward, and of *that*, I can assure you, he informed me himself." (I. xviii. 72)

The peculiar thing about Austen's technique is that though our sympathies are all with Elizabeth against Miss Bingley, Miss Bingley is in fact correct (though she may not "know the particulars") in almost all of what she says, as Elizabeth will later come to understand. Whether because of a satirical impulse or an angry one, Elizabeth often finds herself in the position of overstating her own case; here she is lured into the position of arguing that birth means nothing, an opinion that will be endorsed neither by the novel as a whole nor by Elizabeth's own later self. Conversely, the off-putting Miss Bingley is given the "correct" line on Wickham, a choice echoed in Austen's decision to give Lady Catherine de Bourgh the novel's only explicit criticism of the practice of "entailing estates from the female line" (II. vi. 126).

The "particulars" that will be needed to explode the notion that Wickham's character and behavior are worth defending are delivered to Elizabeth and to the reader simultaneously in the medium of Darcy's letter following the initial marriage proposal. Equally obviously, the plot of the novel as a whole hinges on revelations of partial and prejudiced judgment encapsulated in Elizabeth's painful self-examination following her reading of that letter: "Of neither Darcy nor Wickham could she think, without feeling that she had been blind, partial, prejudiced, absurd" (II. xiii. 185). But while the reader has not been given enough information to come to a more-or-less independent evaluation (such evaluations of course always depend ultimately on the narrator) of the situation, this is not the case concerning another important judgment made by Elizabeth in the novel's first volume. Offended by Elizabeth's refusal of his marriage proposal, Mr. Collins transfers his gallant attentions "to Miss Lucas, whose civility in listening to him, was a seasonable relief to them all, and especially to her friend" (I. xxi. 88). When Elizabeth thanks Charlotte for keeping Mr. Collins in a good humor, Charlotte simply says how satisfied she is to be useful:

This was very amiable, but Charlotte's kindness extended farther than Elizabeth had any conception of; – its object was nothing less, than to secure her from any return of Mr. Collins's addresses, by engaging them towards herself. Such was Miss Lucas's scheme; and appearances were so favourable that when they parted at night, she would have felt almost sure of success if he had not been to leave Hertfordshire so very soon. But here, she did injustice to the fire and independence of his character, for it led him to escape out of Longbourn House the next morning with admirable slyness, and hasten to Lucas Lodge to throw himself at her feet. (I. xxii. 93)

"[T]he fire and independence of his character": the phrase cannot be Elizabeth's, at least as applied to this situation (of which she is completely ignorant), and it is certainly not Charlotte's. By a process of elimination, then, it must be the narrator's own, just as the phrase "admirable slyness" can be ascribed only to the narrator. Yet it remains difficult to locate the narrator *vis-à-vis* the characters, the ironic mode keeping us at an unspecified distance from them. The narrator offers one summing-up in which what are presumably Charlotte's own opinions surface in the third-person voice: "The stupidity with which he was favoured by nature, must guard his courtship from any charm that could make a woman wish for its continuance; and Miss Lucas, who accepted him solely from the pure and disinterested desire of an establishment, cared not how soon that establishment were gained." In a subsequent conclusion, though, more expansive and less audibly satirical, the narrative moves more resolutely into free indirect style to provide Charlotte's own reflections on the occasion of her engagement:

Mr. Collins to be sure was neither sensible nor agreeable; his society was irksome, and his attachment to her must be imaginary. But still he would be her husband. – Without thinking highly either of men or of matrimony, marriage had always been her object; it was the only honourable provision for well-educated young women of small fortune, and however uncertain of giving happiness, must be their pleasantest preservative from want. This preservative she had now obtained; and at the age of twenty-seven, without having ever been handsome, she felt all the good luck of it. (I. xxii. 94)

The language here cannot be apportioned definitely either to Charlotte or to the narrator, but the voice is fairly sympathetic towards what we take to be Charlotte's own position on matrimony, and the decorous Johnsonian diction of "the only honourable provision" and "pleasantest preservative from want" is not mobilized here in an explicitly satirical cause.

Elizabeth Bennet does not seem to have heard or read these sentences, however, and the narrator's treatment of her response to the engagement instead echoes what may be presumed to be her own language on the occasion:

She had always felt that Charlotte's opinion of matrimony was not exactly like her own, but she could not have supposed it possible that when called into action, she would have sacrificed every better feeling to worldly advantage. Charlotte the wife of Mr. Collins, was a most humiliating picture! – And to the pang of a friend disgracing herself and sunk in her esteem, was added the distressing conviction that it was impossible for that friend to be tolerably happy in the lot she had chosen. (I. xxii. 96–7)

The hyperbole of the language here – a hyperbole that we suppose to have been transferred from Elizabeth Bennet's own thoughts into a third-person voice working in the free indirect mode – draws attention to the fact of the judgment's being considerably too harsh. Charlotte Lucas is hardly in a position to make so good a marriage (in a worldly sense) as her younger, better-looking friend, and Elizabeth is unkind to stigmatize her desire to be settled as a sacrifice of "every better feeling to worldly advantage." (Jane is kinder in her judgment, and even comments on the fact that Elizabeth's "language" is "too strong" in speaking of the couple [II. i. 105].) In other words, *Pride and Prejudice* offers no simple equation between who we *like* and who we believe to be *right*, and the novel's argument about the difference between first impressions and real under-standing is developed in and complicated by precisely such passages (another interesting example can be found in the narrator's contrasting Elizabeth's judgments on Charlotte and on Wickham at II. iii. 117).

The sharpest irony in this section of the novel concerns Elizabeth's supreme conviction in the well-foundedness of her own character assess-ments, and the narrator has fun at Elizabeth's expense when it is observed that in Wickham's "manner of bidding her adieu, wishing her every enjoyment, reminding her of what she was to expect in Lady Catherine de Bourgh, and trusting their opinion of her – their opinion of every body – would always coincide, there was a solicitude, an interest which she felt must ever attach her to him with a most sincere regard; and she parted from him convinced, that whether married or single, he must always be her model of the amiable and pleasing" (II. iv. 117). These are Elizabeth Bennet's own words, applied to and by herself, but elsewhere the language associated with Elizabeth displays more of that indirection (often sharply ironic) associated with Austen's preferred style. Only once Lydia has eloped with Wickham does Elizabeth come to understand that Darcy is "[e]xactly the man, who, in disposition and talents, would most suit her" (III. viii. 237): "But no such happy marriage could now teach the admiring multitude what connubial felicity really was," the narrator continues. "An union of a different tendency, and precluding the possibility of the other, was soon to be formed in their family." The painstaking and perhaps self-protectively ironic diction of the second sentence may belong to Elizabeth herself, and so (but only by a great stretch of the imagination) may the Johnsonian phrase "connubial felicity"; if the language originates at this juncture with Elizabeth, though, it is surely not her own in any proper sense, but more likely borrowed either from a widely prevalent notion of the Johnsonian style or from her own father.

What is most noticeable about this pair of practices – the subtle effect of semi-satirical judgment associated with Austen's free indirect style, the striking choice to put incorrect or unfounded judgments into the mouth of the novel's most attractive character while allowing better-founded ones to less attractive characters (Miss Bingley, Charlotte Lucas, Lady Catherine) – is that neither one finds an obvious analogue in either Fielding or Richardson. When Richardson deploys Lady Davers to voice an argument against cross-class marriage, her brother Mr. B. is prompt to refute it, and Pamela herself in her narration of the encounter leaves the reader in little doubt as to how the argument will ultimately be resolved. Similarly, *Tom Jones* offers a complex and wide-ranging argument about the appropriate balance or compromise between parental authority and children's obedience (an analogy that extends all the way from the family to the nation), one that may be thought of as the dynamic summation of a number of characters' beliefs (the attribution of exaggerated political positions to Squire Western and his sister is especially useful), but Fielding does not for the most part allow Sophia or Tom to voice positions (unless, perhaps, out of naïvety) that seriously challenge the settlement of the novel's conclusion. Indeed, in its oblique mode of operating, the Austenian narrator seems to owe something more to Swift's first-person satirical voices, from the projector of *A Tale of a Tub* to Gulliver or the modest proposer.

Austen's novels (it is a strange effect, almost a trick of the eye of the "duck–rabbit" sort) sound distinctly more satirical – more eighteenth-century, as it were – if one reads them immediately following the early unpublished satires. In one sense, this is clearly akin to the ways in which a text like Locke's second *Treatise* looks remarkably different when read in its polemical historical context as opposed to the dehistoricizing context of a political science classroom. In another sense, though, a sense at once superficial and quite profound, the difference arises in part from the irregularities of punctuation and spelling in Austen's manuscripts: a similar effect can be achieved by reading the canceled chapters of *Persuasion*, whose unorthodox accidentals exert an extraordinary influence on readers' perceptions of style and voice. I partly follow the lead here of William H. Galperin, who observes – one of a great many striking insights in his provocative book *The Historical Austen* – that although Austen may have looked to Burney as a model for her third-person narratives, "the realistic practice that she is widely believed to have perfected, with its particular deployment of free indirect style, is less an advancement upon an earlier type of omniscient narration – specifically Fielding's – than a practice that consists equally with aspects of the epistolary mode in which as many as a third of Austen's major fictions may have been conceived." He supports this thesis by citing the "abrupt and disingenuous turn to Fieldingesque omniscience and moral authority" at the end of the alluring epistolary narrative *Lady Susan*, a turn to a summing-up mode which is in this case implicitly rejected – Galperin argues – "as a damping down of the largely indeterminate text that precedes it."[15] He persuasively concludes – again, partly on the evidence of *Lady Susan*, whose ending clearly displays "the metamorphosis of an omniscient narrator into a character with biases and limitations" – that "the achievement of authority was always conflicted in ways that Austen's continued practice of free indirect discourse has managed to obscure."[16] The passage Galperin alludes to in *Lady Susan* puts the tension between epistolary and third-person narration front and center: "This Correspondence," interjects an impatient narrator after only forty-one letters (a minuscule number, considering the usual scale of the eighteenth-century epistolary novel), "by a meeting between some of the Parties and a separation between the others, could not, to the great detriment of the Post office Revenue, be continued longer."[17]

Lady Susan's voice in the letters is charmingly Machiavellian, her schemes announced with such a lack of self-doubt that she endears herself to the reader if not to the other principal letter-writer, her sister-in-law Mrs. Vernon (whose own schemes are equally ruthlessly mounted in aid of the interests of her immediate family). Examples of this charm are legion, but a single passage will convey the flavor of Lady Susan's epistolary style (she is narrating the latest incident in her attempted seduction of Mrs. Vernon's brother Reginald, whom she has most recently alienated by an ethical misstep):

Oh! how delightful it was, to watch the variations of his Countenance while I spoke, to see the struggle between returning Tenderness and the remains of Displeasure. There is something agreable [*sic*] in feelings so easily worked on. Not that I would envy him their possession, nor would for the world have such myself, but they are very convenient when one wishes to influence the passions of others. (p. 232)

Like other English Machiavels, perhaps most notably Shakespeare's Iago and Milton's Satan, Lady Susan's maneuvering (unfolded here, of course, in letters rather than soliloquies or dramatic monologues) challenges the conventional preference for eliciting readerly sympathy towards characters whose morality the work as a whole endorses. Both its brevity and the dominance of the satirical mode in which it operates set *Lady Susan* apart from, say, a more corrosive full-length epistolary narrative such as Laclos's *Liaisons Dangereuses*, but like Iago, whose theatrical management of other people aligns him with the playwright, Lady Susan herself is the closest thing Austen's epistolary narrative offers to an authorial stand-in. The brisk and slightly demented voice of that interrupting narrator at the end is quite distinct, of course, from Lady Susan's letter-writing style, but the two perhaps have more in common than either one has with Mrs. Vernon's manner, which is chiefly made up of self-serving pieties, fiercely partisan sympathies, and a willingness to subordinate others to her own interested designs, as the narrator acknowledges in a late aside concerning "Mr. Vernon who, as it must have already appeared, lived only to do whatever he was desired" (p. 248): a joke about literary conventions as well as about Mrs. Vernon's instrumental view of other people.

Lady Susan's voice, I have said, is distinct from that of the summing-up narrator of the coda. Can we identify, then, any personal qualities belonging to that narrator? Many of these unpublished fictions were composed in Austen's teens and early twenties – might we extrapolate from biography and hear in the delighted abruptness of that cutting-short the lively voice of an adolescent girl? This would be pointless and reductive, though of course biographical knowledge makes itself felt whatever our beliefs about the best ways of reading literary texts: even the most dedicated formalist is probably affected by his or her knowledge of the author's sex. By no means all of Austen's early works are composed in epistolary form, and another early narrator – one about whom we are given little personal information but a revealing amount of psychological–intellectual detail – may clarify aspects of Austen's practice more generally, namely the "partial, prejudiced, and ignorant Historian" who narrates *The History of England*.[18] These well-chosen adjectives put pressure on exactly the things we most frequently imagine we can count on historians *for*: impartiality and information. Austen's historian breaks virtually every rule known to history-writers, observing of Henry VIII and Anne Boleyn, for instance, that "Tho' I do not profess giving many dates, yet as I think it proper to give some and shall of course Make choice of those which it is most necessary for the Reader to know, I think it right to inform him that her letter to the King was dated on the 6th of May" (p. 138): the provision of day and month without year being an instance of following the letter rather than the spirit of the injunction to record dates. Avowals of ignorance are frequent here, and (like *Lady Susan*) the *History* itself is severely truncated in length: "It is to be supposed that Henry was Married, since he had certainly four sons, but it is not in my power to inform the Reader who was his wife"; "Lord Cobham was burnt alive, but I forget what for" (pp. 134, 135). Carelessness about facts and a teasing fondness for withholding exactly the information that might be supposed to provide a rationale for history-writing in the first place are both inherently bound up with the question of bias, as demonstrated by the historian's disarming admission about the Lancastrian Henry VI: "I suppose you know all about the Wars between him and The Duke of York who was of the right side; If you do not, you had better read some other History, for I shall not be very diffuse in this, meaning by it only to vent my Spleen *against*, and shew my Hatred *to* all those people whose parties or principles do not suit with mine, and not to give information" (p. 135). The historian will go even farther in subsequent episodes, observing with regard to Charles I, for example,

The Events of this Monarch's reign are too numerous for my pen, and indeed the recital of any Events (except what I make myself) is uninteresting to me; my principal reason for undertaking the History of England being to prove the innocence of the Queen of Scotland, which I flatter myself with having effectually done, and to abuse Elizabeth, tho' I am rather fearful of having fallen short in the latter part of my Scheme. (p. 144)

It should be clear how much the narrator of the *History of England* has in common with, say, the modern projector whose digressions punctuate Swift's *Tale of a Tub*, but with one important caveat. Swift's projectors are undoubtedly male, but can we say of the *History* that its narrator is either a he or a she? More histories are authored by men than by women in this period, and the impersonal voice associated with much history-writing tends to read as masculine, just as George Eliot's omniscient narrators, like her pen-name, have a distinctly masculine cast. But is it more plausible to think of the partial and ignorant historian as a man gone off the rails or as a woman whose failure to possess the standard properties associated with the identity of historian is actually related to her sex? In one sense it is an absurdity to ask such a question: omniscience in any case refers to a state of knowing, and there is no reason genitals (or chromosomes) should come into it one way or the other. I suppose it is loosely in support of D. A. Miller's argument, though, to observe how infrequently in our reading experience we exist in a state of complete ignorance about the sex associated with a narrative voice.[19]

Without the space to develop here an extended argument about Austen's relationship to Swift, I will conclude with one last suggestive juxtaposition, in this case to the domestic-minded letter-writer Charlotte Lutterell in Austen's "unfinished Novel in Letters" *Lesley Castle*. Austen experiments here with a host of literary conventions, but one of the text's richest aspects lies in the personal voice of this particular letter-writer. Apologizing to her correspondent for a delay in answering, Charlotte explains that she has been caught up in preparing for her sister's wedding:

And now what provokes me more than anything else is that the Match is broke off, and all my Labour thrown away. Imagine how great the Dissapointment [*sic*] must be to me, when you consider that after having laboured both by Night and by Day, in order to get the Wedding dinner ready by the time appointed, after having roasted Beef, Broiled Mutton, and Stewed Soup enough to last the new-married Couple through the Honey-moon, I had the mortification of finding that I had been Roasting, Broiling and Stewing both the Meat and Myself to no purpose. Indeed my dear Freind [*sic*], I never remember suffering any vexation equal to what I experienced on last Monday when my Sister came running to me in the Store-room with her face as White as a Whipt syllabub, and told me that Hervey had been thrown from his Horse, had fractured his Scull and was pronounced by his Surgeon to be in the most eminent [*sic*] Danger.

"Good God!" (said I) "you don't say so? Why what in the name of Heaven will become of all the Victuals! We shall never be able to eat it while it is good. However, we'll call in the Surgeon to help us–. I shall be able to manage the Sirloin myself; my Mother will eat the Soup, and You and the Doctor must finish the rest." Here I was interrupted, by seeing my poor Sister fall down to appearance Lifeless upon one of the Chests, where we keep our Table linen. (p. 110)

Charlotte and her mother can do little else than join "in heartfelt lamentations on the dreadful Waste in our provisions which this Event must occasion, and in concerting some plan for getting rid of them," a "devouring Plan" whose language surely harks back to that of Swift's equally ruthless and sustenance-minded modest proposer:

"Dear Eloisa" (said I) "there's no occasion for your crying so much about such a trifle" (for I was willing to make light of it in order to comfort her), "I beg you would not mind it–. You see it does not vex me in the least; though perhaps *I* may suffer most from it after all; for I shall not only be obliged to eat up all the Victuals I have dressed already, but must if Hervey should recover (which however is not very likely) dress as much for you again; or should he die (as I suppose he will) I shall still have to prepare a Dinner for you whenever you marry any one else. So you see that tho' perhaps for the present it may afflict you to think of Henry's sufferings, Yet I dare say he'll die soon, and then his pain will be over and you will be easy, whereas my Trouble will last much longer for work as hard as I may, I am certain that the pantry cannot be cleared in less than a fortnight." (p. 111)

Charlotte's preoccupation with the domestic affects every aspect of her language. As well as likening her sister's face to "a Whipt syllabub," she describes herself as being "as cool as a Cream-cheese" (p. 125), an apt near-literalization of a familiar cliché, and expresses a particular longing "to go to Vaux-hall, to see whether the cold Beef there is cut so thin as it is reported, for I have a sly suspicion that few people understand the art of cutting a slice of cold beef so well as I do" (p. 124), an unexpected twist on the conventional London-bound epistolary heroine's desire to go abroad on expeditions of pleasure. The paradox here is that Charlotte's attention to the traditionally feminine preserve of housekeeping should so clearly be matched by a humorously pathological block on understanding the motives that lead women to seek out romantic and marital attachments. After speculating as to her sister's possibly setting her cap at another young man, Charlotte writes: "Perhaps you may wonder that I do not consider *myself* as well as my Sister in my matrimonial Projects; but to tell you the truth I never wish to act a more principal part at a Wedding than the superintending and directing the Dinner, and therefore while I can get any of my acquaintance to marry for me, I shall never think of doing it myself, as I very much suspect that I should not have so much time for dressing my own Wedding-dinner, as for dressing that of my friends" (p. 118). Beyond the humor of it, this passage reveals a stubborn detachment from any investment in marriage plots on one's own behalf as opposed to that of sisters, friends and indeed one's "acquaintance" in the broadest sense, so that even a narrator of properties – a letter-writer with a sex, a name, a family, a first-person voice – can be seen to possess something of the neuter or indeterminate quality that may be discerned in Austen's other voices.

NOTES

1 [Daniel Defoe], *The Farther Adventures of Robinson Crusoe; Being the Second and Last Part of His Life, and of the Strange Surprizing Accounts of his Travels Round three Parts of the Globe. Written by Himself* (London: W. Taylor, 1719), pp. 43–4.

2 See, for instance, the disorienting transposition of a number of famous novelistic openings from first- to third-person voice and vice versa in Susan S. Lanser, *The Narrative Act: Point of View in Prose Fiction* (Princeton: Princeton University Press, 1981), p. 11.

3 Ian Watt, *The Rise of the Novel: Studies in Defoe, Richardson and Fielding* (Berkeley and Los Angeles: University of California Press, 1956), p. 32.

4 Michael McKeon, *The Origins of the English Novel, 1600–1740* (Baltimore: Johns Hopkins University Press, 1987), pp. 418, 414.

5 Claude Rawson, "Satire, Sensibility and Innovation in Jane Austen: *Persuasion* and the Minor Works," in *Satire and Sentiment, 1660–1830: Stress Points in the Augustan Tradition* (New Haven and London: Yale University Press, 1994), p. 270. On the theoretical implications of the difficulty, associated with Austen's preferred form of narration, of "distinguish[ing] a character's internal representation of her thoughts and feelings and the narrator's interpretation of them," see also William H. Galperin, *The Historical Austen* (Philadelphia: University of Pennsylvania Press, 2003), p. 221.

6 Rawson, "Satire, Sensibility and Innovation in Jane Austen," pp. 267–98 (p. 278).

7 D. A. Miller, *Jane Austen, or The Secret of Style* (Princeton and Oxford: Princeton University Press, 2003), pp. 32, 55. For Miller, Austen's narrators are profoundly desexualized (neuter, in Roland Barthes's sense), an assertion with which Karl Kroeber disagrees; see "Jane Austen Criticism, 1951–2004," *Studies in the Novel* 38:1 (2006), 108–16 (p. 114).

8 Jonathan Swift, *Gulliver's Travels*, ed. Claude Rawson and Ian Higgins (Oxford: Oxford University Press, 2005), p. 10.

9 B. C. Southam, *Jane Austen's Literary Manuscripts: A Study of the Novelist's Development through the Surviving Papers*, rev. edn. (London and New York: The Athlone Press, 2001), p. 53; further details concerning epistolarity (certain in the case of *Sense and Sensibility*, speculative but highly plausible with regard to *Pride and Prejudice*) are given on pp. 54–9.

10 Gary Kelly, "Jane Austen and the English Novel of the 1790s," in *Fetter'd or Free? British Women Novelists, 1670–1815*, ed. Mary Anne Schofield and Cecilia Macheski (Athens, OH: Ohio University Press, 1986), pp. 285–306 (p. 286 and pp. 297–8).

11 Rawson, "Satire, Sensibility and Innovation in Jane Austen," p. 269.

12 Jane Austen, *Pride and Prejudice*, ed. James Kinsley, intro. Fiona Stafford (Oxford and New York: Oxford University Press, 2004), I. vii. 22. Subsequent references will be given parenthetically in the text by volume, chapter and page number.

13　*Pride and Prejudice*, I. xv. 56; and see also I. xvii. 64–5.

14　Kelly, "Jane Austen and the English Novel of the 1790s," p. 298.

15　Galperin, *Historical Austen*, p. 21.

16　Galperin, *Historical Austen*, p. 121.

17　Jane Austen, *Lady Susan*, in *Northanger Abbey, Lady Susan, The Watsons, Sanditon*, ed. James Kinsley and John Davie, intro. Claudia L. Johnson (Oxford and New York: Oxford University Press, 2003), p. 247. Subsequent references will be given parenthetically in the text.

18　Both *The History of England* and *Lesley Castle* are quoted from *Catharine and Other Writings*, ed. Margaret Anne Doody and Douglas Murray (Oxford and New York: Oxford University Press, 1998); subsequent page references will be given parenthetically in the text.

19　How often is an omniscient narrator gendered female? Asked this question, the writer and science-fiction scholar Justine Larbalestier (in a personal email of March 22, 2007) pointed to the collective female first-person plural voice of Karen Joy Fowler's 2004 novel *The Jane Austen Book Club*, whose indebtedness to Austen suggests that the British novelist may serve as instigator for such experimentation; but instances are certainly fairly rare.

CHAPTER 15

The hungry mouth: eucharistic parody in Hogarth, Goya, and Domenico Tiepolo

Ronald Paulson

HOGARTH

An engraving by William Hogarth of *c.* 1761 called *Enthusiasm Delineated* (fig. 1) shows the inside of a Methodist meeting house filled with a mob of the lower orders devouring images of Christ – a parody Eucharist.[1] It is, ostensibly, a satire on Methodist superstition, the naïve literalizing of the injunction, "Take and eat this in remembrance that Christ died for thee." But the Eucharist was the most sacred sacrament of the Christian church, and Hogarth's print, never published, survives in only two impressions.

Transubstantiation, the belief that Christ's body and blood in heaven and the bread and wine on the altar of the church became a physical identity at the moment of the priest's blessing, was anathema to Protestants. The common-sense Church of England view was expressed in the sixteenth century by Bishop John Jewel when he wrote that "the Body of Christ is to be eaten by faith only, and none otherwise"; we eat the sacrament not literally but "with the mouth of faith":

the sacrament-bread is bread, it is not the body of Christ: the body of Christ is flesh, it is no bread. The bread is beneath: the body is above. The bread is on the table: the body is in heaven. The bread is in the mouth: the body in the heart. The bread feedeth the outward man: the body feedeth the inward man . . . Such a difference is there between the bread, which is a sacrament of the body, and the body of Christ itself.[2]

Protestants rejected transubstantiation, not only because of its "mystery" but because it depended on the function of the priest (as did salvation, or confession, penance, and indulgences).[3] Protestants merely ate the bread and commemorated Christ's original gift of his body and blood. Communion around a table, not before an altar, recalled the Last Supper. What Hogarth shows in *Enthusiasm Delineated* is either an extreme form

251

Figure 1. William Hogarth, *Enthusiasm Delineated* (c. 1761).

of Protestant rejection of popery (everyone is equally devouring Christ — no need for a priest), or a gross materialism that reduces Protestant and Catholic and all Christian theology of the atonement to cannibalism.

At the least, Hogarth is saying what Swift said of Peter and Jack in his *Tale of a Tub*, that however far apart Catholics and Calvinist (read,

Figure 2. William Hogarth, *The Gate of Calais* (1748).

Methodist) enthusiasts wander they keep bumping into each other. The style of preaching in *Enthusiasm Delineated* is Methodist–evangelical, but the preacher, in the excitement of his oratory, dislodges his wig, exposing the skull of a tonsured priest; his robe opens to reveal a Harlequin costume; and he surrounds himself with "idols" that would never have been permitted in a Methodist meeting house or even an Anglican church. It appears that Hogarth is tarring all Christian religion with the same brush; only a Muslim, peering in amazement at the scene through a window, a convention of Enlightenment satires, shows any signs of sanity. (The other non-Christian, a Jew, reading about Abraham's sacrifice of Isaac and sacrificing a flea, participates in, and shares the principle behind, the Eucharist, implying the common basis of both religions.)

Hogarth had satirized the Catholic sacrament of the Eucharist before. In a print of 1748, *The Gate of Calais* (fig. 2), his conceit lay in the analogy between substantial and transubstantial meat. In the distance the Mass is being celebrated by Catholic priests worshiping at a cross under an inn sign of the Dove (the Holy Spirit). The gate of Calais, framing the priests celebrating Mass, resembles a gaping mouth, the portcullis teeth, and two escutcheons the eyes. On this side of the open mouth, a fat priest is savoring a side of beef carried by a skeletal Frenchman to the local English tavern, celebrated in the print's subtitle, "O The Roast Beef of Old England."[4] The English eat substantial amounts of beef, drink beer, and so on; the French starve on spiritual fare alone.

In the sixth plate of *A Harlot's Progress* (1732) a prostitute's body was substituted for the Body of Christ in a parody of a *Last Supper*, and something similar was also implicit in the dissection of Tom Nero's body after hanging in the last plate of *The Stages of Cruelty* ("The Reward of Cruelty," 1751). Unlike *Enthusiasm Delineated*, these plates were structured on the model of a sacrifice, the first the Last Supper (with a table in the form of a coffin, a chalice for the Blood, the coffined Harlot for the Body), the second a literal sacrifice with the dissection-table taking the place of an altar,[5] the chief surgeon supervising the dissection standing in for both the magistrate presiding over an execution and God the Father over a *Last Judgment*.[6] These prints, however, were less a direct attack on religion than a satiric reduction of the religious to the social, the blunt Mandevillian reality of London life in the 1730s where prostitutes did redeem (die for) gentlemen so that they could take their pleasure while shielding their respectable wives.[7] Hogarth's message was that in eighteenth-century England the only atonement is the human one of a whore or a thief and murderer in relation to a vengeful law and a corrupt society. In *Harlot 6* the girl's body was, given the congruence of coffin and dining-table, by implication food: that is, these people are (in a characteristic Hogarthian pun) "eating," "making a meal of" her, as at the end of his career Tom Nero's entrails are being devoured by a dog like the one he had tortured in the first plate.[8] And behind Swift (whose Moderns and spiders live by eating their own excrement) and Hogarth was the common satiric image of devourment, either positive or negative. Negative in the classical sense, when Tantalus challenged the gods by feeding them the body of his son Pelops, testing them to see whether they can tell the difference between celestial and human meat; then, when Pelops' son Atreus avenges himself on his brother Thyestes, by serving him a dish containing the flesh of Thyestes' children. The Latin *cena* or dinner-party, from Horace to Juvenal to Petronius, was based on the difference between moderation and excess, between spiritual and physical hunger: in *The Satyricon* between Trimalchio and Eumolpus, the eater and the eaten, Trimalchio's will and Eumolpus', the dinner Trimalchio forces on his guests and the one Eumolpus forces on the legacy-hunters. Positive in the liberating feasts of Rabelais's giants, Pantagruel's mouth opening to reveal new, undreamt of worlds. Closest to Hogarth's *Harlot* was Swift's *Modest Proposal* (1728) with its metaphor of eating and being eaten: English landlords "devour" the Irish ("I could name a Country, which would be glad to eat up our whole Nation"), so why not their babies? Implicitly, his terms "devour" and "eat" go back to the (Irish) Catholic doctrine of transubstantiation.[9]

In the *Harlot* the implied devouring was of the Body, a substitute for the Host, by so-called respectable society; in *The Gate of Calais*, both the Host and nutriment were at stake, and hunger the subject. The clergy (specifically of course in a xenophobic cartoon, the Roman Catholic) and not the congregation gets the real, the material versus the spiritual food. In this sense the clergy (the gaping mouth of the gate) is "devouring" the hungry congregation – as earlier the respectable Londoners were "devouring" the Harlot. In *Enthusiasm Delineated* the body of Christ is literally being eaten. Being inserted into mouths, the Eucharist has become either cannibalism (as Bishop Jewel and the Protestant reformers had implied) or (closer to Swift's satire on religious enthusiasm in *A Tale of a Tub*) fellatio. This Host is plainly phallic, being fondled as well as mouthed. One recalls Graham Greene's image of the power of the Catholic priest, which, while the words of a Catholic, could have been uttered by Protestants in their penchant for ribald mockery of popery: from a priest the congregation "took God – in their mouths"; the priests were "putting God into the mouths of men."[10] Women taking lovers "in their mouths" would have been Greene's way of describing fellatio. Both readings are present in the overarching metaphor of "hunger," but the sexual sense is supported by the preoccupied lovers in the foreground and, next to them, the Swiftean "pleasure" thermometer that measures religious/sexual enthusiasm in terms of madness, ecstasy, love-heat, and lust-hot.[11] (Hogarth's congregation and its chapel include memories of the madhouse Swift had described in the "Digression Concerning Madness": the roots of religion, or at least enthusiast religion, in a sexually derived self-punishing madness. The setting, as in *A Rake's Progress*, plate 8, which was based on the "Digression," is church-as-Bedlam.)

Appropriately, given the Protestant belief in the Body as sign over the reality of transubstantiation, the phallus is only a dildo.[12] The Host is a *likeness* of Christ, and the figures around the pulpit are other idols – representations of God and Satan, Moses and Ss. Peter and Paul, and Adam and Eve, copied from paintings by Raphael, Rubens, and Rembrandt. That is to say, the papist worshiped the sign in place of what it signified. To the papist, the bread *was* the actual body of Christ; to the English Protestant, it was real bread, only the sign – the memory – of

Christ, but if you were to merge the traditions you would have small replicas of Christ's body. The imagery of eating the Body of Christ, the subject of *The Gate of Calais*, exposes the physical hunger – in the gaping, greedy, needy mouths of the shabby congregation, the reality beneath (and not to be satisfied by) the holy Eucharist, and parallel in that respect to the gin in Hogarth's *Gin Lane* (1751).

Echoing the open mouths below, Hogarth's meeting house is presided over (formally balancing the figure of the preacher in the pulpit and above the heads of the congregation) by a large chandelier in the shape of a globe with an open-mouthed human face inscribed "New and Correct Globe of Hell." On the globe of hell a line marks the equator as "Horrid Zone," and the smaller globe above it is labeled "Part of New Purgatory." On the face, one eye is "Molten Lead Lake," the other "Bottomless pit"; "Pitch and Tar Rivers" cross the face, one running into "Brimstone Ocean," the other toward "Parts Unknown." The mouth, angrily turned down at the corners, is "Eternal Damnation Gulf" or hell-mouth.[13]

Sin and hell were what the 1760s Methodist congregation was primarily concerned with, the subject of the preacher's rant. As well as Swift's "Digression Concerning Madness," Hogarth was recalling the sermons of George Whitefield, the Methodist evangelist, in which he turned the chapel into a literal hell.[14] Sin was identified not so much by its nature as by its punishment, the hell-fire that is the ultimate reach of the evils following upon Adam's sin. You in the congregation, says the preacher, can look to right and left and see two out of three who are damned – by an incredibly angry God (like the hell-face on the globe) who is dangling sinners over the pit of hell as Hogarth's preacher dangles God and Satan. There is nothing specific, only something frightening, as in the description of hell itself as a "furnace," the gaping mouth of the "old serpent" – obscure, and so all the more terrifying and (in Edmund Burke's terminology of the 1750s) sublime. Where part of the evil is in the obscurity, the imagination is free to imagine the horrors of "darkness visible" and eternal fires for ever and ever.

Devouring in *Enthusiasm Delineated* therefore evokes both the medieval hell-mouth and the Eucharist in which (in Graham Greene's words) we eat the body of Christ – a significantly earthy way of describing the holiest sacrament; then, therefore, sheer hunger, and finally, the sense of "devouring" of Dante's *Inferno*, from the pull downward of the vortex of hell, from Circle One down to Nine, to the figures in the lake of ice, Ugolino chewing on the head of Ruggieri, who had forced him to eat his own children, and Satan himself with the ultimate betrayers Brutus,

Cassius, and Judas in *his* mouth. Hell would have been seen by Hogarth, the artist of *The Gate of Calais*, as a metaphor of devourment.[15]

Drawing as it also does on Swift's "Digression Concerning Madness," the message of Hogarth's image of devourment and hell is that religion is a substitute for sex, and sex, we know from Augustine onward, is the original cause of damnation; ergo, the congregation, obsessed with salvation and confusing the Body of Christ with a dildo, is not saved but (surprise!) is in fact damned. You eat Christ's body in lieu of bread, expecting grace and salvation but (as it disappears into hell's mouth) you find instead hell and damnation – in a Bedlam, needless to say, physical rather than spiritual; and, furthermore, religion is in any case a poor substitute for bread. This is a conclusion that applies as well to the preacher, who within the hell-mouth of the meeting house recalls *The Reward of Cruelty*, in which Pieter Brueghel's fish image is invoked – the eater is eaten, the cruel agent becomes the patient for a larger agent.

The two aspects of the Eucharist – the body and the mouth – evoked a skeptical or materialist interpretation of the sort that any satirist might have welcomed. Swift comes dangerously close in his *Tale of a Tub*. Like Hogarth's, his body metaphor should be applied only to the radical evangelical enthusiasts, or (as some Church of Englanders, including the queen, believed) perhaps to the whole Christian religion across the spectrum of Roman Catholic to Evangelical.

Hogarth did not in fact publish *Enthusiasm Delineated*; it was sufficiently liable to prosecution for blasphemy for him to have suppressed it, but in 1762 he revised the image, adjusting it to accommodate a topical scandal. Thriftily, he reused the copperplate, changing the vehicle (the image) while retaining the tenor.[16] He turned *Enthusiasm Delineated* into *Credulity, Superstition, and Fanaticism*, more narrowly a satire of Methodists' belief in both miracles and ghosts. Sexually based "enthusiasm" (the equation of religious belief and sexual desire) is replaced by the safer subject of superstition, though still sexually based. The Christs being devoured have been replaced by the contemporary "Cock Lane Ghost," a young woman who allegedly returned from the dead to condemn her murderer – a fraud recently exposed by Samuel Johnson and others.[17] The images of God and the devil, who brandished respectively a Trinity trivet and a pitchfork (an image of salvation–damnation), are replaced by a witch riding her broomstick and a variety of well-known ghosts (of Caesar, Buckingham, etc.). *Enthusiasm Delineated* showed the sexual origin of religion; *Credulity* shows the *credulous* belief in ghosts and miracles; the congregation – these *credulous* fools – have, by a typical Hogarthian pun, "swallowed whole" the story of the ghost (a pun Hogarth would have felt applied equally to the earlier version of the print with its reference to fellatio).[18]

In the published state the Host has become a Harlot substitute, a female named Fanny Lynes, the "Cock Lane Ghost"; and the bawd-in-ecstasy Mother Douglas has been replaced by the Mary-the-Mother parody of *Cunicularii*, Mary Toft the "Rabbit Woman." Hogarth has taken two aspects of religion – the belief in miracles and in the sacrament of the Eucharist (the greatest miracle) – and placed them in the evangelical preacher's sermon, whose subject is hell; he shows the "miracles" to be in fact Levitical "abominations" (the Boy of Bilson vomiting nails, Mary Toft giving birth to rabbits), and replaces religion with superstition, reflecting the current fad for Old English ballads and folk-tales. Following the New Awakening in the American colonies and Methodism in England, and not long after the advocacy of the sublime of Burke's *Philosophical Enquiry into the Origins of our Idea of the Beautiful and Sublime*, he makes the connection between the aesthetic and (in this case perhaps going back to John Dennis) the religious sublime.

Bernd Krysmanski has offered the most persuasive explanation for the oxymoron in *Enthusiasm Delineated* of Methodist meeting house and idolatrous papist images, a solution that supplements the one just given: that the print is about art; primarily, Hogarth intends a parallel between preacher–congregation and the art auctioneer and the "congregation" of connoisseurs, and he "puts Methodist enthusiasm and the devotion for Old Masters on the same level."[19] Both preacher and auctioneer represent the authority that elicits enthusiast madness. Art, in short, is the subtext of the print, or its real subject.

There is a direct line leading from *Enthusiasm Delineated* back to the first plate of *Marriage A-la-Mode* (1745, fig. 3), whose walls and ceiling are covered with Old Master paintings, baroque scenes of torture and martyrdom by Titian and his followers, showing gods punishing rebellious sons and disobedient creatures; the continuum is religion, Counter-Reformation art, and the origin of both in sexual dysfunction. The preacher of *Enthusiasm Delineated* recapitulates the chief surgeon of *The Reward of Cruelty*, posed as a magistrate in the pose of a God the Father in a *Last Judgment*, the figure Hogarth had earlier laid out in the patriarchal presiding figure of Lord Squander and in the fathers in the paintings he collects and hangs as admonitory images (Zeus, Jehovah, Pharaoh, Louis XIV), based on terror, for the admonition of his son. These are figures of the "Old Masters," painters Hogarth sought to replace with his "modern

Figure 3. William Hogarth, *Marriage A-la-Mode* 1 (1745).

moral subjects." (By "Old Master" or "Dark Master" Hogarth meant conventional, tradition-bound artists.) As early as *A Harlot's Progress*, the parody of the Eucharist was conveyed through echoes of religious art, most obviously in plate 6, paintings and prints of *The Last Supper*, whether by Leonardo or Dürer. In all of his work, the paintings abstract and stifle the humans who live beneath them, morally and literally, into art.

GOYA

Thirty years later in Roman Catholic Spain, in his *Caprichos* (published 1799), Goya also reduced religion to superstition, the spiritual image to the physical (witches riding broomsticks), but here the receiving mouth is that of the priest, usually shown being filled with less spiritual food and drink. In *Capricho* 13 (fig. 4), monks are using their gaping mouths to devour food. The inscription is "Estan calientes" (They are hot): the food they are eating is hot, their mouths are hot, and they are "in heat." Eating the eucharistic wafer becomes, in the mouths of the priests, the eating of

Figure 4. Francisco Goya, *Caprichos* (1799), no. 13, "Estan calientes."

spiced-up food and/or sexual appetite, both gluttony and lust. One preparatory drawing shows a human head being brought in on the platter and adds the caption, "A dream of some Men who were eating us up" – emphasizing the anticlerical aspect of the print – from the priest's devouring Christ to devouring his congregation of worshipers, recalling both Swift's *Modest Proposal* and Hogarth's *Gate of Calais*. Another drawing for *Capricho* 13 gives one monk a huge, phallic nose, evoking the sexual aspect of devourment. Both are primarily, however, about the gaping mouths, spaces echoed in the arch that encloses the scene.

The devouring mouth is Goya's symbol of predation, conflating the Christian sacrament of the Eucharist with the myth of the vampire and the medieval representations of the hell-mouth that swallows the damned in the mystery plays and in the paintings of the Last Judgment and hell. Goya's paintings and prints are pervaded by gaping mouths and the analogous shapes of archways, gates, caves, pits, and dungeons, in courts of the Inquisition, mad-houses, prisons, and bandits' lairs, where rape and murder take place; all are consuming agents, registering a degeneration of the sacred Eucharist into cannibalism, of salvation into damnation.

Goya knew Dante, who had been translated into Spanish as early as the fifteenth century. His patron Jovellanos, if not Goya himself, would have known Milton's priests with "blind mouths."[20] His Enlightenment patrons, the *ilustrados* who collected the English prints of Hogarth and Gillray, would have shared them with Goya. It is unlikely that he could have seen *Enthusiasm Delineated*, but *Credulity, Superstition, and Fanaticism* would have been easily accessible. It is not necessary to my argument, however; the central issue of Roman Catholicism was transubstantiation and the Eucharist, and this laid open to the Enlightenment artist an image of great ambiguity, religious and anthropological, an ambivalent conjunction of religious and folklore imagery.

Goya worked within the tradition of the Spanish folk-tale, in which parents become so poor they cannot feed their children; in order to survive, they abandon the children in the deepest part of a forest, occupied by wolves, witches, and other creatures who wish to eat them. Hunger leads to the children's eating the gingerbread off a witch's house, and she plans to devour them, but she is herself made a meal (the eater is eaten) when the boy pushes her into the oven she has prepared for baking the siblings. As Robert Darnton has shown, the plots of devourment indicated real physical hunger as a motive of the folk-tales and their ways of dealing with the evils of peasant life.[21] These tales, supported by the basic association of hunger with the Eucharist, were ways of coping with the evils (death, suffering, disease, starvation); they project a particularly strong image of evil in the giant who "eats the blood of an Englishman," the wolf who eats both the little girl and her old grandmother, and the witch who would bake and eat children. The Host obviously does not satisfy such physical hunger.

The reference is to the bread and stones of the first temptation of Christ ("man cannot live on bread alone," Matthew 7:3–4). The first

picaresque tale, the anonymous *Lazarillo de Tormes* (1554), consisted of a
series of episodes based on folk-tales.[22] A poor boy, without parents or
sustenance, escapes starvation and death only by attaching himself to a
master who both starves and mistreats him. In the second episode he
encounters a priest, even worse than the blind beggar, "a living portrait
of the utmost niggardliness," who virtually starves Lazaro to death.[23] The
only "food" in the priest's house is "a string of onions locked away
upstairs," but the priest keeps also locked away the loaves of holy bread
for Mass. Lazaro gets into the chest and, "seeing the bread, began to
worship it, but did not dare kiss it, even"; all he can do is "contemplate
there the blessed face of God (as children are wont to call bread)." Mixing
the discourses of the spirit and the flesh, he says: "I opened my bread-
filled paradise and took up in my hands and teeth a loaf of holy bread and
in the time you could say two credos I had made it invisible." He uses the
bread as, it is suggested, it should (as a last resort to the hungry) be used,
preferable to its "spiritualization" by the priest, hypocritical since he eats
the bread himself. Physical versus spiritual hunger is what the Spanish
picaresque was about.

At the heart of Goya's representations, the gaping mouth recovers the
figures around the Christ of the Passion, the story Hogarth had parodied
in his *Harlot's Progress* plates. The model was plate 4, showing the Harlot
in Bridewell Prison beating hemp, in the pose of a *Flagellation of Christ*.
Around the time of the *Caprichos* Goya painted a large altarpiece for the
Cathedral of Toledo of *The Taking of Christ in the Garden* (1798, fig. 5).
Like Hogarth, he used as his model the *Christ Mocked* and *Ecce Homo*
paintings of Netherlandish painters, most strikingly available in the
Quentin Metsys version hanging, where he would have studied it, in the
Spanish royal collection (Madrid, Prado). Metsys shows Christ surrounded
by grotesquely ugly mockers, one of whom shows a gaping mouth. Goya's
painting of the threatening shapes emphasizes the open mouths, shouting,
mocking, and threatening the beautiful, idealized shape of Christ.

The open mouth preparing literally to devour Christ, the Host of the
Mass, is an image from which the open-mouthed figures of the *Caprichos*
follow – and all the caves and archways into which Goya's figures
disappear, all consuming agents, counter-Christs. In both *Enthusiasm
Delineated* and Goya's paintings of Christ, the people (the congregation,
the mockers of Bosch and Metsys) devour Christ, conflating the cruelty of
the *Ecce Homo* pictures and the efficacy of Christ's sacrifice, in the two
senses of "devour." The same people who destroy him are – the irony –
destined to benefit from his incarnation and sacrifice. The earliest of such

Figure 5. Francisco Goya, *The Taking of Christ in the Garden* (1798).

paintings, his *St. Francis Borja Attending a Dying Man* (1788, Valencia Cathedral), shows the man's open mouth from which the spirit issues at death; demons are waiting to seize the soul that emerges from the mouth, while the mouth is reaching out to receive the life-giving blood of Christ that spurts from the crucifix held by St. Francis Borja. The large orifice formed by the moon-shaped window in the background is the first of those gaping, hungry mouths shaped by architecture. Later the gaping mouth of St. Joseph of Calasanz is swallowing the Host, the symbolic body of Christ, in his last communion – again within the larger mouth of the Roman arch which frames the action (1819, San Anton Abad, Madrid).

The reference is to a ritual that promised a way to immortality or paradise, a way out of the problem of evil, which Goya relates also to the sucking perversions of the witches and priests in the *Caprichos*, a way to increase one's own power by eating/sucking someone more powerful. The assumption, as in witch lore, is that power is conveyed by giving and taking the contents of the body. The most spectacular scene of such devourments is Goya's *Saturn Devouring His Son* (1820, fig. 6). If the priest devours the congregation/the Spanish people, then Saturn, the ancient, original god, devours his son – not, as in Rubens's painting, merely bites into him, but swallows his head and upper body.

In the context of the contemporaneous French Revolution, the cutting off of the head recalls, of course, the beheading of Louis XVI and others. The 1790s witnessed the regressive undercurrent of revolutionary imagery, seen in the importance of eating in the very different works of Gillray in England. The French *sans-culottes* fire food into the mouths of other European peoples and sup on the heads of their aristocrats; in England a John Bull gourmandizes warships and both Pitt and Napoleon are devouring the globe; ultimately Goya's Saturn devours his son. Louis XVI was a "father" being beheaded, whereas Goya's son, representing the next stage of the revolutionary scenario, evokes Pierre Vergniaud's *bon mot* that the revolution was "like Saturn, devouring its own children," words that reflected the cyclic quality of the revolution Goya witnessed in Spain, freedom following repression, turning again into repression, and so on in a vicious cycle ending with the tyrant Ferdinand VII back on the throne.[24]

In Goya's images of the Napoleonic war in Spain (the Peninsular War) devourment grows into engulfment. In his sequence, *Desastres de la guerra*, the pits receive the corpses from firing squads, famine, and disease (No. 27, fig. 7). In no. 65 the apocalyptic realism of the burial scenes returns to emblematic scenes (from the *Caprichos*) of clerical and

Figure 6. Francisco Goya, *Saturn Devouring His Son* (1819).

Figure 7. Francisco Goya, *Desastres de la Guerra* (1810–20).

aristocratic follies, beginning with excessive worship of the dead, relics, and holy images. In no. 68 the Church is an institution "fed" with devotional offerings which gives in return only feces. The image of a half-buried corpse, with the familiar shadowy figures of mockers in the background, holds a paper inscribed "Nada" (no. 69), and a vampire bat sucks the life out of a man's body (nos. 71–2). The pits and graves in the *Desastres* in fact are mouths that devour these people – without any promise of an afterlife in heaven; demons are lurking in the background to claim these people. Finally, the "Proud Monster" (*Fiero monstruo*, no. 81), an animal something like a sow, is swallowing her own farrow, recalling the *Saturn* painting and anticipating Freud's words, "Kronos devoured his children, just as the wild boar devours the sow's litter."[25]

In *Saturn Devouring His Son* the father is literally devouring the son, but Goya executed the painting, appropriately and ironically, on the wall of the dining-room in his house, the *Quinta del Sordo* (now in the Prado). On another wall he painted Judith cutting off Holofernes's head, a retaliation; opposite Saturn, two figures are at their dinner, and a demon with open mouth prompts or tempts an old man. By representing with paint these devouring figures on the walls of his own dining-room, where *he* devours food, Goya makes himself both devoured and devourer. He demystifies and exorcises the paternalist Eucharist. And in his contemporary self-portrait with Dr. Arrieta (1820, Institute of Arts, Minneapolis), an *ex voto* picture following his recovery from a serious illness, he paints himself in the composition of a Bellini *Pietà*, but supported not by Mary or an angel but by his doctor, who feeds him life-saving medicine. Demonic heads (of the sort he painted on the walls of his *Quinta del Sordo*) take the place of Bellini angels. Goya is being served the Blood by a physician who replaces a priest, but, unlike the other dying men (Borja and Calanz), Goya's mouth is closed.

In *Totem and Taboo* Freud tells us how by means of murder and cannibalism the sons of Darwin's "Primal Horde" overcome the dominion and threat of the father, and in the act of devouring identify with him. Thus "the company of brothers": "in the act of devouring him they accomplished their identification with him, and each one of them acquired a portion of his strength," so indicating anthropologically a direct line from the cannibalism of the Primal Horde to the Eucharistic devouring of Christ.[26]

Goya shows the father devouring the son, but the son at the same time is dining on the father, in his "Black Paintings" replacing the unity and hierarchy of baroque paintings with his own demotic, grotesque, and caricatural forms. In Hogarth's grim scenario of *Marriage A-la-Mode* there was Lord Squander and his son, and Squander's Old Master paintings, which represented himself and mythological fathers killing their rebellious sons. But on the ceiling was a painting of Pharaoh's host drowned by the closing of the Red Sea, and in the sequel, young Squander has in his own way the last word by producing a daughter (not a son) to whom he has transmitted congenital syphilis and so brought to an end the father's precious genealogical line. And Hogarth, the artist, has transformed the Old Master paintings into his "modern moral subject."

DOMENICO TIEPOLO

Behind Giovanni Domenico Tiepolo, as behind Hogarth and Goya, was the model of Antoine Watteau, who in *L'Enseigne de Gersaint* (Berlin, Charlottenburg) shows the portrait of Louis XIV being packed away, on its way out of Gersaint's shop, which is now hung with paintings in the new rococo style. Watteau's solution to the art of Louis XIV was to replace the gods and heroes with *commedia dell'arte* clowns and contemporary lovers, in particular in *Les Comédiens italiens* (Washington,

National Gallery of Art) the all-white figure of innocence, Pierrot, on a
stage in an *Ecce Homo* composition.

In the last decade before his death in 1804 Domenico Tiepolo, the son
of Giovanni Battista Tiepolo, the great Venetian painter of heroic
Christian and classical subjects, made 104 drawings in pen, brown ink,
and brown wash of the life of the *commedia* clown Punchinello in a
society of Punchinellos.[27] Serial composition, going back to *A Harlot's
Progress* and Goya's *Caprichos* (which drew upon the artistic license of
Giambattista's *Capricci* and *Scherzi di fantasia*), was a familiar mode for
Domenico. His series included his *Via Crucis* and *Flight to Egypt* etchings
and his *Hercules and Antaeus* and *Scenes of Modern Life* drawings. Like
the *Harlot's Progress*, the *Punchinello* drawings are a modern redaction of
the Christian story of incarnation and atonement.[28] The story begins
with the miraculous birth of the father (presumably the miraculous
Giambattista) from an egg and ends with the martyrdom and resurrection
of the son. We might recall Stephen Daedalus's "Ballad of Joking Jesus"
("I'm the queerest young fellow that ever you heard / My mother's a Jew
and my father's a bird"), except that here both parents are birds, as we see
from the absent cock's picture on the wall. There is a *Taking of Christ
before Pilate*, and even a *Flagellation*, a bare-bottomed spanking, a comic
reprise of *Harlot* 4, where the Harlot was beaten.[29] The series ends with a
variety of deaths, by hanging, by firing squad, as well as, finally, a natural
death in bed.[30] And the deaths are followed by an elaborate account of
Punchinello's burial in his parish church and his resurrection – or rather,
more precisely, in the Enlightenment context, his refusal to stay dead
(he returns, attenuated as a *transi*, a fugitive from a tomb).[31]

But Domenico's series was different from Hogarth's *Harlot* in two
important ways: he includes versions other than the Christian story, such as
Ganymede and Jupiter's eagle, and he generously expands in the incar-
national middle with a vast variety of scenes of Punchinello's everyday life –
doing this and that, assuming this and that human role, taking up different
professions, and going on travels to remote (even fabulous) lands. The
various deaths could be taken to be Punchinello continuing his spectrum of
professions – attending an execution, or participating in an execution, of
another Punchinello – or being executed himself by other Punchinellos.

The framing events of the miraculous birth and the resurrection
underline one of the most obvious phenomena of the middle – the parody
of heroic and/or religious stories, a shifting emphasis from the high to the
low, from baroque-rococo history painting of the sort Giambattista
Tiepolo made to paintings of everyday life, Italian equivalents of

Hogarth's English "modern moral subjects."[32] This was a continuation of Domenico's own work in his father's lifetime: he had filled in the commonplace scenes of peasants while his father did the gods and heroes.[33] Throughout the *Punchinello* series the scenes of low life are punctuated with parodies of the paintings of the great Giambattista. Punchinello and Colombina court in the attitudes of Giambattista's painting of Tasso's Rinaldo and Armida. Punchinellos overrun a *Triumph of Flora* and Punchinello the painter is lifted from Giambattista's *Apelles Painting Campaspe*. Punchinello the history painter works on Giambattista's *Sacrifice of Iphigenia* (in the Villa Valmarana, where Domenico worked on the less exalted, everyday subjects). Domenico's *Marriage of Punchinello* recalls Giambattista's *Marriage of Barbarossa* in his magnificently decorated Kaisersaal of the Residenz, Würzburg.[34]

The repetition of Giambattista's compositions has been regarded by art historians as both a habit of long standing (though never done so pervasively) and a sign of Domenico's tired old age. The chief function of the series, however, was a summing up, a retrospective of Domenico's own life and art made at the end of it; and this meant inevitably for him a summing up of his towering father as well, who brought to a climax the tradition of Venetian history painting. His father had died in 1770 at the Spanish court, where he was working, his style replaced by the neoclassicism of Anton Raphael Mengs and his followers, and Domenico, who returned to Venice to continue his father's practice, found commissions even in his native Italy declining in the 1780s. His last paintings, from the early 1790s, were painted on the walls and ceilings of the family villa, and showed Punchinellos mixing with other contemporaries in local and contemporary scenes. There were no paintings after about 1793, the last decade being devoted to serial drawings, including those of Punchinello.

Domenico's title-page for the *Punchinello* series (fig. 8) calls for comparison with that of his religious etchings, *Via Crucis* (1749), which showed an altar labeled "VIA CRUCIS" – on this side a prone cross, on the far side a ladder, an obvious symbol of ascent and resurrection.[35] On this side was also a baluster-shaped vase on which was perched a cock, prefiguring the picture of the cock on the wall in Punchinello's nativity. The *Punchinello* title-page retains the ladder but moves it to the nearer side so that Punchinello can ascend the altar. The title-page implies that the *Via Crucis* and *Punchinello* are two versions of the same story, the ladder a prefiguration of Punchinello's return from death at the end of the series; and it carries ironic memories of resurrection when it reappears in the views of birth, hanging, burial, and return.

Figure 8. Giandomenico Tiepolo, *Punchinello* (*c.* 1800).

But the ladder, a symbol of descent and ascent from and to heaven, is literally, of course, a reference to the way a Punchinello ascended to the stage platform on which he performed. The ladder is also present in the scene of the elder Punchinello's miraculous birth from the egg, presumably referring, in this case, to his descent *from* heaven.

The altar-stage also resembles a tomb, like the one in Nicolas Poussin's *Et in Arcadia Ego* (Chatsworth, Devonshire Collection), or more specifically the tomb in Giovanni Battista Cipriani's *Death Even in Arcadia*.[36] The inscription, however, is not "*Et in Arcadia Ego*" but "*Divertimenti per gli ragazzi*," not one of death but of diversion (for the kids). The ladder invites Punchinello to climb onto his stage, play his pranks – *lazzi* will replace the father's philosophy – entertain the *ragazzi*, and (as the final drawing, no. 77, confirms) mock mortality of the *Et in Arcadia Ego* sort. He carries a doll of a young Colombina, which is being sniffed at by his dog (as death is being eyed by a dog in Giambattista's *Capriccio* of *Death Holding Audience*).

Instead of a funeral urn, the slab holds conical Punchinello hats, turned upside down to resemble cooking pots. Domenico's Punchinello has a picnic hamper, jug of wine, dish of gnocchi, and bundle of faggots.

Figure 9. Giandomenico Tiepolo, *Punchinellos at Dinner* (c. 1800).

George Knox has drawn attention to the gnocchi and noted the omni-presence of appetite in the *Punchinello* series.[37] Gnocchi is fed to the infant Punchinello, and later served to Punchinellos at dinner out of the same gnocchi pot. (The Punchinello habit of eating gnocchi is already apparent in Giambattista's drawings of the 1740s and in at least one painting of Punchinellos cooking.) The Punchinello hats and the gnocchi pots are interchangeable. The hat corresponds to the conical pot (so shaped to provide ample space for the swelling of the gnocchi as they rise), and the Punchinello uses his hat both for protecting his head and for cooking his food (fig. 9). Thus, the shape of the hat is explained by the Punchinello's appetite. But why gnocchi? Because this simple dumpling made of potatoes was a staple of the poor. The appearance of the gnocchi, pot, and fork in processions draws on popular prints of the Triumph of Carnival, but in particular (Knox argues) on the Festival of San Zeno in Verona, which involved the distribution of food and wine to the poor of the parish of San Zeno. In the context of Domenico's mock-heroic satire of atonement, the Punchinellos' gnocchi, "the dumpling shaped like themselves," becomes the popular equivalent of eucharistic bread.[38]

So if the block is both an altar and a *commedia* stage, it is also a table on which the Punchinellos eat. One recalls the sumptuous dinners in

Giambattista's works, but above all the great dinner scenes of his father's model, Veronese; which, we remember, Veronese painted as *Last Suppers*, for the refectories of convents and monasteries, but, because of the heavy emphasis on copious food and drink, and the variety of types, including dwarves and dogs, had to rename (disguise as) a *Marriage at Cana* or a *Dinner in the House of Levi*. Domenico extends Veronese's sort of people who originally attended the Last Supper into the ordinary people he had painted for his father in the annexes to the villas.

The name Punchinello probably derived from *pulcino*, a chicken, so-called because of Pulcinello's beak mask and his strutting walk, and from the fact that his sweetheart in the *commedia dell'arte* was named Colombina: thus Pulcino and Colomba, edible chicken and pigeon (in the drawings, they are mock-heroic turkeys). The egg, besides its connection to *pulcino* and *colomba*, was a natural symbol for the Host: while an egg remains the same on the outside, it is being transformed inside into a whole chicken. An example is the ostrich egg suspended above the Virgin and Child in Piero della Francesca's *Sacra Converzatione* in the Brera, Milan, or the egg of the frontispiece of Hogarth's *Analysis of Beauty*.

In the Punchinello drawings food and eating return to their sacramental function (as in the Roman Catholic ritual but also in the Christian Humanism of Rabelais's Pantagruelism). In fact, in its secularization and popularization, they are coincidentally closer to the Protestant Communion in memory of Christ's sacrifice, as the drawings themselves serve to memorialize Domenico's father. The image of the gaping mouth is reduced to its proper subordination within a scene of carnival and convivial celebration, and so to the "life" of an artist, parodist (imitator of his father's high style), joker, subculture figure, victim, whose story is roughly parallel to – or at least begins and ends with – the essential story of incarnation and atonement.

Domenico Tiepolo is, like Goya, drawing upon popular imagery and a folk culture in which death and resurrection can be related to "the demise of Carnival and the beginning of Lent."[39] Punch was the ultimate anarchist. The English Punch had a phallic nose, chin, hump, and large club, with which he beat Joan (Judy), the police, and all contenders. Domenico's drawings take up the historical context of the French invasion and the fall of the Venetian Republic. The Punchinello figures are shot by a firing squad or hanged in images that are comic versions of those in Goya's *Desastres*. Domenico's Eucharist, like Goya's, plays itself out against the French Revolution and Napoleon's Italian campaigns. Punchinello had become (in some parts of Italy at least) a political figure of the *Lumpenproletariat*, built on his older identity as Lord of Misrule, and in the context of the French occupation he comes to represent Venice.

With Napoleon's armies marching around northern Italy and Venice's Great Council demoralized enough to vote itself out of existence, Domenico recapitulates with irony his father's heroic art. The father *had* "devoured" the son (the son, subservient to the father, did the minor, contemporary parts of the scheme), and now the son absorbs and transmutes the art of the father, representing his surrogates the Punchinellos in the story of incarnation and atonement, at large dinners eating gnocchi, the poor man's bread. Although he may be the emblem of social reality in Venice, Punchinello is also the comment upon the nature of that reality – one that now accepts a clown rather than a god as its hero. The humble Punchinellos eat plebeian gnocchi and polenta instead of the Host, rendering the Mass as a humble, demotic equivalent, as they do the father's art. They substitute imitation for invention, commonplace action for heroic. They can become absorbed in the most frivolous pastimes or turn their backs on the viewer altogether, with no concern for a possible existence as "exempla virtutis."

And yet the father remains the *donné*, the material out of which the son creates his new reality. Long before Domenico took him up, Giambattista was drawing and painting Punchinellos. Punchinello appeared in his *Scherzi di fantasia* etchings as one of the ultimate sages to whom the magicians and witches who populate that series go to seek knowledge. It is appropriate that Punchinello appeared in the *Scherzi*, for he is an emblem of improvisation, *invenzione*, related to the form Giambattista was employing as well as to Giambattista the artist, whose success depended precisely upon his resourcefulness, fantasy, and willingness to please. The self-irony, the family joke (the resemblance to a Punchinello nose in the self-portrait on the Würzburg Residenz ceiling) of the father's paintings and drawing of Punchinello were carried on by the son, including the decoration of the family house, where he presented them, as well as in the drawings, as a family. The difference between the father's Punchinello and the son's is, however, obvious. The son's Punchinello, as we see in the borrowings from his father, is an imitator, not an originator; he is an improvisor of materials already at hand, essentially the forms of the past, now antiquated.

The "realism" of both Hogarth and Domenico Tiepolo is defined by allusions to the past, to Old Master paintings of the baroque. Hogarth's is defined against, first, the theatricality of baroque art, embodied in the paintings on the walls of his scenes, and second, against the contemporary "realism" of the bourgeois theater of George Lillo and Nicholas Rowe. Tiepolo uses instead the costumed fantasy *mise-en-scène* of the *commedia dell'arte* (reducing his father's *opera seria*). The strategy of both artists fulfills Swift's fear in *A Tale of a Tub* of the Moderns' parricide of the Ancients, but also his prophecy (and the Duke of Buckingham's in his model, *The Rehearsal*) that this act of making-new will merely repeat the old in a new key, at a lower level of intensity. The artist incorporates the Old Masters and shows how unreal their style and subjects are, set against their contemporary equivalents as merely a first stage of "realism" (in the novel as well as painting).

Goya, the more radical artist, imposes on his anti-heroic subject-matter not the heroic imagery of the past but the aberrant images of folklore, magic, and the occult, indicating an atavism only glimpsed in Hogarth's *Enthusiasm Delineated*. Goya's concern is with the artist's perception of things ("I saw this," "This is truth"), in a progression from *Caprichos* to *Desastres*, from reportage to satiric outrage ("What more can one do?") to visionary and hallucinatory metamorphosis. Hogarth allowed an exculpatory interpretation – that the Christian symbols, by being burlesqued by the evangelical enthusiasts, are demonized and rendered a kind of Black Mass; it is *they* who are blaspheming the Christian Eucharist. Not the Church but the evangelical heretic has turned the congregation into lunatics who find an outlet for their sexual mania in religious ritual. Goya took the responsibility on his own shoulders: such a scene was what *he* saw in 1780s Spain.

NOTES

1 Bernd Krysmanski, in his encyclopedic study of the allusions in *Enthusiasm Delineated*, has persuasively dated the print 1761 (*Hogarth's "Enthusiasm Delineated": Nachahmung als Kritik am Kennertum* [Hildesheim: Olms, 1996], vol. II, pp. 901–2). The present essay draws upon materials dealt with in my *Hogarth's Harlot: Sacred Parody in Enlightenment England* (Baltimore: The Johns Hopkins University Press, 2003) and *Sin and Evil: Moral Values in Literature* (New Haven: Yale University Press, 2007). For the background of *Enthusiasm Delineated* and *Credulity, Superstition, and Fanaticism*, see Ronald Paulson, *Hogarth's Graphic Works*, 3rd edn. (London: Print Room, 1989), cat. no. 210, and *Hogarth*, vol. 3, *Art and Politics: 1750–1764* (New Brunswick: Rutgers University Press, 1993). On the Eucharist and cannibalism, see Claude Rawson, "'Indians' and Irish: Montaigne, Swift, and the Cannibal Question," *Modern Language Quarterly* 53 (1992), 299–364; *God, Gulliver, and Genocide: Barbarism and the European Imagination, 1492–1945* (Oxford: Oxford University Press, 2001), pp. 48–51, 77–8.

2 John Jewel, *A Reply to Mr. Harding's Answer*, in *Works*, ed. J. Ayre (Cambridge: Parker Society, 1845–59), vol. I, p. 449; *Works of John Jewel, Bishop of Salisbury*, ed. J. Ayre (Cambridge: Parker Society, 1845–59), vol. II, pp. 1, 121.

3 See Horton Davies, *Worship and Theology in England* (Princeton: Princeton University Press, 1975), vol. II, p. 311. For ecclesiastical background, see C. W. Dugmore, *Eucharistic Doctrine in England from Hooker to Waterland* (London: Society for Promoting Christian Knowledge, 1942), especially chapter 6.

4 Hogarth also satirized the Eucharist (reducing salvation according to grace to a lottery) in *The Lottery*, which parodied Raphael's *Disputa on the Eucharist* (Paulson, *Hogarth's Graphic Works*, cat. no. 53).

5 Among images of God the Father in a Last Judgment, see in particular Dürer's scene from his *Apocalypse* series in which God sits in a chair not unlike the one in which Hogarth's surgeon sits. See Paulson, *Sin and Evil*, pp. 113–17.

6 There was a graphic precedent in a Lutheran satire of *c.* 1567, entitled *Anatomia M. Lutheri*, which parodied a Last Supper by turning it into a dissection and eucharistic devouring of Martin Luther's body. As described by Joseph Leo Koerner (my source for this image): "Eleven Protestant reformers, named in the verse commentary by Johann Nasus published below, feast on the naked body of Luther . . . [which] replaces the body of Christ in the Communion meal (in a sense rendering the Eucharist hyper-mundane, in accordance with radical Protestant theology)" – a print that could have been a source for the idea of *Harlot 6* as well as, more particularly with its dissection, of *The Reward of Cruelty*. See Koerner, *The Reformation of the Image* (Chicago: University of Chicago Press, 2004), p. 397, ill. 192, which he identifies as a parody of a Lutheran print of 1567 (ill. 191). Judging by the large sums of money spent by Hogarth on prints (as recorded in his account books), it seems probable that he might have seen, if not owned, this "influential woodcut, which saw several editions" (*ibid.*). Krysmanski points out a more direct source in depictions of dissections: *Hogarth's "Enthusiasm Delineated,"* fig. 94, a print of 1493; a print which could have been a source for the Luther satire of 1567.

7 "The only way to preserve Female Chastity, is to prevent the Men from laying Siege to it: But this Project of the *Publick Stews* is the only Way to prevent Mens laying Siege to it: Therefore this Project is the only Way to preserve Female Chastity." See Bernard de Mandeville, *A Modest Defence of Publick Stews* (London, 1724), pp. xi–xii and 50.

8 See Paulson, *Hogarth's Harlot*, pp. 119–22.

9 Jonathan Swift, *Irish Tracts 1728–1733*, ed. Herbert Davis (Oxford: Blackwell, 1964), pp. 112, 117. Of course, Swift draws upon the commonplace metaphor, as in the opening of Defoe's *Jure Divino* (1706), "If [tyrants] forbear there's Neighbours to devour, / 'Tis not for want of Will, but want of *Power*" (ll. 3–4); and the basic dichotomy of eater eaten, as in his *Robinson Crusoe* (1719).

10 Graham Greene, *The Power and the Glory* (1940; London: Heinemann, 1945), pp. 74, 80.

11 Hogarth had used this earlier in his *Masquerade Ticket* of 1727. For other phallic images in Hogarth's engravings, cf. the tails of the lion and unicorn in *Masquerade Ticket* and the lion's penis in *Sleeping Congregation* (Paulson, *Hogarth's Graphic Works*, cat. nos. 108 and 140).

12 Cf. Rochester's poem from the 1670s, "Signor Dildoe."

13 Krysmanski connects the expression of the globe-face to Charles le Brun's illustration of the "passion" of astonishment (figs. 44, 45), but the expression is more easily interpreted as one of anger, that is, the anger that damns sinners to hell. Astonishment is expressed by the Muslim at the window.

14 Although the building does not resemble either of Whitefield's chapels in London, the Methodism represented is his Calvinist branch rather than Wesley's more Anglican. The association with Whitefield is in the collar of the howling dog, the inscription on the reader's lectern, and the reader's crossed eyes (see Paulson, *Hogarth's Graphic Works*, cat. no. 210). As his biographer has noted, Whitefield "looked upon himself as a loyal son of the Church of England" (Arnold A. Dallimore, *George Whitefield: The Life and Times of the Great Evangelist of the Eighteenth-Century Revival*, [Edinburgh: Banner of Truth, 1980], vol. II, p. 305). An idea of this particular hell can be drawn from Jonathan Edwards's sermon, "Sinners in the Hands of an Angry God," preached in Enfield, Connecticut, in 1741, as part of his "Great Awakening" (see Paulson, *Sin and Evil*, chapter 7).

15 In the late 1750s Hogarth was in effect the first Englishman we know of who read the whole of Dante's *Inferno* in English. His friend William Huggins showed him his translation, asking him to furnish illustrations, which Hogarth declined. Huggins published some passages of his translation, but the MS was lost at his death, and the first published complete Englishing of Dante was by the Rev. Henry Boyd (1802), beginning with the *Inferno* in 1785. See Paulson, *Sin and Evil*, pp. 353–4.

16 As he also used the copperplate of *Gulielmus Hogarth* to make *The Bruiser* (Paulson, *Hogarth's Graphic Works*, cat. nos. 181, 215).

17 See Paulson, *Hogarth, Art and Politics*, pp. 362–6, also pp. 392–3.

18 The pun also, of course, applies to the mouths of *Enthusiasm Delineated*. See Eric Partridge's example, "swallow a gudgeon, to be gulled" (sixteenth century), in Partridge, *A Dictionary of Slang and Unconventional English*, 7th edn. (London: Routledge, 1984). For Hogarth's visual punning, see Ronald Paulson, *Hogarth: The Modern Moral Subject* (New Brunswick: Rutgers University Press, 1991), pp. 261–4. The eating, however, is played down in *Credulity*, where there is only one open mouth (from three in *Enthusiasm*).

19 Krysmanski, *Hogarth's "Enthusiasm Delineated*," vol. II, pp. 901–2.

20 See Ronald Paulson, *Representations of Revolution (1789–1820)* (New Haven: Yale University Press, 1983; reprinted, 1987), pp. 304–6.

21 Robert Darnton, "Peasants Tell Tales: The Meaning of Mother Goose," in *The Great Cat Massacre and Other Episodes in French Cultural History* (New York: Basic Books, 1984), pp. 9–74.

22 Goya painted a scene from the *Lazarillo*, listed in an inventory drawn up in 1812 (see Pierre Gassier and Juliet Wilson, *The Life and Complete Works of Francisco Goya* [New York: Reynal, 1971], p. 381, Appendix A). *Capricho* no. 3, "Que viene el Coco," refers to the scene in which Lazarillo's little brother is scared by the appearance of their mother's black lover. On the folk-tale in *Lazarillo de Tormes*, and specifically hunger and the priest, see Fernando Lázaro Carreter, *"Lazarillo de Tormes" en la picáresca* (Barcelona, 1972); Harry Sieber, *Language and Society in "La Vida de Lazarillo de Tormes"* (Baltimore: The Johns Hopkins University Press, 1978). See also Paulson, *Sin and Evil*, pp. 281–4.

23 *Lazarillo de Tormes*, trans. Mack Hendricks Singleton, in *Masterpieces of the Spanish Golden Age*, ed. Angel Flores (New York: Rinehart, 1957), pp. 41, 45–6.

24 Vergniaud's remark was delivered to the assembly on March 13, 1793, reported in *Le Moniteur universel*, no. 75, March 16, 1793.

25 Sigmund Freud, *Totem and Taboo*, in *Standard Edition of the Complete Psychological Works of Sigmund Freud*, trans. James Strachey (London: Hogarth Press, 1958), vol. XIII, p. 142.

26 Cf. "Mourning and Melancholia," where Freud identifies the origin of melancholy in a loss of one sort or another, a death perhaps – "an object-loss which is withdrawn from consciousness." The ego identifies with "the abandoned object," and therefore "wants to incorporate this object into itself, and, in accordance with the oral or cannibalistic phase of libidinal development in which it is, it wants to do so by devouring it" (*Standard Edition*, vol. XIV, pp. 249–50).

27 The order of the *Punchinello* drawings, so far as external evidence is concerned, depends on penciled numbers which have no authority, have been changed in some cases by another hand, and are in many cases clearly erroneous. It is not even clear that the drawings were still mounted when sold in 1920. The series of drawings survived almost intact until they were sold in 1920 and dispersed. Before the dispersal a few sets of photographs were made. My own thoughts on Domenico Tiepolo go back to "Punchinello in Venice," *Bennington Review* 11 (1981), 58–69; further back to my teaching of the Punchinello drawings in a seminar at Yale, where one of my students, Jill Rubin, contributed to my understanding of the Italian background. My references are to Adelheid Gealt's catalogue, *Domenico Tiepolo: The Punchinello Drawings* (New York: Braziller, 1986).

28 In this sense the Punchinello series is parallel to the much longer series on the life of Christ; for which see *Domenico Tiepolo: A New Testament*, ed. Adelheid M. Gealt and George Knox (Bloomington: Indiana University Press, 2006). For the *Harlot*'s retelling of the New Testament story, see Paulson, *Hogarth's Harlot*. In Plate 1 M[ary?] Hackabout (the Harlot) is the Virgin Mary in a *Visitation*; in Plate 2 the mystery of the conception is revealed (the cuckolding of her keeper with the young lover slipping out of the door behind him), followed in Plate 3 by an *Annunciation*. Plate 4 shows the Flagellation, with

Mary in place of Christ. In Plate 5 she assumes the pose of the grieving Mary the Mother, but also present is an allusion to the soldiers casting dice for Christ's robe at the foot of the cross, which are in fact her clothes (the doctors contest her cure, the landlady plunders her clothes). Finally, in Plate 6 Hackabout's body is congruent with the table of the Last Supper and Communion, the Body next to the Blood (the chalice); she has *become* the Christ-figure – Mary the Mother substituting, in Hogarth's version of the Incarnation, for the Son. The son is present, a mute witness (in fact, his back is turned, he is seated on the wrong side of the table), but it is the *mother* whose body and blood figure in the most holy of sacraments, the Eucharist.

29 *Nativity* (Gealt, *Punchinello*, no. 2), *Taking of Christ*, no. 36, and a sequence of Punchinello before the magistrate, no. 39; in prison, no. 38; and the *Flagellation*, no. 37. Cf. the spanking of the child in Goya's *Capricho* no. 25. There is also a parody of a Harrowing of Hell; released from prison, no. 40, followed by a triumph, no. 41, etc.

30 Death by hanging, no. 72; by firing squad, no. 71; natural death, nos. 73–4, 100–2, 104.

31 Burial, nos. 75–6; and resurrection, no. 77.

32 See Hogarth's *Autobiographical Notes*, in Hogarth, *The Analysis of Beauty*, ed. Joseph Burke (Oxford: Clarendon Press, 1955), p. 216.

33 There is a parallel here to Hogarth's relationship with his spiritual father, Sir James Thornhill, the painter of the *Allegory of the Protestant Succession* in the Great Hall at Greenwich and the *Life of St. Paul* around the cupola of St. Paul's Cathedral.

34 There are many other examples, and sometimes Domenico borrows from Veronese, Tintoretto, and other artists of the great Venetian heroic tradition. He borrows from his own art as well (his *Hercules and Antaeus* series, his satyr drawings, and his *Scenes of Modern Life*).

35 See H. Diane Russell, *Rare Etchings by Giovanni Battista and Giovanni Domenico Tiepolo* (Washington, DC: National Gallery of Art, 1972), figs. 42, 1. Like both *Via Crucis* and *Punchinello*, the title-page focuses on an altar-like slab of stone on which perch several owls; typical of Giambattista, they denote wisdom but, given their sinister looks, also predatory night birds.

36 See Erwin Panofsky, "Et in Arcadia Ego: Poussin and the Elegiac Tradition," in *Meaning in the Visual Arts* (New York: Anchor Books, 1955), p. 310, fig. 93. Cipriani's painting is in the Hagley Hall Collection; a mezzotint was published by Boydell in 1789 (London, Courtauld Institute).

37 Delivered in his lecture at McMaster University in 1980, published as "Domenico Tiepolo's Punchinello Drawings: Satire, or Labor of Love?" in *Satire in the 18th Century*, ed. J. D. Browning (New York: Garland, 1983), pp. 124–46.

38 Gealt, *Punchinello*, no. 164. The gnocchi pot appears in nos. 3, 22, and 70 – the last a carnival procession, a *bacchanale del gnocchi* with Punchinellos brandishing gnocchi forks. No. 11 is a wedding banquet, 21 a supper, 22 a feast; 82 is a birthday party. In no. 20 they are cooking polenta, another plebeian equivalent of the Host. Alessandro Torri's *Cenni Storici . . . il Venerdi*

Ultimo di Carnovale, denominato Guoccolare (Verona, 1818) contains accounts of the authorities trying to keep the festival under control.

39 As Marcia E. Vetrocq puts it, "these correspondences evidence Domenico's understanding that the pageant of Carnival was the archaic prototype for, and the popular transfiguration of, the pageant of Christ's death and resurrection (Vetrocq, *Domenico Tiepolo's Punchinello Drawings* [Bloomington: Indiana University Art Museum, 1979], p. 38).

CHAPTER 16

Beckett in the country of the Houyhnhnms: the inward turn of Swiftian satire

Marjorie Perloff

In a 1975 memoir, the Romanian-born philosopher E. M. Cioran, who, like his friend Samuel Beckett, had lived in exile in Paris since the mid-1930s, recalls the following conversation:

Beckett told me he was re-reading the "Travels," and that he had a predilection for the "Country of the Houyhnhnms," especially for the scene in which Gulliver is mad with terror and disgust at the approach of a Yahoo female. He informed me – and this was a great surprise to me, above all a great disappointment – that Joyce didn't care for Swift. Moreover, he added, Joyce, contrary to what people think, had no inclination whatever for satire. "He never rebelled, he was detached, he accepted everything. For him, there was *absolutely no difference between a bomb falling and a leaf falling.*"[1]

"A remarkable judgment," as Cioran concludes, reminding us that Beckett himself did rebel, was not detached, and, having fought in the Resistance for six years during World War II, was painfully aware of the difference between leaves falling and bombs falling. Like the Swift of *Gulliver's Travels*, his particular "inclination for satire" had less to do with social or political critique or with attempts to provide correctives for human foibles, than with what Claude Rawson refers to as the "radical incurability of the human condition, grounded in the 'nature' of the human animal."[2] Like the Swift of *Gulliver's Travels*, who, in Northrop Frye's words, "shows us man as a venomous rodent [Lilliput], man as a noisome and clumsy pachyderm [Brobdingnag], the mind of man as a bear pit [Laputa] and the body of man as a compound of filth and ferocity [the Houyhnhnms],"[3] the Beckett protagonist is given to declarations like "To contrive a little kingdom, in the midst of the universal muck, then shit on it, ah, that was me all over. The excrements were me too, I know."[4] And, again as in Swift, Beckett's vision of man as "compound of filth and ferocity" is at once comically fantastic and yet so detailed in its realistic precision that readers cannot help recognizing their acquaintances as well as themselves at every turn.

John Fletcher, whose 1962 "Swift and Beckett: A Comparative Study" is still the most thorough treatment of the subject,[5] informs us that Beckett, who had studied Swift at Trinity College, reread the major works intensively in 1933. Swift's presence is explicit in such early stories as "Fingal" and "A Wet Night," as well as in Beckett's first published novel *Murphy*, which contains numerous allusions to *The Drapier Letters* and *A Tale of a Tub* (see Ackerley and Gontarski, p. 550). Fletcher finds much common ground in Swift's and Beckett's treatment of Ireland and of the Catholic Church, in their epistemological skepticism, their critique of pride and vanity, and especially in the mind–body dualism that animates their "excremental" vision and satiric treatment of sexual relations. The major difference between the two, Fletcher posits, is that "Swift looks down on human beings from a lofty height and with a degree of impatience, like Jupiter in his poem about the last judgment, whereas Beckett prefers viewing the world from the dunghill on which his hero lies stretched out under a cold sky." And further: "The Beckettian journey, unlike Gulliver's travels, is a search for one's true being, a search conducted without change of place" (Fletcher, pp. 22–3).

Each of these points – especially the notion that Beckett's journey is a search for "one's true being" – might be, and often has been, debated, but my concern here is less with the extractable ideas and thematic motifs shared (or not shared) by the two great Anglo-Irish writers than with the illumination a reading of *Gulliver's Travels* can give to the enigmatic, indeed often baffling texture, tone, and language of Beckett's fictions. Reading Beckett under the sign of Swift, one can trace the way satire – conventionally the literary mode in which the grotesque and absurd are measured against at least an implicit moral norm – has given way, in the twentieth century, to a much less assured, indeed a free-floating irony. In Beckett's case, at least, the Swiftian penchant for the satiric excoriation of mankind is tempered by a curious lyricism that turns the satiric mirror inward, bringing Beckett close to his other great Anglo-Irish precursor W. B. Yeats. Like the Yeats of "A Dialogue of Self and Soul," Beckett's narrators – Molloy, Malone, the Unnamable, as well as the protagonists of "First Love" or "The Calmative" – are given to "cast[ing] out remorse." It is not a matter, as in Yeats, of the willingness to "Measure the lot, forgive myself the lot," for forgiveness implies that there is someone available – if only the narrator himself – who is willing to do the forgiving. Rather, in Beckett's world one casts out remorse because there is nothing to do but to *go on*, to "Try again. Fail again. Fail better" ("Worstward Ho," vol. IV, p. 471).

For Swift, the very notion of "Fail better" would have been unacceptable: even his darkest writings suggest that man *could*, in theory, be better if only he were to recognize and renounce his pride, his self-deception, and petty stratagems. But in the post-World War II landscape of *Godot*, *Endgame*, and the *Trilogy*, all discourse on what human beings *might* be seems merely beside the point. "I think," Beckett remarked in an interview of 1956, "anyone nowadays who pays the slightest attention to his own experience finds it the experience of a non-knower, a non-can-er."[6] But doubt is not equivalent to pessimism:

> I take no sides. I am interested in the shape of ideas even if I do not believe them. There is a wonderful sentence in Augustine. I wish I could remember the Latin... "Do not despair; one of the thieves was saved. Do not presume: one of the thieves was damned." That sentence has a wonderful shape. It is the shape that matters.[7]

It is a sentence Beckett comes back to again and again. "Take Augustine's doctrine of grace given and grace withheld," he tells Tom Driver in 1961, "have you pondered the dramatic qualities in this theology? Two thieves are crucified with Christ, one saved and the other damned. How can we make sense of this division?"[8]

The acceptance of the inscrutability of the universe is hardly an attitude conducive to satire, whose argument or plot, however fanciful, is aimed at a particular set of circumstances or forms of behavior. But since Swift's own satire in Book IV of *Gulliver* is of a very special kind, Beckett's fascination with its elaborations is not surprising. Swift's satirical manner, Rawson reminds us, "is the opposite of the one practised by Pope (or Fielding or Gibbon), which aims to establish solidarity with the reader against a bad world":

> Swift's way is to disconcert and destabilize, creating a quarrelsome ambience in which the reader is treated as belonging to the enemy... It follows that the narrator and satirist are similarly included... Whatever improvements are available to humankind from good institutions and laws and the practical accommodations of everyday life, the account of humanity at the essential definitional level is bleak and uncompromising. ("Introduction" to *Gulliver's Travels*, p. xxxviii)

It is this "uncompromising" aspect of Swift's satire that undoubtedly appealed to Beckett. F. R. Leavis was one of the first to note that "Even when Swift's ironic intensity undeniably directs itself to the defence of something that he is intensely concerned to defend, the effect is essentially negative. The positive itself appears only negatively – a kind of skeletal presence . . . a necessary precondition, as it were, of directed negation."[9]

The "disturbing energies" thus generated are clearly in evidence in the famous scene (Book IV, 8) singled out by Beckett in which an unsuspecting Gulliver, bathing in a stream, is overwhelmed with disgust by the advances of a female Yahoo: "She embraced me after a most fulsome Manner; I roared as loud as I could, and [my protector the Sorrel] Nag came galloping towards me, whereupon she quitted her Grasp, with the utmost Reluctancy, and leaped upon the opposite Bank, where she stood gazing and howling all the time I was putting on my Cloaths" (pp. 248–9).

When Gulliver had first sighted the Yahoos in chapter 1, he took them to be a species of tree-inhabiting animal:

Their Heads and Breasts were covered with thick Hair . . . they had Beards like Goats, and a Long Ridge of Hair down their Backs, and the fore Parts of their Legs and Feet, but the rest of their Bodies were bare, so that I might see their Skins which were of a brown Buff Colour. They had no Tails, nor any Hair at all on their Buttocks, except about the *Anus*; which, I presume Nature had placed there to defend them as they sat on the Ground, for this Posture they used, as well as lying down, and often stood on their hind Feet . . . The Females were not so large as the Males; they had long lank Hair on their Heads, and only a sort of Down on the rest of their Bodies, except about the *Anus*, and *Pudenda*. Their Dugs hung down between their fore Feet, and often reached almost to the Ground as they walked. (p. 209)

It is only much later that Gulliver comes to recognize that, however flat these creatures' noses, however thick their lips, hairy their breasts, and long their finger- and toe-nails, the Yahoos, as they are called, exhibit "a perfect human Figure" (p. 210). In the eyes of his Houyhnhnm master, Gulliver is an anomaly, a not-quite-typical Yahoo. "[The Master] knew not," for example, "what could be the Use of these several Clefts and Divisions in my Feet behind; that those were too soft to bear the Hardness and Sharpness of Stone without a Covering made from the Skin of some other Brute" (p. 225). Gulliver's body – the human body – is gradually defamiliarized. But the full connection is not made, either by Gulliver or by the Houyhnhnms, until the female Yahoo identifies the nude man swimming as one of her kind and lunges for him: "This was Matter of Diversion to my Master and his Family, as well as of Mortification to my self. For now I could no longer deny that I was a real *Yahoo*, in every Limb and Feature, since the Females had a natural Propensity to me as one of their own Species" (p. 249).

Why a "Diversion" to the Houyhnhnms? Are these virtuous, rational horses perhaps a trifle malicious, enjoying the suffering of the anomalous creature that is Gulliver? Or are they right to make fun of Gulliver's pride, his conviction that *he*, at least, is "above" Yahoo sexual desires? A similar comedy is played out in Beckett's fictions. Again and again, a passive male narrator, who presumably wants only to be left alone, is accosted by an ugly, aggressive, and unappetizing female, who has sexual designs on him. In the early work – *More Pricks Than Kicks* and *Murphy* – such sexual couplings are the material for slapstick or farce, but, beginning with *First Love* (1946), the erotic Yahoo union in question takes on a darker – and also more comic – dimension. Unlike Swift's black-haired Yahoo, who is said to be "no more than eleven years old," Beckett's female aggressors are withered, old, or at best ageless women, the persistence of whose desire serves only to emphasize the absurdity and grotesqueness of sexual union. But unlike Gulliver, who fends off the female Yahoo aggressor, Beckett's narrators usually succumb to "love," at least briefly, thus having to own up to their own sexual instincts. Indeed, in Beckett country, as opposed to Houyhnhnmland, one is identified as a Yahoo, not by physical attributes alone, but by one's Yahoo actions. Then again, Beckett's "I," which he himself aptly called the "narrator/narrated," has so amorphous a "self," so incoherent and conflicted an identity, that "acting like a Yahoo" is itself ambiguous. [10] In what follows, I want to consider how the Yahoo paradigm functions in two of Beckett's key fictions of the late 1940s: *First Love* and *Molloy*.

THE DREAD NAME OF LOVE

Beckett's short story *First Love* was written in French as *Premier amour* in 1946 but not published in Paris until 1970 and in English by Grove Press in 1974. It was the first of four postwar stories (the others are *The Expelled*, *The Calmative*, and *The End*) – stories that, as I have suggested elsewhere, deal much more specifically and substantively than is usually thought with Beckett's years in the Resistance, first in the Gloria cell in Paris, then in hiding in Roussillon in Provence, and finally in St.-Lô in Normandy where, in 1945–6, Beckett worked for the Red Cross, building a new hospital. [11] In all four stories, as in *Molloy*, which Beckett wrote in 1947, the narrator is unaccountably evicted from his dwelling place, hides in cowsheds or in fields, and is victimized by various authority figures, whether policemen, strangers, or predatory women.

The sexual paradigm found in the war stories and in *Molloy* also has a biographical dimension. In 1937, Beckett was pursued by the wealthy and

openly promiscuous art patroness Peggy Guggenheim and had a brief
but intense affair with her. In her memoir *Out of This Century* (1946),
Peggy describes her obsessive love for "Oblomov," as she playfully refers
to the passive Sam, admitting that her passion was not returned. But they
did see a lot of each for the next month or two and remained friends
thereafter. Peggy, as James Knowlson notes in his biography of Beckett,
was by no means attractive. Eight years older than Sam, "she had a high
brow, a bulbous nose (partly the result of facial surgery that had gone
wrong), and thin, spindly legs: she often wore socks and sandals."[12]

This relationship – and there were others like it[13] – may have been at
the back of Beckett's mind when he wrote *First Love* and the Lousse
section of *Molloy*, although, as Beckett's biographers have shown, we can
never take Beckett's caricatures of women (or, for that matter, caricatures
of himself as dirty, miserable old man) literally. The "first love" motif
invokes, of course, a long literary tradition, from Dante's *Vita Nuova*
(one of Beckett's sacred texts), to Joyce's *Portrait of the Artist*, but perhaps
the most intriguing fictional source for Beckett's story is Ivan Turgenev's
classic 1860 novella "First Love," which Beckett surely must have known.[14]
In the Turgenev story, the innocent sixteen-year-old hero falls in love
with, and is ultimately rebuffed by, the beautiful, aristocratic, and
capricious "older girl" next door. Only years later, when Zinaida is dead,
does the narrator learn that it was not one of his fellow suitors with whom
she was in love, but his own late father.

The opening sentence of Beckett's *First Love* parodies this love triangle:
"I associate, rightly or wrongly, my marriage with the death of my father,
in time" (vol. IV, p. 229). For Beckett, the two events merely *happen* to
coincide: it is not that the principals ever knew one another – if indeed
the father and Lulu (or Anna, as the narrator later calls her) can be said to
be characters at all. Rather – and here the Swift connection comes in – the
dates on the gravestone become part of an absurd counting game whereby
the narrator tries to establish his age at the time of his "marriage," even as
the Gulliver of Lilliput counts out the sticks to construct his miniature
"theatre" with a handkerchief (*Gulliver*, p. 35). The graveyard setting of
Beckett's story, moreover, is distinctly Swiftian:

The smell of corpses, distinctly perceptible under those of grass and humus
mingled, I do not find unpleasant, a trifle on the sweet side perhaps, a trifle
heady, but infinitely preferable to what the living emit, their feet, teeth, armpits,
arses, sticky foreskins, and frustrated ovules . . . The living wash in vain, in vain
perfume themselves, they stink. (pp. 229–30).

If Beckett's narrator prefers the smell of corpses to that of the living, it is, no doubt, because in Yahooland, as the Houyhnhnm master explains to Gulliver sometime before the pivotal Yahoo encounter, the living, especially in heat, emit a noxious odor: "a Female *Yahoo* would often stand behind a Bank or a Bush, to gaze on the young Males passing by, and then appear, and hide, using many antick Gestures and Grimaces; at which time, it was observed, that she had a most *offensive Smell*"; such a creature, Gulliver is told, will then "run off into some convenient Place where she knew the Male would follow her" (p. 245). But because, like Gulliver, Beckett's narrator also fancies himself a thinking being, his report from the graveyard is not wholly about fecal matter and smells: he reads the inscriptions on the gravestones and pens his own:

> Hereunder lies the above who up below
> So hourly died that he survived till now. (vol. IV, p. 230)

This absurd version of the life–death dialectic – under/above, up/below, died/survived, hourly/now – culminating in the rhyme of "below"/"now," is put forward in full recognition that the second line "limps a little perhaps." And to show off his intelligence even further, the narrator compares the pathetic graveyard where his father is buried to the "infinitely preferred" Ohlsdorf cemetery on Prussian soil (in Hamburg), "with its nine hundred across of corpses packed tight, though I knew no one there, except by reputation the wild animal collector Hagenbeck" (p. 231). Is a cemetery then rated according to the number of its graves? It takes a moment to realize that the "corpses packed tight" in this German cemetery, with its "Groves, rottoes, artificial lakes with swans," are those of soldiers killed in World War I and hence reminders of Beckett's own war experience. "I was afraid I'd die," he remarks, "I turned aside to vomit, I envied them."[15]

Graveyard, war, and finally, as is typical in these Beckett fictions, expulsion and exile: upon the death of his father, "they" demand the narrator's removal:

One day, on my return from stool, I found my room locked and my belongings in a heap before the door. This will give you some idea how constipated I was, at this juncture. It was, I am now convinced, anxiety constipation . . . Or am I confusing it with the diarrhoea? It's all a muddle in my head, graves and nuptials and the different varieties of motion. (p. 232)

The Yahoo nature of man, the defecating animal, is always kept before us; at the same time – and here Beckett teases out Swift's implications – man is distinguished from his humanoid counterparts in that he is the animal that suffers. During those "long cruel sessions in the necessary house" where he strains ("heave! ho! heave! ho!") in the privy, the narrator gazes dully at the "almanac hanging from a nail before my eyes with its chromo of a bearded stripling in the midst of sheep, Jesus no doubt." Jesus' pain is his own: it is he who, wearing his "traveling costume, I mean shoes, socks, trousers, shirt, coat, greatcoat, and hat," sees himself as expelled and pursued by those inside his former home: "men, women and children, and the voices, the sights, the smiles, the hands, the keys in the hands, the blessed relief . . . come let's eat, the fumigation can wait" (p. 232).

Gulliver's delusional pains, which Swift treats comically, come *after* he has been banished from the country of the Houyhnhnms, when, on the journey home, he cannot bear contact with his own Yahoo kind. In Beckett, by contrast, suffering is continuous, there being no before and after in the display of man's inhumanity to man. It is in the context of the painful expulsion from his previous domicile (itself hardly a paradise) that the narrator now meets Lulu – the name evoking, not only the resourceful but doomed prostitute of the Franz Wedekind–Alban Berg opera, but also – in an especially subtle stroke – the demonic child through whose voice the medium (Mrs. Henderson) speaks in Yeats's *Words upon the Window-Pane*, the séance-play in which Lulu becomes the agent exorcising the spirit of Jonathan Swift ("that bad old man!"), presented as torn between Vanessa and Stella.[16]

The meeting of the future lovers is first treated as slapstick: "She also disclosed her family name, but I've forgotten it. I should have made a note of it, on a piece of paper. I hate forgetting a proper name" (p. 233). The future lovers meet on a bench on the bank of the canal, although again the narrator doesn't remember which canal since "our town boasts two." "To the fore," he remarks, "a few yards away, flowed the canal, if canals flow, don't ask me" (p. 233). But of course it makes no difference which of two canals is behind the bench; canals, moreover, have little visible "flow"; their water – one thinks of the protagonist of Eliot's *Waste Land*, "fishing by the dull canal" – appears stagnant in keeping with the non-identity of this Lulu (if that is indeed her name?).

Lulu's first words, indeed among the few words we ever hear her speak directly, are "Shove up." So startled is the protagonist by this off-color locution (as in "shove it up your ass") that he stays, moving over a little, and listens to the woman sing "*sotto voce*, as to herself . . . disjointedly." And although Lulu soon leaves, this "most tenacious woman" returns night after night, soon urging the man "to put your feet on my knees." "I didn't want to be asked twice," he tells us, "under my miserable calves

I felt her fat thighs. She began stroking my ankles. I considered kicking her in the cunt" (p. 234). The reader, startled by the aggressiveness of this ugly remark, is disoriented, even as is the "gentle reader" in Gulliver's account of his return home from Houyhnhnm land. The narrator now declares that, much as he feared the "dulling of the self," he succumbed:

Man is still today, at the age of twenty-five, at the mercy of an erection, physically too, from time to time it's the common lot, even I was not immune, if that may be called an erection. It did not escape her naturally, women smell a rigid phallus ten miles away and wonder, How on earth did he spot me from there? One is no longer oneself on such occasions, and it is painful to be no longer oneself, even more painful if possible than when one is. (p. 234)

Here is Beckett's parodic version of Gulliver's encounter with the female Yahoo: whereas Gulliver immediately cries out, longing to escape, in Beckett's case, the "Tincture of Reason" (Swift's phrase, Gulliver, p. 254) gives way, under the power of the erection, as the woman, able to "smell a rigid phallus ten miles away," knows. "One is no longer oneself on such occasions," although being "oneself" is quite bad enough. What, moreover, is man's self? Note that although Lulu is the aggressor, it is man who has the "aggressive" erection necessary for sexual union to occur. Beckett is in this respect more negative than Swift: his protagonist may be repulsed by the Yahoo encounter, but there is no way out: "When she had finished and my self been resumed, mine own, the mitigable, with the help of a brief torpor, it was alone" (vol. IV, p. 234). So much for one night, but the coupling now becomes routine: "In the daytime I foraged for food and marked down likely cover" (p. 235). A Yahoo existence indeed!

With the coming of the cold weather, the narrator repairs to a deserted cowshed, "littered with dry and hollow cowclaps"; here he can dream of his Lulu. Dirt, dung, feces: these are regularly associated, as by Swift, with Ireland: "wherever nauseated time has dropped a nice fat turd you will find our patriots." As in Gulliver the "savage" Irish penchant for dirt becomes part of the Yahoo paradigm:

Yes, I loved her, it's the name I gave, still give alas, to what I was doing then. I had nothing to go by, having never loved before, but of course had heard of the thing, at home, in school, in brothel, and at church, and read romances, in prose and verse under the guidance of my tutor, in six or seven languages, both dead and living, in which it was handled at length. I was therefore in a position, in spite of all, to put a label on what I was about when I found myself inscribing the letters of Lulu in my old heifer pat or flat on my face in the mud under the moon trying to tear up the nettles by the roots. They were giant nettles, some full three foot high, to tear them assuaged my pain . . . (p. 237)

Here the sly catalogue – home, school, brothel, and church – and the absurd notion that Lulu's homeless lover has read, with his tutor, romances in "six or seven languages both dead and living" – comically offsets the actual account of Yahoo love-making, replete with mud, cowpat, and nettles. Beckett doesn't reject the value of learning as does Swift, for whom it is almost always shallow and misguided; he merely remarks on the anomaly of the well-educated student making his bed, so to speak, in a place of mud, nettles, and "cowshit," with the likes of Lulu. But, as it develops, the love scenario has to take in both aspects of "love": thus the narrator, who decides to rename Lulu, Anna,[17] can, echoing Anchises' words at the funeral of his grandson Ascanius, "divellicate urtica *plenis manibus*" (scatter from full hands a tropical nettle-like *urtica* plant), even as he feels "under my tossing head, her thighs to bounce like so many demon bolsters" (p. 238).

Lulu/Anna has not yet been described physically. Only some time later does the narrator come across his beloved on their familiar bench, "her hands buried in a muff." Interestingly, the muff, an appurtenance of well-dressed ladies, who, like Gulliver, dress themselves in the skins of other animals, makes the Beckett protagonist weep, no doubt because, for the first time in this story of first love, the female Yahoo's "shapeless, ageless, almost lifeless" figure is humanized. Then too Lulu/Anna now sings a song about "lemon trees or orange trees" – perhaps Mignon's song, "Do you know the land where the lemon trees grow?" from Goethe's *Wilhelm Meister*. And now for the first time the narrator notices her face: "the eyes were crooked, but I didn't know that till later. It looked neither young, nor old, the face, as through stranded between the vernal and the sere." These poetic allusions to wet and dry foliage are now qualified by the awareness, when Lulu takes him to her rooms, of her squint – it becomes her defining feature, no matter how slowly and teasingly she undresses for him. And Lulu/Anna now seduces the narrator in a real bed: he wakes up to find her beside him, "naked naturally. One shudders to think of her exertions. I still had the stewpan [makeshift chamberpot] in my grasp. It had not served. I looked at my member. If only it could have spoken! Enough about that. It was my night of love" (p. 243).

Again, the overtures and exertions are all the woman's. From then on, Anna brings him his meals and looks in now and again, between, as it turns out, satisfying her customers, for she is now (or had she always been?) working as a prostitute. The affair might have continued, had Anna not announced, one day, that she was pregnant. Now all falls apart, as she plagues him "with *our* child, exhibiting her belly and breasts" (p. 245). "What finished me," responds the narrator, "was the birth." The death–life cycle comes full circle, life – the infant's cry signifying the death of the "marriage." The narrator can't stand witnessing a birth: the cries, whether the infant's or its mother's, "pursued me down the stairs and out into the street" and they continue to haunt him: the cries never cease.

Is the puling infant the narrator's offspring? The reader knows only that, in Beckett's scheme of things, when "love" leads to conception and birth it is no longer desired. There have been ingenious psychoanalytic explanations of this state of mind, but the story makes perfectly good sense in Swiftian terms.[18] Mating, both in Yahooland and here, is just that: it exists for sexual gratification: any byproduct like a child would trouble animal (more properly, Yahoo) pleasure with the intrusion of conscious thought. The guilt experienced by Beckett's narrator implies that he cannot quite live according to Yahoo norms. Then again – and here is a telling irony – when it comes to parental love, the Houyhnhnms are deficient too: "They have no fondness for their Colts or Foles; but the Care they take in educating them proceedeth entirely from the Dictates of *Reason*. And I observed my Master to shew the same Affection to his Neighbour's Issue that he had for his own" (*Gulliver*, p. 250). In the "Elysium of the roofless" (vol. IV, p. 236), which is the dung-filled graveyard world of *First Love*, there are, of course, no Houyhnhnms, no one to help the narrator learn what a "proper" kind of love might be.

Still, for all its bleakness and grotesque comedy, Beckett's tale is finally less pessimistic than Swift's. For unlike Gulliver, who resists the Yahoo girl and fancies himself fit company for the Houyhnhnms, with whom he engages in discussion about issues of great ethical and political moment, the narrator of *First Love* knows he is no better than the woman who smells him out, knows indeed that he has come to depend on her: "She disturbed me exceedingly, even absent. Indeed she still disturbs me, but no worse than the rest" (vol. IV, p. 235). And for this condition – the human condition – there is no solution beyond the admission of failure: "I didn't understand women at that period. I still don't for that matter. Not men either. Not animals either. What I understand best, which is not saying much, are my pains. I think them through daily, it doesn't take long, thought moves so fast" (p. 235).

What distinguishes the human animal, in Beckett's scheme of things, is this capacity for suffering, and, more important, the capacity for remembering that suffering and, in Gertrude Stein's words, for "telling it again and again." Yahoos, after all, have no memory, no way of relating past to present. But at the end of *First Love*, when the narrator says, "I could have done with other loves perhaps. But there it is, either you love or you don't" (p. 246), the reader, whom the narrator now addresses directly, knows that the story is to be continued.

THE INEXHAUSTIBLE FACULTY OF NEGATION

If the Lulu/Anna of *First Love* is largely a cipher, the receptacle for her lover's seed and perhaps the product of his imagination, the Lousse of *Mollo* is somewhat more sinister – and more comic as well. In the course of the picaresque adventures that take place as the crippled Molloy, crutch on the handlebar of his bicycle in crucifix shape, is tooling down the road, ostensibly *en route* to visit his mother, he runs over and kills a dog. Like Gulliver in Brobdingnag, he is just trying to run away from the scene of the crime, when he is stopped, in this case, "by a bloodthirsty mob of both sexes and all ages . . . and they were preparing to tear me to pieces" (vol. II, p. 28). But the lady who owns the dog intervenes and forgives Molloy, explaining that she had been on her way to the veterinary to have "poor Teddy," as the dog is called, "put out of his misery" (p. 28). Indeed, this "Mrs. Loy . . . or Lousse, I forget, Christian name something like Sophie" (p. 29) now invites Molloy to her house so that he can help her bury the dog. Given the choice between Lousse and "the unavoidable police constable" who is getting ready to make trouble for him, Molloy easily chooses the lady. An astonishing burial scene follows, in which the "onelegged" Molloy, unable to "dig" the required hole, because his other "rigid" leg will not support him, must leave the job to the lady:

I was virtually onelegged, and I would have been happier, livelier, amputated at the groin. And if they had removed a few testicles into the bargain I wouldn't have objected. For from such testicles as mine, dangling at mid-thigh at the end of a meager cord, there was nothing more to be squeezed, not a drop. So that non che la speme il desiderio, and I longed to see them gone, from the old stand where they bore false witness . . . (p. 31)

Here the shift from Leopardi's lyric cry – *non che la speme, il desiderio è spento* ("not only the hope but the desire is spent") – to Molloy's longing to remove his testicles from the bodily frame where they bear "false witness," is as painful as it is hilarious, what with its punning on speme/sperm and testify (witness)/testicles. Indeed, Molloy's insistence that he has only "one leg at his disposal" recalls the whore in Joyce's *Nighttown* who asks Bloom, "How's your middle leg, mister?" Is that perhaps the stiff one? And of course Sophie (wisdom) Lousse (lost, loose, louche) is presented as a Circe figure. The grave she is digging for her little dog is also Molloy's own.

After the funeral, Molloy is "plied with delicacies" of food and drink and "welcomed" into Lousse's cluttered, over-furnished and frilly parlor, where her lady-like demeanor is oddly offset by the voice of her parrot exclaiming, at regular intervals, "Fuck the son of a bitch." "He must have belonged to an American sailor," our naïve narrator concludes (p. 33), or perhaps a French sailor since the only other sentence at his disposal is the French "*Putain de merde.*" In this setting of sinister – but also comic – Yahoodom, Lousse removes Molloy's hat from his head – a signal of the loss of identity Molloy now suffers. For when he wakes up after a long sleep, he is "in a bed in my skin," his clothes nowhere to be found, the room's door locked and windows barred. His beard has been shaved, his body washed. And he realizes he is not, after all, nude, but "wearing a nightdress, very flimsy. If they had told me I was to be sacrificed at sunrise I would not have been taken aback" (pp. 33–4).

If this emasculation at first seems the very opposite of the embrace the Yahoo female gives Gulliver, it is soon seen to be similar. The removal of one's clothes and emptying of one's pockets is a common theme in *Gulliver's Travels*, and we recall Gulliver's shame in IV, 3, when the Houyhnhnm master demands that he undress and, Gulliver complying, declares that "it was plain I must be a perfect *Yahoo*; but that I differed very much from the rest of my Species in the Whiteness and Smoothness of my Skin, my want of Hair in several Parts of my Body, the Shape and Shortness of my Claws behind and before, and my Affectation of walking continually on my two hinder Feet" (p. 221).

Like Gulliver, Molloy eventually gets his clothes back from Lousse's valet, but, like the Gulliver of *Lilliput*, he finds that his pockets have been emptied: his sucking stone is gone, as well as a knife he may or may not have had. Now comes the confrontation in the garden with the mistress of the house, who admits that she has arranged things so as to force Molloy to stay with her:

I threw the bicycle back in the bush and lay down on the ground, on the grass, careless of the dew, I never feared the dew. It was then that Lousse, taking advantage of my weakness, squatted down beside me and began to make me propositions, to which I must confess I listened absent-mindedly, I had nothing else to do, I could do nothing else, and doubtless she had poisoned my beer with something intended to mollify Molloy, with the result that I was nothing more than a lump of melting wax, so to speak. (vol. II, p. 42)

Mission evidently accomplished. Part Circe, part Hecate, overperfumed with the lavender she grows in her moonlit garden, Lousse is nevertheless closer to Swift's Yahoo female than to either of these figures, for there is nothing even remotely attractive or appealing about this sexless old woman, nothing that a Molloy/Gulliver in his right mind could want. Towards the end of his account of his stay with Lousse, where he is confined to house and garden, not allowed to venture out into the street – a stay which may have been "a few months, perhaps a year" (p. 46) – Molloy finally gives us a brief physical description of his mistress:

Lousse was a woman of an extraordinary flatness, physically speaking of course, to such a point that I am still wondering this evening, in the comparative silence of my last abode, if she was not a man, rather or at least an androgyne. She had a somewhat hairy face, or am I imagining it, in the interests of the narrative. The poor woman, I saw her so little, so little looked at her. (vol. II, p. 51)

And he recalls another woman named Ruth, "or perhaps the name was Edith," whom he had once "loved" – a "woman "eminently flat," who "moved with short stiff steps, leaning on an ebony stick." As in the case of Lousse, "it was she who started it in the rubbish dump, when she laid her hand upon my fly" (p. 53). And after further speculation on the relationship of this "affair" to real love and how his mother's image merges with those of Ruth/Edith and of Lousse, Molloy concludes the episode by remarking, "I left Lousse at last, one warm airless night, without saying goodbye" (p. 54).

In *God, Gulliver, and Genocide*, Claude Rawson points out that in the visual representations of Hottentot women (well known to Swift from contemporary travel literature), the familiar image of the "savage" woman with hanging breasts, "naturally associated with past (and sometimes even present) child-bearing, often acquires secondary associations of the monstrous or unnatural. There is a subtype . . . of androgynous old women with long hair and masculine features, including a powerfully emphatic musculature."[19] The large "flat" body with "somewhat hairy" face: here is the "witch" or "warrior-woman" Yahoo variant that seems to haunt Beckett's imagination.[20] As in Swift, it is she, with her "miserable molys . . . administered in infinitesimal doses probably to draw the pleasure out" (vol. II, p. 49) who forces herself upon the unenthusiastic lover, claiming him, at least for the moment, as her own. "A mug's game," as Beckett puts it, "and tiring on top of that."

What I am calling the Yahoo figure in *Molloy* has most frequently been understood as a mother surrogate: Molloy himself, after all, declares, as he contemplates his relations with Lousse and then Ruth/Edith, "God forgive me, to tell you the horrible truth, my mother's image sometimes mingles with theirs, which is literally unendurable, like being crucified, I don't know why and I don't want to" (vol. II, p. 55). The novel begins "in my mother's room," presumably after her death, with Molloy declaring, "I sleep in her bed. I piss and shit in her pot. I have taken her place. I must resemble her more and more. All I need now is a son" (vol. II, p. 3). But the Freudian aspects of Beckett's novel, with its varied and obsessive representations of the son's conflicted feelings for his mother, are, I think, more properly understood as part of Beckett's larger ethos, an ethos surely shaped, not only by the Oedipal drama and private fantasies that had so markedly colored his early life, but also by his experience of the previous seven years – years of hiding and running, as the war played itself out.

And here the comparison to *Gulliver* is instructive. Unlike Molloy or the unnamed narrator of *First Love*, Gulliver fends off the Yahoo female; indeed, the very notion of having sexual relations with a Yahoo is taken to be not only repugnant but out of the question. Gulliver, so far as the reader knows, remains chaste to the end, or rather beyond the end, of his journey, for when last viewed in the *Travels*, he has gone no further than to allow his wife "to sit at Dinner with me at the farthest End of a long Table; and to answer (but with the utmost Brevity) the few questions I asked her" (p. 276). Indeed, "the smell of a *Yahoo* continuing very offensive, I always keep my Nose well stopt with Rue, Lavender, or Tobacco-Leaves" (p. 276). Lavender: we recall that this is Lousse's preferred flower and that she plants large beds of it in her garden. "If I had not lost my sense of smell," Molloy remarks, "the smell of lavender would always make me think of Lousse, in accordance with the well-known mechanism of association" (vol. II, p. 43).

Swift is not, of course, identical to Gulliver – and certainly the latter cuts a rather ridiculous figure in the final chapters of "A Journey to the Houyhnhnms." But the famous concluding disquisition on *Pride* links the author to his character:

> My reconcilement to the *Yahoo*-kind in general might not be so difficult if they would be content with those Vices and Follies only which Nature hath entitled them to. I am not in the least provoked at the Sight of a Lawyer, a Pick-pocket, a Colonel, a Fool, a Lord, a Gamester, a Politician, a Whoremunger, a Physician, an Evidence, a Suborner, an Attorney, a Traytor, or the like. This is all according to the due Course of Things. But, when I behold a Lump of Deformity, and Diseases both in Body and Mind, smitten with *Pride*, it immediately breaks all the Measures of my Patience . . . (p. 276).

Here Swift powerfully attacks on both fronts: his catalogue of professions takes care to find just about everyone in his society guilty of the "Vices and Follies" of Yahoodom. But in singling out pride as the cardinal Yahoo sin, Gulliver, in Ian Higgins's words, "embodies the 'absurd Vice' as he preaches against it" (see Notes to *Gulliver*, p. 362). It is Swift's point, Higgins suggests, that "Gulliver has, as he feared, relapsed into human corruptions since leaving Houyhnhnmland" (p. 362).

But this is to forget that as early as chapter 5, the Houyhnhnm master argued that Gulliver was, in a sense, worse than the actual Yahoos on the island, explaining that "although he [the master] hated the Yahoos of this Country, yet he no more blamed them for their odious Qualities than he did a Gnayh (a Bird of Prey) for its Cruelty, or a sharp Stone for cutting his Hoof. But, when a Creature pretending to Reason, could be capable of such enormities, he dreaded lest the Corruption of that Faculty might be worse than Brutality itself" (pp. 230–1). The corruption of reason is an acute instance of pride, the corrupted taking himself to be above the fray.

Gulliver's pride takes the special form of considering himself exempt from Yahoo status, even though he recognizes his body as a Yahoo one. The exemption takes the form of refusing the Yahoo female – or any Yahoo female; Gulliver never doubts for a moment that he is *above* this defining Yahoo act. And Swift must place his protagonist above, or at least outside, that act if the satirical thrust of *Gulliver's Travels* is to have its full force. The satirist's eye and ear for folly and vice must be directed outward so that readers may distance themselves from the "fiction" related by the narrator. Indeed, by the time Gulliver prepares to leave the country of the Houyhnhnms, he is using Yahoo skins to make his canoe, sails, and shoes, as if the Yahoos were, after all, purely Other.

Beckett's characters, born into a very different world, suffer from no such delusion. On the contrary, the caricaturing of others is largely a phantasmagoria within which the narrator's own self is burlesqued and held up to ridicule. However grotesque, absurd, and disgusting a Lulu or a Lousse might be – and Beckett's portraits are certainly malicious and unflattering – the narrator knows that his own actions – more properly, antics – are comic, absurd, and self-defeating. The "I" of *First Love* who can't sleep at Anna's until he moves all of the furniture out of the room, the Molloy who, in a Chaplinesque moment, pretends to be angry at Lousse's valet, who has removed his clothes, presumably to be cleaned (vol. II, p. 38) – these are comic characters, likable in their all-too-human self-deceptions:

For to want my clothes, and I thought I wanted them, was no reason for pretending to be angry, when they were refused. (vol. II, p. 38)

Even the skeleton of this sentence – "For to want my clothes was no reason to be angry, when they were refused" – is puzzling: why shouldn't someone be angry under the circumstances? But the qualifying clause "and I thought I wanted them," as well as the introduction of the participle "pretending" make a mockery of the whole sentence. If one thinks one wants X, does one in fact want it? And if there is no real anger felt, why pretend to it?

The self-mockery expressed by such locutions is quite unSwiftian. In the sardonic sequence in which Molloy tries to remember "the system, after the great English schools, and the guiding principles of good manners, and how to proceed," he wonders how to relate those principles to his actual habits such as "the finger in the nose, the scratching of the balls, digital emunction and the peripatetic piss" (p. 21). "It is in the tranquility of decomposition," he concludes, "that I remember the long confused emotion which was my life, and that I judge it, as it is said that God will judge me, and with no less impertinence" (p. 21).

God's judgment an impertinence? Or is it impertinent to think it an impertinence? These are the ironies for which Beckett is famous – ironies that have no outlet in any sort of Modest Proposal, but that give us pleasure by their very formulation. Here are Hamm and Clov in *Endgame*:

> HAMM. That old doctor, he's dead naturally?
> CLOV. He wasn't old.
> HAMM. But he's dead?
> CLOV. Naturally.
> [Pause]
> *You* ask *me* that? (vol. III, p. 209)

What remains to be satirized in this "endgame" except the refusal, intentional or otherwise, to understand what the other is saying? Hamm takes as a given the doctor's old age and asks about his death. Clov responds with the irrelevant, "He wasn't old." When Hamm impatiently repeats the question, Clov replies "Naturally," which may be just a sarcastic repetition of what Hamm has said but may also imply that the "naturalness" of the old doctor's death in somehow in question. And the final turn, "*You* ask *me* that?" is open to any number of interpretations, some funny, some quite sinister. The referents of these lines remain indeterminate, but the dialogue has a perfect shape. And we recall Beckett insisting that when it comes to sentences, "It is the shape that matters."

"The Use of Speech," as Swift's Houyhnhnms understand it, "[is] to make us understand one another, and to receive Information of Facts"

(*Gulliver*, p. 222). Are Beckett's narrators, voices who, it would seem, provide little "information" and frequently "*say the Thing which is Not*," therefore to be considered no better than Yahoos? The question is moot, for, to paraphrase Wittgenstein, "If a Yahoo could speak, we would not understand him."

NOTES

1 E. M. Cioran, "Encounters with Beckett," *Partisan Review* 43:2 (1976), reprinted in Lawrence Graver and Raymond Federman (eds.), *Samuel Beckett: The Critical Heritage* (London: Routledge & Kegan Paul, 1979), p. 367.
2 Claude Rawson, "Introduction," in Jonathan Swift, *Gulliver's Travels*, ed. Claude Rawson and Ian Higgins, Oxford World Classics (Oxford: Oxford University Press, 2005), p. xxxviii. All references to *Gulliver's Travels* in this essay are to this edition.
3 Northrop Frye, *Anatomy of Criticism: Four Essays* (Princeton: Princeton University Press, 1957), p. 235.
4 Samuel Beckett, "The End," *Samuel Beckett: The Grove Centenary Edition*, 4 vols. (New York: Grove Press, 2006), vol. IV, *Poems, Short Fiction, Criticism*, p. 292. All references to Beckett are to this edition: see vol. I, *Novels: Murphy, Watt, Mercier and Camier*; vol. II, *Novels: Molloy, Malone Dies, The Unnamable, How It Is*; vol. III, *Dramatic Works*.
5 John Fletcher, "Swift and Beckett: A Comparative Study" (1962), "The Modern Word: Samuel Beckett Apmonia," www.themodernword.com/beckett/paper_fletcher.pdf/. For related studies of Swift and Beckett, see Frederik N. Smith, *Beckett's Eighteenth Century* (New York: Palgrave Macmillan, 2002); John Pilling, *Samuel Beckett* (London: Routledge, 1976), pp. 141–5; J. Ackerley and S. E. Gontarski, *The Grove Companion to Samuel Beckett: A Reader's Guide to His Work, Life, and Thought* (New York: Grove Press, 2004), pp. 549–51. In *Gulliver and the Gentle Reader: Studies in Swift and Our Time* (1973; rpt. Atlantic Highlands, NJ: Humanities Press International, 1991), Claude Rawson cites Beckett a number of times but does not develop the comparison.
6 Israel Shenker, "An Interview with Beckett," *New York Times*, May 1956; reprinted in Graver and Federman, *Samuel Beckett: The Critical Heritage*, p. 148.
7 See Beckett, "Conversation with Harold Hobson" (1956), in *Beckett at Sixty*, ed. John Calder (London: Calder and Boyers, 1967), p. 34.
8 Tom Driver, "An Interview with Beckett" (1961), in Graver and Federman, *Samuel Beckett: The Critical Heritage*, p. 220.
9 F. R. Leavis, "The Irony of Swift," in *The Common Pursuit* (1952; Harmondsworth: Penguin, 1962), pp. 74–5.
10 On the "narrator/narrated," see Hugh Kenner, *A Reader's Guide to Samuel Beckett* (1973; Syracuse University Press, 1996), p. 94.
11 Perloff, "In Love with Hiding: Samuel Beckett's War," *Iowa Review* 35:1 (2005), 76–103.

12 James Knowlson, *Damned to Fame. The Life of Samuel Beckett* (New York: Simon & Shuster, 1996), p. 263.

13 According to Knowlson – and Anthony Cronin confirms this in his *Samuel Beckett: The Last Modernist* (London: HarperCollins, 1997) – Suzanne Deschevaux-Dusmenil, Beckett's wife, whom he met in 1929, moved in with in 1938, and married in 1961, was also eight years older than Beckett; like Peggy Guggenheim, she was the aggressor, visiting him in the hospital after he was accidentally stabbed on the street in January 1938, and then making a home for him for the next half-century, no matter how unresponsive to her he may have been at various times in their life together. But unlike Peggy, Suzanne was more companion than lover and the demands she made on Beckett were more psychological than sexual. Later in life, Beckett was pursued by more attractive women, for example, Barbara Bray, the BBC editor who moved to Paris to be near him.

14 For a survey of "first love" narratives from Turgenev and Hardy to Beckett, see Maria diBattista, *First Love: The Affections of Modern Fiction* (Chicago: University of Chicago Press, 1991).

15 Beckett, vol. IV, p. 231. The word "rottoes" in the above sentence is not a misprint, but a neologism used to remind the reader of those "rotting" in the ground below those pretty groves.

16 See W. B. Yeats, *The Words upon the Window-Pane*, in *The Collected Plays of W. B. Yeats* (London: Macmillan, 1953), pp. 597–617. In German idiom, "Lulu" means "peepee" – an appropriate tag for this "first love."

17 In "Writing in the Shit: Beckett, Nationalism and the Colonial Subject," David Lloyd suggests that the name change "from the repetitive 'Lulu' to the chiastic 'Anna'" reinforces the notion that "the prostitute embodies the anxiety of dispossession, perpetually self-alienated in exchange for money." See *Anomalous States: Irish Writing and the Post-Colonial Moment* (Durham: Duke University Press, 1993), pp. 50–1. But Lulu, as long as she is called by that name, is not overtly identified as a prostitute; it is only Anna, perhaps the parodic St. Anne, who is.

18 In "Le Père, l'amour, l'exil," *Cahiers de l'Herne: Samuel Beckett* (Paris: Editions de l'Herne, 1976), pp. 256–68, Julia Kristeva reads "Premier Amour" as a mock-Oedipal drama in which the father is killed only to reappear as the son – a reversal of the Christ-story.

19 Claude Rawson, *God, Gulliver, and Genocide: Barbarism and the European Imagination, 1492–1945* (Oxford: Oxford University Press, 2004), p. 111. And further: "The equations between Hottentot and Irish and between Hottentot and Yahoo are received lore, and naturally interpenetrate deeply with the Yahoo-Irish equation" (p. 111). Rawson observes that "androgynous hag" was extensively studied by Cesare Lombroso, in his widely read ethnographic study *La Donna delinquente: La prostituta e la donna normale* (1893). Cf. Vivian Mercier, "Samuel Beckett and the Sheela-na-Gig," *Kenyon Review* 23 (1961), pp. 299–324, where the Lousse–Ruth/Edith figure is related to the ancient Irish stone-carvings known as "Sheela-na-gigs," the female figures

who have in common "an ugly masklike or skull-like face, with a huge scowling mouth; skeletal ribs; huge genitalia held open by both hands; bent legs" and "either shrunken breasts or none" (p. 305).

20 Notice that Ruth (Hebrew for "friend") turns into Edith (Old English for "spoils of war"), a name appropriate for the Yahoo witch. See Mary Bryden, *Women in Samuel Beckett's Prose and Drama* (New York: Barnes and Noble, 1993), pp. 166–83, passim.

Index